**Keep this book. You will
need it and use it throughout
your career.**

About the American Hotel & Lodging Association (AH&LA)

Founded in 1910, AH&LA is the trade association representing the lodging industry in the United States. AH&LA is a federation of state lodging associations throughout the United States with 11,000 lodging properties worldwide as members. The association offers its members assistance with governmental affairs representation, communications, marketing, hospitality operations, training and education, technology issues, and more. For information, call 202-289-3100.

LODGING, the management magazine of AH&LA, is a "living textbook" for hospitality students that provides timely features, industry news, and vital lodging information.

About the American Hotel & Lodging Educational Institute (AHLEI)

An affiliate of AH&LA, the Educational Institute is the world's largest source of quality training and educational materials for the lodging industry. AHLEI develops textbooks and courses that are used in more than 1,200 colleges and universities worldwide, and also offers courses to individuals through its Distance Learning program. Hotels worldwide rely on AHLEI for training resources that focus on every aspect of lodging operations. Industry-tested videos, CD-ROMs, seminars, and skills guides prepare employees at every skill level. AHLEI also offers professional certification for the industry's top performers. For information about AHLEI's products and services, call 800-349-0299 or 407-999-8100.

About the American Hotel & Lodging Educational Foundation (AH&LEF)

An affiliate of AH&LA, the American Hotel & Lodging Educational Foundation provides financial support that enhances the stability, prosperity, and growth of the lodging industry through educational and research programs. AH&LEF has awarded millions of dollars in scholarship funds for students pursuing higher education in hospitality management. AH&LEF has also funded research projects on topics important to the industry, including occupational safety and health, turnover and diversity, and best practices in the U.S. lodging industry. For more information, go to www.ahlef.org.

MANAGEMENT of FOOD and BEVERAGE OPERATIONS

Sixth Edition

Educational Institute Books

MANAGEMENT of FOOD and BEVERAGE OPERATIONS

Sixth Edition

Jack D. Ninemeier, Ph.D.

AMERICAN HOTEL & LODGING
EDUCATIONAL INSTITUTE

Disclaimer

This publication is designed to provide accurate and authoritative information in regard to the subject matter covered. It is sold with the understanding that the publisher is not engaged in rendering legal, accounting, or other professional service. If legal advice or other expert assistance is required, the services of a competent professional person should be sought.

> —*From the Declaration of Principles jointly adopted by the American Bar Association and a Committee of Publishers and Associations*

The author, Jack D. Ninemeier, is solely responsible for the contents of this publication. All views expressed herein are solely those of the author and do not necessarily reflect the views of the American Hotel & Lodging Educational Institute (AHLEI) or the American Hotel & Lodging Association (AH&LA).

Nothing contained in this publication shall constitute a standard, an endorsement, or a recommendation of AHLEI or AH&LA. AHLEI and AH&LA disclaim any liability with respect to the use of any information, procedure, or product, or reliance thereon by any member of the hospitality industry.

Contents

Preface

HAS THE WORLD of food and beverage management changed since 2010 (the year the previous edition of this text was published), and is there a need to revise the book so soon? For several reasons, the answer to both questions is "Yes!" First, managers have become very resourceful in their efforts to define and deliver what guests (in for-profit operations) and consumers (in not-for-profit organizations) want in their food service experiences. This creativity allows their operations to succeed and remain viable food service alternatives in the marketplace. Second, technology has provided managers with new opportunities to market to and please guests, decrease costs, and focus on priority concerns rather than perform back-office number-crunching activities. Third, today's electronic media allow practicing managers and such industry observers as academics and students to keep up with the rapid pace of change in ways that were never before possible.

These are among the reasons that a new edition of this book is in order. Today's managers are implementing changes in all segments of the industry. Today's and tomorrow's managers will be working in an industry where change is commonplace.

It is very gratifying to know that the first five editions of *Management of Food and Beverage Operations* have been used by students of and employees in the food service industry throughout the United States and around the world. I hope that this sixth edition will continue to contribute to the knowledge and success of today's and tomorrow's leaders in our industry. This new edition has been written to ensure that the text continues to address its goals effectively. These goals are:

- To provide an up-to-date introduction for those who are considering a management career in commercial or noncommercial food service.

- To reinforce basic knowledge and provide fresh perspectives for those who currently manage food service operations.

- To provide a source of information useful in food and beverage training programs.

While the general chapter topics in the new edition have remained basically the same, the content within each chapter has been modified significantly to reflect current issues confronting the ever-changing food service industry.

What's new in the text? Readers will find that the discussion of food service technology has been integrated where applicable into each chapter. Today, as never before, technology is important to the way things are done in food and beverage operations. Automation in operations and financial management, for example, is increasingly commonplace and is discussed in this edition. Electronic advancements in marketing (alerting potential guests to the operation and determining, often on a very individual basis, the products and services they desire) and in service (how guests order food and beverage products) have been especially fast-paced and are detailed in applicable chapters. Another topic growing in importance for industry professionals and of concern to an increasing number of their guests, "green" restaurants (which encompasses the subject of sustainability), is addressed in this edition. Of course, statistics, references, exhibits, and Internet site lists have been updated, and every effort has been made to ensure that all information is as current as possible at the time of printing.

I owe thanks to the many people who have contributed to the development of this book. First, while the text has changed significantly over the years, the input from those special individuals who helped with the earlier versions still shapes the book's organization and philosophy. In addition, the authors of other books, authors of magazine and journal articles, presenters at educational sessions, academic colleagues, students, and businesspeople with whom I have met and/or exchanged correspondence both in the classroom and at their food and beverage operations are acknowledged for their contributions to the book.

The author acknowledges the guidance of Senior Vice President George Glazer, Senior Director of Academic Publications Tim Eaton, and editors Jim Purvis and Peter Morris of the American Hotel & Lodging Educational Institute. I have truly enjoyed my many-years-long relationship with this most professional organization and appreciate its emphasis on publication standards of the highest level.

In closing, I am flattered that many of you will encounter this book as you take another step on a lifelong journey of professional and personal development. I sincerely hope it helps you to better prepare for and achieve your career and personal goals.

Jack D. Ninemeier
Hilo, Hawaii

About the Author

DR. JACK D. NINEMEIER is professor emeritus in *The* School of Hospitality Business at Michigan State University. He holds a Ph.D. from the University of Wisconsin, Madison. His food service industry experience includes more than thirty-five years of teaching at Michigan State University and the University of New Orleans, seven years of service as a state-level administrator of a feeding program serving more than 350,000 meals daily, and four years of experience in various positions in commercial food service operations. Additionally, Dr. Ninemeier was a Research Consultant for the American Hotel & Lodging Educational Institute for twelve years.

Dr. Ninemeier is the author, coauthor, or editor of seventy-two books related to various aspects of food service and healthcare management. He also has written more than 300 articles in trade journals, developed more than 200 training monographs on all areas of food service management, and conducted numerous seminars nationally and internationally.

Part I
Introduction

Chapter 1 Outline

Food Service: A Diverse Industry
    Commercial Operations
    Noncommercial Operations
Food Service Origins
    Hotel Restaurants
    Freestanding Restaurants
    Food Service in Noncommercial
      Facilities
Organization of Commercial Operations
    Independents
    Chain Restaurants
    Franchises
Noncommercial Operations and Contract
    Management Companies
The Future of the Food Service Industry

Competencies

1. Distinguish between commercial and noncommercial food service operations. (pp. 3–9)

2. Outline the origins and development of food service in hotels, restaurants, and institutions. (pp. 9–13)

3. Identify and describe the three basic organizational categories of commercial food service operations, and discuss the use of for-profit contract management companies to run noncommercial operations. (pp. 13–17)

4. Identify trends likely to affect food service in the coming years. (pp. 17–18)

The Food Service Industry

WHEN YOU HEAR the term *food service*, you may picture a dining room with starched white tablecloths in an expensive restaurant. But do you also picture a truck stop on a busy interstate, or a concession operation in a professional sports arena? How about dietary services in schools, colleges, hospitals, nursing homes, and other institutions? And are you aware that military food service facilities and country clubs are also part of the food service industry? As you can see, the food service industry is vast, encompassing every type of food service operation that provides meals to people away from their homes and sometimes even in their homes.

Exhibit 1 presents a few interesting facts about the U.S. restaurant industry. Another way to get an idea of the industry's scope is to look at the food service giants. Exhibit 2 shows the largest quick-service and full-service chains. Quick-service restaurants are those with a low check average and limited menu items and service (frequently featuring self-service counters and drive-through service). Full-service restaurants have a higher check average and typically offer alcoholic beverage service.

Food Service: A Diverse Industry

Food service organizations can be divided into two broad segments: commercial and noncommercial. Sales generated by commercial organizations are significantly larger than the sales from noncommercial organizations. Exhibit 3 provides an overview of the food service industry. Note that the food service industry is part of the hospitality industry, and that the commercial and noncommercial segments are composed of many different types of organizations.

Commercial Operations

Commercial food service operations attempt to maximize profits through the sale of food and beverages. Examples of commercial operations include freestanding restaurants, food service in lodging properties, and numerous other types of facilities.

Freestanding Eating and Drinking Places. Freestanding eating and drinking places can be independent properties and chain properties, including those in Exhibit 2, or franchises. These organizational alternatives will be discussed later in the chapter. Freestanding eating and drinking places include white-tablecloth (high-check-average), casual-dining, family-service, and quick-service restaurants. They can provide indoor and/or outdoor table service and a wide variety of

3

Exhibit 1   Facts About the U.S. Restaurant Industry

America's Restaurants:

Small Businesses with a Large Impact on Our Nation's Economy

- Restaurant industry sales are projected to total $709.2 billion in 2015 and equal 4 percent of the U.S. gross domestic product.
- Restaurant-industry job growth is projected to outpace the overall economy for the sixteenth consecutive year in 2015.
- The restaurant industry is projected to employ 14 million people in 2015—about one in ten working Americans.
- The restaurant industry is expected to add 1.7 million jobs over the next decade, with employment reaching 15.7 million by 2025.
- More than nine in ten eating-and-drinking place businesses have fewer than fifty employees.
- More than seven in ten eating-and-drinking places are single-unit operations.
- $83,561 sales per full-time-equivalent employee at eating-and-drinking places in 2013.
- Average unit sales in 2011 were $874,000 at full-service restaurants and $777,000 at quick-service restaurants.

Cornerstones of Career and Entrepreneurial Opportunities

- One-half of all adults have worked in the restaurant industry at some point during their lives, and one out of three got their first job experience in a restaurant.
- Eight in ten restaurant owners say their first job in the restaurant industry was an entry-level position.
- Nine in ten restaurant managers started in entry-level positions.
- 58 percent of first-line supervisors/managers of food preparation and service workers in 2013 were women, 13 percent were black or African-American, and 19 percent were of Hispanic origin.
- Restaurants employ more minority managers than any other industry.
- The number of black- or African-American-owned restaurant businesses jumped 188 percent between 1997 and 2007, compared to a 36 percent increase for all restaurant businesses.
- The number of Hispanic-owned restaurant businesses increased 80 percent between 1997 and 2007, while the number of Asian-owned restaurant businesses grew 60 percent.
- The number of women-owned restaurant businesses rose 50 percent between 1997 and 2007.

An Essential Part of Daily Life

- Nine in ten consumers say they enjoy going to restaurants.

Exhibit 1   *(continued)*

> • Half of consumers say restaurants are an essential part of their lifestyle.
>
> • Seven in ten consumers say their favorite restaurant foods provide flavors that can't easily be duplicated at home.
>
> • Eight in ten consumers say going to a restaurant with family and friends is a better use of their leisure time than cooking and cleaning up.

Source: National Restaurant Association, *2015 Restaurant Industry Factbook;* available at www.restaurant.org (click on "News & Research"). The *Factbook* is updated annually.

Exhibit 2   Largest Quick-Service and Full-Service Restaurant Chains

Rank	Company/Chain Name	2013 U.S. Systemwide Sales (Millions)	Total Units in 2013
Quick-Service			
1	McDonald's	$35,856.3	14,278
2	Subway	$12,735.0	26,427
3	Starbucks	$11,723.0	11,457
4	Wendy's	$8,787.0	5,791
5	Burger King	$8,502.5	7,155
6	Taco Bell	$7,800.0	5,769
7	Dunkin' Donuts	$6,700.0	7,677
8	Pizza Hut	$5,700.0	7,846
9	Chick-fil-A	$5,052.6	1,775
10	KFC	$4,300.0	4,491
Full-Service			
1	Applebee's	$4,515.6	2,019
2	Chili's Grill & Bar	$3,795.0	1,265
3	Olive Garden	$3,615.0	831
4	IHOP	$2,825.9	1,593
5	Outback Steakhouse	$2,459.0	768
6	Red Lobster	$2,360.0	679
7	Denny's	$2,336.4	1,599
8	Cracker Barrel	$2,104.7	626
9	The Cheesecake Factory	$1,688.0	169
10	TGI Friday's	$1,622.0	416

Source: Adapted from *QSR Magazine,* "The QSR 50" (August 2014); retrieved 5-26-15; available at qsrmagazine.com; and *FSR Magazine,* "FSR 50: The Numbers" (August 2014); retrieved 5-28-15; available at fsrmagazine.com.

Exhibit 3   A Close Look at the Food Service Industry

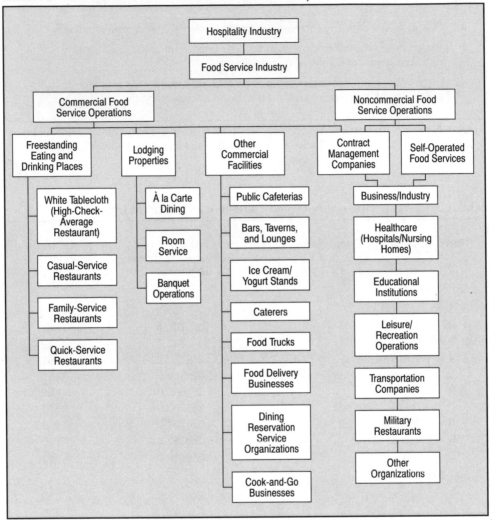

menu items. They may be open for only one meal period or for twenty-four hours daily. Some offer a *California style* menu: items that are usually served for breakfast, lunch, or dinner are offered at all times. Most white-tablecloth and many casual-dining restaurants serve alcoholic beverages.

Family-service properties offer **comfort foods** in a relaxed setting, typically without the availability of alcoholic beverages.

Lodging Food Service Facilities. Food service facilities are available in lodging operations ranging from the smallest bed-and-breakfast inns to the largest hotels, resorts, and conference centers. Just as with freestanding eating and drinking places, there are many types of hotel food service facilities, such as à la carte dining in coffee shops, family restaurants, specialty restaurants, and gourmet rooms.

Room service is frequently available, and many lodging operations also provide banquet services.

Historically, when hotels were classified according to food service, there were two types: full-service properties, which offered food and beverage services, and limited-service properties, which did not offer food and beverage services. This distinction is now blurred because many limited-service properties offer complimentary breakfast services, ranging from coffee and simple fruit or pastry items to more extensive, hot breakfast items. The term **lobby food service** has evolved to describe these offerings.

Many hoteliers realize that food and beverage departments cannot generate required profits on the basis of sales to in-house guests only. Extensive patronage from the local community is often necessary for hotel food and beverage operations to realize financial goals, and hoteliers aggressively market to the community and compete with other food service operators in the area.

A new option in lodging food services enables hotel guests to purchase food items at deli-bar or other sandwich/snack service areas and take the products to their rooms. Also, the availability of pizza and beer through room service allows hotels to compete with food and beverage operations outside the property.

Other Commercial Facilities. These include public cafeterias, bars, taverns, ice cream and frozen yogurt stands, and caterers. Public cafeterias are often similar to full-menu restaurants and lunchrooms because they offer a wide variety of menu items, but table service may be limited. Bars, taverns, and lounges serve alcoholic beverages, but typically offer limited or no food services. Ice cream and frozen yogurt stands offer primarily frozen dairy and related products. Caterers prepare meals for large or small banquets and may provide food service in on- or off-site locations.

Food trucks are a relatively recent addition to the food service marketplace. Traditionally offering snacks and limited menu offerings such as sandwiches and other simple items, the food truck concept has expanded to, for example, quick-service restaurants using trucks at large sports venues, and local chefs offering special items—even gourmet foods—at various locations (some of these chefs use Twitter and other social media to announce where they will be each day).

Food delivery businesses provide a service to guests who place online orders with restaurants by delivering their restaurant orders to them. Many properties have significantly increased their business with this new type of "take out" service system. Grub Hub (https://labs.grubhub.com) is a leader in this type of food delivery system.

Dining reservation service organizations offer restaurant management software that allows guests to make reservations at any time from the restaurant's website, Twitter account, or Facebook page, among other alternatives. Open Table (www.opentable.com) is an example of an organization offering these services.

"Cook-and-Go" businesses make available the ingredients and all cooking equipment needed for popular recipes. At these businesses, customers can prepare their own meals (guidance and classes are available) and take them home for consumption. Other organizations do the reverse: they prepackage weighed and measured fresh ingredients for popular recipes and ship the ingredients to the customer's location.

Noncommercial Operations

Noncommercial food service operations exist in properties for which providing food and beverage service is not the primary mission. Usually, but not always, noncommercial food service operations seek to minimize expenses while paying special attention to providing nutritious meals. Examples of facilities that provide food services include business/industry, healthcare, educational, leisure/recreation, and transportation organizations and private clubs.

Traditionally, noncommercial food service operations have focused on nutrition and other noneconomic factors. After all, people in some of these facilities receive 100 percent of their daily food intake at the facility (hospital patients, for example). This makes it especially important to protect the health and well-being of those being served. Trained dietitians are often retained on a full-time or consulting basis. In some cases, dietitians actually manage the food service operation; in others, they assist operating managers.

Food services in noncommercial operations can be offered by a for-profit contract management company or, alternatively, may be operated by the noncommercial organization itself.

Business/Industry Organizations. Programs for business/industry organizations range from vended services in manufacturing plants to gourmet dining facilities in the executive dining rooms of large banks, insurance companies, and other businesses. Food service programs for employees can exist in almost any type of work situation. Sometimes programs are subsidized by employers who offer them as a fringe benefit to employees.

Healthcare. Hospitals and nursing homes of all types make up an important part of the noncommercial food service market. Some of these facilities are privately owned; others are run by a government agency. In addition to acute-care hospitals where patients typically stay for only a short time and nursing homes that provide permanent care for their residents, there are homes for the blind, for orphans, and for mentally and physically handicapped people.

Educational Institutions. Food service for schools, such as public and private elementary and secondary schools and post-secondary schools (vocational schools, colleges, and universities), is a big business. Some public school systems in large cities serve hundreds of thousands of meals daily. Elementary and secondary schools may participate in the federally subsidized National School Lunch Program and other child-nutrition programs. In addition to traditional school lunches, school food service programs may include school breakfasts, meals at community events, and senior citizen meals.

Private Clubs. Private clubs can be member-owned and governed by a board of directors elected by the members. Alternatively, they can be nonequity clubs that are owned by individuals or corporations. Country (golf) clubs, city clubs, athletic clubs, and military, tennis, and yacht clubs are examples of facilities that provide food and beverage (and other) services to members who pay an initiation fee and subsequent monthly charges and membership dues.[1]

Leisure and Recreation Operations. Food service in amusement and theme parks, sports arenas and stadiums, and race tracks is a large and exciting part of noncommercial food service. Leisure operations that provide food service also include bowling alleys, summer camps, and hunting lodges.

Transportation Companies. Food services offered in transportation terminals and on airplanes, trains, and ships are included in this segment. Services range from vended operations to sandwich and short-order preparation to extravagant gourmet meals.

Military Restaurants. Food services provided to military personnel are varied and include cafeterias, dining rooms, and retail sales outlets, among others.

Other Organizations. There are many other organizations that offer food service to people away from their homes, including prisons, religious groups, athletic facilities, casinos, and cruise lines.

Food Service Origins

This section takes a brief look at the origins of hotel restaurants, freestanding restaurants, and food service in noncommercial facilities.

Hotel Restaurants

Food service operations as we know them today in hotels and other lodging operations evolved from early inns and other rest shelters for travelers. Just like travelers today, travelers in ancient times needed bed and board. The first innkeepers were families with houses located along popular travel routes who, for a fee, invited travelers to join them for food and a bed. Later, along with sleeping accommodations and food, inns also provided alcoholic beverages and entertainment for their guests. Innkeepers prepared meals from whatever food was available. There was usually plenty of wine and beer, plus cheese, vegetables, and a variety of cakes and buns. Meat, if available, included goat, pork, lamb, and fish. By the time of the Roman Empire, inns were commonplace.

The Roman Catholic Church. In the Middle Ages, the Roman Catholic Church maintained hospices (a type of inn), monasteries, and other religious houses that provided rest for travelers. In effect, the Church operated the first hotel chain.[2]

English Inns. In England, there were a few inns or *ale houses* that rented rooms as early as 1400. They were located in large towns, at major crossroads, at ferry landings, and along well-traveled roads. Whether travel was by foot, horseback, coach, or canal boat, travelers had to rest and eat, and inns provided necessary services for these travelers. Some inns were actually private homes with one or two extra bedrooms. Others were large buildings with many rooms.

American Inns. The evolution of inns and taverns in the United States was similar to the English pattern. While the food was often simple, it was plentiful; beer and rum were usually served also.[3] A tavern known as Cole's Ordinary was opened in Boston in 1634 by Samuel Cole; it was probably the first tavern in the American colonies. In America, as elsewhere, lodging and food service accommodations followed travel routes.

Hotels in the Twentieth Century. During the early 1900s, large hotels were constructed in nearly every large city in the United States. These hotels became very popular with travelers. Community events and special occasions often centered on the hotel and its food and beverage operation.

In the 1950s, the public perceived a decline in the quality of hotel food and beverage operations in many lodging properties. The mid-1970s saw a rebirth in the purpose and quality of hotel food service operations. Today, hotel restaurants are an integral part of the profit plan at many properties. Prime hotel space such as the lobby/atrium is often allocated to food and beverage outlets. Experienced chefs, high-quality food and beverage products and services, and well-planned community promotions have helped to create a new positive image for hotel food and beverage operations.

Freestanding Restaurants

An early form of restaurant, the coffeehouse, appeared in England in the mid-1600s. By the early eighteenth century, there were several thousand coffeehouses in London.

Restaurants as we know them today began in France in the late eighteenth century. Before then, public food services were offered by inns and catering operations. The caterers, called *traiteurs*, formed a guild (union) with limited membership. When a vendor created a soup made of sheep's feet and white wine sauce, he was brought to court by the guild because of alleged competition. However, the court ruled that this specialty dish did not compete with any dish prepared by the guild, and the vendor was allowed to continue. The soup vendor merchandised the soup as *le restaurant divin*—the divine restorative (which gave us the word *restaurant*).[4]

In the United States, credit for the first restaurant is generally given to Delmonico's, established in New York City in 1827. The Delmonico family operated nine restaurants until 1923 that were known for lavish banquets and extensive menus. Relatively few cities could support restaurants like Delmonico's, which offered high cuisine at high prices. Then, as now, the vast majority of American eating places offered simpler, less expensive food items.

The first big chain restaurant operator was Fred Harvey; by 1912, his company operated a dozen large hotels, sixty-five railway restaurants, and sixty dining cars. John R. Thompson was another early chain operator. By 1926, he had more than 100 self-service restaurants in the Midwest and the South.[5]

By the 1920s, there were enough automobiles in the United States to support a new type of food service facility: the drive-in restaurant. People could eat in their cars with curb service provided by carhops. In the 1960s, this innovation was largely replaced with indoor quick-service franchise operations. Today, many casual-service (and other) restaurants generate a significant amount of revenue from the sale of items sold to guests for at-home consumption. These guests may pick up their food at the restaurant via a drive-through window or may be provided with restricted parking spaces outside a separate restaurant door dedicated to take-out orders. Some operators even offer a new form of curb service by having service personnel take orders out to the guests' cars when guests arrive to pick up their food.

Quick-Service Franchise Operations. Nothing has had a greater impact on the food service industry than quick-service (also called *fast-food*) franchise operations. Quick-service franchising dates back to at least the 1920s and 1930s when A&W Restaurants and Howard Johnson's franchised some of their units.[6]

Sandwiches, primarily hamburgers, rule the quick-service segment of the industry. Hamburgers' origins can be traced back to medieval times, but they were first served on a bun at the St. Louis World's Fair in 1904. Quick-service chain restaurants that feature hamburgers, such as McDonald's, Wendy's, and Burger King are increasingly familiar throughout much of the world.

Food Service in Noncommercial Facilities

There are many types of noncommercial food service programs; to cover the origins of them all is beyond our scope. However, we will look at three institutions especially important to the development of noncommercial food service: businesses, hospitals, and schools.

Businesses. Robert Owen has been called "the father of industrial catering." As a young mill operator in Scotland, Owen was appalled by the exploitation of workers in the British textile industry. About 1815, as part of a general program to improve the working conditions of his employees, he established a large "eating room" for employees and their families. Owen's methods were so successful that they spread throughout the world.

By the 1890s, some factories, insurance companies, banks, and other businesses in industrialized countries provided food service for employees. Cafeteria service was not introduced to businesses until 1902, when a building housing a kitchen, two cafeterias, and recreational facilities was built for the Plymouth Cordage Company in Plymouth, Massachusetts.

Today's Food Services Offer Something for Everyone

Drive-throughs are common in quick-service operations and can account for 50 percent or more of the total revenue in some quick-service units. Food courts in shopping malls provide shoppers with many different types of food choices in one convenient location. An increasing number of grocery stores, convenience stores, and gas stations devote a significant amount of space to self-service salads, sandwiches, snacks, and other items that can be taken out or consumed on-site in sit-down or stand-up locations. Quick-service operations, once found only in freestanding buildings, now occupy space in hotels, department stores, airline terminals, military installations, healthcare facilities, schools and colleges, and elsewhere.

The options made available to the dining-out public continue to expand. Do you want table- or quick-service offerings of ethnic foods? How about restaurants featuring very small entrée portions so guests can order several samples? Many guests want low-fat, low-carbohydrate, and other healthy foods, and many restaurants in the commercial segment offer these to their guests. (In fact, some offer only these.)

World War I saw an increase in the number of businesses that offered food service to workers. As manufacturing plants expanded and workers became scarce, providing food service was a means of attracting and keeping good workers. Cafeteria service became more popular, since large numbers of workers could be fed quickly, fewer people were needed to run a cafeteria, and workers could select the food they wanted at the prices they were willing to pay.

World War II saw another leap in the number of businesses providing food service. By the end of the war, approximately one-third of all industrial workers were being fed on the job.

Of course, business food service programs have changed in many ways since 1945. The coffee break was introduced widely during World War II and is now a business standard. Many businesses provide coffee to employees throughout the workday for free or for a modest fee. Many vending service companies and other vendors provide **office coffee service** for client companies. It is not just the industry giants who provide food service today; small businesses are also establishing food service programs to improve employee morale and productivity. Programs range from gourmet dining to food available from vending machines. Meals can be prepared on-site or catered in. Nutrition is increasingly emphasized; more business food service programs provide nutritious menu alternatives and educate employees about eating properly.

Hospitals. India and Egypt had crude hospitals as early as 600 B.C. In early Greece and Rome, the sick took refuge in temples; as with hospitals today, food was provided for patients. England's first hospital was established in A.D. 1004. The first hospital on the North American continent was established in Mexico in 1524.

An emphasis on a therapeutic diet designed to help restore patient health became important in hospitals in the mid-1800s. It was during this period that an English nurse, Florence Nightingale, created the beginnings of modern hospital organization. She is considered the first modern hospital administrator and dietitian.

In early hospitals in the United States, food preparation was the responsibility of a cook, the head housekeeper, or the head nurse. As the relationship of nutrition to a patient's recovery and good health became apparent, doctors began to seek people in food service to assist in creating healthy diets for their patients. At an 1899 Home Economics Conference, the title of *dietitian* was given to people who entered this new profession.

Menus offering patients a selection of items are the norm for most hospitals today. Centralized kitchens make food preparation more efficient. Many hospitals have cash cafeterias for employees and visitors. In an increasing number of hospitals, contract management companies run the food service operation under the guidance of a dietitian. Modern hospital food service programs feature extensive menus, high-quality food products, and modern preparation and service equipment. Many hospital food service programs are comparable in many ways with commercial food service operations. In fact, some hospital food service facilities compete with commercial operations by offering take-home food for employees and those visiting patients.

Schools. Although schools existed in ancient times, there are few records of their methods of food service. The universities that were established in Europe during the twelfth century typically did not provide food service. Students boarded with residents of the local community and were responsible for their own meals. Students at Oxford (founded in England in the latter part of the twelfth century) and Cambridge (established in the thirteenth century) had living quarters on campus, but had to make their own meals with the help of their servants. Eventually, dining halls were established at these universities. In these halls, a very formal evening meal was provided.

English public schools such as Rugby, Eton, and Harrow evolved from religious institutions established during the Middle Ages. (Because of their character and approach to education, public schools in England are the equivalent of private schools in the United States.) These and other public schools were not known for their food service. Charles Dickens paints a bleak picture of public schools and the food they served in *Nicholas Nickleby* and other novels.

American schools were patterned after English schools. By 1776, ten universities were established in the American colonies. From the beginning, various forms of food service were provided at each university. School food services in elementary and secondary schools began in the mid-1800s and evolved into modern programs reaching millions of students daily during the school year. In 1935, Congress first made federal funds available to subsidize school food programs. Federal support programs have continued and expanded in the years since.

Early school food service at the university level tended to be table service. Today, universities (as well as elementary and secondary schools) prefer cafeteria service. Food service in residence halls, student unions, and lunchrooms can be provided by the schools themselves or by contract management companies. Care is usually taken to provide (or at least make available) well-balanced meals. Commercial food service operations have been built near college campuses for hundreds of years. As many readers of this chapter know, food service offerings in post-secondary school facilities can be extensive. Students may have access to numerous menus in residence halls and other locations throughout campus. In addition, there may be à la carte restaurants, take-out operations, home (room) delivery, convenience stores, snack bars, quick-service units (independent or school- or franchise-operated), vending, concessions, banquet operations, and others.[7]

Organization of Commercial Operations

Commercial food services can fall into three basic categories: independents, chain units, and franchises.

Independents

An **independent operation** is owned by an owner or owners who have one or more properties with no chain relationship. If multiple units are owned, menus may not be identical among properties, food purchase specifications may differ, operating procedures may vary, etc. These properties are sometimes referred to as "mom and pop" operations.

New operators are lured into the restaurant business for many reasons. "People have to eat; why shouldn't they eat at my place?" is a thought that has launched many restaurants. New entrepreneurs are further encouraged because many restaurants require relatively little capital to get started. Land, facilities, and equipment can be leased, and the minimal amount of inventory needed to open a restaurant can often be purchased on several weeks' credit. However, a large number of restaurants that open are not in business five years later, and the statistics work against independent operators.

In an industry increasingly dominated by chain restaurants and franchise operations, is there still a place for an independent operator? The answer is *yes*. Entrepreneurs who can spot a market whose wants and needs are not currently being met may be able to capture that market and prosper—if they consistently provide value and good service to guests.

Chain Restaurants

Chain restaurants are part of a multi-unit organization. They often have the same menu, purchase supplies and equipment cooperatively, and follow operating procedures that have been standardized for every restaurant in the chain. A chain restaurant may be owned by a parent company, a franchise company, or by a private owner or owners.

Some people incorrectly believe that a chain and a franchise operation are the same. They are not. While a franchise property is affiliated with a chain, a chain property is not necessarily a franchise; it may be company-owned, for example.

What are the advantages of restaurant chains? Large chains can readily acquire cash, credit, and long-term leases on land and buildings. This is not as feasible for many independent properties. Chains can afford to make more mistakes than independent operators can, so it is easier for chains to experiment with different menus, themes, designs, and operating procedures. After it discovers the correct "mix," the chain can develop a package for use by all its properties. The independent operator has limited opportunities to undertake extensive experimentation.

Restaurant chains also have a personnel advantage. Chains can afford staff specialists who are experts in finance, construction, laws, operations, and recipe development. Independent operators must handle most, if not all, of these responsibilities on their own or must retain the services of accountants, attorneys, and other professional specialists as necessary.

Chains have another advantage from a control perspective. They are able to generate internal financial information that can be used as a basis of comparison among properties. Independent operators usually know how well their restaurants *are* doing, but are frequently unaware of how well their restaurants *should be* doing. A restaurant chain operating many properties within a specific geographic area can more easily generate information that can be used to set revenue and cost goals, as well as to identify problems in specific properties.

On the other hand, there are also disadvantages to restaurant chains. It can be difficult for chains to keep up with changing markets and economic conditions. As chains grow, a bureaucracy involving a large amount of paperwork, rules, and procedures can slow them down. Top management may lose the motivation to keep up, and what is best for the company might not always receive the highest priority.

Commercial Organizations Can Be Complex

The typical guest who visits the à la carte dining room of a chain-affiliated hotel has no idea (nor does he or she care) how the property is organized. Consider, however, that the hotel:

- Can be owned by one or more investors (or organizations).

- May be affiliated with a franchisor (chain) selected by the owner(s). The chain has a brand (Hilton, Marriott, or Sheraton, for example), and a visitor to the property associates that brand with his or her experience while visiting the property.

- Might be managed by a contract management company.

- Could have sub-contracted food services in the à la carte dining room to a fourth party (for example, an independent restaurant operator in the community).

Note that this arrangement does not shield the owner(s) from food service–related problems. A diner who experiences problems in the restaurant will not be upset with the independent restaurant operator. The diner's perception is likely to be of the brand that operates the restaurant. You can begin to see why the brand (franchisor) must have some control over the standards that drive the operation of the hotel, including its restaurants.

Franchises

Franchises are a special category of chain operations. With a franchise, the **franchisee** (the owner of a specific property) pays fees to a **franchisor** (or franchise company) in exchange for the right to use the franchisor's name, building design, and business methods. Furthermore, the franchisee must agree to maintain the franchisor's business and quality standards. The franchisor expands its franchise chain by signing up franchisees. Franchisees are often local businesspeople with investment funds. However, large companies seeking investment options may also purchase a franchise.

The franchisee is usually responsible for generating funds to start the business. In addition to initial franchise fees, the franchisee may be required to pay royalty fees assessed on the basis of a specified percentage of revenue or other factors, as well as advertising costs, sign rental fees, and other costs such as stationery and food products. (It may be against the law to stipulate as part of the franchise agreement that the franchisee must buy products of any kind from the franchisor. However, the franchisor can establish quality requirements that product suppliers providing items to the franchise must meet.)

The benefits of owning or managing a food service franchise typically include:

- Start-up assistance.

- Company-sponsored training programs for management staff and training resource materials for employees.

- National contributions toward local advertising campaigns.

- More revenue because of more extensive advertising, greater name recognition of the franchise chain, and the consistency of products and services among chain properties (guests know what to expect).

- Lower food costs due to volume purchasing by the chain.

- Tested operating procedures that specify how things should be done.

- Name recognition that often makes it easier to recruit new staff members.

Many food service franchisors and franchisees have been tremendously successful. When franchisors are successful, they can command high fees and there may be long waiting lists to buy a franchise. Often, the franchisees are screened, and there may be little choice in the areas (territories) that are available for purchase.

There are also disadvantages to owning or managing a food service franchise. The contract is often very restrictive. The franchisee has little choice about the style of operation, the products served, services offered, and even methods of operation. The menu might be set, along with the decor, required furnishings, and production equipment. Since the franchise agreement is drawn up by the franchisor, the document generally favors the franchisor. The agreement may leave little room to negotiate. This causes problems if there are disagreements between the two parties.[8] Most typically, a franchisee operates a unit such as a McDonald's or Dunkin' Donuts in a freestanding building or in rented space to which the public has access (for example, in a shopping mall, a hotel lobby, or an airport terminal). However, some franchisees use a **co-branding** tactic in which, for example, two noncompeting brands (such as McDonald's and Dunkin' Donuts) share the building, parking lot, and dining space.

Noncommercial Operations and Contract Management Companies

Today, as pressures for cost containment accompany lower revenue and bottom lines, there is a need to manage noncommercial food service operations as professional businesses. An increasing number of organizations are using for-profit contract management companies to operate their food service programs. There are some advantages to their use:

- Large nationwide management companies have greater resources to solve problems.

- Management companies can save money through effective negotiations with suppliers.

- Management companies can often operate noncommercial food service programs at a lower cost than their self-operated counterparts.

- Facility administrators, trained in areas other than food service operations, can delegate food service responsibilities to professional food service managers. (Large institutions often retain a *food service liaison* with industry management experience to represent them in initial negotiations and ongoing operations with management company personnel.)

There are also potential disadvantages to using contract management companies:

- Some management companies may assume too much control in matters that affect the public image of the institution, long-range operating plans, and other important issues.

- Some people dislike having a profit-making business involved in the operation of a healthcare, educational, or other noncommercial food service program.

- There may be concerns that a management company will decrease food and beverage quality.

- The organization may become dependent on the management company. What happens if the management company discontinues the contract? How long will it take to implement a self-operated program or select another management company?

The Future of the Food Service Industry

No one can accurately predict how the complex and diverse food service industry will evolve. Several impacts of the global recession that began in 2008 and affected almost all businesses everywhere have shown staying power. With the Great Recession officially over, food service owners and managers continue to seek ways to provide higher levels of guest value (price relative to the quality of the products and dining experience provided), and they continue to aggressively market their organizations to consumers. Additionally, they have worked hard to find ways to reduce operating costs without sacrificing quality standards. This effort to eliminate unnecessary costs continues, and often provides a competitive edge that reduces the need to increase selling prices. Other food service trends include the following:

- In the commercial food service sector, many observers believe that home meal replacements will continue to increase in popularity. Consumers are looking for convenience, and have (or want to spend) less time at home preparing meals. Restaurants and supermarkets are competing aggressively with each other to capture this market. Both can offer fully cooked, ready-to-eat or ready-to-heat food items that could make up a major part of a meal or serve as the entire meal. An increasing number of restaurants offer carry-out or delivery services; more supermarkets are offering prepared items in close-to-the-door locations for guests on the go. The food delivery and "cook-and-go" businesses introduced earlier in the chapter result from this trend.

- In the quick-service segment of the industry, look for new foods and higher-quality items that emphasize value. Some observers also predict more consolidation (quick-service chains buying other chains) and more creative marketing strategies in this segment.

- In casual-dining operations, look for more entertainment (sometimes termed *eatertainment*), the goal being to provide a total dining entertainment experience for guests.

- Convenience stores, which in the past have served mostly snack foods, will gain market share. One way is through co-branding. For example, they may share store space with a well-known quick-service brand. This may quickly change the public's perception about the variety and quality of food available in convenience stores.

- For restaurants, expect changes in menu items. Comfort foods, new ethnic-fusion preparations that combine two or more ethnic cuisines into one dish, and more healthy food choices are among restaurant trends expected to unfold in the near future.

- **Green restaurants** will become more popular with the industry and the public, and will increasingly emphasize sustainability practices that reduce energy usage and minimize waste.

- The industry will continue to look for and invest in ways that allow technology to improve operations. The use of technology is increasing in food service organizations today. Additional innovations will enable food service decision-makers to more proficiently and effectively perform their jobs. Creative use of social media will enable food service organizations to pinpoint the focus of their advertising efforts.

Endnotes

1. Readers interested in private clubs should see Joe Perdue and Jason Koenigsfeld, editors, *Contemporary Club Management,* 3rd ed. (Lansing, Mich.: American Hotel & Lodging Educational Institute, 2013).

2. Jack D. Ninemeier and David K. Hayes, *Menu Planning, Design, and Education: Managing for Appeal and Profit,* 2nd ed. (Richmond, Cal.: McCutchan Publishing Corp., 2008), p. 5.

3. Readers desiring more information about the history of the food service industry should see Gerald W. Lattin, Thomas W. Lattin, and James E. Lattin, *The Lodging and Food Service Industry,* 8th ed. (Lansing, Mich.: American Hotel & Lodging Educational Institute, 2014), Chapter 7.

4. Lattin, p. 133.

5. Donald E. Lundberg, *The Hotel and Restaurant Business,* 6th ed. (Boston: CBI, 1979), p. 203.

6. Lundberg, p. 297.

7. Much of this section is based on material in John W. Stokes, *Food Service in Industry and Institutions* (Dubuque, Ia.: Brown, 1960), pp. 1–15.

8. More information on franchise contracts is available in Jack P. Jefferies and Banks Brown, *Understanding Hospitality Law,* 5th ed. (Lansing, Mich.: American Hotel & Lodging Educational Institute, 2010).

Key Terms

chain restaurant—A restaurant that is part of a multi-unit organization. Chain restaurants often have the same menu, purchase supplies and equipment cooperatively, and follow operating procedures that have been standardized for every restaurant in the chain.

co-branding—A food service arrangement in which two noncompeting brands are offered to consumers in the same building location.

comfort foods—Familiar foods that remind consumers of the foods they ate during childhood or the foods they prepare at home.

commercial food service operation—An operation that sells food and beverages for profit. Independent, chain, and franchise properties are all commercial food service operations.

franchise—A special type of chain operation in which a facility owner (the franchisee) pays fees to a franchisor in exchange for the right to use the name, building design, and business methods of the franchisor.

franchisee—Someone who owns (or leases) a property and building and purchases the right to use a brand name for a specified period of time and at an agreed-upon price. The price includes royalties based upon revenues and contributions to regional and/or national advertising programs.

franchisor—Someone who owns and manages a brand and sells the right to use the brand name.

green restaurants—Restaurants that implement practical solutions to reduce their environmental impacts.

independent operation—An operation owned by an owner or owners with one or more properties that have no chain relationship—menus might not be identical among properties, food purchase specifications might differ, operating procedures are varied, and so on.

lobby food services—Complimentary food/beverage alternatives provided to guests, typically in lobbies or public areas of limited-service lodging operations.

noncommercial food service operation—A food service operation within an institution such as a business, hospital, or school. Traditionally, noncommercial food service operations have focused on nutrition and other noneconomic factors; today, as costs mount, there is a need to manage noncommercial food service operations as professional businesses.

office coffee service—A vendor-provided service that delivers coffee and other beverages and snacks to offices and other workplaces.

 Review Questions

1. Freestanding eating and drinking places include what types of operations?
2. What are some trends in hotel food service?
3. What are some examples of noncommercial food service operations?
4. Who had the responsibility for food preparation in early hospitals? Who typically has that responsibility today?

5. What are three basic types of commercial food service operations?

6. What are some of the advantages and disadvantages of chain restaurants? franchises?

7. What are the advantages and disadvantages of using a management company to run a noncommercial food service operation?

8. What food service trends might we see in the future? What factors affect food service trends?

Internet Sites

For more information, visit the following Internet sites. Remember that addresses can change without notice. If the site is no longer there, you can use a search engine to look for additional sites.

Food Service Publications

Chef
www.chefmagazine.com

Fast Casual
www.fastcasual.com

Food Management
www.food-management.com

Food Service Director
www.foodservicedirector.com

Food Service News
www.foodservicenews.com

FSR Magazine
www.fsrmagazine.com

Hotel F&B Magazine
www.hotelfandb.com

National Restaurant Association
  SmartBrief
www.smartbrief.com/restaurant

Nation's Restaurant News
www.nrn.com

QSR Web (Quick-Service Restaurants)
www.qsrweb.com

Restaurant Business
www.restaurantbusinessonline.com

Restaurant Hospitality
www.restaurant-hospitality.com

Restaurants & Institutions
www.rimag.com

Food Service Professional Associations

American Culinary Federation
www.acfchefs.org

American Dietetic Association
www.eatright.org

Club Managers Association of America
www.cmaa.org

International Food Service Executives
  Association
www.ifsea.com

North American Association of Food
  Equipment Manufacturers
www.nafem.org

Restaurant/Food Online Communities

FohBoh
www.fohboh.com

Food and Beverage Underground
www.foodandbeverageunderground.com

Contract Management Companies

Aramark
www.aramark.com

Sodexo
www.sodexousa.com

Compass Group USA
http://compass-usa.com

Chapter 2 Outline

People in Food Service
  Management Staff
  Production Personnel
  Service Personnel
Sample Organization Charts
Career Paths in Food Service
  Your Future in the Industry

Competencies

1. Identify a variety of managerial, production, and service positions that are typical of the food service industry, and describe the roles these positions play in providing food service. (pp. 23–35)

2. Explain the purpose of an organization chart, and identify the organizational structures of various kinds of food service operations. (pp. 35–38)

3. Describe several critical issues that a person should consider before starting a career in food service. (pp. 38–42)

2

Organization of Food and Beverage Operations

THIS CHAPTER focuses on the organizational structures of food service operations. Organizations are created to achieve objectives, some of which are financial. Commercial properties want to maximize profits; most noncommercial operations want to minimize expenses in order to reduce or eliminate sponsor subsidies. An organization can have numerous other objectives as well. Food and beverage quality; human relations, including employee training; and societal contributions are among them.

The way an organization is structured affects its ability to achieve objectives. If, for example, supervisors must direct the work of too many employees, they are less likely to provide the individual attention necessary to foster effective interactions with employees, and human relations objectives might be unattainable.

All objectives of a food service operation must be considered as long- and short-term plans for the organization are developed. For example, assume a hospital food service operation wants to ensure that nutrition requirements are met in all meals, that proper nutrition education is provided for all patients or residents, and that community outreach efforts are successful. It is then necessary to create the employee positions to cover these responsibilities. Employees must be recruited, selected, and trained for these positions.

An **organization chart** is a diagram showing the formal relationships among various employee positions in an operation. In this chapter, we will review organization charts for various types of food service operations. First, however, let's take a look at some food service positions and learn what production and service personnel do in their jobs.

People in Food Service

The food service industry is **labor-intensive**: a large number of people is required to do the work necessary to attain food service objectives. Technology has not changed this basic fact. There was experimentation with computerized kitchens as early as the 1960s, but, while this effort has introduced some automated and specialized equipment as it has evolved, no one has found a way to replace people with equipment to any significant degree in most food service operations. Even if this was possible, the "service" component in food service and hospitality means that many consumers want to be served by people, not machines. Also, while technology is available to provide relatively high-quality convenience foods, today's *fresh is best* philosophy in many industry segments eliminates this alternative that could potentially reduce food production labor costs. Most guests want human service and will pay for it; automation may not significantly reduce service labor costs in the foreseeable future in most types of food service operations.

Food service employees fall into three general categories: managers, supervisors, and entry-level production and service personnel. This chapter reviews the responsibilities of some of these staff members. Note that the position titles used in the following sections may vary from operation to operation, and not all of the positions described are found in every operation.

Management Staff

In general, there are three levels of managers in a specific operation: top managers, middle managers, and supervisors. The positions constituting each level vary by property, as do the duties assigned to each position. Whether department heads are considered top or middle managers, for example, depends on the organization's size. Chefs are top managers in some operations and middle managers in others. Exhibit 1 illustrates the relationships between employees in a single-unit food service operation.

Note that two levels of managers (top- and mid-level) are shown in the exhibit. The former might include people with such job titles as general manager and assistant general manager. In a large operation, they may need assistance from staff personnel with accounting, purchasing, and human resources responsibilities. In this technical capacity, **staff personnel** provide advice to those in the chain of command, but do not make decisions for them. The chart also indicates that top-level managers direct the work of mid-level managers, who may include department heads responsible for food production, beverage operations, and dining-room service.

Exhibit 1   Relationships Between Staff Members in a Single-Unit Operation

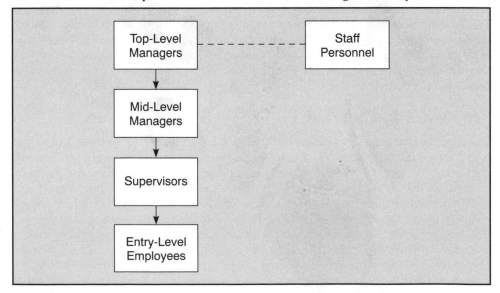

Top-level managers are concerned with long-term plans and goals. They focus more than other managers on the external business environment in general. They watch for environmental opportunities and threats, such as competitors' changes in strategy, a sluggish economy, and changes in consumer preferences.

Middle managers are in key positions through which communication flows up and down the organization. They are concerned with shorter-term goals, and typically are less concerned with large issues affecting the business environment. They manage the work of supervisors.

Supervisors are sometimes referred to as *linking pins*. They must represent higher levels of management to employees and, at the same time, transfer employee wishes and concerns upward. A supervisory position is the first level of management. Supervisors generally use their technical skills more than other managers, and they are concerned with such short-term goals as preparing employee schedules and helping employees through the busy times that occur during almost every meal period.

Entry-level employees who exhibit superior knowledge and skills and who desire positions with more responsibility often become supervisors. That position is complex and certainly not for everyone, but it is an interesting position to which employees can aspire.

In large multi-unit chain corporations, top management may begin with a board of directors elected by stockholders (see Exhibit 2). The board of directors is responsible for the long-range strategic planning of the corporation and for

Exhibit 2   Top Managers in a Corporation

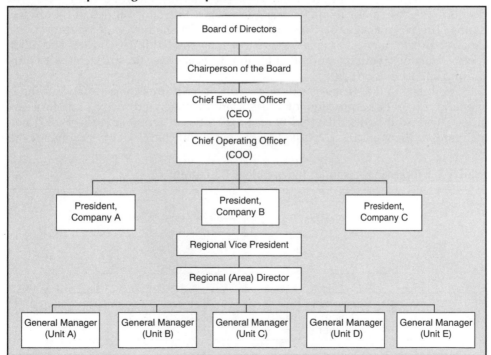

high-level evaluation and decision-making activities that affect current operations. The board may elect or appoint a chairperson to coordinate the board's work. Many operations also retain a chief executive officer (CEO) who serves as an intermediary between the board of directors and lower-level managers. One person may hold the titles of chairperson of the board and CEO. Sometimes a chief operating officer (COO) assumes some of the CEO's responsibility for direct control over operational aspects of the business.

Very large organizations that own several food service companies, and, perhaps, have business interests in non-food service areas as well, may have presidents to assume responsibility for specific companies. As shown in Exhibit 2, each president may have regional vice presidents who supervise regional or area directors. They, in turn, oversee the work of general managers, who manage individual properties. (Large restaurant chain organizations frequently refer to the managers of their restaurants or units as *unit managers* rather than *general managers*. Since the duties are virtually the same for both unit and general managers, we will use the term *general manager* throughout the chapter.)

Even though it is contrary to the impressions of employees in specific food service properties, in large corporations it is common to refer to the general managers of individual restaurants or hotels as middle management, not top management. Exhibit 2 shows why this is so; general managers are relatively far down on the corporation's organization chart.

Exhibit 3 shows top managers in an independent restaurant. The general manager oversees five department heads, as well as a controller (a staff position concerned with the restaurant's finances). The chef is concerned with food production. The restaurant manager has guest service responsibilities in the dining rooms. The bar manager assumes responsibility for the beverage operation, the catering director manages tasks relating to selling and holding banquets and other special functions (both on- and off-site), and the executive steward deals with purchasing and sanitation.

Exhibits 4 and 5, respectively, show **job descriptions** for a restaurant manager and a hospital's equivalent of a restaurant manager: a director of dietary services. These exhibits describe typical responsibilities of general managers and also list many of their specific job tasks. As the person in charge of operations for the

Exhibit 3   Top Managers in an Independent Restaurant

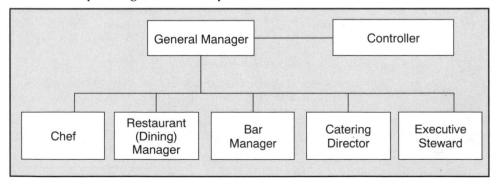

Exhibit 4   Job Description—Restaurant Manager

I.   Basic Responsibilities

Responsible for meeting all budget goals; for ensuring that quality standards for food and beverage production and service to guests are constantly maintained; for meeting with clients and booking special catered events; for supervising, scheduling, and training the food and beverage controller and assistant managers; for delegating general management tasks to assistant managers; for verifying through analysis of source documents that all revenue due is collected from food and beverage sales; for designing/improving existing cash security and recordkeeping/accounting systems; for meeting budgeted cost goals; and for supervising department heads in absence of Assistant Restaurant Managers.

II.   Specific Duties

A. Develops (with department head assistance) and approves operating budgets.

B. Monitors budget to control expenses.

C. Serves as restaurant contact for all advertising/marketing activities.

D. Supervises, schedules, and trains Food and Beverage Controller and Assistant Restaurant Managers.

E. Provides information required by the controller for payroll, tax, and financial statement and related purposes.

F. Reviews all operating reports with department heads; conducts regular and special meetings to correct operating problems.

G. Meets with prospective clients; plans and prices special catered events.

H. Designs and improves restaurant revenue security and cash disbursement systems.

I. Conducts cost-reduction/minimization studies.

J. Audits source documents to ensure that all revenue due has been collected.

K. Delegates miscellaneous administrative tasks to assistant managers.

L. Serves as restaurant's contact with insurance agent, attorney, banker, and accountant.

M. Reviews department reports; makes recommendations and follows up to ensure that all problems have been corrected.

N. Is available to provide assistance as needed during busy periods.

O. Addresses special problems as assigned by owner.

III.   Reports to

Owners.

IV.   Supervises

Assistant Restaurant Managers, Food and Beverage Controller; department heads in absence of Assistant Restaurant Managers.

V.   Equipment Used

Must be able to operate and perform minor repairs on all equipment in restaurant and know how to operate, generate, and interpret reports from the property's point-of-sale system.

VI.   Working Conditions

Works in all areas of restaurant; long hours, standing, and walking are routine components of the job.

VII.   Other

Must know how to operate and do minor maintenance and repair work on food production and service equipment and building heating, ventilating, air conditioning, plumbing, and electrical systems. Must be tactful and courteous in dealing with the public.

Exhibit 5   Job Description—Director of Dietary Services

I.   General Functions

Responsible for managing the entire department; for maintaining functional relationships between Administration, Nursing Services, and other departments and departmental staff of Dietary Services; for implementing and maintaining a system of quality assurance; for developing and administering a policy and procedure manual for all Dietary Services activities; and for preparing necessary financial and operational reports as required.

II.   Specific Responsibilities

A. Develops departmental regulations in conformance with administrative policies and procedures and sets standards for the organization and supervision of Dietary Services.

B. Meets at least weekly with Assistant Directors of Dietary Services to determine standardization and management effectiveness.

C. Coordinates the development and administration of a training program for management and supervisory personnel.

D. Develops policies and procedures governing the handling and storage of food and supplies and equipment.

E. Maintains financial records as required by Administration, including monthly cost reports.

F. Meets with staff to review progress and make future plans for Dietary Services.

G. Monitors daily operations to ensure quality and nutritional food services to patients, employees, and visitors.

H. Maintains safety and sanitation standards to ensure compliance with all regulatory agencies.

I.   Prepares realistic budgets for each cost center. Monitors the budget for conformance. Takes necessary action when there is a deviation from the budget.

J. Reviews and evaluates the performance of supervisory staff.

K. Administers the preparation of job descriptions, scheduling manuals, and guidebooks covering all phases of the Dietary Services operations, and interacts with the facility's human resources personnel to ensure applicable policies are implemented.

L. Attends professional meetings and conferences to keep informed of current ideas, issues, and trends in the field of healthcare food services.

M. Performs other related duties as requested by the Vice President of General Services.

III.   Education

Must have a minimum of a Bachelor of Science degree in Food Service Management, Nutrition, or Business Administration. A Master's degree is preferred.

V.   Experience

Must have a minimum of five years' experience in all phases of hospital food service preparation and administration.

property, whether a freestanding restaurant, hotel food and beverage department, or noncommercial food service operation, the general manager is basically responsible for all aspects of the operation. Much of this work involves setting objectives, creating plans to reach those objectives, and evaluating the extent to which objectives have been attained.

Exhibit 6 is a job description of a hotel beverage manager. Beverage managers are typically considered middle management.

Line and Staff. Line managers typically have authority within or over one or more revenue-generating departments that directly provide goods or services to guests. Staff managers provide support and advice to line managers. Staff managers and their departments do not have a direct impact on bringing in revenue. Rather, they are technical specialists who provide advice and services to managers in line positions. Staff managers and specialists in many large food service operations include the following, who were briefly noted earlier:

- *Human resources manager.* Large food service operations often have a human resources department with specialists supervised by a manager or director. Among other duties, the human resources manager recruits applicants for vacant positions, conducts preliminary employee selection activities, and makes hiring recommendations to line managers. The final hiring decisions rest with the line managers of the departments in which the employee will work, not with the human resources manager. This staff specialist may also develop and conduct orientation programs, know and provide up-to-date information about labor-related laws, and develop guest-service and other generic training programs.

- *Controller.* The controller typically reports to the general manager, but sometimes to area or regional directors above the general manager. Controllers and their staffs develop and interpret financial statements to help line managers make effective decisions. Controllers also help determine menu selling prices, audit point-of-sale data, and develop specialized records and reports for use by line managers as they make operating decisions.

- *Purchasing agent.* This staff specialist obtains information about food and other products required by the operation, selects suppliers, expedites incoming orders, and makes buying decisions, among other tasks.

- *Other staff specialists.* Large restaurant chains may have corporate-level attorneys, real estate specialists, and construction experts at their headquarters to assist in the chain's expansion efforts. Many noncommercial food service operations have such staff specialists as dietitians or nutritionists who help plan menus to ensure that nutrition requirements are met. Healthcare facilities may employ therapeutic dietitians to audit patients' diets.

Production Personnel

Production employees, also called back-of-the-house or heart-of-the-house employees, are concerned primarily with food production and usually have relatively little contact with guests. Certain basic production tasks must be assigned

Exhibit 6   Job Description—Hotel Beverage Manager

I. Overview

Responsible to the Food and Beverage Director for the successful and profitable management of the lounges and bars within the hotel and for the operation of beverage-only hospitality suites and group functions.

II. Specific Responsibilities

Responsible for:

A. Maintaining warm, hospitable relations in all guest contacts.

B. Developing and meeting or exceeding budgeted goals in revenues, costs, and profits for the beverage operation.

C. Developing accurate and aggressive long- and short-range financial objectives relating to alcoholic beverage sales.

D. Implementing an effective program to serve alcoholic beverages responsibly.

E. Maintaining housekeeping and sanitation standards in lounges and bars.

F. Planning and implementing sales promotion programs in lounges and bars.

G. Knowing the competition and keeping current with industry trends.

H. Maintaining effective revenue and cost controls in the Beverage Department.

I. Implementing and supporting company policies and procedures.

J. Maintaining a high level of professional appearance, demeanor, ethics, and image of self and subordinates.

K. Implementing professional development activities for self and subordinates.

L. Communicating effectively between the department and the Food and Beverage Director within areas of responsibility.

M. Operating in compliance with all local, state, and/or federal laws and government regulations.

N. Maintaining fair wage and salary administration in the department in accordance with corporate policies and applicable laws.

O. Assessing and reviewing the job performance of subordinates and maintaining personnel records of assigned employees as described in the Personnel Policy Manual.

P. Conducting and attending regular department meetings.

Q. Directing and coordinating the activities of all assigned personnel and meeting department responsibilities.

R. Hiring, orienting, training, and supervising assigned personnel to meet department responsibilities.

S. Maintaining positive employee relations in a supportive environment.

T. Interacting with staff in other departments to ensure a harmonious working relationship.

U. Ensuring good safety practices of employees and guests throughout the property and assisting in the maintenance of proper emergency and security procedures.

V. Performing special projects as requested.

to employees regardless of a food service operation's type or size. As production volumes increase, positions become more specialized. Then typical production personnel include the following:

- Executive chefs and assistant chefs
- Cooks and assistant cooks
- Bakers (pastry chefs)
- Pantry (cold food) staff
- Chief stewards and stewards who have cleaning and related responsibilities
- Storeroom and receiving employees

Executive Chefs and Assistant Chefs. Executive chefs are managers in charge of production personnel in the kitchen. In large operations, an executive chef may perform managerial duties only, while other chefs assume production duties. In smaller operations, the executive or head chef (he or she may be the only chef) has both managerial and production duties. Executive chefs may plan menus with the food and beverage director and/or the restaurant manager, be responsible for recipe standardization and overall food quality, assist in developing food purchase specifications, prepare daily entrées, plan and oversee special events, develop procedures for food production, and perform miscellaneous food-related planning and production tasks. Executive chefs may directly supervise a number of different types of chefs, including sous chefs (assistants to the executive chef), chefs garde-manger (chefs in charge of cold food production), and banquet chefs (who prepare food for group functions).

Cooks and Assistant Cooks. Cooks assist chefs by preparing soups, sauces, and food items to be sautéed, baked, poached, steamed, braised, roasted, grilled, broiled, or fried. They carve and cut meats and prepare cold meat and seafood salad plates, cold sandwiches, hors d'oeuvres, and canapés. Types of cooks include soup cook, sauce cook, fish cook, roast cook, pastry cook, and relief cook. In large operations, cooks may specialize in specific food items; in small operations, cooks are likely to prepare all menu items.

Assistant cooks help cooks prepare food. They may trim, peel, clean, grind, shape, mix, or portion foods before cooking, and may do simple cooking under the guidance of cooks or chefs.

Bakers (Pastry Chefs). Bakers include head bakers, bakers, and baker's assistants. Head bakers are managers who specialize in all phases of bakery preparation and must be able to prepare a wide variety of bakery products following standard recipes. Bakers prepare less complex bakery products such as bread, rolls, pies, and plain cakes and may assist head bakers with other tasks. Baker's assistants help head bakers and bakers prepare various bakery products. Large facilities may retain pastry chefs for elaborate cake decorating, artistic petit fours, and chocolate carving, among other creative tasks.

Pantry (Cold Food) Staff. Pantry-service assistants supply dining room and banquet pantries with such necessary items as utensils, china, glassware, flatware, and

What Is a Chef?

Some persons use the terms "cook" and "chef" to mean the same thing. However, food service professionals understand that there are no agreed-upon standards for "cooks." In contrast, specific and defined levels of experience, skills, and knowledge have been established by the American Culinary Federation (www.acfchefs.org) for chefs in the United States. ACF develops and administers fourteen professional certification programs for those in the culinary profession. The list that follows is for Cooking Professionals. Other programs include those for personal cooking professionals, bakery and pastry professionals, culinary administrators, and culinary educators.

Cooking professionals as defined by ACF includes the following:

- Certified Culinarian (CC): An entry-level culinarian within a commercial food service operation responsible for preparing and cooking sauces, cold food, fish, soups and stocks, meats, vegetables, eggs, and other food items.

- Certified Sous Chef (CSC): A chef who supervises a shift or station(s) in a food service operation. Equivalent job titles are sous chef, banquet chef, garde manger, first cook, a.m. sous chef, and p.m. sous chef.

- Certified Chef de Cuisine (CCC): A chef who is the supervisor in charge of food production in a food service operation. This could be a single unit of a multi-unit operation or a freestanding operation. He or she is in essence the chef of the operation with the final decision-making power as it relates to culinary operations.

- Certified Executive Chef (CEC): A chef who is the department head; usually responsible for all culinary units in a restaurant, hotel, club, hospital, or food service establishment. In addition to culinary responsibilities, other duties include budget preparation, payroll, maintenance, controlling food costs, and maintaining financial and inventory records.

- Certified Master Chef (CMC): The consummate chef. A CMC possesses the highest degree of professional culinary knowledge, skill, and mastery of cooking techniques.

What's the difference between a cook and a chef? The answer is: "A lot!" Food service professionals consistently use the proper terms.

other supplies. These employees may also prepare beverages and assist in serving food when required.

Chief Stewards and Stewards. Chief stewards are managers who typically oversee porters, dishwashing employees, and related personnel. A chief steward may also be in charge of purchasing at some operations. Stewards and their staffs perform cleaning tasks to maintain a high level of cleanliness and sanitation. They may also scrape, wash, and store pots, pans, and other cooking utensils and equipment. Additional duties may include performing janitorial and special cleaning tasks in food and beverage areas and cleaning and storing china, glass, flatware, and related equipment according to acceptable sanitation procedures.

Storeroom and Receiving Employees. Storeroom employees assist in storing, checking, and issuing storeroom supplies. Receiving clerks help suppliers unload food and other supplies and verify that the quality, size, and quantity of incoming products meet the property's specifications. They also check to make sure the prices of items ordered are correctly recorded on the suppliers' invoices.

Service Personnel

Also called front-of-the-house employees, service personnel have significant contact with guests and perform numerous activities. Positions include:

- Dining room (restaurant) managers
- Hosts/receptionists
- Food and beverage servers
- Buspersons
- Bartenders
- Other service personnel

Dining Room (Restaurant) Managers. At small properties, the dining room manager oversees the dining room and performs receptionist duties. At large properties, the dining room manager directly supervises an assistant, whose title may be assistant dining room manager, host, receptionist, or something similar. The dining room manager greets guests during busy times and supervises other service employees. The dining room manager has many other duties including:

- Checking the physical condition of the dining room before it opens
- Checking the place settings on tables and the condition of the china, glassware, and flatware (if appropriate; for example, quick-service and some other restaurants do not pre-set tables)
- Ensuring the menus are in good condition
- Noting reservations that have been made
- Assigning table sections to service staff
- Rearranging tables to accommodate large guest groups
- Scheduling service personnel according to estimated business volume
- Evaluating the job performances of service employees
- Making sure that guests are satisfied and following up on guest complaints
- Performing normal supervisory responsibilities
- Taking appropriate action in case of an emergency or an accident
- Dealing with intoxicated or hard-to-handle guests in a discreet and appropriate manner
- Providing special services to guests as required
- Maintaining a pleasant dining room atmosphere

- Managing dining room closing duties
- Providing reports and other data requested by upper management

Hosts/Receptionists. Hosts, called dining room captains, maître d's, or receptionists at some properties, directly supervise service employees. Hosts check all phases of dining room preparation; complete *mise en place*—a French term meaning "put [everything] in place"; and discuss menu specials, expected regular guests, and anticipated total number of guests with servers and other service employees. During service, the host may greet and seat guests, present menus, and take guest orders. Other tasks can include serving wines, planning for and providing tableside preparation, helping servers when necessary, and preparing flaming desserts. The host may also offer after-dinner drinks and coffee to guests and present the check.

Food and Beverage Servers. These employees serve food and beverages to guests. The skills food servers need depend on the operation. Guest service at a table-service restaurant is more complex than guest service at a coffee shop. At an elegant restaurant, servers may need to know how to serve wine and flaming desserts; servers in family-service restaurants may only need basic serving skills. Servers who work at an operation that uses automated revenue management equipment will need to develop different skills from servers who work at an operation that uses a simple handwritten guest check system.

Buspersons. Typical responsibilities for buspersons include setting tables and removing dirty dishes, linens, and other items from tables. They may also perform *mise en place* before the meal period begins and clean up dining room and service areas afterward.

Bartenders. Bartenders prepare alcoholic beverages and serve them directly to guests or to servers who then serve the guests. There are two basic types of bars: public bars and service bars. Bartenders working at **public bars** prepare and serve beverages directly to guests sitting or standing at the bar and to servers who take the beverages to guests seated in the lounge. Bartenders working at **service bars** do not serve beverages directly to guests; they pass beverages to servers who present them to guests in the lounge or the dining room. Many bars are combination public/service bars.

Other Service Personnel. Beverage servers provide food and beverage items to guests in lounge areas. Cashiers may take reservations, and collect guest payments as guests depart. A few operations use an expediter during busy periods to help production and service personnel communicate. This person, often a manager, controls the process of turning in orders and picking up food items. The expediter can monitor production times, resolve disputes about when an order came in, and coordinate the interaction among cooks and servers. Another service-related employee increasingly used in many restaurants is the curbside food server who takes preordered food to guests waiting in their cars.

Public cafeterias and similar facilities in noncommercial operations may have cafeteria line workers who portion foods ordered by guests passing through the serving line. Runners may be used in self-service cafeteria operations to replenish foods as they are consumed by guests.

Sample Organization Charts

The sample organization charts show how different types of food service operations can be organized. They can help you better understand where and how the personnel positions just discussed may fit into various types of organizations.

Exhibit 7 shows the simple organization of a small restaurant. In this case, the restaurant manager is the owner. The cook, bartender, and host/cashier report directly to the owner/manager. A third level of the organization consists of an assistant cook and dishwashers (supervised by the cook), beverage servers (supervised by the bartender), and food servers (supervised by the host/cashier). Of course, every operation is different. The owner/manager of a very small operation will prefer a *flat* organization. In that case, every person, regardless of position, would be supervised directly by the owner/manager (see Exhibit 8).

As a food service organization grows, it likely needs more employees. It also must make the work more specialized, so additional positions become necessary. Exhibit 9 shows a possible organization chart for a large restaurant. In this example, the general manager directly supervises two positions: the controller (responsible for cashiers and a receiving/storeroom clerk) and the assistant manager. The assistant manager directly supervises four department heads: a chef or head cook (responsible for food production), the chief steward (responsible for sanitation), a head bartender (responsible for beverage production and service), and a dining room manager (responsible for food service). Each of these department heads supervises employees. Because of the increased number of levels, a greater amount of direction and communication is necessary in this operation than in those shown in Exhibits 7 and 8. All operations must meet the same needs: purchasing, preparing, and serving food and beverages, and cleaning up. The number of employees, the degrees of specialization, and the number of organizational levels account for the differences between the organizational structures of small and large operations.

Exhibit 7   Organization Chart for a Small Restaurant

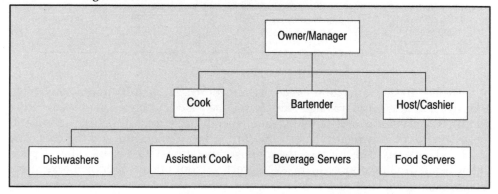

Exhibit 8   Organization Chart for a Small Restaurant with a Flat Organization

Exhibit 9   Organization Chart for a Large Restaurant

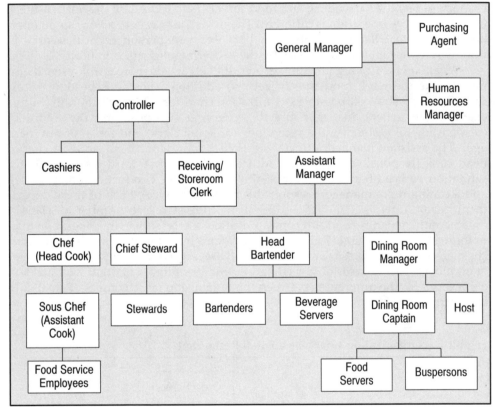

Exhibit 10 shows an abbreviated organization chart for a 200-room hotel. Note that the hotel's general manager supervises the food and beverage director who, in turn, supervises an assistant food and beverage director. The assistant food and beverage director manages the bar and dining room managers and the chef. The food and beverage director is on the same organizational level as the other department heads (maintenance chief, sales director, front office supervisor, executive housekeeper, and controller).

Exhibit 10   Organization Chart for a 200-Room Hotel

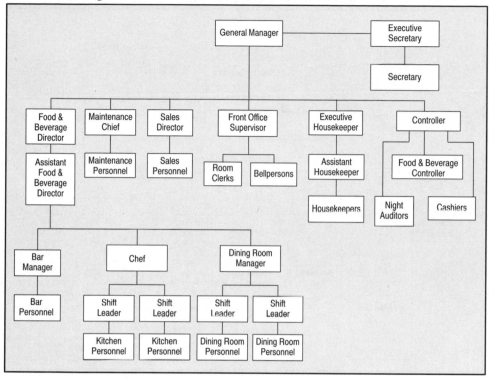

The organization chart for a country club food service operation (see Exhibit 11) shows something not found in the organization charts we have seen previously: the members (guests) are in charge. At a typical country club, the club's members elect a board of directors that appoints an executive committee. The executive committee hires and supervises the club's general manager, who works as a COO to implement the board's policies. Alternatively, a contract management company might be hired to operate the club. The assistant manager of the food and beverage department directly supervises the manager of the specialty dining outlet, executive chef, executive steward, dining room manager, catering manager, and bar manager.

Exhibit 12 shows a large university residence hall's food service operation. The director of the department of university housing has overall responsibility for the residence halls, including their food service programs. The coordinator of food services for the university is in a staff or advisory relationship to the director. The food service coordinator is responsible for numerous tasks, including menu and recipe development, training programs for food service personnel, and operation of the test kitchen. An associate director links the residence hall manager to the director of university housing. The residence hall manager (somewhat equivalent to a restaurant's general manager) supervises the food service manager who, in turn, supervises personnel with responsibilities for food production, service,

Exhibit 11   Organization Chart for a Country Club Food Service Operation

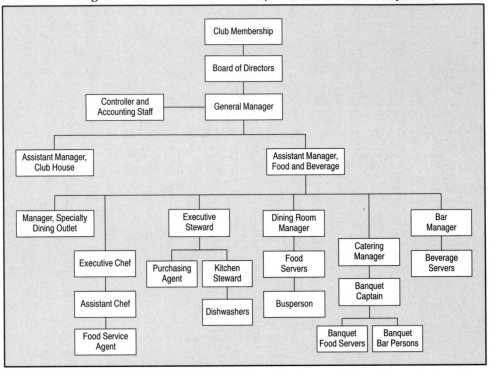

and student employees. In some university organizations, the food service manager is directly responsible to the coordinator of food services. There are several residence halls, each of which is supported by an area manager and administrative personnel in the director's office. At a small college, the food service manager might undertake menu planning and purchasing in addition to coordinating all the activities required in the day-to-day operation of food services.

Exhibit 13 shows the organization of a hospital food service operation or dietary department. Note that one assistant director coordinates production and special functions activities and supervises the lead or head cafeteria server. The second assistant director oversees the transporting and serving of food to patients and also coordinates the therapeutic work performed by dietitians.

Career Paths in Food Service

We have discussed many food service positions and how they relate to each other in various operations. Where do you begin and how do you advance within the food service industry? There are many career choices available. Everyone has different interests, knowledge, and abilities and, therefore, different career aspirations and opportunities.

Exhibit 12   Organization Chart for a University Food Service Operation

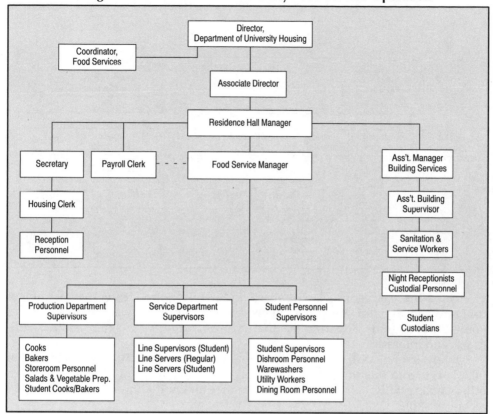

Courtesy of Michigan State University, East Lansing, Michigan.

One way to help get your career started is to obtain experience in the industry while you are a student. Not only will you learn things that can be useful later, you will also:

- Bring experiences to class that will help put facts in perspective.

- Make contacts with professionals who can help you find employment after graduation.

- Show that you are genuinely interested in making a career in the food service industry.

If you are already a food service employee and want to know where you can go next, you can look at your operation's organization chart for advancement opportunities. As you move up the organizational ladder, job requirements become greater and work tasks more challenging, but pay and benefits also generally increase.

Exhibit 13   Organization Chart for a Hospital Food Service Operation

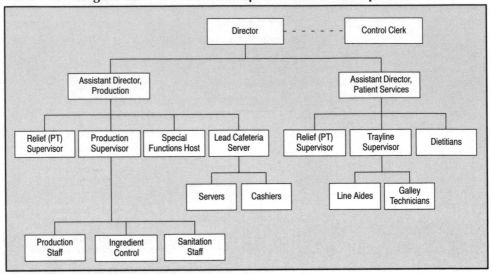

Since there are no established or industry-required career advancement routes, where and how far you go depends on (1) what you want to do, (2) where you are now, (3) the opportunities that evolve, and (4) your skills, abilities, attitudes, and interests.

Interpersonal skills are very important at all organizational levels. In the people-centered business of food service, the ability to work with and through others will usually help you get ahead more quickly than just concentrating on technical skills.

Your Future in the Industry

Projected growth in almost every segment of the food service industry, along with a continuing labor shortage for some positions, will yield a large number of job opportunities of all types and responsibility levels. If you want to become involved in this exciting industry, chances are very good that there will be a place for you.

Perceptions of the Industry. Some misconceptions exist about what work in the food service industry is like. For example, some people believe there is a significant emphasis on technology and marketing in lodging and quick-service restaurants and that there is less concern about these issues in independent and noncommercial food service operations. This is not true.

It is important for those thinking about a new or different career in food service to learn as much as possible about all positions they consider. Let's try to clarify some points. First of all, food service jobs can be challenging, no matter what the position or organizational level. At lower organizational levels, jobs may be physically difficult. At higher organizational levels, the work is different, but still difficult; many important and far-reaching decisions must be made. Work hours can be long for all food service employees, and, in many organizations, food service employees must work when other people want to be entertained: evenings, weekends, and holidays. Noncommercial food service opportunities, which are often underrated by people aspiring to food service positions, usually count among their benefits more traditional work hours (at least for management staff). Weekends, holidays, and vacation times are more likely to be free of employment responsibilities.

Some people may feel that service positions are by definition unattractive. There is no question that the food service industry involves serving guests, patients, residents, and others. If you think there is a negative image or lower social status attached to providing service to others, a position in the food service industry may not be for you. On the other hand, the opportunity to help others is a drawing card for many people.

Some observers also complain that food service comprises many dead-end jobs. However, entry-level positions are *not* dead-end jobs. People can advance within the organization; when people become proficient in a position, opportunities for promotion are likely to become available.

Salaries and Benefits. Wage and salary compensation and benefits for entry-level food service positions are often higher than minimum wage, especially in areas with labor shortages. The average entry-level salary for college and university food service graduates is generally higher than the entry-level salaries available to the graduates of liberal arts and many other college programs. However, as is true when deciding on any career, the question should not be, "What is the starting pay?" but rather, "What will I be receiving in compensation and benefits five years from now?"

The answer to this question is that food service industry careers are competitive with other industry careers. Graduates starting in entrance positions in fast-track operations in quick-service chains and other rapidly expanding companies can easily become department heads earning very attractive salaries—often with incentive plans that provide additional compensation. Benefit packages, including health care and retirement plans, are often competitive with those in other industries, and increasingly include tuition, vacation lodging, and meals-at-work reimbursements. Of course, salaries and benefits are influenced by company, region of the country, responsibilities of the position, experience, training, and related factors.

An indirect benefit of working in the food service industry has to do with geography. Since food service operations are prevalent throughout the world, an employee's geographic preference is generally an easier objective to attain in the food service industry than in many other fields. Where do you want to live? Wherever it is, there are likely to be opportunities in the food service industry.

Challenges and Opportunities. Regardless of the industry segment you enter, the challenges of the job are a tremendous incentive. Do you want an opportunity to make decisions that will affect many people and many dollars over a long period of time? A young person managing a multi-million dollar business is a common occurrence. The challenge and excitement of dealing with large numbers of employees and guests can also be a draw.

How do you get involved in food service work? You might already be employed in a food service position. If so, you should talk with your immediate supervisor, if you have not already, about professional development opportunities within your operation.

Maybe you are a college student who is already convinced that food service is for you. Where can you get more information? Talk to your school faculty and placement officers and with managers in local properties about career opportunities.

If you are interested in the food service industry and are not a college student, contact a school or college in your area that offers a hospitality education program. You may be able to take courses or obtain placement advice from them. You can also study at home. The American Hotel & Lodging Educational Institute offers courses that cover all major areas of hotel, motel, and food service operations. Designed so you can study at your own convenience, Educational Institute courses offer a planned, career-long program of professional growth and development.[1] You should also check with local hospitality operations about employment opportunities. Your primary objective should be to get your foot in the door. After that, there will be many career possibilities for you to consider as you gain experience and learn more about the industry.

Endnote

1. For more information, contact the American Hotel & Lodging Educational Institute, 2113 North High Street, Lansing, MI 48906, or go to www.ei-ahla.org.

Key Terms

chief steward—Manager who typically oversees porters, dishwashing employees, and related personnel. May also be in charge of purchasing.

job description—An organizational tool that lists the most important tasks that must be done by someone working in a specific position.

labor-intensive—Requiring a large amount of human labor as opposed to equipment or technology.

line manager—A manager with decision-making authority within or over a revenue-generating department that directly provides services or products to guests.

organization chart—A diagram that shows the relationships among various positions in an operation.

public bar—A bar where bartenders prepare alcoholic beverages and serve them directly to guests and food servers. Guests can order and pick up their own beverages at public bars.

service bar—A bar where bartenders prepare alcoholic beverages for food servers who then present them to guests in the dining room. Guests typically do not order or pick up their own beverages at service bars.

staff personnel—Employees who serve in a technical, advisory, or support capacity to line managers.

? Review Questions

1. Into what three general categories can food service employees be grouped?
2. What are examples of the chief concerns of top managers? middle managers? supervisors?
3. What is a typical way to organize top managers in a large corporation?
4. What sorts of tasks do restaurant or general managers typically perform?
5. What is the difference between line and staff managers?
6. What production personnel typically work in food service operations?
7. What are typical duties of a host?
8. What is a flat organization?
9. What is the major difference between a country club organization and other types of organizations that provide food service?
10. What are some misconceptions about the food service industry?
11. What are some challenges and opportunities in the food service industry?
12. How does compensation in the food service industry compare to that in other industries?

Internet Sites

For more information, visit the following Internet sites. Remember that Internet addresses can change without notice. If the site is no longer there, you can use a search engine to look for additional sites.

Basic Job Search Website (advice on careers, job searches, résumés, interview tactics, and much more)

www.careerbuilder.com

monster.com

Hospitality Positions for Job Searchers

Foodservice.com
www.foodservice.com/employment

Hotel Jobs.com
www.hoteljobs.com

Hcareers
www.hcareers.com

Hospitality Online
www.hospitalityonline.com

Hospitality Jobsite
www.hospitalityjobsite.com

Position Vacancies in Specific Organizations

Most large hospitality organizations feature Employment or Career Opportunities pages on their websites. For example, see the following:

Aramark
www.aramark.com

Olive Garden
www.olivegarden.com

Marriott
www.marriott.com

Walt Disney
www.disneycareers.com

McDonalds
www.mcdonalds.com/careers

Hospitality Job Descriptions

Dictionary of Occupational Titles (DOT)
www.occupationalinfo.org

Other Job Search Information

Enter the following terms into your favorite search engine:

- career planning
- employment interviewing
- hospitality job descriptions
- how to write a résumé
- job search skills

Chapter 3 Outline

What Is Management?
    The Management Process
    Integrating the Management Process
Managerial Responsibilities and
    Relationships
        Primary Groups
        Secondary Groups
The Importance of Hospitality

Competencies

1. Define *management* and list the steps in the management process. (p. 47)

2. Describe the management tasks involved in planning, organizing, coordinating, staffing, directing, controlling, and evaluating. (pp. 47–57)

3. Contrast primary and secondary groups, and describe management's role in providing hospitality to all guest groups. (pp. 57–60)

3

Fundamentals of Management

THIS CHAPTER EXAMINES the basics of management. First it defines management and takes a look at the management process. Then it discusses the responsibilities managers have to guests, owners, employees, and others. The chapter closes with a discussion of the special importance of hospitality to food service managers.

What Is Management?

What is **management**? What does a manager do? Managing involves using what you have (resources) to do what you want to do (attain organizational objectives).

Many types of resources are available to a food service manager, including the following:

- People
- Money
- Time
- Energy
- Products
- Equipment and space
- Procedures

All resources are in limited supply. Managers never have enough people, money, and time, for example, to do everything they would like to do. Therefore, their job is to determine how best to use the limited resources that are available.

This responsibility is implemented by making decisions. A good manager can allocate resources wisely and make good decisions when solving problems critical to the operation. An ineffective manager is unable to make the best allocation and problem-solving decisions.

The Management Process

The management process comprises seven basic activities or tasks: planning, organizing, coordinating, staffing, directing, controlling, and evaluating (see Exhibit 1). You will be involved in all or most of these activities when you manage a food service operation.

Planning. Planning is the management task of creating goals and objectives and programs of action to reach them. Goals and objectives indicate what you want

Exhibit 1   The Management Process

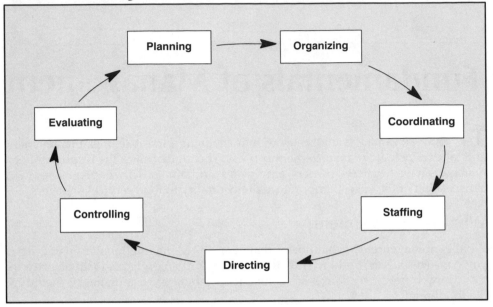

to do; action plans tell how you propose to do it. Planning should be done before other management tasks are undertaken.

Every manager, regardless of position or type of food service organization, must plan. At the highest management levels, executives undertake a sequence of planning to help determine the food and beverage operation's goals and the best ways to attain them. Exhibit 2 identifies basic planning responsibilities of top-level managers.

At intermediate management levels, managers develop operational plans to attain short-term goals. For example, department heads work with chefs to plan menus that will please guests and generate revenue. At lower management levels, supervisory planning involves the day-to-day process of running the operation. Examples of this include developing employee schedules and determining quantities of food to purchase and produce.

Let's look at how planning might take place at a large restaurant company with many units. At top management levels, the board of directors, the board chairperson, and the chief executive officer may set long-term goals that may not be achieved until two, three, five, or even ten years into the future. For example, such a goal might be: "To be the number-one restaurant chain in gross revenues in the Midwest region within ten years." Intermediate levels of management—unit managers and department heads within specific units—focus on meeting annual budget objectives and on short-term economic planning. At lower levels of management, supervisors in each department within the unit pre-cost the next month's banquets, plan the next week's labor schedule, or set goals to be attained within a short time period.

Exhibit 2   The Sequence of Planning for Top-Level Managers

Planning is a process that involves the development of six management tools. Some managers incorrectly believe that these tools can be developed independently of one another. However, effective planning requires that they be developed in the following order:

A vision is a vague idea about what the food and beverage operation would be like if it were ideally effective. For example, a hotelier planning an à la carte restaurant in a lodging property may envision the best dining alternative in town that serves a specific type of cuisine. The mission statement for the dining outlet begins to quantify the vision and becomes a second very important planning tool. A mission statement driven by the vision just discussed might be "to offer traditional examples of the cuisine in an authentic environment and attract families and young adults with the value pricing that will be offered."

The long-range plan identifies what the hotelier will attempt to do over the next five years to move toward the mission. A financial goal tied to the long range plan may be to generate revenues that are 30 percent greater than those estimated when the new concept was initially introduced. The business plan indicates the planned results for the first year of the long-range plan. In our example, first-year revenue goals would be estimated in concert with the five-year goal identified in the long-range plan. The business plan may also indicate strategies and action steps along with responsibilities for their implementation to help ensure that business plan goals are attained.

The marketing plan indicates how the revenue goals in the business plan will be met. Marketing, advertising, and promotion tactics, among others, could be listed along with an implementation calendar.

The operating budget repeats the business plan's revenue goals, identifies the estimated expenses required to generate the revenue, and, very importantly, forecasts the bottom-line operating results that will be of critical importance to the general manager.

As illustrated above, the marketing plan and operating budget are very closely related. For example, revenue goals in the operating budget cannot be met without effective marketing, and the costs of marketing activities are included in the operating budget.

Whether the organization is a multi-unit chain or a single property, planning must start with the highest-level managers. Only when they establish a definite course of action can **subordinate** managers at all organizational levels develop plans that fit into the organization's long-range plans.

Other factors in effective planning include:

- *Information.* One must have access to complete information to plan effectively. A chef, for example, cannot effectively plan a menu without having information about the estimated ingredient costs for items to be prepared from the menu.

- *Communication.* Managers at all levels should communicate with each other when developing plans. For example, when a food service manager develops an operating budget, it is wise to get input from each department head and the property's accountant (controller). Whenever possible, managers should also communicate with employees when making plans that affect them. Employees are more likely to follow plans they have helped develop because they become "our plans," not "management's plans."

- *Flexibility.* Plans should be flexible. Some food service managers develop plans and then refuse to make changes even though conditions warrant them. One obvious example is the operating budget. What if revenue is less than what was projected in the budget? Managers may have to make changes to lower costs and/or generate increased business.

- *Implementation.* Obviously, plans must be implemented to be effective. Sometimes a lot of time and discussion go into putting a plan together, but the plan is never implemented or is only partially carried out. This is a waste of limited resources and is frustrating for staff members who provided input.

Managers should not plan only when they get around to it. Time should be set aside regularly for managers at each organizational level to establish objectives, create plans to attain them, and make revisions as necessary. If managers do not set aside regular time for planning, the organization may experience one crisis after another, with managers moving from one unexpected situation to the next to combat problems they could have avoided if they had planned effectively.

Organizing. The management activity of **organizing** answers the question, "How can we best assemble and use our limited human resources to attain our objectives?" Organizing involves establishing the flow of authority (power) and communication among people.

In any organization, care should be taken to make sure each employee has only one supervisor. If an employee has two bosses, problems can occur if conflicting orders are given. What, for example, should a dishwasher do if the head cook says, "We need dishes," and the restaurant manager says, "We need help cleaning up a spill in the front of the house"?

The number of employees each supervisor should manage must be carefully determined. The right number of employees for each supervisor depends on many variables, including the supervisor's experience, the complexity of the work, the amount of supervision employees require, the frequency with which problems are likely to occur, and the amount of help the supervisor can expect from higher-level managers. What is important is that supervisors not be responsible for more people than they can handle.

The authority to make decisions about using resources should be available at the appropriate level. It is inefficient for a supervisor to have the responsibility to do something, but not have the authority necessary to get it done. Supervisors should not need to seek higher management approval for tasks that they must routinely do as part of the job. Increasingly, entry-level employees are given **empowerment** to make decisions as well; for example, a food server might be given the discretion to replace, or *comp*, an incorrectly prepared meal rather than be required to check with a manager first.

An organization's structure evolves throughout the life of the business, but many food service operations have organization charts that do not reflect current operating procedures. For example, an organization chart can indicate that the cook's supervisor is the chef when in fact a kitchen manager now directs the work of some cooks. The organization chart should be updated regularly so that it gives a current, accurate picture of how the operation's human resources are organized.

Coordinating. Coordinating is the management task of assigning work and organizing people and resources to achieve the operation's objectives.

Coordinating depends on communication. There must be effective channels of communication to transmit messages up, down, and across the food and beverage operation. It is also necessary for peers (those at the same organizational level) to communicate with each other. Achieving the organization's goals can happen only if there is open communication between department heads and other department managers.

Delegation is an important aspect of coordinating. Delegation is authority that is passed down the organization. Ultimate responsibility or accountability, however, cannot be delegated. For example, the food and beverage director is responsible to the hotel's general manager for all aspects of the food and beverage department's operating budget. The director may, in turn, delegate the authority to make some decisions about food and beverages to the head chef and the beverage manager. However, the director will still be responsible to the general manager for meeting budget goals.

Staffing. Staffing involves recruiting and hiring applicants.[1] The goal of staffing is to find the best-qualified employees for the food service operation. At large properties, managers may be asked to select from applicants screened by the human resources department. At smaller properties, the general manager may give managers total responsibility for finding, screening, and hiring applicants.

Application forms, selection tests, reference checks, and other screening tools, including computerized tests, can all be a part of the recruitment and selection process. However, some operations do very little screening; instead, they hire the first person who walks through the door after an employee quits.

It is important to match the applicant to the vacant job rather than hire someone and then determine what he or she can do. To this end, jobs must be defined in terms of the tasks to be performed. Job descriptions list required tasks for each job; they can make it easier to match applicants to jobs.

E-Recruitment and E-Selection Technology

Technology has enabled food service employers (and all others) to move beyond the traditional recruitment methods of newspaper advertising, word-of-mouth advertising, and posting "Help Wanted" signs in windows. Food service employers increasingly use Monster.com and hospitality-industry-specific job search websites to widely announce position vacancies. Online recruiting is popular with both employers and job applicants.

The extent to which an organization uses such technology depends upon the number of employees it has. Organizations typically use more-sophisticated technology applications to recruit candidates for higher-level vacancies and less-sophisticated technology to recruit entry-level staff members. Online applications with automated entry into databases are increasingly popular. Web interviewing that asks common questions of all applicants may be available. Potential employers, or those they **outsource** for this purpose, can search computerized criminal databases. Background checks can also involve searches of credit and driving records. Many hospitality organization websites feature employee recruitment pages. Multi-unit organizations can share recruitment information.

Employers increasingly use online personality tests and other tests during the employee-selection process. Such tests can reveal a candidate's occupational interests, behavioral traits, ability to work with a team, initiative, and problem-solving skills. Employers can use the tests to predict a candidate's potential sales success, guest-service abilities, and other major traits. Also available is job-match testing, which can compare job candidates' qualities to the attributes of the most successful employees. Employers can use this selection data to electronically screen applicants for suitability for other positions in the organization. Employers can use all such information in reports and database development, and include it as part of documentation for employee records.

Job specifications list the personal qualities necessary to perform jobs effectively. We all bring different amounts of knowledge, experience, and common sense to a job. A job specification indicates the personal attributes judged necessary for successful job performance.

Consider all possible sources of job applicants. Personnel from human resources departments in large properties may recruit from within the organization. They can also ask currently employed staff members for suggestions, work with employment service agencies, and advertise.

Some managers think that the more applicants who apply, the more work it will take to sort them out, so they try to limit the number of applicants. From the perspective of the total organization, this is a poor strategy. The chance of finding the right person for the job increases if a large number of people are encouraged to apply and effective screening procedures are used.

Part of staffing is making sure new hires get off to a good start. An employee's early experiences on the job strongly affect his or her relationship with the organization. A well-planned employee orientation program is necessary to properly introduce new employees to supervisors, coworkers, and the organization in general. For example, the property's mission statement can be explained during the orientation session(s) as can other information all employees should know. Examples include the organization's emphasis on guest service, the need to consistently use work practices that incorporate sanitation and safety concerns, and the procedures to be followed if emergencies arise.

Directing. Directing is a big part of most food and beverage managers' jobs. Effective leaders are able to get work done through other people. This is certainly true in the labor-intensive food service industry. Employees are absolutely critical to the success of every food service operation. All human beings are complex and at times difficult to understand. However, understanding employees' wants, needs, and expectations helps managers direct the employees more effectively.

Directing includes supervising, scheduling, and disciplining employees. Supervising comprises all the ways managers relate to their employees when work is being done. When supervising employees, managers should know how to motivate, inspire cooperation, give orders, and bring out the best in people. It is important to find ways to mesh organizational goals with employees' goals. Employees can be motivated when their personal needs are addressed on the job. Whenever possible, employees should have input regarding decisions that affect them.

Unfortunately, many commercial and noncommercial food and beverage operations experience high levels of employee turnover. This often occurs because of the way staff members are managed by their supervisors. For example, many hospitality employees believe that their employers do not appreciate them. An entry-level employee's relationship with his or her immediate supervisor can have a significant impact upon whether the employee has a positive on-the-job experience and, in turn, will influence whether he or she will remain with the operation.

Fortunately, there are many commonsense and no- or low-cost tactics that can be used to effectively interact with employees. Perhaps the most important is for managers to treat employees the way they would want their own boss to treat them. Many employees are interested in promotion opportunities; training to help prepare these staff members for new and better-paying positions will interest them. Ongoing interaction with employees can reinforce a relationship of respect, recognition, and reward.

Scheduling employees effectively is very important. Managers must know exactly how much labor is needed, then be able to work within those parameters and treat all employees fairly.[2]

Disciplining employees is a task many managers dread. However, it can be a positive experience if managers keep in mind that discipline does not necessarily involve punishment. Rather, discipline is a way to address, correct, and reinforce behavior and help employees become productive members of the organization. Discipline can consist of informal coaching and counseling sessions as well as more serious meetings between the manager, employee, and perhaps a higher-level manager or (in large organizations) someone from the human resources department. Written warnings and suspensions may be necessary in some situations. Following a formal, written disciplinary action program is the best way an organization can protect itself against charges of favoritism, discrimination, and unfair practices.

Directing people is complex and sometimes difficult. In many directing situations, it is useful for managers to think about how they would like to be treated. Chances are, employees share many of the same concerns managers have.[3]

Controlling. There is no guarantee that goals will be attained just because effective plans have been developed, resources have been organized, staff has been selected, and directions have been carried out. For this reason, managers must attend to the **controlling** function of management, which includes developing and implementing control systems.

Many food and beverage products pass through a food service operation. Therefore, control procedures for purchasing, receiving, storing, issuing, preparing, and serving products are necessary.

Control includes much more than just the physical tasks of locking storeroom doors, checking standard recipes, or weighing incoming products on a

---

Organizational Culture and Successful Food Service Organizations

Organizational culture is the understandings shared by food service employees that influence the operation's decision-making. This culture is passed on to new members of the group. Organizational culture is impacted by top-level managers' beliefs and ethics that help drive the operation's rewards and recognition activities and its processes and procedures.

The desired long-term performance of food service employees is best ensured when everyone is committed to the operation's success and works together to maximize it. Staff members agree upon operational goals such as striving to discover what guests want and then provide it. They work together to minimize or eliminate the problems and barriers that impact the consistent delivery of memorable products and services. The organizational culture creates an environment in which long-term plans are made, policies and procedures are developed, operating plans are determined, and each individual guest is best served.

Core values are the foundations of a culture because they describe how all employees are asked to act. They guide the planning, decision-making, problem-solving, and prioritizing of actions that transform plans into reality. They define the organization's direction and answer the question, "How do we want to act and behave?"

Core values determine the commitments that should be made and drive each leader's and employee's interactions with the organization's stakeholders; a stakeholder is anyone who is impacted by the food service operation.

There are several critical core values that are generally applicable to all organizations, including those in the hospitality industry. One is a genuine concern for customers; others include a genuine respect for all employees and a desire to consider the ethical implications of managerial and other organizational decisions. Still another universal core value is the emphasis on quality: the output of products and services that meet predefined standards based on customer expectations.

scale. The process of control actually begins with establishing a budget. A budget indicates expected revenue and cost levels. Managers may look at recent financial statements—especially income statements—or use statistics developed in-house as a base to project anticipated revenue and expense levels. Once the budget is established, managers must measure the extent to which budget goals are met. If the variance between expected results and actual results is excessive, corrective action must be taken and the results evaluated to assess whether the corrective action was effective.[4]

Exhibit 3 shows the basic steps in the control process. To understand the steps, assume that a cafeteria manager estimates revenues of $20,000 for a specific week. This goal becomes the standard (amount expected). At the end of the week, the total amount of revenue generated is determined. Measuring actual operating results is the second step in the control process. Assume that the actual amount of revenue generated was $18,000, and a comparison in step 3 between actual operating results and the standard reveals the negative variance of $2,000. The cafeteria manager will probably want to take corrective action (step 4) after determining if the revenue goal was achievable and, if it was, why it was not attained. Corrective

Exhibit 3   Basic Steps in the Control Process

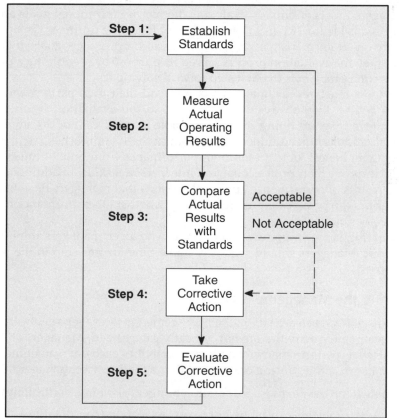

action may include, for example, implementing procedures to ensure that guests do not leave without paying and that all revenue from the cashier is accounted for. Procedures can then be evaluated to determine if they are effective (step 5). This last step in the control process helps the manager to refine corrective actions so he or she can better attain goals.

Managers should develop control systems to alert them to problems on a timely basis. Obviously, it is not ideal to learn many weeks after it started that a control problem (apparent theft of inventory in storage, for example) exists. Food service managers often develop daily or weekly control procedures to supplement monthly budget information provided by their accountants or bookkeepers.

Be aware that controls must be worth more than they cost. For example, using a system that costs $50 weekly to save $35 weekly is not a good idea. On the other hand, spending $500 for a piece of equipment that will save $50 per week is reasonable because the payback period is only ten weeks ($500 ÷ $50 = 10).

Evaluating. **Evaluating** is the management task that involves determining the extent to which planned goals are achieved. Managers evaluate as they: (1) review the operation's progress toward achieving overall organizational goals, (2) measure employee performance, and (3) assess the effectiveness of training programs. The constant question for managers must be, "How well are we doing?"

Managers must continually evaluate whether organizational goals are being attained because failure to do so can spell trouble for the future of the operation. If goals are on target, managers can move on to accomplish new goals. If goals are not being met, the evaluation process served its purpose by identifying a problem. Awareness of a problem is the first step toward solving it.

Managers must also evaluate themselves and their own performance. Some managers believe they always do a good job, so self-evaluation is unnecessary. Others believe they are doing the best possible job and cannot do any better—again, evaluation is judged unnecessary. Both of these approaches are unproductive. Taking an honest look at their own performance from time to time can help managers improve their professional and interpersonal skills. In addition, considering the results of performance appraisal sessions that managers have with their own superiors can be very helpful in assessing whether job performance improvements are possible.

Evaluating is too important to be left to whenever managers think there is time to do it. Managers should regularly make time for this step in the management process.

Integrating the Management Process

We have discussed each activity in the management process separately. In the real world, management activities are not so neatly categorized. Managers at all organizational levels perform many management activities each day, sometimes simultaneously. For example, during one typical day, a food service manager might:

- Help develop the next year's operating budget (planning, controlling).
- Deal with problems caused by improper delegation (coordinating).

- Work with a colleague in another department to plan an upcoming special event (planning, coordinating).

- Revise job descriptions and job specifications (organizing, staffing).

- Carry out routine supervisory activities (directing).

- Revise standard food and labor cost estimates (controlling).

- Conduct employee performance reviews (evaluating).

As managers gain and learn from experience, they are better able to perform all the various management activities and tasks that arise every day.

Managerial Responsibilities and Relationships

The people with whom food service managers typically interact fall into two basic categories: primary groups and secondary groups (see Exhibit 4). The primary groups can include guests, owners, boards of directors, area and regional directors, lower-level managers, and employees. These are the people to whom the manager has the greatest and most direct responsibility. The manager also has a more indirect responsibility to the secondary groups: suppliers, the local community, and government regulatory agencies. Let's examine the manager's responsibilities to each of the constituencies in both of these groups.

Primary Groups

Guests. Managers of commercial and noncommercial operations have equal concerns about those to whom their services and products are provided. These

Exhibit 4 Food Service Manager Relationships—Primary and Secondary Groups

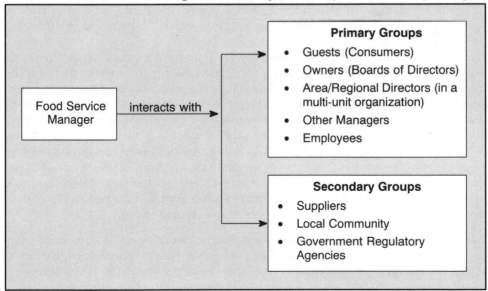

persons may be called guests in commercial operations, and patients, students, residents, or employees in noncommercial operations; however, it is always important to emphasize the needs of those being served.

Managing for guests is challenging because no two guests are alike. Guests in commercial operations typically have different reasons for visiting a food service operation. Some may want a quick meal; others desire a leisurely dining experience. Some may want to escape from their day's activities, while others want to discuss a business deal. Guests also may visit a restaurant or hotel food and beverage operation for special occasions, discovery of new places and new food items, and the opportunity to feel important. Similarly, no two patients in hospitals, residents in retirement centers, students in educational facilities, and employees in business and industry settings are the same. They also have special concerns about and perceptions of food service and want to have their individual needs and desires satisfied during their food service experience.

Managers first address their guests' needs by providing them with a clean, safe place to eat. Treating guests hospitably is also important. Then, managers must determine what guests want and need when they visit the operation. A quick-service giant like McDonald's has teams of researchers to help it discover what its guests want and need. An independent restaurant manager may use guest comment cards, surveys, and personal interviews or observations. Once guest needs are determined, managers must try to meet them to build a loyal guest base that will ensure the continued success of the operation.

Owners. Owners of commercial operations and boards of directors of noncommercial facilities are vitally concerned about their operations. In a corporation, the owners are stockholders; in a partnership, the owners are two or more people with investment interests; in the case of a single owner, the owner is frequently the manager as well. In a noncommercial operation, the "owners" of the organization for which food service is provided may be a government agency, a for-profit or not-for-profit corporation headed by a board of directors, or another entity.

What are the objectives of the owner(s)? Usually the primary objective is to maximize profits (in commercial operations) or to minimize expenses (in noncommercial operations). Owners of commercial operations may also have more personal objectives that involve ego needs or the desire for accomplishment. Those with top-level responsibility for noncommercial operations may be concerned about societal, financial, healthcare, and other issues.

A manager's primary responsibility to the owner(s) is to make the food service operation an economic success or to ensure that it meets other goals that drive the reasons for its existence. Often this means meeting or exceeding the property's operating budget or profit plan. The many factors that go into making an operation an economic success define the challenge of management.

Area/Regional Directors. Food service managers working for a large multi-unit chain organization have an immediate supervisor not yet mentioned: the area/regional director. This person has the same concerns about the performance of a unit manager that the owner has about the manager of a single-unit operation.

Managers. The food service manager who works at a large property probably assists a higher-level manager. The food service manager's job is to meet job responsibilities and perform other tasks as directed by his or her manager, who is responsible for evaluating employees' performance. Sometimes it is easy to resent one's boss or misunderstand the boss's motives. Keep in mind that the boss probably shares many concerns with the employees. The boss is also trying to satisfy performance requirements imposed by an owner or a higher-level manager, while at the same time fulfilling personal needs and wants.

Employees. Food service managers not only manage employees, they manage *for* employees. Managerial decisions have an impact on making the operation a success, which provides employees with a place to earn a living, make friends, and plan a future. In other words, food service managers manage for their employees' well-being as well as their own.

Secondary Groups

Suppliers. Responsibilities to suppliers include establishing a reasonable working relationship and being fair and ethical in all dealings with them. Food service managers must guard against having an "I win—you lose" attitude toward suppliers. Such an approach is shortsighted at best. Instead, a relationship stressing fairness and mutual satisfaction should be fostered. This can lead to trust, cooperation, and good service from suppliers.

There are at least two other reasons for maintaining a good relationship with suppliers: (1) suppliers and their employees are potential guests of the food service operation, and (2) they may discuss how they are treated at the operation with others who may be potential guests.

Local Community. The community in which a food service organization operates is involved in an ongoing relationship with it. In many instances, entire sections of communities may be revitalized, or may deteriorate, due to the status of nearby hospitality operations such as hotels and restaurants.

A community may have common concerns that managers should be aware of, including the following:

- *Nuisance concerns.* Excessive noise and rowdy guests gathering in the parking lot are nuisances that managers should deal with.

- *Environmental concerns.* Managers should ensure that their property's grounds are free from litter, and that no litter from the property gets onto neighboring properties. Using biodegradable detergents and disposable supplies is another way a property can show its sensitivity to environmental concerns.

- *Entertainment concerns.* In operations that book singers, comedians, and other entertainment, managers should try whenever possible to provide entertainment that is desirable to and appropriate for the community.

- *Civic concerns.* Managers can show their support for the local community by supporting charitable, educational, and other civic groups.

Our list of examples could continue, but the message is clear: the food service operation is a citizen of the community, and managers must run the operation in a responsible manner if they want to enjoy the patronage and goodwill of community residents.

Government Regulatory Agencies. Government regulatory agencies collect taxes and other fees and ensure that applicable laws and regulations are followed. Concerns of government agencies include sanitation, safety, building codes, employees, licenses, and taxation, among others. Food service managers must understand the significant role government regulatory agencies play and manage their operations so that they comply with all applicable federal, state, and local laws.

The Importance of Hospitality

The food service industry is truly a "people business." The food service manager's job is not to unlock the door and wait for the cash register to ring. The manager must first provide products and services that guests will enjoy. Then the manager must train and supervise the staff to provide these products and services in a hospitable way that will encourage guests to return.[5]

Hospitality—the cordial reception of guests—is easy to discuss, but difficult to consistently practice. Problems caused by lack of concern for guests are evident in too many food service operations.

Let's look at what can happen when an attitude of hospitality does not exist. Have you ever watched a television commercial that shows smiling employees at a quick-service restaurant inviting you to visit the property? What happens when you visit the property and the employees do not act like the smiling, courteous employees pictured in the commercial? You will likely feel disappointed, even if only on a subconscious level. Contrast this example with a restaurant where friendly employees seem genuinely happy that you have chosen to visit their property.

Is the difference between friendly and unfriendly employees only a matter of personality? The ability to relate to people can be influenced by personality. However, it is also likely that friendly employees have a friendly manager who has concern for guests and who serves as an excellent **role model**, promoting an attitude of hospitality in the employees. Even though they have a million other things to do, wise managers identify regular guests by name, remember the table they prefer, and provide any special attention that is practical. They set an example for their employees so their guests will have a positive experience.

Endnotes

1. For more information about staffing, see Robert H. Woods, *Managing Hospitality Human Resources*, 5th ed. (Lansing, Mich.: American Hotel & Lodging Educational Institute, 2012).

2. Readers interested in more information about determining and maintaining labor requirements in food and beverage operations should read Chapter 14 in Jack D. Ninemeier, *Planning and Control for Food and Beverage Operations*, 8th ed. (Lansing, Mich.: American Hotel & Lodging Educational Institute, 2013).

3. For more information on directing employees, see Jack D. Ninemeier and Raphael R. Kavanaugh, *Supervision in the Hospitality Industry*, 5th ed. (Lansing, Mich.: American Hotel & Lodging Educational Institute, 2013).

4. For more information on food and beverage control, see Ninemeier, *Planning and Control*.

5. The Educational Institute has numerous educational and training resources that address guest service issues, including CD-ROMs, videos, seminars, and workshops. For more information, phone the Institute at 1-800-349-0299 or review the Institute's website at www.ei-ahla.org.

🔑 Key Terms

controlling—The management task of measuring actual results against expected results, such as measuring actual sales against expected or budgeted sales. Controlling also refers to safeguarding the operation's property and revenue.

coordinating—The management task of assigning work and organizing people and resources to achieve the operation's objectives.

directing—The management task of supervising, scheduling, and disciplining employees. Supervising includes such functions as training and motivating employees.

empowerment—The redistribution of power within an organization that enables managers, supervisors, and employees to perform their jobs more efficiently and effectively. The overall goal is to enhance service to guests and increase profits for the organization by releasing decision-making responsibility, authority, and accountability to every level within the organization.

evaluating—The management task of determining the extent to which planned goals are attained.

hospitality—The cordial reception of guests.

job specification—A staffing tool that identifies the personal qualities necessary to perform a job effectively.

management—The use of resources to attain organizational objectives.

organizing—The management activity that attempts to best assemble and use limited human resources to attain organizational objectives. It involves establishing the flow of authority and communication among people.

outsource—Contracting an outside person or organization to perform jobs or services that would otherwise be done by a business's employees.

planning—The management task of creating goals, objectives, and programs of action to reach those goals and objectives. Planning should be done before undertaking other management tasks.

role model—A person whose behavior or success on the job can be imitated by others.

staffing—The management activity of recruiting and hiring applicants.

subordinate—A person at a lower level in rank or authority.

⟨?⟩ Review Questions

1. What is the management process?

2. What resources does a food service manager have available to meet the organization's goals?

3. Why is it important to set aside time for planning?

4. What is the purpose of an organization chart?

5. Recruiting and hiring are part of which management activity or task?

6. Should a large number of people be encouraged to apply for a job opening? Why or why not?

7. Where does the process of controlling begin?

8. Managers' responsibilities extend to which primary groups?

9. How can a restaurant positively affect a community? How can it negatively affect a community?

10. What are examples of aspects of food service operations that are regulated by government agencies?

11. Why is the principle of hospitality important to every food and beverage operation?

💻 Internet Sites

For more information, visit the following Internet sites. Remember that Internet addresses can change without notice. If the site is no longer there, you can use a search engine to look for additional sites.

Hospitality Publications Illustrate Management in Action

Chef
www.chefmagazine.com

Fast Casual
www.fastcasual.com

Food Management
www.food-management.com

Food Service Director
www.foodservicedirector.com

Food Service News
www.foodservicenews.com

FSR Magazine
www.fsrmagazine.com

Hotel F&B Magazine
www.hotelfandb.com

National Restaurant Association
  SmartBrief
www.smartbrief.com/restaurant

Nation's Restaurant News
www.nrn.com

QSR Web (Quick-Service Restaurants)
www.qsrweb.com

Restaurant Business
www.restaurantbusinessonline.com

Restaurant Hospitality
www.restaurant-hospitality.com

Basic Management Skills

About.com
(enter "management and leadership"
in the site's search box)

Businessballs
www.businessballs.com

Free Management Library
www.managementhelp.org

Mind Tools
www.mindtools.com

Managing Guest Services (Hospitality)

Customer Service Zone
www.customerservicezone.com

Hospitality Net
www.hospitalitynet.org

Karten Associates
www.nkarten.com

KnowThis.com
www.knowthis.com

Chapter 4 Outline

Marketing: Focus on Guests
Feasibility Studies
    Identifying Market Area
      Characteristics
    Evaluating the Proposed Site
    Analyzing the Competition
    Estimating Demand
    Projecting Operating Results
    Staying Current
Marketing Research
    Property Analysis
    Competition Analysis
    Market Analysis
The Marketing Plan
Implementing the Marketing Plan
    Sales Efforts
    Advertising
    Contemporary Electronic Advertising
    Public Relations and Publicity
Marketing Tactics for Noncommercial Food
    Service Operations

Competencies

1. Explain marketing in terms of delivering guest-pleasing service. (pp. 65–67)

2. Describe the steps involved in developing a feasibility study, and list the three types of marketing research that should follow such a study. (pp. 67–73)

3. Describe the elements of a complete marketing plan, focusing on the roles of sales, traditional and electronic advertising, public relations, and publicity; and compare public relations and publicity for hospitality operations. (pp. 73–87)

4. Describe marketing tactics that a noncommercial food service operation might use. (pp. 87–88)

Food and Beverage Marketing

FOOD AND BEVERAGE marketing is a complex, fascinating subject with many components so this chapter can provide only a brief introduction. After an overview of guest-related concerns, the chapter discusses feasibility studies and addresses preopening and ongoing marketing research. It then discusses marketing plan development and the major tools to use to achieve a marketing plan's objectives: sales, advertising and promotions, public relations and publicity. The increased use of social media for restaurant marketing is explored, as is the use of guest loyalty programs and gift cards.[1] The chapter concludes with a brief look at marketing for noncommercial operations.

Marketing: Focus on Guests

A simple definition of marketing is *seeing the business from the perspective of the guests*. While it is easy to understand that food and beverage managers *should* always be concerned about guests, sometimes this is not the case, because other management concerns intrude: "What will it cost?" "What will employees resist least?" "What would the owner like best?" and so on. Yet, a marketing emphasis on excellent guest relations is a significant key to every hospitality operation's success.

Emphasizing the guests makes obvious sense for commercial food service operators. After all, the public has choices, and people can express their displeasure by visiting a competitor's property. The possible consequences of failing to recognize guests' needs apply to noncommercial food service managers as well. Increasingly, students and businesspeople, for example, have choices when they consider food service options in schools and business/industry organizations. Self-operated food services that cannot attain financial and other goals may be administered by a contract management company. Even a contract management company can be replaced by another company if the food service program that it operates in a noncommercial setting is unsuccessful.

Some observers may believe that consumer concerns are less important in, for example, correctional facilities and healthcare facilities where there is a captive market. However, where do prison riots frequently begin? In the dining area. What do patients in hospitals and residents in long-term facilities frequently voice displeasure about? Again, the answer involves the quality of the food services offered.

As you can see, then, marketing—the process of considering the food service operation from the point of view of those being served—is critical.

The most important ingredient in a successful guest-service effort is top-level commitment. Food service managers who are committed to marketing do the following:

- Use strategies that focus on what is best for their guests.

- Talk about service routinely.

- Implement guest-friendly service systems.

- Exemplify all aspects of excellent guest relations as they personally talk about and interact with guests.

- Balance high-tech with high-touch; that is, they temper systems and methods with the personal factor.

- Market service to their guests.

- Emphasize service in employee training programs and reward staff members who consistently deliver exemplary guest service.

- Measure service and make the results available to their employees.

Wise food service managers know that their first responsibility is to meet or exceed the wants and needs of their guests. If they do this, success is more likely to follow. Food service managers should be able to effectively answer the following questions:

- How important is service in my organization?

- How do I emphasize service during employee recruitment and selection and during employee orientation and training sessions?

- How do I tell/show my staff about service-related concerns?

- How do I evaluate service levels?

- What are my service strategies?

- What are my service procedures?

- How do I reinforce service strategies?

- Is service a *program* or a *philosophy* at my property?

- Does my staff manage **moments of truth**—any opportunities a guest has to form an impression about the property? Are all possible moments of truth favorable?

- Do I emphasize service all the time or only after a service-related problem arises?

Food service managers must incorporate concerns about the guests into all of their activities. While this is easy to say, it is difficult to do consistently. Food service operations succeed by making a continuous, never-ending journey toward service excellence. The first step is to recognize that service is important. A second step is to develop guest-friendly processes that consistently deliver products and services that meet organizational standards. A third step is to continually assess and respond to guests' ever-changing preferences.

Feasibility Studies

A **feasibility study** should be conducted before a proposed food service operation is constructed or an existing facility is purchased or leased. Potential investors decide whether to finance a project by evaluating the results of the feasibility study. This input guides the planners and architects of the project, and assists managers as they develop marketing plans and prepare initial operating budgets.

Feasibility studies are generally prepared by organizations such as public accounting firms, real estate companies, or management consulting organizations commissioned by the developers or potential owners. Although developers and potential owners may conduct feasibility studies themselves, an independent consultant usually conducts the study if outside financing is necessary.

While the scope of a feasibility study varies from project to project, the following functions are common to most studies:

- Identifying market area characteristics
- Evaluating the proposed site
- Analyzing the competition
- Estimating demand
- Projecting operating results

Identifying Market Area Characteristics

Market area characteristics include **demographic information** about potential guests of the new operation. This frequently involves those in the general area of the proposed site. However, in the case of destination (vacation) operations, a much broader scope will be needed. Useful information about potential guests includes age, gender, level of education, marital status, number of children, family income, type of employment, and location of residence. Other helpful information often includes the area's volume of retail sales, the number and types of industrial and commercial businesses, the impact of tourism, and available transportation.

In addition to presenting current market area statistics, a feasibility study analyzes positive and negative trends that may affect demand for the proposed facility. For example, the economic stability of the area's commercial and industrial enterprises can have a direct bearing on the future success of the operations, especially if those enterprises were primary demand generators for the property. Also, if the communities surrounding the proposed site are experiencing an economic decline or upswing, it can affect the desirability of the proposed project.

Evaluating the Proposed Site

The site for a proposed food service facility is one of the most important variables determining the eventual success or failure of the operation. A restaurant that

---

Technology and Feasibility Study Information

Increasingly, technology provides important ways for restaurant owners and investors to gather potential-customer information or to search for possible business-expansion locations. For example, Internet-based applications can provide demographic maps and reports for all areas and addresses within the United States. Owners and investors can obtain information based on postal zip codes, driving times, or distances that reveals potential-guest age groups, household facts, and average household expenditures. The information can include household spending for food consumed away from home, number of dining-out occasions, and location of competitors, among numerous factors. All such information can be generated in tables, maps, or graphs as well as in standard written reports.

Computerized marketing data can also help restaurant managers learn about potential customers. For example, managers can obtain information useful in planning food delivery routes, and learn the best, most effective ways to advertise to potential guests (such as social media, billboard ads, or direct mail).

---

offers quality food and friendly service in an inviting atmosphere with beautiful decor will typically fail if it is in a poor location. On the other hand, a poor-quality restaurant may succeed *in the short run* if it is in a great location such as a **restaurant row** in a suburban area.

A feasibility study evaluates the project site and the area surrounding it by researching the number of people living or working (1) in the surrounding metropolitan area, (2) within walking distance, and (3) within easy driving distance. Other factors the study can analyze include the availability and convenience of parking, traffic flow patterns, distances from exits off main highways, and the location of other attractions that draw guests, such as shopping malls, movie theaters, and other food service operations.

The study should also analyze the accessibility of the proposed site. Turning against oncoming traffic or having to cope with one-way streets may be bothersome, but not necessarily damaging to business. However, in a highly competitive market, restrictions on turns into and out of the site and inadequate on-site or nearby parking, as well as other accessibility inconveniences, may lower guest demand.

Analyzing the Competition

The competition analysis section of a feasibility study presents an inventory of all competing food and beverage facilities in the project's market area. Competition may consist of not only freestanding establishments, but also food service operations in office buildings, private clubs, and social and fraternal organizations.

Additional competition may come from department, grocery, and convenience retail stores, as well as gas stations that increasingly dedicate significant space to the sale of sandwiches, soft drinks, and related items. Retail stores such as Target, Wal-Mart, and numerous others frequently lease space to and/or receive a percentage of revenue generated by branded quick-service restaurants located within their stores. Examples of food outlets established in stores include

Little Caesars, McDonald's, Taco Bell, Pizza Hut, Starbucks, Sonic, KFC, and other national, regional, and local (independent) operations. These units compete directly with freestanding restaurants including their own brands. Other retail shops may offer their own food services ranging from upscale outlets to kiosks selling sandwiches and mobile carts selling hot dogs, ice cream novelties, and other foods along with beverages.

Sometimes the analysis of competition is confined to the immediate vicinity of the proposed site. However, when the facility is planned to be especially unique, it is likely to attract guests from a wider area.

A feasibility study generally analyzes information about each competitor, including:

- Location (closeness to the proposed site)
- Type of restaurant
- Source and volume of business
- Days and hours of operation
- Menu prices
- Guest check average
- Type of service
- Number of seats
- Availability of alcoholic beverage service
- Entertainment
- Promotional efforts
- Chain affiliation

The feasibility study should also show how long each competitor has operated at its location, the business volume of each competitor at various meal periods on different days of the week, and how current guests feel about the food and service provided by each establishment.

The competition analysis helps establish preopening marketing strategies for the proposed food service facility. For example, the results of a feasibility study can help determine the following:

- The type and volume of demand for food and beverage services
- The adequacy with which the competition satisfies the current demand
- The strengths and limitations of the competition
- The points of difference that must be established between the proposed facility and the competition

The results of the competition analysis can also be useful in guiding the design of the proposed facility, planning the menu and the type of service, establishing prices, determining hours of operation, and developing advertising and promotion strategies.

Estimating Demand

Developing an estimate of demand for a commercial food and beverage operation begins with an analysis of the market area's restaurant and bar sales. This provides an overview of dining trends and market demands. Data for this analysis can be gathered by surveying potential guests about their restaurant, banquet, and meeting room needs.

Surveying can be accomplished through personal interviews or direct mail questionnaires. Increasingly, potential operators or owners considering expansion retain third-party organizations that use computer-assisted survey technology to conduct surveys. Potential guests are asked about their food preferences; how often they dine out; how far they are willing to travel to do so; how much time they spend on breakfast, lunch, and dinner; and how much money they are willing to spend for each meal period.

Projecting Operating Results

Most feasibility studies project **pro forma** financial results for the first, second, and (sometimes) third year of operation. Potential investors need this information so they can decide whether to finance the project.

Generally, investors want to examine forecasts of food and beverage revenue and estimates of expenses for such costs as administration, labor, marketing, facility maintenance, energy, rent, insurance, and property taxes. While not all consultants use the same methods, nor give the same amount of detail, the feasibility study should clearly explain the basis of the estimate for each major revenue and expense category. This information can guide managers in planning the budget for the facility's first year of operation.

Staying Current

Feasibility studies are often conducted long before construction actually takes place (for newly constructed facilities) or a new operation is opened in an existing building. Given the dynamics of the economic environment, a feasibility study completed six months ago may be of little value unless the data collected has not significantly changed. It is often difficult to determine this without conducting further studies. The fact that feasibility studies can become dated so quickly emphasizes the need for food service managers to conduct ongoing marketing research.

Marketing Research

After a food service facility is in operation, ongoing marketing research helps to ensure that the business meets the needs and wants of guests. This research also provides the basis for developing an effective marketing plan. Ongoing marketing research typically includes a property analysis, a competition analysis, and a market analysis. Combined, these analyses answer questions related to the operation's strengths, weaknesses, opportunities, and threats, and constitute a **situation analysis**.

Property Analysis

A property analysis is a written, unbiased appraisal of a food service operation's production and service areas, products, and services. This analysis is used to assess the strengths and weaknesses of the operation. The building's exterior, the landscaping, and the property's signage should be included in the analysis. The building and site should be carefully evaluated in terms of traffic flow, accessibility, visual appeal, and compatibility with local surroundings.

The property analysis should also assess the operation in terms of the categories used in the feasibility study (location, type of restaurant, source and volume of business, and days and hours of operation, for example). These statistics will enable managers to make meaningful comparisons between the property and the competition.

A property analysis should be more than a simple checklist. It is important to think about the property from the guest's perspective. In other words, the analyst should try to envision the facility as guests see it. Friends of management and the staff can be invited as guests during selected meal periods to provide the kind of feedback that property insiders may be incapable of providing.

Competition Analysis

While a property analysis is extremely important, it is equally necessary to know what the competition is doing. A competition analysis should cover the same categories listed in the feasibility study.

While forms and checklists are useful for analyzing the competition, it is far more effective to actually experience what the competition has to offer. Food service managers and staff should visit competitors' operations at a variety of times (breakfast, lunch, and dinner as well as slow and peak business periods, for example) to completely understand the service and atmosphere the competitors provide.

Market Analysis

A market analysis identifies the food service operation's current markets and examines marketplace factors and trends that provide opportunities or pose threats to the operation. A **market** is a group of guests with similar needs, wants, backgrounds, incomes, and buying habits. Market analysis involves guest profile research and identification of marketplace factors and trends.

What Is a Brand?

Simply defined, a *brand* is the name of a multi-unit food service organization. For example, almost everyone is familiar with such brands (organizations) as McDonald's, Pizza Hut, and Olive Garden. However, brands also relate to a company's reputation as well as the stereotypes and images that guide someone's perception of the company. Consistency of product, service, advertising, and even basic facility design can be part of a brand's image. Brands create a promise of what guests can expect and help guests to identify with the company and the brand.

Guest Profile Research. Data on a guest's age, gender, frequency of visits to the property, and employment can be important in **positioning** or repositioning the food service operation. If research indicates that the operation draws business-people at lunch and families in the evening, for example, managers can plan menus that will appeal to each group. Similarly, if most lunch guests are business-women, the operation might want to appeal to them with an eye-catching salad bar and specially priced small lunch portions for light eaters.

The manager, host, or food servers can gather guest profile information sim-ply by talking with guests. They can gather more information by observing such details as briefcases that identify guests as businesspeople, shopping bags that identify guests as patrons of a nearby shopping mall, and sports bags that identify guests as members of a local health club.

A property's website can be a good source of guest profile information. Infor-mation might be provided in return for coupons or "points" in a frequent diners' club (discussed later in the chapter). Analysis of electronic ordering system infor-mation may yield a "picture" of guest locations that, in turn, may suggest socio-economic data of use to planners.

Special **promotions** can also be used to obtain important guest profile infor-mation. For example, a special promotion could request business cards of guests as entry forms for a free meal drawing. One or more cards can be drawn on speci-fied dates and each winner given a complimentary meal. This type of promotion is a cost-effective way to obtain names, occupations, and telephone numbers of current guests.

Detailed **guest surveys** or short **guest comment cards** can be excellent sources of information helpful in planning menus and developing promotions for specific guest groups. Completed guest surveys may also help management with pricing decisions and provide clues about markets still untapped.

The types of questions asked may vary with the meal period. For example, if the operation caters to businesspeople at lunch, the lunch survey could ask ques-tions relating to favorite food selections, speed of service, interest in mobile phone and internet ordering, and other factors that would make the operation more attrac-tive to businesspeople. Surveys vary according to management's objectives. A ques-tionnaire can focus on food preparation (preferences for fried, broiled, or steamed items) or on the preferred type of service (buffet or table service).

To encourage guests to fill out questionnaires or comment cards, servers can draw attention to the form and tell guests that they will receive a bonus gift or discount coupon if they turn in the completed form when making payment. Management can make it easy to fill out the form. For example, it can provide a complimentary pen or an envelope for the completed survey. Guests who have received less-than-perfect food and/or service may feel intimidated when turning in unflattering comments to food servers. In these cases, an envelope helps deal with the problem and may be the key to obtaining more detailed responses from guests. Restaurant websites can draw comments from those who have visited the property and allow more exploratory questions to be asked. For example, an operation might ask, "On a scale of 1–5, to what extent would you be attracted to a restaurant because it offers a take-home salad bar?"

Marketplace Factors and Trends. A market analysis also identifies environmental opportunities and problems that can affect business. Changes in demographics; positive and negative events in the community, region, state, and nation; the cost and availability of energy; government regulation; and the cost of travel are just a few of the marketplace factors that can influence business volume and check averages. Statistics for projecting environmental effects on business can be found in census data, information from industrial commissions such as the state or city department of economic development, and industry reports. Exhibit 1 highlights a selection of potential resources for this data.

A recurring trend that food service operators confront in both commercial and noncommercial segments relates to nutrition and lifestyle concerns. A significant increase in consumer demand for healthy menu options can prompt managers to make significant changes in their businesses.

The Marketing Plan

The **marketing plan** translates ongoing marketing research into strategies and tactics. As shown in Exhibit 2, creating a marketing plan involves selecting target markets, determining objectives, creating action plans to meet those objectives, and monitoring and evaluating those plans to measure their success and help set new objectives.[2]

Although many restaurateurs promote their restaurants as if they are appealing to a single market, in reality many restaurants appeal to a number of markets. As mentioned previously, the guest mix at lunch may be very different from the guest mix at dinner. While managers should keep this diversity in mind, they should also remember that it is impossible to be all things to all people. Restaurateurs should first identify which major markets their operation already appeals to by using guest surveys, guest comment cards, and other information-gathering techniques. They can then devote marketing efforts to maintaining and increasing the number of guests from those markets before trying to attract new ones.

After target markets are selected, the next step in developing a marketing plan is to establish specific marketing objectives. Ideally, there should be objectives for each market and each meal period. From these marketing objectives, specific sales objectives and quotas can be set. For best results, marketing objectives should be:

- *In writing.* Everyone has the same information when objectives are put in writing.

- *Understandable.* Objectives will not be reached unless managers and employees can understand them.

- *Realistic yet challenging.* Objectives should not be set so high that staff members give up before they start; conversely, objectives should not be set so low that they present no challenge.

- *Specific and measurable.* Objectives should be as specific and measurable as possible. For example, rather than say "Increase lunch business," the marketing objective should say "Increase lunch business during June by increasing the guest count by five percent and the average guest check by $2."

Exhibit 1   Marketplace Resources

AREA ATTRACTIONS

Chamber of Commerce (local)

Convention and Visitors Bureaus

COMMERCIAL & INDUSTRIAL ACTIVITY

State Banking Department

See department websites and governmenta pages under state name.

U.S. Treasury

Comptroller of the Currency, found on the web and listed in governmental pages under "United States."

Chamber of Commerce (local)

State Department of Commerce

DEMAND

U.S. Department of Commerce Directories

Local Chamber of Commerce Statistics

Hotel Sales Tax Figures (if available)

Monthly and Yearly Lodging Reports

Convention and Visitors Bureaus

Local Hotel Managers

DIRECT COMPETITION

On-Site Inspections

Directories (chain, AAA, Mobil)

Hotel and Restaurant Managers

INCOME/EMPLOYMENT

State Commerce and Economic Development Department

Division of Economic Development found on the web and in governmental pages under state name.

MARKET SUPPLY/DEMAND

Local Hotel and Lodging Association

Convention and Visitors Bureaus

Hotel/Restaurant Managers and Operators

POPULATION AND DEMOGRAPHICS

State Office of Demographics and Economic Analysis (sometimes called the Division of Research and Statistics)

Found on the web and in governmental pages under the state name.

POTENTIAL COMPETITION

Building Permits

Local Department of Buildings, found on the web and in governmental pages under county or state.

Project Status

Local Department of Buildings in conjunction with local banks.

RETAIL STATISTICS

State Office of Demographics and Economic Analysis

State Commerce Department

Division of Economic Development

First Data InfoSource/Donnelly Marketing

SITE ADAPTABILITY

Community Planning Agencies

TOURISM

State Highway Department

State Department of Transportation, Traffic and Safety Division; found on the web and in governmental pages under state name.

Local Airport Authorities

State Department of Transportation, Public Transportation Division; found on the web and in governmental pages under state name.

Area Attractions

Area Hotels

Note: Technology companies providing demographic and related data are listed at the end of the chapter in the "Internet Sites" section.

Exhibit 2   Creating a Marketing Plan

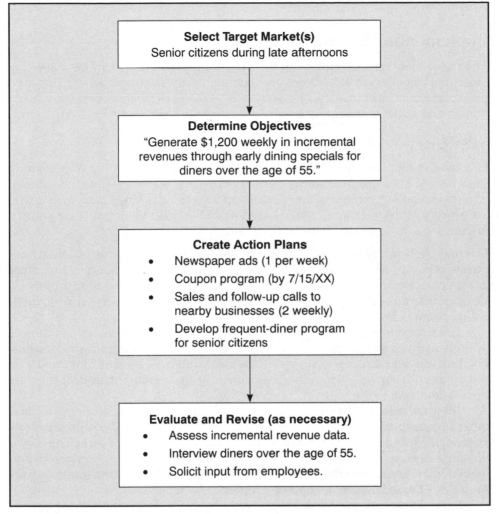

After marketing objectives are established, action plans with target dates must be created to reach them. Employees should be encouraged to contribute their ideas. Action plans can be simple, perhaps involving only one employee, or relatively complicated, involving many employees. Action plan expenses must be included in the marketing budget. Responsibility for performing each action or seeing that it is carried out should be assigned to specific individuals to allow for more effective accountability and monitoring.

The more carefully action plans are monitored and evaluated, the easier it will be to set future marketing objectives and action plans, because managers will learn what works and what does not. Also, if action plans are monitored regularly, there may be time to take corrective action(s) if a plan is not working. Evaluation and timely corrective action may prevent costly mistakes and can lead to more effective marketing plans in the future.

Implementing the Marketing Plan

The major tools used to implement the marketing plan and to achieve marketing objectives are sales efforts, advertising, contemporary electronic advertising, and public relations and publicity. This section also discusses the increased use of technology and social media, guest loyalty programs, and gift cards.

Sales Efforts

Few marketing plan objectives can be attained without maintaining or increasing sales efforts. Two broad categories of sales efforts are internal selling and external or personal selling. Internal selling focuses on increasing revenue from guests who are already at the restaurant. External selling can be used to identify new sources of business.

Internal Selling. Internal selling is any effort made to increase revenue from guests who are already visiting the food service operation. Service and other guest-contact employees often can generate additional sales and repeat business through internal selling. Types of internal selling include suggestive selling, internal merchandising, and special promotions.

Food servers may use suggestive selling techniques to sell such additional or higher-priced menu items as appetizers, wine, premium liquors, and desserts. Food servers who effectively suggest these items can have a significant impact on the operation's success, the guests' enjoyment of the restaurant, and, if they are tipped employees, on their own compensation.

Internal merchandising involves the use of in-house signs, displays, and other promotional material to increase sales. In-house signs and displays include posters, table tent cards (see Exhibit 3), wine displays, and dessert carts. The power of suggestion can be overwhelming when, for example, a food server rolls a cart loaded with mouth-watering desserts directly to a guest's table or a trained server prepares a flamed dessert at another guest's nearby table.

Special sales programs are limited only by one's imagination. Food service managers use such programs for many purposes: increasing the public's awareness of the operation, attracting new guests, keeping regular guests happy, increasing business during slow periods, and spotlighting special events. Examples include the following:

- Couponing
- Product sampling
- Contests
- Packages
- Premiums
- Gift certificates/gift cards

Exhibit 3   Sample Table Tent Card

December Events

Sunday, December 5, 12, and 19
Holiday Brunches with *Santa* and
Special Guest *SpongeBob Squarepants!*

December 7-10 and 14-17
Holiday Luncheon Buffet

Friday, December 31
New Year's Evening Glow À la Carte Dinner
Featuring *The Victor Trachsel Jazz Trio*

Coming in January and February!

Early Bird Specials
Tuesday, Thursday, Friday and
Saturday Night Dining
Enjoy Chef Findley's home cooked
favorites, all under $12.00!

Tuesday, January 18
Cooking Class–*Hearty Winter Soups*

Friday, January 28
Jazz Night featuring the *Ray Kamalay Quartet*
With Special Guest *Cary Kocher, Vibraphonist*

Friday, February 11
Gourmet Wine Dinner featuring the
Wines of France

Monday, February 14
Valentine Dinner featuring
Five Deep Jazz Combo

Courtesy of University Club, Michigan State University, East Lansing, Mich.

- Discounting
- Bonus offers
- Product bundling
- Frequent guest programs

Coupons are often printed with a special offer to attract potential guests. Coupons can be handed out, included in direct mail advertising, printed in newspapers and magazines, available for printing from the property's website, or even sent to guests' mobile telephones. Coupon books are also available on websites (see www.restaurant.com and www.groupon.com, for example). In one format, a purchaser pays a small fee for a higher-value coupon. For instance, a coupon for a $25 meal can be sold for $10. While quick-service restaurants have traditionally offered couponing, higher-check-average properties, including those offering casual service, also offer coupons, especially during difficult financial times. (Managers should be aware of bogus coupons printed from websites not affiliated with the restaurant.)

Product sampling can acquaint guests with new food items. For example, after seating guests, servers may pass around samples of an appetizer to interest them in ordering the appetizer from the menu.

The cost of a *contest* can be justified if it increases sales enough to offset the cost of prizes given to the contest winners. Winners could receive a cash prize or a dinner for two. Quick-service chains frequently have contests or games with large grand prizes with the hope that they will bring additional guests into their establishments nationwide.

Packages can be used to combine several items at a discount price to attract new guests and to increase total revenue. Two examples are dinner/theater packages combining dinner for two with two theater tickets, and hotel weekend packages combining food and beverages with hotel rooms.

Premiums are gifts for guests who pay the regular price for food and beverages. To encourage business on a slow night, for example, a free mug could be given to each adult who orders dinner. Quick-service chains generally use premiums more than any other type of food service operation. They offer gifts to children and hope that the children will ask their parents to take them to one of the chain's fast-food outlets to receive the gifts. A large soft drink glass featuring popular children's cartoon characters is an example of a premium.

Gift certificates and gift cards are handled the same way as gift certificates sold in retail stores. Quick-service chains like to sell gift certificates in small denominations, especially around holidays. These allow children who are on limited budgets to buy gifts for their parents and other relatives. Some gift card recipients might never have visited the operation before, while others might be repeat guests who will be inspired to spend more when they use their gift cards to settle their checks (that is, the restaurant's check averages may increase). Some food service operators sell gift cards in "gift card mall" display racks situated in such central locations as supermarkets or drug stores for customer convenience. Other restaurants place special kiosks on restaurant premises to let purchasers bypass the point-of-sale procedures otherwise required.

Some restaurants sell gift cards that purchasers can personalize, perhaps with a downloaded photo. Other organizations use gift cards as *stored value cards*. That is, once they register online, customers who purchase a specific number of items or spend a specific amount of dollars may receive a free menu item or other reward. Such online registration gives the restaurant an opportunity to communicate with cardholders; for example, the restaurant might send special offers to those who have registered.

Discounting involves lowering the price of food and beverage items to attract more guests and increase total sales. There are a variety of ways to discount: a manager can offer $1 off any large pizza, provide pitchers of beer for $2.50 on Monday nights, or reduce the price of chicken dinners by 50 percent.

There are many ways to offer guests a *bonus* for buying an item at regular price. For example, a restaurant could offer guests three dinners at the regular price and a fourth dinner free, two drinks for the price of one on Thursday nights, or one large pizza at the regular price and a second pizza at half price.

Product bundling occurs when several items are combined into a single product sale. For example, quick-service restaurants often offer a complete meal (sandwich, french fries, and beverage) at a selling price that is less than when each item is ordered individually.

Frequent-guest programs are similar in concept to the very popular airline-sponsored programs. With the latter, one accumulates points (miles) redeemable for free airline tickets. Restaurant-related promotions may award points to frequent guests that equate to complimentary meals, percentage discounts, birthday or anniversary specials, or numerous other benefits. As is true with so many other aspects of modern food service operations, technology is improving frequent-guest programs. Paper-based programs typically use punch cards, stamps, stickers, or other materials that can be easily (and fraudulently) duplicated. Such duplication is not possible with electronic programs.

External Selling. **External selling** (also called personal selling) has traditionally used salespeople to make sales calls to generate additional business. For example, catering companies may make sales calls to promote holiday or other banquets, and hotel sales personnel may contact organizations about large food and beverage functions. External selling is a marketing technique that is increasingly used in the food service industry. In some properties, it is an integral part of a manager's job. Other properties may hire salespeople to generate leads and make personal sales calls.

External sales efforts are often required to maximize banquet bookings and revenue. Banquet salespeople send out brochures, banquet menus, or letters about special packages to prospective groups and follow up these mailings with personal sales calls. They also handle group inquiries and personally discuss the details involved with banquets or meetings. Banquet salespeople work with the chef and other managers to design banquet menus and packages. Then they sell these menus and packages to help increase total revenues.

Representatives of contract management companies and vending organizations make numerous sales calls to prospective new accounts offering noncommercial food service. The websites of those to which calls are being placed can provide helpful planning information. Another example of a noncommercial sales call occurs when food service representatives visit departments in a large health-care, education, or business/industry organization to encourage people to order carry-out food options or to cater a department coffee break or larger function.

Social Selling. Technology, especially social media, is increasingly used to interest new and existing customers in the products and services offered by food service operations. Social selling is a modern form of personal selling because it enables one-on-one communication between the food service representative and potential new guests for one-time banquet and other events and for repeat-business dining. Social selling can be fast and cost-effective, reach an incredible number of targeted persons, and provide seemingly unlimited opportunities for creativity.

As is true with any type of selling effort, planning is needed for social selling. What are the goals? How and when will selling be done and on what predetermined schedule? How will success be measured? Like any type of sales message, social selling messages must add value (the messages must indicate "what's in it" for the potential guests).

There are many social media platforms available today and new platforms become available frequently. Most food service managers find it helpful to at least utilize LinkedIn, Twitter, and Facebook. They listen in on social media because these connections help them learn the thoughts and opinions of those in the marketplace. For example, negative comments about competitors may identify weaknesses that can be taken advantage of, and problems noted for one's own operation become improvement opportunities.

The best social selling tactics involve presenting relevant content and providing information that suggests how one's operation can provide value and benefit those receiving the messages. Social selling tactics to build new markets are, in many ways, similar to those used in advertising (discussed in the next section).

Advertising

Advertising is another major tool food and beverage managers can use to achieve marketing objectives. Managers use advertising to inform the public about their food service operation and persuade guests to visit it. Advertising takes many forms, each of which must be carefully evaluated when managers determine how best to use the property's advertising dollars.

When deciding which advertising medium to use, managers should look for the one whose target audiences most closely match the property's. The operation's ongoing marketing research defines who its guests are and where they are located; once the target markets are defined, managers should select the advertising methods that best reach the markets at the lowest cost.

Managers can use traditional or more contemporary electronic advertising methods. Traditional advertising comprises outdoor advertising, newspapers, magazines, radio, television, direct mail, and other tactics.

Outdoor Advertising. Food service operations sometimes use outdoor advertising to attract the attention of passersby by employing eye-catching, bold, and dynamic ads. Examples include public transit signs posted in commuter rail stations or affixed to buses and advertising kiosks located along public sidewalks or in shopping malls.

Two popular outdoor advertising media are property signs and billboards. Property signs identify the property and attract guests. Billboards are located at roadsides away from the property to attract guests.

Advantages of outdoor advertising can include:

- *Low cost.* Signs and billboards can be fairly expensive to produce, but rental or upkeep costs are relatively low.

- *Long life span.* Outdoor advertising can have a life span of thirty days to several years.

- *Broad reach.* Hundreds, thousands, or even tens of thousands of people may see property signs and billboard messages each day.

Disadvantages of outdoor advertising include:

- *Limited message length.* Messages must be extremely brief and can make only a few points.

- *Waste coverage.* Thousands of people who see the sign will have no interest in the property or an opportunity to visit it.

- *Zoning laws.* Legal restrictions about the type and size of property signs may create problems that are costly and time-consuming to resolve.

Newspapers. Advertising in newspapers is often attractive. For example, a family restaurant can reach many families in the area through a local newspaper, and restaurant chains can obtain effective coverage by advertising a common message.

Newspapers are often divided into several sections, and many restaurants advertise in the entertainment section or target businesspeople in the business section.

Newspapers in large metropolitan areas may have several geographic editions, such as north side and south side, and a small restaurant on the city's north side may advertise only in the north side edition of the newspaper.

Newspaper ads can be placed quickly and can run for varying times. They are also easy to cancel or repeat.

Disadvantages to advertising in newspapers may include that newspaper readers typically skim through pages rapidly and may only glance at or skip ads entirely. The poor quality of newsprint can be problematic because food service managers who want to depict mouth-watering menu items, elegant table settings, or beautiful decor are severely limited by newspaper reproduction capabilities.

Magazines. Magazine ads can last a week or even longer and, because they are available in public places, ads may be read by many times the number of people in the magazine's circulation.

Magazines can reach a select group of readers and often there is a magazine designed for whatever target market a property wishes to reach. Many readers are impressed by the high quality of paper and the excellent reproduction magazines offer. A food operation can use magazines to show off its appetizing food items and beautiful food service facilities.

Magazine advertising also has disadvantages. For instance, magazine ads generally have much higher production costs than newspaper ads, and a full-color ad may require weeks or months to produce. Magazines also have deadlines well in advance of their distribution, so an ad must be submitted far in advance of when it will appear.

Radio. Radio ads can potentially saturate an entire area, and the cost per person reached is low in comparison to other media. Radio ads can be produced very quickly and used almost immediately. A food service property can sponsor a high school sports game, local weather broadcast, or a daily special interest show. Placing opening or closing ads for news broadcasts is another possibility. Pricing is based upon the number of listeners. Drive time (6:00 A.M.–10:00 A.M. Monday through Saturday) typically has a large listener base. A broadcast of a local sporting event may also draw many listeners.

The cost of writing and producing radio ads must also be considered. Formats can range from a simple spoken message to an elaborate production with background music.

Radio ads can be targeted to reach people within convenient driving distance of the property. Managers can try to ensure that ads reach a property's specific target markets by matching the radio station's format and the time of day the ad is broadcast to the markets. If the operation features jazz entertainment in its lounge, it might reach its target market by advertising on the local jazz station. Ads can be repeated many times during the day on several different radio stations. Quick-service chains with new promotions often use radio stations to repeat their message continually.

Radio ads have short life spans: once aired, ads are gone forever unless they are repeated. Therefore, radio ads are generally useful only for messages advertising events scheduled in the near future, such as an upcoming Mother's Day brunch.

Television. Television provides extensive coverage; a commercial can run several times a day on several stations to reinforce the operation's message. The operation can choose television shows and time periods that appeal to an audience matching its target markets. If the operation is a quick-service or family restaurant, for example, it might want to run its television commercials during cartoon shows to reach the children's market. Sports bars may advertise during sporting events.

High cost is a major disadvantage of television advertising. A large commercial food service operation could spend several hundred thousand dollars—or more—to produce one television commercial. A one-minute commercial aired during prime time on national television can cost $1,000,000 or more! Even on local television, airtime can cost thousands of dollars per minute. Rates for cable television are typically lower, but many operations would still consider them too expensive.

Direct Mail. This type of advertising involves sending advertising messages (brochures, coupons, letters, postcards, and other announcements) through the mail. The messages may present specific special offers or may announce changes in the facility, staff, or menu (see Exhibit 4).

Exhibit 4   Sample Direct Mail Letter

NINO PERNETTI

C A F F E   B A C I

To all our friends ......

For the past three years, I have enjoyed my position as the manager of Caffe Abbracci. I was delighted when Nino asked me in May to become the new general manager of Caffe Baci. It is not every day that something like this happens.

The beautifully renovated Caffe Baci is something to be proud of. **Some things never change...Caffe Baci just got better.** As you enter the charming foyer, you will enjoy the ambiance of our new marble wine bar. Next you will want to be seated in the "Il Giardino Room" that has been decorated in unique Italian bisque tiles and accented by a magnificent vaulted skylight. The center of attraction is an imported Tuscany wood burning oven. During the day we serve an executive lunch as well as a variety of thin-crust pizzas. At dinner, we still serve the same wonderfully classic Italian cuisine that made Caffe Baci famous. We have also introduced creative specialties, prepared in the Tuscany oven. To tempt your palate I have enclosed a copy of the menu.

I trust that you will find these new changes a welcome addition for your dining pleasure. I look forward to greeting you soon.

Ciao,

Paolo

AMERICAN EXPRESS **Cards**
We Welcome The American Express® Card

VALET PARKING NOW AVAILABLE

2522 Ponce de Leon Blvd.   •   Coral Gables, FL 33134   •   442-0600   •   Fax 442-0061

This letter from Caffe Baci's manager informs readers that the restaurant's renovation is complete. A menu was enclosed with the letter. (Courtesy of Caffe Baci, Coral Gables, Florida)

Direct mail's main advantage is audience selectivity and specific target marketing. Private clubs illustrate this point well. The club's membership represents its total market since nonmembers cannot patronize the club; promotional information is mailed to members only.

Restaurant managers can develop a selective mailing list by collecting guests' business cards. People who respond to website surveys and reservation requests also provide information to construct focused conventional or electronic mailing lists. Another opportunity to use direct mail advertising to target a specific market arises when food service managers with banquet rooms send wedding package information to couples whose engagement announcements appear in the local newspaper.

With direct mail, managers can measure how well an ad or promotion succeeds. If an operation sends out 1,000 discount dinner coupons, for example, the number of coupons redeemed will indicate the promotion's success.

Producing a high-quality brochure or information packet is expensive. Other costs are for envelopes, postage, and labor. The overall cost per potential guest reached is generally greater than for other advertising mediums. Another major disadvantage is the "junk mail" image associated with most direct mail.

Other Tactics. Limited-service hotels that do not provide on-site food services might allow nearby restaurants to advertise their products and services to hotel guests. For example, a restaurant could provide menus to the hotels to place in guestrooms. Lobby displays, menu books at front desks, and even inserts in the key slots of electronic door locks provide other ways to advertise restaurants to hotel guests.

Other traditional tactics that restaurants use to advertise include the following:

- Ads in sporting event programs
- Name placement on a sponsored sports team's uniforms
- Telephone book display ads
- Specialty advertising items like pencils, pens, magnets, calendars, and penlights
- Flyers and brochures on community bulletin boards

All food service operations receive the benefit of, or suffer negative consequences from, another type of advertising: word-of-mouth. Many people tell their families, friends, and business associates about their dining experiences. Unfortunately, guests with unpleasant experiences tend to repeat details of their visits (perhaps exaggerating the problem with each telling) more often than do those with positive experiences. Food service professionals know that it is important to discover and correct problems when they occur and certainly before guests leave the premises. When staff members show that they care by performing timely corrective actions, guests take notice and are more likely to revisit the property. Repeat guests can help spread positive word-of-mouth messages throughout the community.

Contemporary Electronic Advertising

Today, few aspects of food service operation have been affected by technology as much as marketing and advertising within the increasingly high-tech marketplace. This section examines website and other Internet advertising, mobile marketing, and other electronic advertising tactics.

Websites. The Internet has fostered an entirely new e-commerce industry devoted to taking advertising messages to Internet users. An organization's website is an important part of its electronic advertising opportunities.

Establishing direct links to guests and potential guests is an important focus of e-commerce in the food service industry. Restaurant websites can be designed to enroll visitors in frequent-diner programs as a means of providing highly personalized service based on specified customer preferences. A member of a frequent-diner program that is accessible through the restaurant's website can create a personal profile that helps the restaurant target its marketing and promotion activities. News reports, coupons, cooking class invitations, and promotional offers can be e-mailed to enrolled members. Managers hope that the development of one-on-one guest relationships will translate into increased guest loyalty and enhanced revenues. Some websites show a live web camera (webcam) broadcast of the bar or a dining area. Menus posted on these sites may allow guests to preorder meals for sit-down or carry-out. Some restaurant managers send simple "we miss you" e-mail messages to frequent guests when, for example, they have not visited in a certain length of time. Modern technology allows managers to send newsletters conveying information and advertising messages and permits guests to make reservations at one of many restaurants (for example, in a chain operation for a location anywhere in the country on a date months into the future).

Contemporary websites are carefully designed to communicate as well as advertise. Details about community and regional histories, recipes with family-sized yields, general information useful for those planning banquets, and detailed information about wines are examples of features that can round out a website and provide incentives for consumers to visit the site frequently.

Other Internet Advertising. Food service operations can advertise in other ways besides on their websites. Banner or click-through ads are the Internet's equivalent of billboards. By placing a banner ad on an Internet page that features related content (for example, advertising a nearby restaurant on a site devoted to a community theater), advertisers can better target their messages and reach more qualified buyers. Nearly all banner ads also allow users to click on them to go immediately to the advertiser's own website. Such clicks typically are tallied automatically for advertisers, giving food and beverage establishments an easy way to measure an ad's ability to generate initial interest.

Mobile-Marketing Technology. Hundreds of millions of cell phones are in use in the United States, and many cell phone users read ads featuring specials or coupons for local businesses, including restaurants. Food service operators increasingly use Twitter (www.twitter.com) to solicit guest opinions or announce daily specials and menu changes. Since only those who request this information will view it, this type of message is not unsolicited e-mail. Many observers view cell phone media as the "third screen" for advertising (after television and personal computers). Guests need only bring up a coupon on their cell phone screen and present it at a participating restaurant to redeem the coupon. Demographic information about guests using cellular coupons is available to the restaurant.

Mobile marketing technology also allows visitors to get directions to restaurants and to settle transactions when they wave their cell phone screens at a special meter terminal.

Social Media Advertising. Many food service managers use Facebook for marketing and advertising purposes. They design their Facebook cover by thinking like a guest and then providing information that their guests will want to know about. Examples include photos of new menu items, alerts about menu specials, photos of guests having fun, and directions to their locations. Some managers plan sweepstakes and contests to generate awareness, and others insert videos of interviews with customers and chefs, or provide video tours of the property.

Another social media advertising strategy involves linking restaurant menus to Twitter tweets and offering deals—for example, free desserts with a meal purchase can be announced, and this tweet can be shared with a guest's friends. Other restaurants send out tweets close to the time of a meal period to announce a last-minute special-deal meal.

Of course, more than one social media outlet can be employed during an advertising campaign. For example, a food service manager developing an advertising campaign to roll out a new menu can use Twitter to alert readers about an important upcoming message. This can be followed with a second Twitter message that indicates a very special coupon on the property's Facebook page. When viewed, the Facebook page announces the new menu, shows photos of new items, and provides access to a coupon for a meal discount, complimentary appetizer or dessert, or other promotion.

Public Relations and Publicity

Public relations and publicity are marketing tools managers use to retain current guests and attract new ones. Both are more indirect and subtle than sales and advertising activities.

Public relations involves communicating favorable information about the operation to the public to create positive impressions. Its ultimate purpose is to create goodwill and increase the number of guests who patronize the operation. Restaurant managers should maintain good relations with guests, the media, competitors, the chamber of commerce, the convention and visitors bureau, business groups and other community organizations, trade associations, and government groups, among others. Satisfying current guests and properly handling their problems and complaints is a major contribution to good public relations and to the success of the operation.

Satisfied guests can provide positive word-of-mouth referrals to others. Even handling emergency situations such as fires and accidents in the best possible way can create a favorable impression.

Charity work is a typical public relations activity. Food service operations help charities by collecting donations from employees, sponsoring fund-raising activities, supporting telethons, and contributing company funds. Other examples of public relations activities are sponsoring local sports teams, Boy Scout and Girl Scout troops, and other community organizations.

Publicity is free media coverage of an operation, its staff, or special property events. Coverage can include such items as food, beverages, service, atmosphere, table settings, prices, personnel, or physical surroundings. Unlike advertising, publicity usually appears in the medium's editorial section because the medium, not the operation, controls the message and provides the space or airtime. The food service operation controls the content and placement of advertising in the media, but cannot directly control publicity about the food service operation.

Managers should try to generate positive publicity. They can inform the media of upcoming events at their properties in hopes of getting coverage. The media usually consider the grand opening of an operation or the celebration of a significant anniversary a newsworthy event.

Media personnel can also be informed of significant accomplishments of food service employees. For example, the media might cover a story about an employee who saves a guest from choking. This story would focus favorable attention on the employee and the food service establishment.

Managers can think about activities that the media may consider newsworthy. For example, they can plan parties at the operation to celebrate special events and invite the media to attend. Managers might also provide cooking demonstrations, host food and/or wine club events, and participate in the local restaurant organization's Taste of the Town or **progressive dinner** events.

Some publicity is unplanned and unexpected. In a typical case, a reviewer arrives unannounced to evaluate the food service operation. After the visit, the reviewer publishes or broadcasts his or her review. This type of unplanned publicity can be favorable or unfavorable. The annual Zagat Survey guides that compile survey information provided by frequent diners offer another example of unplanned publicity. New or previously unlisted properties receiving high ratings often experience dramatic increases in their business. This type of media attention can influence a restaurant's eventual success or failure.

Marketing Tactics for Noncommercial Food Service Operations

Most of this chapter has focused on marketing activities for use in commercial food and beverage operations. However, noncommercial food service managers

---

Boosting Public Image

Burger King has a strong statement about its corporate responsibility positions on its website: www.bk.com. It explains its positions and activities concerning numerous issues, including the following:

- Our Commitment to Food
- Our Commitment to People
- Our Commitment to the Environment
- Our Commitment to Corporate Governance

To view the information, go to the website and search for "Company Information," then scroll down to "Burger King Corporate Responsibility."

are just as concerned about marketing and often are just as creative when they plan ways to determine what their consumers desire and then to deliver it.

Market feasibility studies are often undertaken as, for example, decisions are made to self-operate or contract with a management company. Ongoing surveys of people participating in food services are conducted to determine menu item preferences.

The number and types of food services offered by large noncommercial organizations require management creativity to plan and manage. Consider, for example, a large hospital food service program operated by the facility itself or by a contract management company. Procedures will be in place to prepare and deliver meals to patients throughout the facility. Patients may receive attractive menus providing options that address their nutritional concerns. Hospital physicians and staff typically have access to a cash cafeteria operation along with patients and visitors. Hard-copy brochures and/or intranet advertising may be used to attract visitors to the cafeteria. Once there, menu boards and signage advertise menu item availability. Some healthcare food service operations offer catering for large events and even for departmental luncheons and special occasions. Prepared menus, printed newsletters, and brochures are used to advertise and promote these services.

Endnotes

1. A more detailed discussion of marketing can be found in Ronald A. Nykiel, *Marketing in the Hospitality Industry,* 5th ed. (Lansing, Mich.: American Hotel & Lodging Educational Institute, 2011).

2. Some of the information in the marketing, sales, advertising, and public relations and publicity sections is adapted from James R. Abbey, *Hospitality Sales and Marketing,* 6th ed. (Lansing, Mich.: American Hotel & Lodging Educational Institute, 2014).

Key Terms

demographic information—Data relating to age, gender, marital status, ethnicity, income, and occupation that helps to describe a person or a market.

external selling—A marketing technique that involves hiring salespeople to generate leads and make personal sales calls outside the food service operation itself.

feasibility study—A form of market research that analyzes the possible site, relevant demographic statistics, probable competitors, and projected financial success of a proposed food service operation.

guest comment card—A short questionnaire completed by guests and used by food service managers to define current markets and to improve the operation.

guest survey—A questionnaire completed by guests and used by food service managers to define current markets and to improve the operation. Managers may talk guests through the survey or leave it with them to fill out. Questionnaires may be long, and some questions may require detailed answers.

internal merchandising—The use of in-house promotional materials such as posters, table tent cards, wine displays, and dessert carts to promote additional sales.

internal selling—Specific sales activities of employees in conjunction with an internal merchandising program to promote additional sales and guest satisfaction.

market—A group of guests with similar needs, wants, backgrounds, incomes, and buying habits.

marketing plan—A business plan that translates ongoing market research into strategies and tactics. Creating a marketing plan involves selecting target markets, determining marketing objectives, creating action plans to meet those objectives, and monitoring and evaluating those plans to measure their success and help set new objectives.

moments of truth—Any opportunity that a guest has to form an impression of the food and beverage operation.

positioning—Tactics used by an organization to create an image or identity for the brand or organization in the minds of their target market.

pro forma—A financial projection based on assumptions.

progressive dinner—An event in which guests visit one property for appetizers, a second property for dinner, and a third property for dessert.

promotions—Marketing activities an organization uses to communicate with guests.

publicity—Free media coverage of a food service operation, its staff, or special property events.

public relations—The process of communicating favorable information about a food service operation to the public in order to create a positive impression.

restaurant row—A location with many restaurant, entertainment, and other businesses catering to tourists and locals.

situation analysis—A study that helps to assess an organization's strengths, weaknesses, opportunities, and threats.

Review Questions

1. What is a feasibility study?

2. If you were asked to invest in a new commercial food service operation, what would you expect a feasibility study to show in relation to proposed location, demographic statistics, probable competitors, and projected financial success?

3. What three analyses typically are included in ongoing marketing research? What type of information does each provide?

4. How can a food service operation gather guest profile information?

5. What are the major tools used to reach marketing objectives?

6. What are three types of internal selling?

7. What are some advantages and disadvantages of advertising in newspapers and magazines, and on the radio and television?

8. What types of social media would be most useful to specific types of food service operations? Why?

9. With what groups should a food service operation try to maintain good public relations?

10. How does publicity differ from advertising?

11. What marketing tactics can noncommercial operations use?

Internet Sites

For more information, visit the following Internet sites. Remember that Internet addresses can change without notice. If the site is no longer there, you can use a search engine to look for additional sites.

Food Operations Rating Guides

Michelin Restaurant Guide
(Enter "Michelin Restaurant Guide"
in your favorite search engine)

Zagat Survey
www.zagat.com

Yelp
www.yelp.com

Interactive Restaurant Websites

Note: Every large restaurant has a website, as do many smaller ones. Use a search engine to look up your favorites.

Feasibility Study (Information) Technology Companies

Intelligent Direct, Inc.
www.intelligentdirect.com

Market Maps
www.marketmaps.com

General Marketing Information

Free Management Library
www.managementhelp.org
(Enter "marketing" or "advertising" in the site's search box)

Part II

Menu Management

Chapter 5 Outline

Nutrition: The Science of Food
    The Six Basic Nutrients
    Nutrition Guidelines
Nutrition and Food Service Operations
    Menu Planning
    Nutrition Concerns in Purchasing
    Nutrition Concerns in Storing
    Conserving Nutrients During Food
        Preparation
    Standard Recipes and Nutrition
    Nutrition and Food Service
    Nutrition and Legislation
Contemporary Dietary Concerns
    Calories
    Fats and Cholesterol
    Sodium
    Food Allergies
    Vegetarian Meals
    Organic Foods

Competencies

1. Explain the importance of good nutrition, and list and define the six basic nutrients. (pp. 93–100)

2. Describe the value of recommended dietary allowances, the MyPlate program, and nutrition labeling. (pp. 100–102)

3. Describe nutrition concerns as they relate to food service functions, including menu planning, purchasing, storing, preparation, recipe development, and serving food to guests. (pp. 102–110)

4. Discuss menu-labeling laws. (p. 111)

5. Identify dietary concerns related to calories, fats and cholesterol, sodium, food allergies, vegetarian meals, and organic foods. (pp. 111–116)

5

Nutrition for Food Service Operations

EVERYONE REQUIRES a nutritious, well-balanced diet to be healthy. Both the quantity and quality of food are important factors in a proper diet. Few commercial food service managers are nutritionists or trained dietitians. However, they must have some knowledge of nutrition as they plan menus and train staff members to purchase, store, produce, and serve food. Noncommercial food service operations, such as those in correctional facilities, nursing homes, and boarding schools, provide all or most of the food consumed in the operation. Nutrition is of obvious concern in these cases. Some commercial food service operators may feel they are not responsible for addressing nutritional issues because their guests are free to choose where they want to eat and how frequently they visit a particular restaurant.

Today, however, guests are increasingly concerned about nutrition, and many carefully consider dining alternatives relative to nutritious options available. In the case of noncommercial operations, food service managers must *provide* consumers with nutritious meals. In commercial facilities, managers should *offer* items that are nutritious and that appeal to guests who want such items. In both noncommercial and commercial food service operations, nutrition is an important factor that must be addressed as food service plans are developed, implemented, and evaluated.

Many principles of effective food service management directly affect the nutritional quality of food. It is not necessary, therefore, to rethink each component in food operations to address nutritional concerns. Rather, the best strategy is to understand some basics of nutrition and to modify current procedures in practical ways to help ensure that these important nutritional concerns are addressed.

For example, production personnel should understand the following:

- Why it is important to carefully follow recipes

- How menu ingredients might be substituted per guest requests

- Procedures for properly receiving and storing food products

- Pre-preparation, preparation, and holding suggestions that help ensure the maximum retention of nutrients during food processing

Service personnel should understand the following:

- How menu items are prepared and what ingredients are used

- How to suggest substitutes for menu items or ingredients to help guests who express nutritional or other dietary concerns

- The importance of providing feedback to their managers about guest reactions to menu items and their dietary preferences

Unfortunately, many food service professionals who have studied nutrition and use the information on the job do not take care of their own personal health. As you read this chapter, consider how the information can benefit you personally and professionally.

Nutrition: The Science of Food

Let's begin our study of nutrition by defining two terms: food and nutrition. **Food** is material of plant or animal origin that people eat. Once consumed, food nourishes the body and enables us to grow. Everyone needs food to live.

Nutrition is essentially the science of how living beings use the nutrients in food for nourishment. When we study nutrition, we learn about the food we eat and how our bodies use it to stay alive, to grow, to support good health, and, in general, to make us look and feel good. Good health is impossible without good nutrition. This is true not only when we are young and growing, but for every day of our lives. Good nutrition allows us to function efficiently and resist infection and disease. Nutrition even influences how we look. For example, it affects our hair, eyes, complexion, teeth, and gums.

Children who do not receive proper nutrition before birth or as infants may suffer mental and physical consequences. Therefore, the dietary intake of a mother is important to the health and well-being of her unborn child. The direct correlation between the mother's health and that of her child continues even after the baby is born if the mother nurses her child.

Nutrition can affect one's personality. Irritability can result when a nutritional deficiency develops. Our physical and mental efficiency is affected by nutrition. People who do not eat breakfast may not perform well later in the morning. Reaction time and work output can suffer. Overweight people may show changes in their personality because of self-consciousness.

It is important for you—as a person and a food service manager—to understand how food provides for energy, growth, maintenance, and repair. Your knowledge of food and nutrition will help you eat proper foods in the right amounts to stay healthy. It will also help you on the job as you apply this knowledge to meeting the needs of your health-conscious guests.

The Six Basic Nutrients

Food contains nutrients (see Exhibit 1). The six types of nutrients that supply energy, promote cell growth and repair, and regulate the body processes are proteins, carbohydrates, fats, vitamins, minerals, and water.

Proteins. Proteins are essential elements in all living body cells. Proteins are required to build, maintain, and repair all body tissues. They also assist with

Exhibit 1   Major Nutrients and Their Functions

NUTRIENT	PURPOSE	GOOD SOURCES
Protein	• Builds and repairs body tissues. • Is a part of almost all body secretions (enzymes, fluids, and hormones). • Helps maintain the proper balance of body fluids. • Helps the body resist infection.	Protein of the best quality is present in eggs, lean meat, fish, poultry, cheese, and milk. Good quality protein is also found in soybeans and dried beans, peas, and nuts. Useful protein is present in cereals, breads, grains, and some vegetables; however, protein from these sources should be eaten with foods containing better protein.
Carbohydrate	• Supplies energy for physical activity, bodily processes, and warmth. • Helps the body use fat efficiently. • Saves protein for tissue-building and repair.	Starches: Cereals and cereal products such as bread, spaghetti, macaroni, noodles, and baked goods; rice, corn, dried beans, and potatoes; dried fruits and bananas. Sugars: Sugar, syrup, honey, jam, jellies, candy, confections, frostings, and other sweets.
Fat	• Supplies energy in concentrated form (over twice as much as an equal weight of carbohydrates). • Helps the body use fat-soluble vitamins (A, D, E, and K). • Supplies elements of cell membrane structure of all body tissues.	Cooking fats and oils, butter, margarine, mayonnaise, salad dressings, fatty meats, fried foods, most cheeses, whole milk, egg yolks, nuts, peanut butter, chocolate, and coconut.
Riboflavin (vitamin B_2)	• Helps body cells use oxygen to obtain energy from food. • Helps keep eyes healthy. • Helps keep skin around mouth and eyes healthy and smooth.	Milk and milk products, liver, heart, kidney, lean meats, eggs, dark green leafy vegetables, dried beans, almonds, and enriched breads and cereals. (Also present in a wide variety of foods in small amounts.)
Niacin (vitamin B_3)	• Helps body cells use oxygen to obtain energy from food. • Helps maintain healthy skin, digestion, and nervous system. • Helps maintain the life of all body tissues.	Tuna, liver, lean meat, fish, poultry, peanuts, whole grain enriched or fortified breads, cereals, and peas.
Vitamin D	• Helps the body use calcium and phosphorus to build and maintain strong bones and teeth. • Promotes normal growth.	Fish liver oils, vitamin D-fortified milk, irradiated evaporated milk, liver, egg yolk, salmon, tuna, sardines. (Direct sunlight also produces vitamin D.)
Vitamin B_6	• Helps the body use protein to build tissue. • Helps the body use carbohydrates and fats for energy. • Helps keep skin and the digestive and nervous systems healthy.	Pork, liver, heart, kidney, milk, whole grain and enriched cereals, wheat germ, beef, yellow corn, and bananas.

(continued)

Exhibit 1 *(continued)*

NUTRIENT	PURPOSE	GOOD SOURCES
Folic Acid	• Helps the body form red blood cells. • Aids metabolism within the cell.	Liver, lettuce, and orange juice.
Vitamin A	• Helps keep eyes healthy and increases ability to see in dim light. • Helps keep skin healthy and smooth. • Helps keep lining of mouth, nose, throat, and digestive tract healthy and resistant to infection. • Aids normal bone growth and tooth formation.	Liver, deep yellow and dark green leafy vegetables, cantaloupe, apricots, and other deep yellow fruits, butter, fortified margarine, egg yolk, whole milk, and vitamin A-fortified milk.
Vitamin C	• Helps hold body cells together. • Strengthens walls of blood vessels. • Aids normal bone and tooth formation. • Aids in healing wounds and broken bones. • Helps utilize iron. • Helps resist infection.	Citrus fruits and juices, strawberries, cantaloupe, watermelon, tomatoes, broccoli, Brussels sprouts, kale, and green peppers. Useful amounts are also in cauliflower, sweet potatoes, white potatoes, and raw cabbage.
Thiamine (vitamin B_1)	• Promotes normal appetite and digestion. • Helps the body change carbohydrates in food into energy. • Helps maintain a healthy nervous system.	Lean pork, heart, kidney, dry beans and peas, whole grain enriched breads and cereals, and some nuts.
Vitamin B_{12}	• Aids in normal function of body cells. • Helps body develop red blood cells.	Liver, kidney, milk, eggs, fish, cheese, and lean meat.
Calcium	• Helps build strong bones and teeth. • Aids in normal functioning of nerves, muscles, and heart. • Helps blood to clot normally.	Milk, cheese, ice cream, sardines, and clams. Useful amounts are in dark green leafy vegetables and oysters.
Iron	• Combines with protein to form hemoglobin that carries oxygen to all parts of the body. • Helps cells use oxygen. • Prevents iron deficiency anemia.	Liver, heart, shellfish, lean meat, dark green leafy vegetables, egg yolk, dried peas and beans, dried fruits, whole grain and enriched breads and cereals, dark molasses.
Iodine	• Helps the thyroid gland function properly. • Helps prevent some forms of goiter.	Iodized salt, saltwater fish, and seafoods.
Phosphorus	• Helps build strong bones and teeth. • Necessary part of all body cells. • Aids in normal functioning of muscles. • Helps the body utilize sugar and fat.	Meat, poultry, fish, milk, eggs, milk products, nuts, and dried beans and peas.

many other functions. Proteins help form chemicals that build resistance to disease. Enzymes, hormones, and hemoglobin contain protein.

Proteins are made of building blocks called amino acids. After digestion, proteins are broken down into separate amino acids that the body then rearranges to build required tissues.

Protein can be used as an energy source. This occurs when the diet does not provide enough energy from carbohydrates and fats or when more protein is consumed than is needed for other activities.

Which foods contain protein? Complete protein foods come from animal sources and include meat, poultry, fish, eggs, milk, and cheese. The term *complete protein* refers to foods that supply essential amino acids in amounts closely approximating the body's requirements for proteins. Essential amino acids are those that cannot be manufactured by the body and must be supplied in the diet. Incomplete protein foods are those that lack one or more essential amino acids needed to adequately meet body needs. Incomplete protein foods include nuts, dried peas and beans, soybeans, breads, and cereals. Fruits and most vegetables contain very little protein.

Carbohydrates. Carbohydrates supply energy. They are the main source of fuel used for such body processes as digestion and respiration. They also help maintain proper body temperature and eliminate the need for the body to use protein as an energy source. Carbohydrates are necessary to form certain body compounds that regulate many body activities. They include starches, sugars, and cellulose, and come from such plant sources as fruits, vegetables, and grains. Some are also available in animal products; for example, milk contains lactose (milk sugar). Carbohydrates are the second-most abundant type of nutrient in American diets; only water is consumed in greater quantities.

Carbohydrates provide a large percentage of the total calories consumed by most Americans. A **calorie** is a measure of the energy contained in food. The body needs a certain amount of calories to work and perform effectively. However, when more calories are consumed than the body needs, the body stores them in the form of fat. People who consume more carbohydrates than they need are often overweight.

The term **obesity** refers to a condition characterized by an excessive amount of body fat in relation to lean body mass, or a body weight that is 30 percent over the ideal weight for a specified height. Obesity is a major cause of preventable death in the United States. Weight gain and obesity are most commonly caused by consumption of a diet high in fat and calories, a lack of physical activity, or a combination of the two. Overweight and obese people are at a higher risk of developing numerous health problems, including type 2 diabetes, cardiovascular disease, stroke, and hypertension.[1]

Americans consume a considerable amount of their calories in the form of carbonated sodas, salty chips and other snacks, desserts, alcoholic beverages, and pastries, often termed **empty-calorie foods** because they contain many calories but few nutrients. By contrast, healthy foods such as vegetables and fruit account for a smaller percentage of caloric intake in the typical U.S. diet. One result is that people do not consume enough vitamins and minerals.

Many Americans are interested in reducing carbohydrate consumption and are aware of problems associated with excessive consumption of fats. An increasingly large number of people now have diet and nutrition concerns that are significant enough to make them change their eating habits, at least temporarily. Commercial and noncommercial food service managers must be aware of this emphasis on improved nutrition that is changing many people's views about what is good to eat.

Fats. Fat is another nutrient that provides energy. Fats may be saturated (which contain much hydrogen and are solid at room temperature) or unsaturated (which contain little hydrogen and are liquid at room temperature). Visible fats include butter, margarine, vegetable oil, and fat layers in meat. These fats provide approximately one-third of the fat in the American diet. Hidden fats in ice cream, cheese, whole milk products, meat, and egg yolks provide two-thirds of the fat in the American diet.

Fats serve as concentrated sources of heat and energy for the body. They provide more energy (calories) per unit than any other nutrient. Second, fats help the body absorb certain vitamins. Third, fats contribute to the flavor, aroma, and palatability of food.

Many Americans eat too much fat. A rich diet is a significant cause of overweight. Eating too much fat is especially troublesome if people do not exercise to burn up some of the excess calories they consume.

Vitamins. There are many different **vitamins** that perform various functions. Vitamins:

"Stealthy Healthy" Foods in Quick-Service Restaurants

Today, many quick-service restaurants are offering a number of food items on their menus that are perceived as more healthy or nutritious than traditional fast-food fare. Industry observers believe that this increased emphasis on nutrition is here to stay. Public image concerns and the desire on the part of many customers for healthier menu choices are among the reasons for quick-service restaurants to embrace the healthy-eating trend. Examples of some of the changes quick-service restaurants are making include more salad offerings, more nutritious items for children's meals, and changes in preparation methods (e.g., baking some items rather than frying them, using lemon juice as a partial substitute for salt, etc.).

Ironically, while many quick-service restaurants are offering more nutritious items, they may not use "nutritious," "healthy," or similar terms in their advertising or on their menu boards. Why? Some consumers (incorrectly!) believe that "healthy" foods have little flavor. Therefore, some quick-service restaurants prefer to simply use a term such as "fresh" (for items that indeed are fresh) to describe their healthier offerings, since "fresh" suggests that the item is more desirable. Carefully considered terminology is just one strategy that quick-service restaurants are employing as they add "stealthy healthy" foods to their menus.

- Are substances that are needed in very small amounts for the body to function properly.

- Cannot be made by the body (with the exception of vitamin D); they must be provided by foods or supplements.

- Promote growth, aid reproduction, help with digestion, enable the body to resist infection, prevent certain diseases, and help maintain mental alertness.

Vitamin-deficiency diseases can occur. Most frequently, these diseases are caused by an inadequate intake of a vitamin, although in some cases a person's body may fail to properly absorb vitamins. Problems can also arise when too much of certain vitamins are ingested.

Vitamins can easily be destroyed. Proper food handling techniques are important to preserve vitamins and other nutrients.

There are two basic categories of vitamins: fat-soluble and water-soluble.

Fat-soluble. Fat-soluble vitamins are absorbed into the body where they are stored and can be used as needed. Since they can be stored, fat-soluble vitamins need not be consumed with the same regularity as water-soluble vitamins. The fat-soluble vitamins are A, D, E, and K.

- Vitamin A has many important functions. Bones fail to grow to their proper sizes without vitamin A. It helps people see in dim light, keeps the skin soft and smooth, and helps the linings of the mouth, nose, throat, and digestive tract remain healthy. Vitamin A promotes fertility by assisting in sperm production in men and helping fetuses reach full term within the mother. Vitamin A also plays a role in tooth development and hormone production.

- Vitamin D helps the body absorb calcium and phosphorus needed to form bones and teeth. Unfortunately, it is not found naturally in many foods. In the United States, milk fortified with vitamin D provides a very important source of the vitamin. The best source of vitamin D is the sun. When the sun strikes the skin, it changes compounds normally found in the skin into vitamin D.

- Vitamin E functions include preventing the destruction of vitamins A and C and helping protect body fats and fatty substances from destruction.

- Vitamin K assists with blood coagulation. The best source of vitamin K is leafy dark green vegetables. Vitamin K is also formed in the intestines by microorganisms that live in our bodies.

Water-soluble. Water-soluble vitamins (those that can be dissolved by water) are absorbed into the bloodstream but are not generally stored in the body. Therefore, they must be consumed on a regular basis. The water-soluble vitamins are the B-complex vitamins and vitamin C.

B-complex vitamins help the body build protein and use carbohydrates for energy. There are several vitamins in the B complex. Three important B vitamins are thiamine, riboflavin, and niacin.

- Thiamine, or vitamin B_1, helps body cells obtain energy from food, maintains nerves in healthy condition, and promotes good appetite and digestion.

- Riboflavin, or vitamin B₂, helps body cells use oxygen to release energy from food. It helps keep the skin around the mouth and nose healthy, and it also affects vision.

- Niacin, or vitamin B₃, helps body cells use oxygen to produce energy. It promotes the health of the skin, tongue, digestive tract, and nervous system.

Vitamin C is called ascorbic acid and is used to hold body cells together. It strengthens the walls of blood vessels and helps in healing wounds and resisting infections. Vitamin C produces healthy gums and helps increase the absorption of iron in the diet.

Minerals. **Minerals** are building materials and body regulators. Only a small percentage of normal body weight is composed of minerals, but they are essential for building muscle, bones, teeth, and hair. They help maintain the correct amount of water in each cell and allow certain chemical reactions to occur within the body. Enzymes and hormones that help carry out many bodily functions contain minerals. Other minerals send nerve messages and contract muscles. The list of minerals used by the body is long and includes calcium, phosphorus, potassium, sulfur, sodium, chlorine, magnesium, iron, manganese, copper, iodine, bromine, cobalt, and zinc. Some minerals perform only one known essential function; others are involved in various essential and often unrelated functions.

Minerals are often found in food in a water-soluble form. Some of the same food preparation techniques (discussed later in this chapter) to conserve water-soluble vitamins also help to conserve the mineral content of foods.

Water. There is water in every body cell, outside every cell, in the blood, and in other body fluids. In fact, about 60 percent of an adult's and 70 percent of a baby's body is water. People can live longer without food than they can without water.

Water performs many important functions. It serves as a solvent so other nutrients can be used by the body. Water transports waste from the body through the lungs, kidneys, and skin. It is also used as a building material for cells. Water regulates body temperature; it allows perspiration to occur, and it serves as a heat carrier as air is lost through breathing. Water is also essential as a body lubricant. Saliva helps us to swallow foods, and other liquids made up largely of water help move food through the gastrointestinal tract.

Nutrition Guidelines

As you can see, there are many nutrients in a wide variety of foods that are important for health and well-being. It is important that the correct amount of each nutrient be provided in our diets. However, the amount of each nutrient necessary for proper health varies with each person's own unique needs. These needs are influenced by a person's sex, age, health, activity level, and other factors. Therefore, only general nutrition guidelines can be presented here.

Recommended Dietary Allowances. **Recommended dietary allowances (RDAs)** have been established by the Food and Nutrition Board of the National Academy of Sciences—Institute of Medicine. These RDAs establish amounts of essential nutrients that experts believe to be adequate for the nutritional needs of most healthy people.

In addition to the RDAs established by the Food and Nutrition Board, the federal Food and Drug Administration (FDA) has established a set of allowances that are used as a basis for nutritional labeling of food products. Manufacturers can use this information to determine the percent of daily allowances a specific portion of their product provides.

MyPlate. In 2011, the United States Department of Agriculture (USDA) implemented a new educational program called MyPlate (www.choosemyplate.gov) to help consumers make healthier food choices. The program's purpose is to prompt consumers to think about building a healthy plate at meal times and to encourage them to seek more information to manage their diet, weight, and health. The practical information provided is offered with the goal of empowering individuals to make healthier food choices at a time when there is increased concern about the obesity problem in the United States. The MyPlate icon (see Exhibit 2) emphasizes the fruit, vegetable, grain, protein, and dairy food groups.

Exhibit 2   USDA MyPlate

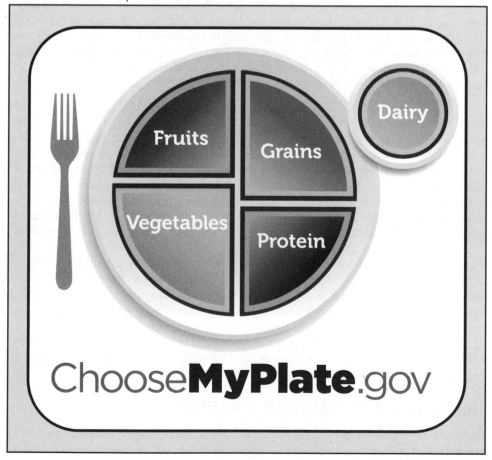

The ChooseMyPlate.gov website provides information about proper nutrition and offers several interactive tools helpful for personalizing the MyPlate program and implementing its basic principles. The site provides information about:

- *Food groups.* This section provides an overview of basic food groups and detailed information about fruits, vegetables, grains, protein foods, dairy, and oils.

- *Weight management.* The section on weight management provides details about tactics to manage one's weight. It provides a personal body mass index (BMI) calculator and a personal "Super Tracker" program that enables users to (1) calculate and track food and beverage consumption, and (2) develop a personalized dairy intake plan.

- *Physical activity.* This section discusses the need for, and how to plan the proper amount of, physical activities to facilitate the success of the dietary intake plans developed by participants. Also provided in the physical activity section: a chart of calories burned during different lengths of time spent on various physical activities, and tips to increase one's daily physical activities.

ChooseMyPlate.gov includes other information, such as recipes and resources that one can use to learn more about the topics of diet, health, and exercise. The website also provides educational tools that professionals can use to plan and implement educational programs. Food service managers and trainers will find this website useful if they plan programs for their staff members that address diet, health, and exercise. The website can also be shared with employees who express concerns about their health or the health of family members and friends.

Nutrition Labeling. To help consumers plan their diet, the vast majority of packaged-food labels now provide information about nutritional content. In the United States, the Nutrition Labeling and Education Act of 1990 (NLEA) requires nutrition labeling for most foods (except meat and poultry) and authorizes the use of nutrient-content claims and appropriate Food and Drug Administration (FDA)-approved health claims. Food service managers in noncommercial operations, especially those dealing with various types of special diets, need this information. Nutrition information is also of increasing importance to commercial operators.

There is scientific evidence that consumption of saturated fats, trans fats (vegetable oil with added hydrogen), and cholesterol raises low density lipoprotein (bad cholesterol) levels that increase the risk of heart disease. Since 1993, the FDA has required that saturated fat and cholesterol be listed on food labels. Information about trans fat has been required since January 2006. Thus, consumers now have the information they need to make heart-healthy food choices.

Exhibit 3 shows a sample Nutrition Facts food label. Notice that the label provides basic information about serving size; servings per container; and calories, protein, carbohydrates, and fats per serving.

Nutrition and Food Service Operations

As noted earlier, managers of many noncommercial food service operations *must* meet the nutritional needs of those they serve. Their counterparts in commercial

Exhibit 3   Sample Nutrition Facts Food Label

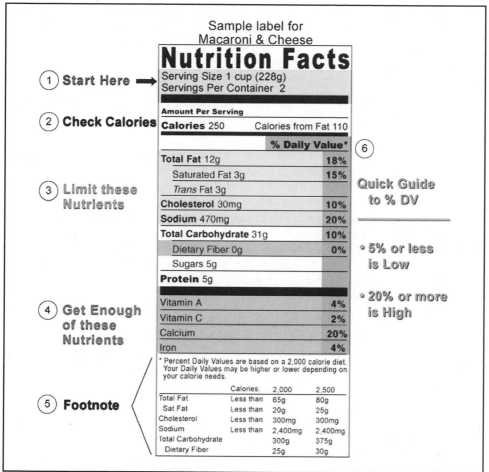

Source: FDA Center for Food Safety and Applied Nutrition, "How to Understand and Use the Nutrition Facts Label." Available online at www.fda.gov/Food/LabelingNutrition/ConsumerInformation/ucm078889.htm.

facilities *should* also be concerned about offering nutritious menu choices. A primary reason is the competitive advantage this increasingly offers as a large percentage of the dining-out public becomes aware of and concerned about the importance of proper nutrition as they make food selection decisions.

If commercial food service managers decide to offer menu items that emphasize nutrition, they should make sure these items are appealing. Guests who want food that is good for them also want that food to look and taste good. Commercial managers cannot serve nutritious food that is unappetizing if they want guests to keep returning to their properties.

Making nutritious foods appealing is also important to noncommercial managers, but for a different reason. While a commercial manager's goal is to maintain or increase sales, a goal for most noncommercial managers is to safeguard the health of consumers. Food that is served but not eaten will not contribute to a balanced meal or to a person's nutritional intake. Therefore, managers in noncommercial food service facilities also want to provide nutritious food that tastes good.

Menu Planning

Using standard reference works, trained specialists in noncommercial operations can calculate the amount of each nutrient contained in each menu item offered. They can also regularly conduct a nutrition audit (an assessment of a meal's nutrient value) assuming the entire meal is consumed.

There are many factors for managers of commercial food service operations to consider when planning menus. For those managers who have health-conscious guests, one factor is nutrition. The USDA MyPlate program previously discussed can be an excellent guide. Meal planners can offer complete meals that have at least one serving from each food group. An à la carte menu can be planned so that all food groups are represented, and guests who want a nutritious meal can choose appropriate menu items. A buffet menu can include several items from each food group.

When planning menus, managers can implement a wide range of strategies that recognize nutrition concerns. For example, they can:

- *Reduce fat and cholesterol in menu items.* Offer lean fish, chicken, turkey, and veal alternatives. Most fish and shellfish are low-cholesterol choices.

- *Reduce sodium.* Many consumers wish to avoid high-sodium (salt) items. To help these consumers, reduce the use of salt in recipes (guests who desire salt can add it at the table), and offer sauces and marinades in low-sodium varieties.

- *Use strategies to reduce calories.* Reduce the amount of fat and sugar used in menu items and offer more low-fat and low-sugar fruits and vegetables. Also, consider reducing portion sizes, which at many restaurants are much larger than the government's recommended sizes. While managers and chefs understand they are "supersizing" portion sizes, they believe that many guests expect large portions when they are dining out. In fact, restaurant portion sizes have increased in concert with the rise of obesity rates.

- *Use strategies to reduce sugar.* Often sugar can be reduced in baked items without sacrificing flavor. Sometimes such spices as cinnamon and nutmeg can add sweetness to these items. Offer sugar-free beverages and fruit desserts instead of sweet desserts. On breakfast menus, make unsweetened cereals available.

Menu planning in noncommercial operations may include the offering of nontraditional food items. Consider, for example, the USDA National School Lunch Program, in which participating organizations may offer items with a significant nutritional emphasis including potato pancakes, blueberry burgers, dried plum barbecue sauce, and asparagus salsa. Like every other food service manager, school menu planners must recognize the food and flavor preferences of students while they consider nutritional needs.

Restaurant Portion Sizes

Portion sizes in restaurants have grown larger. According to information on the ChooseHealthLA website, the average restaurant meal has increased more than four times in size since 1960. The same source reports that the surface area of an average dinner plate has increased 36 percent since that time.

For those diners concerned about portion size and the amount of food they consume when eating out, here are some tips for choosing less food when eating in a restaurant:

- Ask about the availability of half-size portions

- If you order a full entrée, box up half of it before you begin eating

- Share your food with family or friends

- Start with a cup of soup or small salad

Source: ChooseHealthLA (www.choosehealthLA.com), Public Health Department, County of Los Angeles; retrieved 8-6-2014. This site contains a wide variety of diet and health information.

When planning menus, commercial food service managers should consider how special dietary requests can be honored. Service and production staff members often can satisfy guest requests for items that are charbroiled rather than pan fried and can provide salad dressings on the side rather than on the salads. Managers should actively seek feedback from guests and service staff and use this knowledge when planning menus.

It is important to tell the truth on the menu. Words such as *light, low-calorie,* and *sodium-free* have specific meanings defined by the FDA and cannot be used carelessly. Likewise, one should be very careful about providing too-specific nutrition information. For example, stating that a menu item contains a specified number of calories is probably not warranted unless the chef always uses very precise measurements of ingredients that meet exacting food purchase specifications and always uses precision portion-control tools. Busy chefs and cooks in high-volume operations are not food scientists in test kitchens, and, even when following standard recipes, they do not always use precise measurements, nor is it generally possible. It is better to indicate that items are made with margarine rather than butter, that egg yolks can be omitted, and that no additional salt will be used than to make dietary claims that production staff members cannot consistently meet.

Food trends are another factor that commercial food service managers should consider when planning menus, but they are different from food fads. Food fads usually identify certain foods as cure-alls. For example, grapefruit, cranberry juice, and oat bran have been popularized by the media for having special qualities. Food fads surface quite frequently but are generally short-lived.

Food trends, on the other hand, are basic, long-term changes in the public's eating habits. Many recent food trends reflect the public's growing concern with nutrition and healthy eating. For example, there has been a trend in the United States away from red meat and toward seafood. Another trend is decreased consumption of alcoholic beverages. The fresh-is-best trend is also popular. Wise food service managers keep up with food trends and try to incorporate them into their menus.

Although the trend today is toward healthier eating, there will always be guests who are relatively unconcerned about nutrition and who want traditional menu offerings like steak, french fries, and rich desserts. Perhaps these guests regularly consume these items or maybe they do so only on special occasions. Regardless, most commercial operations include items on the menu that appeal to this group of guests.

Nutrition Concerns in Purchasing

Concerns about nutrition that are incorporated into the menu as it is planned must continue at the time food is purchased. When handled correctly, fresh foods typically are the best nutrient sources, although modern processing methods retain nutrients and are also very healthful.

When purchasing low-fat and non-fat dairy milk products (including margarine), nutrition-conscious managers make sure these items are fortified with vitamins A and D. Whole-grain cereals and bread products can be purchased where applicable.

Managers should keep in mind that dark chicken and turkey thigh and leg meat, while typically less expensive than white breast meat, is higher in fat content. Skinless poultry products contain less fat than their counterparts with skin.

When purchasing beef, managers should remember that lower-grade cuts contain less fat than higher-grade items. (However, managers should also keep in mind that lower-grade beef is less tender and less flavorful.) Many food service operations use ground beef. Health-minded managers should consider purchasing ground beef products with less than 10 percent fat by raw weight. Ground round is generally the leanest ground beef; ground chuck is the highest in fat content.[2]

Additional purchasing pointers for managers concerned about nutrition include the following:

- Select skim milk cheeses.

- Use sodium-free soups and sauce bases.

- Avoid packaged foods containing such ingredients as animal fat, palm oil, and coconut oil.

- Purchase canola and/or olive oil for use in food preparation.

- Be informed about the ingredients in convenience food items because they are frequently high in sodium and sometimes saturated fats. (Read labels if available.)

Products should be purchased from reputable suppliers and, when possible, from suppliers that are concerned about nutrition. Many suppliers can provide excellent information about the nutritional content of the items they sell. Remember that the operation's dollars are spent on more than just products because

Government-sponsored websites such as the USDA Food and Nutrition Information Center (www.fnic.nal.usda.gov) make it easy to locate current information useful for educating consumers and training food service staff.

service and information are also important. Suppliers can also offer suggestions about the development of food purchase specifications that can emphasize nutrition concerns.

Nutrition Concerns in Storing

Purchasing high-quality, nutritious foods is pointless if they are not correctly stored, because improper storage conditions can destroy the nutrients contained in these foods. For example, vitamin losses can occur in just several hours, even under proper refrigeration. Significant nutrient losses can occur in fresh produce in just one or two days.

Managers can train employees to use procedures such as the following to reduce nutrient losses during storage:

- Minimize the time between product delivery and use. For example, in the case of fresh fruits and vegetables, delivery every day would be ideal. Proper receiving practices should be followed to make sure that the fruits and vegetables delivered are actually fresh. Those who routinely receive should be trained to recognize the proper quality requirements.

- Handle fresh products carefully to avoid bruising.

- Date incoming products to help make sure that the items received earliest are used first. *First in, first out* should be the rule.

- It is best to store most products in their shipping containers.

- Keep fresh items wrapped or covered to minimize exposure to air, humidity, and light.

- Minimize the storage time of partially processed fruits and vegetables, which are more susceptible to nutrient losses. Pre-preparation, such as preparing salads the shift before they are served, may be good for productivity but bad for preserving nutrients.

- Make sure that the proper storage temperature, humidity, and air-circulation requirements are consistently met. While different products ideally should be stored at different temperatures, this is frequently not practical. This reinforces the need to minimize the time that food products are in storage.

- Dry-storage items should be kept in a cool, dry, well-ventilated area. The storage temperature should be between 50°F and 70°F (10°C and 21°C).

- Fresh fruits and produce items should be stored at refrigerated temperatures and loosely packed; a relatively high humidity is better. The ideal refrigerated storage temperature is approximately 41°F (5°C), which is also the recommended temperature for minimizing the growth of microorganisms.

- Proper frozen storage temperatures should be at 0°F (–18°C) or colder. Even at frozen temperatures, fruits and vegetables can lose nutrients. Freezing, thawing, and refreezing frozen foods also destroys nutrients; these steps should be done with great caution and only when necessary, to help maximize nutritional value and to reduce the possibility of food safety concerns.

Conserving Nutrients During Food Preparation

Mishandling food during preparation can also diminish its nutritional content. To protect food's nutritional value, food service managers must make sure that employees practice basic principles of food preparation designed to retain nutrients, such as the following:

- *Cleaning and trimming.* Food should not be cleaned or trimmed more than necessary. Vegetables should not be heavily pared since nutrients are located just below the skin. If the skin and some of the underskin is removed, many nutrients are lost.

- *Oxidation.* Some nutrients are destroyed on contact with oxygen. Cutting food into small pieces, grinding it, or exposing large surfaces to air can cause vitamin loss. Storage for an excessive amount of time can also cause oxidation.

- *Light.* Sunlight destroys some color pigments and nutrients. Riboflavin (vitamin B$_2$) and pigments such as keratin (yellow) are especially susceptible to damage when exposed to sunlight.

- *Heat.* Heat can change or destroy some nutrients such as vitamin C and thiamine. Therefore, the longer food is cooked, the greater the chance of destroying these nutrients. Heat can also damage proteins.

- *Water.* Many vitamins and minerals dissolve in water, so food should not be soaked, if possible. To maximize the retention of nutrients, foods that are soaked in water should be cooked in the same water. After the food is cooked, the water can be added to the stockpot or used in soups, sauces, gravies, and related products. Cooking food in the least amount of water for the least amount of time can also help preserve nutrients.

- *Misuse of ingredients.* Some vitamins are destroyed in an alkaline medium. For this reason, baking soda should not be used in excess when baking, nor should it be added to green vegetables during cooking.

Standard Recipes and Nutrition

Standard recipes are at the heart of quality control processes in food preparation. Food service managers should address nutrition concerns such as the following as they develop recipes:

- Try to use items that are low in calories, such as fresh fruits and vegetables; carefully consider portion sizes as recipes are developed; substitute foods such as low-calorie salad dressings, artificial sweeteners, and whipping agents when possible to avoid adding calories from fat.

- Recipe procedures can be developed for items to be sautéed and browned in a nonstick pan, allowing them to be cooked with little or no added fat; cooks can broil with foods suspended to allow fat to drain off the product during cooking.

- Chill cooking liquids to remove fat before using them in sauces; trim fat from meat.

- Reconsider using recipes that require organ meats, which are high in cholesterol.

- When baking, try to reduce recipe fat amounts by one-third to one-half. Substitutions for fats, including applesauce, can add moisture and texture to baked goods.

- Minimize the use of salt in recipes; instead, substitute herbs and spices.

Nutrition and Food Service

Food servers must know how to respond to guests' concerns about nutrition when they order menu items. A basic component of food server training can address such issues as the following:

- Alternatives to offer when guests ask questions about the caloric, sodium, or fat content of menu items, for example.

- Alternative food preparation methods. ("If you prefer, you can order the seafood steamed or broiled.")

- How to identify with guests' needs and desires during their dining-out experience. For example, overweight guests may not be diet-conscious and nutritional information about menu items should not be provided to them unless they ask questions. Other guests may like to consume nutritious entrées and reward themselves with high-calorie desserts.

- How to describe items accurately and appealingly and to know when to obtain additional product information from food production personnel. ("What kind of oil is used to pan fry the fish special this evening?")

Remember that servers are often the best source of information about guests' preferences and concerns. Wise managers ask servers about these issues with such questions as "What do guests typically say about our menu?" and "What comments do they make about items they do or do not select?" Such information can be helpful in the menu-planning process.

Nutrition and Dining Out

Most restaurants want to please their guests and try to assist them with reasonable nutrition-related requests, such as when guests ask:

- For sauces and salad dressings on the side and/or ask for lower-calorie dressings

- For salsa, mustard, or flavored vinegars in order to enjoy fat-free flavor

- For half-portions at a reduced price, or ask for a doggie bag to take home half of the meal

- That foods be prepared with olive or canola oil instead of butter, margarine, or shortening

- That foods be broiled or grilled instead of fried

Nutrition and Legislation

The rise in obesity rates, along with increases in the quantity of foods consumed in quick-service restaurants and the public's concern that most quick-service restaurant meals are not healthy, have prompted the proposal of menu-labeling laws around the country. As with no-smoking legislation, the laws proposed or passed in different jurisdictions vary widely, resulting in an assortment of legislative initiatives requiring the posting of certain information in one area and other information in another. This makes it difficult for organizations with numerous properties within these jurisdictions to comply. For instance, some legislation requires that calorie-count information be posted, sometimes specifying that the information placed on menu boards must be in the same-sized print as the menu items. Other legislation does not specify the information's location, size, or print. Still other legislation notes the need for information about trans fats, monosodium glutamate, saturated fats, carbohydrates, and so on.

Some quick-service restaurants provide nutrition information for each menu item on their websites and on within-unit fliers or posters. Legislation in some areas may require that nutrition information be posted on menu boards, which are often already difficult to read because of size limitations and the variety of menu items posted. As restaurants increasingly use digital menu boards, they might program them to show slides of menu items and prices on one screen and specific menu items with applicable nutrition content on another. Electronic kiosks located within restaurant public areas or on tabletops could also display required data.

Contemporary Dietary Concerns

Proper nutrition is only one factor in a healthy diet. As scientific evidence continues to link diet and disease, many consumers are making changes in their eating habits in an effort to live longer, healthier lives. Contemporary dietary concerns include those related to calories, fats and cholesterol, sodium, food allergies, vegetarian meals, and organic foods.

Where Do Restaurants Obtain Nutrition Information?

Where do restaurants obtain nutrition information for their specific menu items as required by menu-labeling legislation? Large multi-unit organizations typically employ dietitians and other professionals who can determine this information. Smaller properties might use electronic tools instead of external laboratories for analysis. For example, MenuCalc (www.menucalc.com) is an online source that can quickly calculate the nutritional content of menu items prepared from recipes. Restaurant managers can post the resulting information on company websites or within restaurants.

Software developers also provide programs that perform nutritional analysis. See, for example, ESHA Research (www.esha.com) and The Nutrition Company's FoodWorks (www.nutritionco.com).

Calories

Most people watching their calories want to lose weight. An important concern for most diet- and health-conscious people is that food taste good but not be fattening. Overweight people tend to have more health problems and shorter life spans. There is also strong social pressure to be thin.

A calorie is a measure of energy contained in food. In general, people who consume more calories than they need gain weight; those who consume fewer than they need lose weight. If calorie intake equals energy expenditure, one's weight remains stable.

How many calories should a person consume? This varies with a person's age, sex, body type, and other variables. Calorie needs decline as people grow older. Women need fewer calories than men because women tend to have a higher proportion of body fat and because they seem to be more efficient users of calories. Activity is another important factor in deciding how many calories a person needs. Professional football players need far more calories than executives who work behind desks much of the time. Other factors may include body and environmental temperature and one's health condition.

What if you are not at your ideal weight? There are fad diets, pills, or even surgeries for reducing weight, and many people are willing to try them. For most people, however, the best way to lose weight is to consume fewer calories and increase activity.

Food service managers can meet the needs of people concerned about calories by offering such low-calorie menu alternatives as fresh fruit and vegetables, diet beverages, sugar substitutes, low-fat milk, and reduced-calorie salad dressings. Menus should include information of interest to dieters, such as preparation methods, substitute ingredients, and smaller portion sizes.

Fats and Cholesterol

As mentioned, fats can be saturated or unsaturated. Saturated fats are found primarily in animal foods, such as meats, lard, butter, whole milk, and eggs. Palm and coconut vegetable oils are also highly saturated. Unsaturated fats are found mostly in foods from plant sources—olives, nuts, corn, and soybeans—and oils made from these and similar foods.

People who wish to lose weight should avoid fats, since they contain more calories (nine) per gram than any other nutrient. As a rule of thumb, 30 percent or less of a person's daily calories should come from fats, and no more than 10 percent of these should be from saturated fats. Saturated fats increase cholesterol levels. A high cholesterol level may lead to cardiovascular disease. Unsaturated fats are healthier and may even reduce cholesterol levels in some individuals.

Lawsuits have been filed against quick-service restaurant chains claiming that people have been influenced by the restaurants' advertising campaigns to consume excessive amounts of high-fat foods offered by those companies, and that health problems occurred as a result.

Cholesterol is a fatty substance found in all animal foods. Humans need a certain amount of cholesterol to live. The human body uses cholesterol to make vitamin D, bile, and various hormones. It is an important part of brain and nerve cells. In fact, the human body manufactures its own cholesterol in small amounts. However, when large amounts of animal foods are consumed, especially those high in saturated fats, the body's cholesterol level can become too high. When this happens, cholesterol may collect in the walls of arteries and block the flow of blood to the heart and other vital organs. Cardiovascular disease and heart attacks may result.

Although the role of cholesterol in causing heart disease and other health problems such as high blood pressure and dementia may not be completely understood, experts generally agree that it is best to keep the dietary intake of cholesterol as low as possible. Food service managers can provide alternatives to foods that are high in cholesterol, such as skim milk rather than whole milk, or egg whites rather than whole eggs. Some egg yolks may be eliminated from some recipes. Salad dressings or gravy can be served on the side so guests on low-cholesterol diets can control how much goes onto their food. A variety of low-cholesterol or so-called "good" cholesterol spreads are available as substitutes for butter and margarine.

Sodium

Sodium is a mineral component of table salt, which is used in seasoning or preserving food. Table salt is valued because it heightens the flavor of foods. Too much sodium in the diet, however, can contribute to hypertension (high blood pressure), irregular heartbeat, and kidney disease.

Food service managers can meet the needs of people concerned with moderating their sodium intake by providing low-sodium menu selections. Table service restaurants can place a salt substitute next to the salt and pepper shakers if they are available on dining tables.

Many people on a low-sodium diet prescribed by a doctor are on a no-added-salt diet. With this diet, salt may be used lightly in cooking, but no salt should be added at the table. Also, foods and condiments high in sodium such as pickles, olives, sauerkraut, ham, bacon, hot dogs, crackers, ketchup, soy sauce, and garlic salt must be avoided. With a little planning it is not difficult for food service managers to meet the needs of most people on no-added-salt diets.

Food Allergies

Some guests must avoid certain foods because they have a food allergy or a food intolerance to them. A food allergy involves a reaction of a person's immune system

---

Fast Food Nutrition Tracker

Do you want to learn about the nutritional content of the meals that you have or will consume at many quick-service restaurants? If so, check out the following website:

www.fastfoodnutrition.org

Enter the name of the restaurant and the menu items you did (or will) consume, and basic nutritional content information will be calculated for you.

to a food item in much the same way that some people respond to insect stings. A food intolerance is a reaction that does not involve the body's immune system.

Most signs of food allergies involve the skin (such as hives or itching) or the gastrointestinal tract (such as vomiting or abdominal pain). Many food allergy reactions are caused by milk, eggs, legumes, nuts, shellfish, and wheat. Guests typically know the foods that create discomfort for them and ask about ingredients before they place their orders.

Celiac disease, an autoimmune disorder affecting digestion that is triggered by the presence of glutens in food, is receiving increasing attention. Since wheat, barley, and rye grains all contain glutens, those affected by celiac disease are severely limited in what they can consume while dining out. These grains are ingredients in numerous menu items, including convenience foods, the exact content of which many food production and service personnel might be unaware. Some restaurants are discovering a new market niche: a growing segment of the population interested in ordering special meals made without glutens, nuts, dairy products, and shellfish.

Anaphylaxis (a life-threatening allergic reaction) can occur in persons with severe food allergies. Therefore, providing correct information to guests asking about food ingredients can literally be a life-saving precaution. Anaphylactic shock can occur as quickly as five minutes after food is consumed. Therefore, it is important to take food allergies seriously and to recognize that there are no shortcuts to accommodating persons with food allergies. One management plan for dealing with food allergies comprises the following steps:

- Designate a point person (for example, the manager) to take charge of interacting with guests who have food allergies.

- The point person speaks with the guest to determine special needs, and then consults with the chef.

- The chef checks ingredients and communicates the need for extra precautions to kitchen staff who prepare the meal.

- The manager, server, or chef takes the meal to the guest and confirms that it has been prepared to meet the guest's needs.

- The person serving the meal should check back with the guest to make sure the meal is satisfactory.

Check out the Food Allergy Research & Education website (www.foodallergy.org; enter "restaurant" in the search box) for more information.

Vegetarian Meals

Many guests prefer vegetarian meals. While some people want to reduce their consumption of meat for dietary reasons, others do so because they do not want to eat foods that require the death or discomfort of animals. All types of vegetarians avoid animal meat, but vegetarians can be divided into several categories based on what they eat in addition to the basic vegetarian diet of vegetables, fruits, grains, and proteins (soy-based foods, legumes, and nuts):

- Vegans are vegetarians who eat absolutely no foods of animal origin, including milk, cheese, and honey

- Lacto-vegetarians are people who add dairy products to their vegetarian diets

- Ovo-vegetarians are people who add eggs to their vegetarian diets

- Lacto-ovo-vegetarians are people who add dairy products and eggs to their vegetarian diets

- Pesco-vegetarians, or pescetarians, are people who add dairy products, eggs, and fish to their vegetarian diets. (Note: not all vegetarians consider pesco-vegetarians to be vegetarians).

As you can see, when a guest requests a vegetarian meal, it is important to determine exactly what the guest can and cannot eat. Servers can also offer a meal that consists only of vegetables, fruits, grains, and nonanimal proteins. When informed about what type of vegetarian the guest is, chefs can typically offer a tasty, nutritious, and attractive meal that meets the guest's needs.

Organic Foods

An increasing number of Americans are eating more organic food products. The term *organic* generally refers to plants or animals raised without the use of chemicals and foods that have been processed from organic crops grown without the use of chemicals and preservatives, artificial flavor, or color.

Reasons for the increased consumption of organic foods include beliefs that they are better for the environment and one's health and that consumers can better

---

Farm-to-Fork Movement

The farm-to-fork (also commonly called farm-to-table) movement is sometimes aligned with an interest in organic or "natural" food. "Farm-to-fork" has different meanings, but elements in the concept typically include local purchasing, a "fresh is best" philosophy, and interactions with specific growers of produce and other food products.

Most farm-to-fork suppliers produce food on a small scale, and their products typically reach a restaurant and its guests much faster than is possible from vendors of mass-produced food and large feedlot supplies.

Proponents of farm-to-fork products believe these items to be fresher, more nutritious, and tastier. They also have an interest in supporting local businesses and perceive that they are making a contribution to sustainability and an eco-friendly environment.

There is an increasing interest in farm-to-fork consumption, and many restaurants emphasize, when possible, menu items containing farm-to-fork ingredients. There are also some restaurants that make sure that all or almost all of the foods they use are farm-to-fork foods and cater exclusively to those customers who desire these products.

support small or local farmers. A perceived improvement in product quality and taste are additional reasons.

According to a Mayo Clinic publication, there is no conclusive evidence that supports the belief that organic food is more nutritious than food grown conventionally.[3] While the USDA certifies organic foods, it does not claim that they are safer or more nutritious. Therefore, while many food service operations purchase organic food products because their guests prefer them, it is probably inappropriate to make nutrition claims about them.

Produce is the largest category of organic food. Other products include bread/baked goods; non-dairy beverages; eggs; dairy products; packaged foods such as soup, pasta, meat, and frozen and other prepared items; and even baby foods. Some restaurant managers have discovered a new market of guests who will pay a premium for the generally higher-priced organic foods. Other restaurants feature some organically grown foods in salads or ingredients on a salad bar.

Endnotes

1. ObesityinAmerica.org. www.obesityinamerica.org.

2. Sandy Kapoor, *Professional Health Cooking* (New York: Wiley, 1995), p. 16.

3. Mayo Clinic Staff, "Organic Foods: Are They Safer? More Nutritious?" MayoClinic. com. (Enter "organic foods" in the site's search box.)

Key Terms

calorie—A measure of heat energy. As applied to food, a calorie (also called a kilogram calorie or a kilocalorie) is defined as the amount of heat needed to raise the temperature of 1 kilogram of water 1°C at 1 atmosphere pressure.

carbohydrates—Basic nutrients that are the main source of fuel for body processes such as digestion and respiration. They also help maintain proper body temperature and eliminate the need for the body to use protein as an energy source.

cholesterol—A fatty substance in the human body and in foods derived from animal products that has been linked to heart disease.

empty-calorie foods—Foods that contain many calories but few nutrients.

fats—Basic nutrients that serve as concentrated sources of heat and energy for the body.

food—Material of plant or animal origin that people eat.

minerals—Basic nutrients that serve as tissue-building materials and body regulators.

nutrition—The science of how living organisms use food for nourishment; the process of assimilating and using the nutrients in food for nourishment, growth, and regeneration.

obesity—Body weight that is much greater than what is healthy, according to the U.S. National Institutes of Health; it is characterized by a much higher amount of body fat than lean muscle mass.

proteins—Basic nutrients made of building blocks called amino acids. During digestion, proteins are broken down into separate amino acids that are then rearranged by the body to build tissue. Complete protein foods supply essential amino acids in amounts that closely approximate the body's protein requirements.

recommended dietary allowances (RDAs)—The amounts of essential nutrients that experts believe are adequate for the nutritional needs of most healthy people.

sodium—A mineral used to season and preserve food.

standard recipe—A formula for producing a food or beverage item specifying ingredients, the required quantity of each ingredient, preparation procedures, portion size and portioning equipment, garnish, and any other information necessary to preparing the item.

vitamins—Basic nutrients that promote growth, help digest foods, prevent certain diseases, and perform a number of other important functions for health and well-being.

 Review Questions

1. Why should commercial food service operators be concerned about providing nutritious food for guests?

2. What are some important points that commercial food service managers should consider when assessing the nutritional content of food served in their operations?

3. How does each of the six basic nutrients contribute to a person's health and well-being?

4. What are some food sources of proteins? of carbohydrates? of fats?

5. Why is it important for a health-conscious individual to know the difference between fat-soluble and water-soluble vitamins?

6. Why is it important for food service managers to know about recommended dietary allowances established by the Food and Nutrition Board?

7. Why would a nutrition audit be more valuable to institutional food service operations than to commercial food service operations?

8. What are some of the ways nutrients can be lost through mishandling during storage or preparation?

9. How many calories should a person consume?

10. How can food service operations help people who need to control their intake of fats and cholesterol?

11. How are food service operators affected by menu labeling legislation? What position should they take on this legislation? Why?

12. What procedures should a restaurant manager establish that would apply when a guest states that he or she suffers from a food allergy?

 ## Internet Sites

For more information, visit the following Internet sites. Remember that Internet addresses can change without notice. If the site is no longer there, you can use a search engine to look for additional sites.

General Nutrition Information

American Dietetic Association
www.eatright.org

American Heart Association
www.heart.org

Dietary Guidelines for Americans
www.health.gov/dietaryguidelines

FDA Center for Food Safety & Applied
   Nutrition
www.fda.gov/Food

FDA Food Labeling and Nutrition
www.fda.gov (enter "food labeling" in
the site's search box)

The Nutrition Source (Harvard University School of Public Health)
www.hsph.harvard.edu/nutritionsource

Restaurant Nutrition Information

McDonald's
www.mcdonalds.com (click on "Food"
and then "Nutrition Choices")

Yum! Brands
www.yum.com (scroll to "Responsibility" and click on "Nutrition" in the
drop down)

Food Allergy Information

Food Allergy Research & Education
www.foodallergy.org

MyFoodMyHealth
www.myfoodmyhealth.com

Other Nutrition-Related Websites

Organic Consumers Association
www.organicconsumers.org

Vegan Society
www.vegansociety.com

Chapter 6 Outline

Commercial Menu Pricing Styles
    Table d'Hôte
    À la Carte
    Combination
Noncommercial Menu Styles
Menu Schedules
    Fixed Menus
    Cycle Menus
Types of Menus
    Breakfast
    Lunch
    Dinner
    Specialty
Menu Planning
    Know Your Guests
    Know Your Quality Requirements
    Know Your Operation
    Selecting Menu Items
    Menu Balance
Menu Design
    Copy
    Layout
    Cover
    Common Menu-Design Mistakes
Evaluating Menus
    General Menu Evaluation Tactics
    Menu Engineering

Competencies

1. Identify the three basic categories of menu pricing styles, and describe the two varieties of menu schedules. (pp. 121–125)

2. Describe the differences in breakfast, lunch, and dinner menus, and list some of the most common specialty menus. (pp. 126–131)

3. Explain the steps involved in menu planning and menu design. (pp. 131–147)

4. Discuss general menu evaluation tactics and menu engineering. (pp. 147–150)

6

The Menu

ONE FAVORITE food service expression is that "it all starts with the menu." The menu dictates much about how an operation will be organized and managed, the extent to which it will meet its financial and other goals, and even how the building itself should be designed and decorated.

For guests, the menu is much more than just a list of available foods. The menu also communicates the operation's image and contributes to the overall dining experience by helping to set a mood and building interest and excitement.

For production employees, the menu dictates what foods must be prepared. The tasks of service employees are also influenced by the items offered on the menu.

For managers, the menu is the chief in-house marketing and sales tool. The menu also tells them what food and beverages must be purchased, the types of production and service equipment needed, the number of workers they must hire, and the skill level of those workers. In short, the menu has an impact on almost every aspect of a food service operation.

Managers must ensure that the menu conveys the right message. In an elegant restaurant with a romantic atmosphere, an elaborate menu tied with gold cord and printed on expensive paper with a leather cover can help set the tone for the guests' dining experience. Even the condition of the menu conveys a message. If the operation's managers allow torn and soiled menus to be distributed, what other areas of the operation are they neglecting?

This chapter looks at menu pricing styles, menu schedules, and the different types of menus. Menu planning and menu design principles follow. The chapter continues with information about evaluating menus and concludes with a discussion of menu management software options. Most of the information and ideas discussed in the chapter can apply to noncommercial food services because almost all of these operations use some type of menu to communicate item availability to consumers.

Commercial Menu Pricing Styles

Menus come in all shapes and sizes, reflecting the extreme diversity of food service operations. Some are printed on parchment; others are written on a blackboard; still others are spoken by the server or made available on an electronic kiosk. But all menus in commercial operations can be categorized by how their menu items are priced. Three basic categories of menus are:

- Table d'hôte
- À la carte
- Combination table d'hôte/à la carte

Table d'Hôte

A **table d'hôte** (pronounced "tobble dote") **menu** offers a complete meal for one price. Sometimes two or more complete meals are offered on the menu, with each meal having its own price. Some table d'hôte menus offer guests limited choices within the meal they select; for example, a guest may choose between a soup and a salad, or a restaurant may offer a choice of desserts. But, for the most part, a meal on a table d'hôte menu is set by the menu planner, and guests are given few, if any, choices. Table d'hôte menus are sometimes called **prix fixe** ("pree feeks") **menus.** (Prix fixe means *fixed price* in French, the originating language for many culinary terms.)

À la Carte

With an **à la carte menu**, food and beverage items are listed and priced separately. Guests need not choose a meal that has been planned for them; they can choose from the various appetizers, entrées, side dishes, and desserts listed to make up their own meal. The prices of the menu items they select are added together to determine the cost of the meal.

Combination

Many operations have menus that are a combination of the table d'hôte and à la carte pricing styles. Table d'hôte menus may offer a selection of individually priced desserts; many à la carte menus include a choice of salads, dressings, vegetables, and potatoes or rice with the price of the entrée.

   A few operations have combination menus that offer an extensive list of complete meal packages and an extensive à la carte section. Chinese and other ethnic restaurants are most likely to feature this type of combination menu.

Noncommercial Menu Styles

Many noncommercial food services offer the same types of menus as do their commercial counterparts. Consider, for example, the private club with an à la carte or table d'hôte menu that is as elaborate and creative as a similar menu in a hotel or restaurant. Consider also the quick-service operation in a hospital or residence hall cafeteria or in a dining area in a business or industry setting. The menu may be written on a presentation board with à la carte pricing and may feature a daily special comprising an entrée and its accompaniments that is actually the operation's table d'hôte offering.

   Some noncommercial operations use a menu without pricing. Consider, for example, those offered to patients in hospitals, residents in retirement centers, and businesspeople in executive dining rooms.

Menus on the Internet

Most food service operations feature their menus on their websites. Those planning and designing menus can get many ideas by using the Internet to review other menus, especially the menus of their competitors. For a sample of some great menus in several industry segments, check out the following:

Casino Hotels and Resorts
Borgata Hotel Casino & Spa (www.theborgata.com)

Casual-Service Restaurants
Olive Garden (www.olivegarden.com)

Catering Food Services
Gourmet 45 (www.gourmet45.com)

Cruise Lines
Princess Cruise Lines (www.princess.com; click on "Learn About Cruising" and then "Onboard Experience" and then "Food & Dining")

Family-Service Restaurants
Denny's (www.dennys.com)

Full-Service Hotels (Catering Menus)
Beach House Hotel (www.beach-house.com; click on "Half Moon Bay," then "Meeting," then "Catering Menus")

Full-Service Hotels (International)
Altira Macau (www.altiramacau.com; click on "Aurora" under the "Dining" tab and then click on "Menu")

Full-Service Hotels (Room Service Menus)
Beverly Wilshire (www.fourseasons.com/beverlywilshire; click on "Dining," then "In-Room Dining")

Health Spas
Mii Amo: A Destination Spa (www.miiamo.com; click on "Cuisine" and then "Menus")

Hospital Food Services
Robinson Memorial Hospital (www.robinsonmemorial.org; click on "Medical Service," then "Nutrition Services," and then "Room Service Menu")

Long-Term Care Facilities
Heritage Commons (www.heritagecommons.com; click on "dinner" and then "Menu")

Pizza Restaurants
Pizza Hut (www.pizzahut.com)

Quick-Service Restaurants
Sonic (www.sonicdrivein.com; click on "Our Food")

University Food Services
University of Illinois at Urbana-Champaign (www.housing.illinois.edu; click on "Current Dining")

Upscale (Fine Dining) Restaurants
The French Laundry (www.frenchlaundry.com; be sure to also review the wine list)

All menus in all types of operations have two things in common: they inform guests about items that are available, and they drive management planning for all resources that are required to produce and deliver the items.

Menu Schedules

Menus can also be categorized by how often they are used. Some operations have a **fixed menu**, a single menu that is used daily, or a menu for each meal period. Other operations use a cycle menu. A **cycle menu** changes every day for a certain period of days; when the period ends, the cycle repeats.

Fixed Menus

Restaurants such as those in hotels and chain restaurants often use a single menu for several months or longer before replacing it with a new fixed menu. Daily specials may be offered to give frequent guests some menu variety, but a set list of items still forms the basic menu. Fixed menus work best at food service establishments where guests are not likely to visit frequently, or where enough items are listed on the menu to offer an acceptable level of variety for repeat guests.

Cycle Menus

Cycle menus are designed to provide variety for guests who eat at an operation frequently, perhaps even daily. Noncommercial operations, both self-operated and those that are operated by contract management companies in schools, health-care facilities, business and industry facilities, and other settings, frequently use cycle menus (see Exhibit 1). Commercial operations whose guests are likely to visit every day, such as restaurants in isolated resorts or downtown cafeterias, may also use them.

Typical cycles range from a week to four weeks, but some are longer. Establishing the right cycle length is important. With too short a cycle, the menus may repeat too often and guests may become dissatisfied. If the cycle is too long, production and labor costs involved in purchasing, storing, and preparing the greater variety of foods may be excessive. The optimum cycle length varies by type of operation and how often its guests are expected to eat there. Some casino hotels in Las Vegas use a seven-day cycle menu because most guests do not stay long enough to notice the repetition. A resort whose average guest stays two weeks may plan a two-, three-, or four-week cycle menu, depending on how concerned the management is with providing variety for guests who stay longer than average. In a large university, a cycle menu of twenty-eight days may be appropriate.

The daily menus used in a cycle can be à la carte or table d'hôte. Schools, hospitals, prisons, and other institutions may use table d'hôte menus in the cycle; that is, they may offer one set meal for breakfast, lunch, and dinner each day (although noncommercial operations are increasingly using menus that offer a choice). Commercial operations that use cycle menus may offer à la carte menus; a hotel restaurant on a seven-day cycle could rotate seven different à la carte menus, for example.

Exhibit 1 Sample Cycle Menus

WEEK 1	MONDAY	TUESDAY	WEDNESDAY	THURSDAY	FRIDAY
ENTREES Choose 1	Hamburger with bun Chili	Submarine Sandwich Ground Beef and Gravy	Pizza Cheese Sandwich Bologna	Spaghetti w/ Meat Sauce Tunafish Sandwich	Tacos Sloppy Joes with Bun
FRUITS AND VEGETABLES Choose 2	French Fries Celery Sticks Applesauce	Mashed Potatoes Cabbage-Apple Salad Fruit Cocktail	Buttered Green Beans Carrot Sticks Fruit Gelatin	Tossed Salad Buttered Spinach Apple Crisp	"Round-about" Potatoes Orange Juice Banana

WEEK 2	MONDAY	TUESDAY	WEDNESDAY	THURSDAY	FRIDAY
ENTREES Choose 1	Toasted Cheese Sandwich Meatloaf w/ Gravy	Pizza Turkey–Ham Sandwich	Fish in Bun Chicken or Turkey Supreme	Hamburger and bun Macaroni and Cheese	Lasagna Hot Dog and Bun
FRUITS AND VEGETABLES Choose 2	Mashed Potatoes Vegetable Soup Sliced Peaches	Buttered Corn Tossed Green Salad	French Fries Confetti Cole Slaw	Tater Tots Beets in Orange Sauce	Buttered Green Beans Finger Relishes
BREAD OR SUBSTITUTE	Hot rolls (with meatloaf)				
BONUS!					

WEEK 3	MONDAY	TUESDAY	WEDNESDAY	THURSDAY	FRIDAY
ENTREES Choose 1	Tacos Egg Salad Sandwich	Hot Dog and Bun Meat Turnover with Gravy	Spaghetti and Meat Sauce Turkey Sandwich	Pizza Tunafish Sandwich	Hamburger and Bun Ravioli

WEEK 4	MONDAY	TUESDAY	WEDNESDAY	THURSDAY	FRIDAY
ENTREES Choose 1	Sloppy Joes with Bun Beef Stew	Baked Fish Beefaroni	Hamburger and Bun or Cheeseburger	Baked Chicken Toasted Cheese Sandwich	Pizza Submarine
FRUITS AND VEGETABLES Choose 2	Celery Sticks Buttered Corn Orange Slush				
BREAD OR SUBSTITUTE	Cheese Biscuit with Butter				
BONUS!	Peanut Butter Cup				
MILK Whole or 2%	Milk				

WEEK 1	MONDAY	TUESDAY	WEDNESDAY	THURSDAY	FRIDAY
ENTREES Choose 1	Hamburger with bun Chili	Submarine Sandwich Ground Beef and Gravy	Pizza Cheese Sandwich Bologna	Spaghetti w/ Meat Sauce Tunafish Sandwich	Tacos Sloppy Joes with Bun
FRUITS AND VEGETABLES Choose 2	French Fries Celery Sticks Applesauce	Mashed Potatoes Cabbage-Apple Salad Fruit Cocktail	Buttered Green Beans Carrot Sticks Fruit Gelatin	Tossed Salad Buttered Spinach Apple Crisp	"Round-about" Potatoes Orange Juice Banana
BREAD OR SUBSTITUTE		Saltines (with Chili)	Roll (with Ground Beef)		Italian Bread (with Spaghetti)
BONUS!			Peanut Butter Cookie		Oatmeal Cookie
MILK Whole or 2%	Milk	Milk	Milk	Milk	Milk

These cycle menus are used at a middle school. Note that the menus are on a four-week cycle and provide limited choices.

Types of Menus

Three basic types of menus are breakfast, lunch, and dinner menus. In other words, these menus are designed around the three traditional meal periods. There are also a large number of specialty menus designed to appeal to a specific guest group or meet a specific marketing need. The types of menus a food service operation offers depends on the number of meals it serves and the type of operation it is. Many operations have a separate breakfast menu with a cutoff time for serving breakfast. Combining lunch and dinner menus is a common practice. Whether to offer specialty menus depends on the operation and its clientele. An upscale restaurant may feel that a separate wine or dessert list adds to its image, for example.

Let's look at some common types of menus.

Breakfast

Breakfast menus are fairly standard. Many operations in both the commercial and noncommercial segments offer choices of fruits, juices, eggs, cereals, pancakes, waffles, and breakfast meats like bacon and sausage. Sometimes regional specialties, such as grits, are offered.

The watchwords for typical breakfast menu items are *simple, fast*, and *inexpensive*. Many guests are more price-conscious at breakfast than at other meals. They are also likely to be in a hurry to get to work or otherwise start their day, so they want fast service. To keep prices down and make quick service possible, most breakfast menus are relatively limited.

Lunch

Like those at breakfast, lunch guests are often in a hurry. Therefore, lunch menus must also feature menu items that are relatively easy and quick to make. Sandwiches, soups, and salads are important in many lunch menus.

Lunch menus must have variety; many guests eat lunch at the same restaurant several times a week because it is located close to where they work or go to school. To provide variety, most lunch menus offer daily specials. These can be printed on a separate piece of paper and clipped onto the lunch menu. Or a cycle menu can be used to provide variety, in which case the entire menu changes daily for a certain number of days.

Lunch menus usually offer smaller portions than dinner menus, because most guests do not want to feel full and sleepy during the afternoon. Lunch menus are usually less elaborate than dinner menus. If appetizers are offered at lunch, they are simpler to make and fewer in number. Lunch menus usually include desserts.

Dinner

Dinner is the main meal of the day for most people, and menu items offered at dinner may be heavier in character and more elaborate than those offered at breakfast or lunch. Dinner is more likely to be eaten in a leisurely fashion than breakfast or lunch because guests are often seeking a dining experience or celebrating a special occasion at dinner.

Guests are willing to pay more for dinner than for lunch, but they also expect a greater selection of menu items and place a greater premium on service, atmosphere, and decor. Therefore, dinner menus usually offer a wide variety of selections. Steaks, roasts, chicken, seafood, and pasta dishes like lasagna and linguine are typical dinner entrées. Wines, cocktails, and exotic desserts are more likely to be on a dinner menu than on a lunch menu.

Specialty

There is a wide range of specialty menus, from poolside menus to those for afternoon teas. Some of the most common specialty menus are:

- Children's
- Senior citizens'
- Alcoholic beverage, including wine
- Dessert
- Room service
- Take-out
- Banquet
- California
- Ethnic

Children's. Children's menus do not necessarily have to blend in with the restaurant's theme or decor; the important things are to ensure that the menu is entertaining and that items appealing to children are offered at a value price. (To see a large selection of children's menus, get on the Internet and enter "images of children's menus" in your favorite search engine.) The goal is to occupy the child long enough for the parents and other guests to eat in peace. Children's menus can be shaped like cartoon characters, dinosaurs, or rocket ships. Many children's menus feature bright colors, cartoons, pop-up designs, or black and white drawings that the child can color. Menus that fold into hats, masks, or other toys are good for small children; puzzles, word games, stories, and mazes can work for older children.

The food offered on children's menus should be familiar, simple, and nutritious. Portions should be small and prices should be modest.

Tassels, staples, or other potentially dangerous materials that can be removed and swallowed should never be part of a children's menu.

Some hotel restaurants offer creative children's menus. For example, Ritz-Carlton hotels offer "Ritz Kids Menus," which present a wide variety of menu items to their young guests. In addition, some Ritz-Carlton properties offer "healthy choice" menus that present attractive and creative ways to provide nutritious items that are also "fun" to youngsters. Ritz-Carlton properties may also offer a special dining program for children twelve and under that includes breakfast, lunch, and dinner with unlimited fountain drinks during meals at selected hotel dining outlets for a single price per child per day. (To learn more about these children's menus and food service options, just enter "ritz kids meals" into your favorite search engine.)

Children's menus at fine-dining restaurants can be upscale. How about mini-steaks or small portions of grilled seafood with broccoli, a glass of milk, and perhaps a cookie for dessert?

Senior Citizens'. Menus that appeal to the special wants and needs of senior citizens are increasingly important. **Senior citizens' menus** can be separate menus or separate sections of regular menus. They can also be selections of menu items placed throughout the regular menu.

Some seniors, especially those who may be living on fixed incomes, are more price-conscious and appreciate being able to receive smaller portions of popular items at reduced prices.

Other seniors have dietary prescriptions or recommendations from their doctors. Most revolve around weight control, diabetes, cardiovascular problems or precautions, and gastrointestinal disorders. Other seniors are just more conscious of the need to eat properly. Seniors watching their weight and those who are diabetic need simple, light snacks, entrées, and desserts. A piece of fresh fruit served stylishly can allow a diabetic to enjoy dessert with others at the table.

Many seniors are on a no-added-salt diet. With this diet, it is fine to use salt lightly in cooking, but no salt should be added to the food when it reaches the table. Many good-tasting menu items can be prepared without sodium-rich condiments and foods.

Noting ingredients when items are described on the menu can help seniors make appropriate selections. Knowledgeable service staff can pick up where the menu leaves off by providing ingredient and preparation information to guests with special dietary concerns who request this information.

Alcoholic Beverage. Cocktails and wines can be listed on a separate **alcoholic beverage menu** or included on the regular menu. Sometimes, for example, menu descriptions for entrées suggest suitable wines. If included on the regular menu, the drink list should come before the food selections so guests desiring a drink before ordering their meal will have the necessary information. Operations that offer separate alcoholic beverage menus often have separate cocktail menus and wine lists. Separate beverage menus can be used in the lounge as well as in the dining room.

Food service operations should list alcoholic beverages in large, readable type, with brand names and prices included. Today many beverage menus include no- or low-alcohol drinks creatively named and described to help promote their sale.

Disney Menus

Want to see current menus, including those for children, from Disney Operations all around the world? Go to www.allears.net.

The site also provides information about Disney restaurants, special dietary needs, special dining events, and dinner shows.

Dessert. At the end of the meal, many guests will not recall the dessert items they saw listed on the main menu. Food servers at some operations use dessert trays or carts to remind guests of desserts. Some operations have a separate **dessert menu** so that food servers have something to give to guests at the end of the meal to remind them of the desserts available. Many family- and casual-service restaurants place dessert menus in tabletop holders so that they are visible to guests throughout the meal.

The advantages of having separate dessert menus include the following:

- The operation may sell more desserts.

- There is more room for bold graphics and descriptive copy.

- If dessert items or prices change, operations do not have to reprint the main menu.

- More space is available on the lunch and dinner menus for information applicable to those items.

The types of desserts offered vary with the type of operation. Some elegant restaurants feature flaming desserts prepared tableside, many family restaurants offer cake and ice cream, and quick-service restaurants offer such simple dessert items as ice cream cones, cookies, and other items that can be eaten without utensils. Upscale restaurants often include after-dinner wines, brandies, and liqueurs on the dessert menu.

Room Service. Many full-service hotels offer room service (often called "in-room dining") to guests. With a few exceptions, such as those found at luxury hotels, **room service menus** offer a limited number of menu items. They may offer selected items from the hotel's regular menu or feature items not on the regular menu.

Most room service menus are limited because it is difficult to offer high-quality food that does not deteriorate during delivery from the production area to the guestroom, suite, or outlying guestroom area. This is a problem in every lodging operation, especially in high-rise hotels where service staff must contend with elevators and in resort-type properties where food servers must use a vehicle to transport the food to guestrooms that may be far from central kitchen areas.

One type of room service menu is the doorknob breakfast menu. A **doorknob menu** lists a limited number of breakfast items and times that the meal can be served. Guests indicate what they want to eat and when they want the food delivered, and hang the menu outside the door on the doorknob. The menus are collected overnight, and the orders are prepared and sent to the rooms at the requested times. Most lodging properties now use electronic door-locking systems, and some properties insert announcements about the availability of room service or about room service specials in these card slots. Room service menus are increasingly available on in-room televisions and, in many properties, guests can place orders via this medium.

Take-Out. An increasing number of table-service restaurants offer **take-out menus** to capture consumer dollars that otherwise might be spent at quick-service establishments or on convenience foods in supermarkets and convenience stores.

"Grab-and-Go" Room Service

In the traditional room service model, a guest in his or her room orders desired food and beverages by, for example, telephone, television, or doorknob menu, and those items are delivered to the guestroom. Some hotels now offer a grab-and-go style of room service to replace (or in addition to) traditional room service. With this method, guests desiring food and beverage products select them and pay for them in the hotel lobby or some other public area. There might, for example, be one or more kiosks or other retail spaces at the hotel where these products are available. Limited-service properties often have "pantry" areas where grab-and-go items are available. Microwave ovens may be available in these areas if they are not available in the guestroom. Guests may pay for these items when purchased, or the products may be added to their guestroom folio for payment at checkout.

In the United States, home-meal replacement is a popular concept. For many, a traditional take-out meal has involved calling a property to order from a take-out menu. The guest then drives to the property, parks the car, and goes inside the restaurant to the bar or host stand. Today some properties are designed with a dedicated take-out food service counter, sometimes with a separate entrance. Increasingly, staff members are available to carry preordered meals curbside to guests waiting in their cars. This version of the quick-service restaurant's drive-through is quickly gaining popularity in many commercial restaurants.

Some organizations dedicate parking spaces for those ordering curbside delivery, and most accept credit cards at curbside. Some chains including Applebee's, Ruby Tuesday, and Outback Steakhouse now generate a significant percentage of their total revenues from curbside sales. Advantages for guests include greater menu variety and higher-quality items than are generally available in quick-service properties, along with obvious time-saving benefits.

Like room service menus, take-out menus should feature items that can maintain an acceptable level of quality over a long period of time. Guests will not be satisfied unless the food they have purchased still looks and tastes good when they consume it.

Take-out menus should be inexpensive to produce since guests take them home. Some operations use their take-out menus as direct mail advertising pieces.

Modern technology certainly supplements and often replaces paper take-out menus. For example, restaurants feature take-out menus on their websites. Smartphone apps are available, and some properties make on-site dining and take-up menus available in community dining resources that are often web-based. Social media including Facebook and Twitter are often sources of information about take-out dining options, ranging from placement of entire menus (Facebook) to a quick note about today's special (Twitter).

Banquet. Hotel food and beverage operations and restaurants that do extensive banquet business often develop preset **banquet menus** in varying price ranges from which guests may choose desired items. They can also plan custom banquet menus when guests request them.

The pricing style for banquet menus is usually table d'hôte—a set meal with few, if any, choices offered at a set price. The meal can be elaborate, with appetizers, soups or salads, wine, and fancy desserts served along with the entrée and its accompaniments. Many banquet operations recognize that some guests require or desire special meals for religious, medical, or other reasons and make efforts to accommodate these requests.

Managers who plan banquet menus must be careful to select food that can be produced in quantity and still hold its quality until the last guest is served.

California. Some restaurants offer breakfast, lunch, and dinner menu items on one menu, with all the items available at any time of the day: if guests want spaghetti for breakfast or pancakes for dinner, they can order it. This concept originated in California, so this type of menu is called a **California menu.** Obviously, an operation with no restrictions about when it will serve breakfast, lunch, or dinner items also gives up the production and scheduling convenience these restrictions provide.

Ethnic. Ethnic menus are offered by restaurants to appeal to guests who like a particular cuisine. Restaurants that feature Italian, Chinese, Greek, or Mexican foods are familiar to most of us. Ethnic restaurants offering Japanese, Middle Eastern, Scandinavian, Korean, Indian, and Thai cuisines are also popular.

An ethnic menu typically features a variety of dishes popular in the applicable country or area; it may also offer items for the more adventurous diner. The names of the dishes are often listed in the original language and translated into English. The main ingredients of each dish should be listed. How authentic should the menu items be? If most of the restaurant's guests are of the ethnic background to which the menu seeks to appeal, the dishes should closely follow traditional recipes. However, if most of the clientele are from other ethnic backgrounds, the recipes can be less traditional. For example, spices can be changed and some ingredients may be eliminated so the resulting dishes will be more readily acceptable to a broader range of guests.

Menu Planning

The success of a food service operation is largely in the hands of its menu planning team. Work will flow more smoothly, guests will be served more effectively, and financial goals will be easier to attain when the menu has been properly planned. The opposite is also true: a poorly planned menu will cause significant operating problems that will affect guests, employees, and ultimately the financial health of the operation.

Not all food service managers plan or help plan a menu. Those in multi-unit quick- or casual-service restaurants, for example, may not do any menu planning at all; their menus will likely be developed at corporate headquarters after extensive market research. In hospitals and schools, menus may be planned by staff dietitians. At a large independent restaurant, the menu may be planned by a team that includes the restaurant manager, the head chef, and the purchasing director. Menu planning may be done by the owner, chef, and/or head cook at a small restaurant.

Menu planning is complex, and requires knowledge of the entire operation. Fortunately, it is rare that a menu planner has to start from scratch. Most menu planners revise a current menu. This means that the menu's pricing style—table d'hôte, à la carte, or a combination of the two—has already been chosen; a fixed or cycle menu is already in place; and the type of menu—breakfast, lunch, dinner, or specialty—has already been determined.

For most menu planners, therefore, menu planning consists of considering and selecting new menu items for an existing menu. How does a menu planner go about making these selections? The answers vary from operation to operation and from planner to planner, but three rules are basic: know your guests, know your quality requirements, and know your operation.

Know Your Guests

The relevance of all decisions about the menu depends on knowing your guests well. What kinds of guests visit your operation? What do they want to eat? What are they willing to pay for a meal? If one of your primary markets is teenagers, your menu will probably look very different from the menu of a restaurant whose main market is married couples with children.

Some menu planners assume that their personal preferences are the same as their guests'. This is not necessarily true. When selecting menu items, menu planners must consider the guests' preferences, not their own. Menu planners can learn guest preferences by, among other things, talking with guests; reviewing feedback that guests have handwritten or entered online; and studying production and sales records. Wise managers should also discuss menu item preference with service staff, since they come into frequent contact with guests, and even with buspersons and dishwashers, who know what products are brought back to the kitchen for disposal. Exhibit 2 reviews some basic guest-related concerns in menu planning.

Know Your Quality Requirements

Exhibit 2 also emphasizes the importance of quality when menus are planned. Only items meeting the operation's quality requirements should be included on the menu. Characteristics including flavor, consistency, texture, form, shape, nutritional content, visual and aromatic appeal, and temperature all have quality implications. Sometimes a **make-buy analysis** is undertaken to determine the quality equivalents when items can be prepared on-site or purchased as convenience foods. Regardless, if an item's quality does not meet the property's standards, it cannot be offered on the menu.

Know Your Operation

The type of operation helps determine what kinds of menu items are appropriate. Several factors have a direct impact on what kinds of menu items the operation can offer:

Exhibit 2   Priority Concerns of the Menu Planner

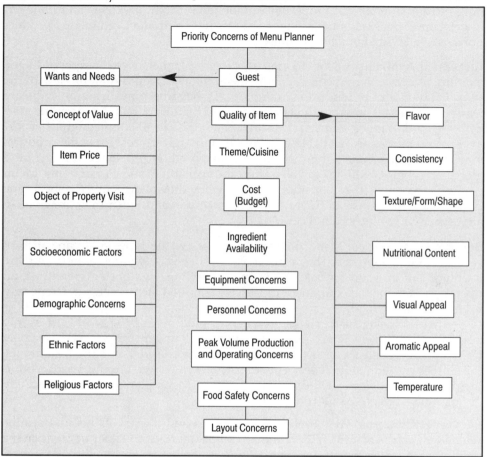

- Theme or cuisine
- Cost (budget)
- Ingredient availability
- Equipment concerns
- Personnel concerns
- Peak volume production and operating concerns
- Sanitation concerns
- Layout concerns

Theme or Cuisine. The restaurant's theme or cuisine helps determine what types of menu items are appropriate. An ethnic restaurant has a menu that is very different from a menu at a family-oriented or quick-service chain restaurant.

Cost (Budget). Menu planners must recognize financial constraints when planning menus. Commercial properties cannot attain profit objectives and noncommercial operations cannot minimize expenses unless product and related production costs fall within budgetary limits.

Ingredient Availability. Not too long ago, menu planners were hampered by the inability to obtain ingredients for some menu items during certain months of the year. High-quality produce, for example, may have been available only during warm months, and other products were affected by the ups and downs of the marketplace. Today, however, most items in common use in all but the highest-check-average properties are available year-round, although the cost for some products may vary significantly during the year. Transportation problems, weather, and global economic conditions can also affect the availability and cost of items. Menu planners recognize these potential concerns when they plan menus for short time periods (quarterly instead of annually, for example) and when they are creative about menu item substitutions.

Equipment Concerns. Menu planners must know the types and capacities of equipment in the kitchen. They can choose a wider variety of menu items if there is equipment on hand for baking, steaming, broiling, frying, etc. In contrast, an operation with limited equipment must have a limited menu unless it extensively uses convenience foods.

When choosing menu items, planners should spread the workload evenly among the equipment. For example, if most menu items are deep-fried, fryers may be overloaded while the ovens and broilers are underused. For many restaurants, the entrées chosen should reflect a good distribution between frying, baking, broiling, roasting, and other methods of preparation. Menu planners are increasingly giving diners options about cooking methods.

Personnel Concerns. The number of employees and their skills help determine what items can be placed on the menu. Menu planners should not put items on the menu that the kitchen staff does not have the skills to prepare.

Just as with equipment, menu planners want to avoid overwhelming some kitchen personnel while leaving others with little to do. Careful menu item selection can help spread the workload evenly among kitchen personnel.

Peak Volume Production and Operating Concerns. Equipment limitations affect the quantity and variety of food that can be produced, as do food preparation processes. For example, menu planners can select menu items that are prepared to order and include those that can be prepared in small quantities several times during a meal period. They can also incorporate items that are produced in large quantities only once for each dining period. Planners can determine the best way to make each menu item, and the available kitchen equipment and staff members must be able to efficiently produce the correct number of items when they are required.

Food Safety Concerns. Food safety is an ever-present priority. Food service managers should recognize sanitation concerns when menus are initially planned. If a potentially hazardous food such as hollandaise sauce or a seafood dish cannot be appropriately held on the serving line, it cannot be offered unless there is a way to produce it on an as-ordered basis. This is not generally practical in many food preparation settings.

Layout Concerns. Menus in existing operations are typically influenced by the kitchen layout and space available to produce the required items. Consider, for example, a suggestion to add fresh-baked bread to the menu of an operation that does not have the proper design or square footage to accommodate the baking operation. Consider also problems that the menu planner in a small pizza restaurant may encounter when he or she decides to add a two-crust pizza to the menu. Workflow can slow significantly if a top crust must be added to the pizza at the end of the production station.

Selecting Menu Items

Numerous books, manuals, and training lessons have been written on the art and science of selecting menu items for menus.[1] What follows is a simplified discussion of this complex subject.

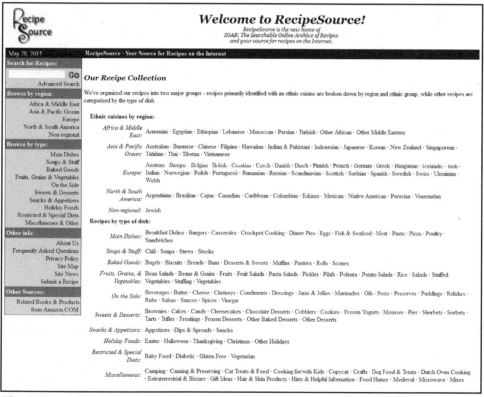

The Internet has helped put thousands of recipes within easy reach of food service professionals who are developing menus that will appeal to guests' palates and pocketbooks. (www.recipesource.com)

The items listed on a menu often can be categorized as appetizers, salads, entrées, starch items (potatoes, rice, pasta), vegetables, desserts, and beverages. How do menu planners create a pool of possible menu items in each of these categories from which to create or revise menus? There are many possible sources:

- *Old menus.* The operation's own previous menus may list menu items that were once popular but were dropped from the current menu for one reason or another. It may be time to reconsider them for the revised menu.

- *Books.* There are seemingly innumerable books for the food service industry devoted to recipes and new menu item ideas.

- *Trade magazines.* Trade magazines, including e-versions, can be excellent sources of recipes for new menu items.

- *Cookbooks for the quantity food and home markets.* Hard-copy cookbooks featuring quantity recipes are readily available, and many are produced by chefs' organizations. Cookbooks for home use can provide many new ideas for salads, soups, garnishes, entrées, and desserts. Of course, once chosen, the recipes will have to be modified to yield larger quantities.

- *Websites.* A growing number of food service websites now catalogue a wide variety of recipes gathered from all over the world. One good starting point is the list of several recipe websites at the end of this chapter.

Only those new menu items that marketing research has indicated that guests may like should be considered. Once the pool of possible menu items has been narrowed down to items the guests may like, some items must be eliminated because of the following:

- Cost
- Incompatibility with the operation's theme or cuisine
- Unavailable equipment
- Insufficient equipment capacity
- Inadequate kitchen space
- Insufficient number of employees
- Incompatibility with employee skills
- Inconsistent availability of some ingredients
- Inability to meet the operation's quality standards
- Potential sanitation problems

After menu planners have considered these and other factors, they can select the items they wish to offer.

Entrées. Entrées are usually selected first when a menu is planned. Menu planners must determine what kinds of entrées to offer: beef, pork, fish, entrée salads, etc. Planners may feel that the restaurant should have something for everyone and, therefore, may be tempted to provide a wide range of entrées. This approach can create many operating problems. For example, a wider variety of food and ingredients must be ordered, received, stored, issued, prepared, and held for service. More equipment and more personnel with the necessary skills must be available. Production and service problems are more likely. The reverse, offering only a few entrées, reduces these problems. Many quick-service, specialty, and theme restaurants offer relatively few entrées. This minimizes in-house production and serving problems. The best approach is to consider the items that the majority of guests will prefer and then offer other entrées as necessary. For example, a restaurant featuring steak may offer a few seafood and entrée salad choices to accommodate diners who do not prefer beef entrées.

As indicated earlier, menu planners must consider methods of preparation when selecting entrées. Production problems and service delays occur when all or most of the entrées are prepared the same way.

Appetizers and Soups. Appetizers include cheese, fruit, seafood items such as shrimp cocktail, and an ever-expanding list of specialty items such as nachos, buffalo wings, bruschetta, and deep-fried foods served with dips or sauces. Appetizers are supposed to arouse the appetite before dinner, so they are generally small in size and spicy or pleasantly biting or tart. The number and variety of appetizers on a menu is determined by the type of operation and its guests. Quick-service operations typically do not have appetizers, while elegant restaurants may devote a whole page of their dinner menus to appetizers.

Many restaurants offer a limited selection of soups. Sometimes a soup du jour (soup of the day) is listed. If more than two or three soups are offered, they are often listed separately on the menu rather than combined with the appetizers. The kinds of soups offered are determined by the type of operation. Seafood restaurants usually offer soups like clam chowder and shrimp or lobster bisque, while Italian restaurants often serve minestrone soup. Upscale restaurants may offer chilled soups such as vichyssoise and others classically prepared from the meat stocks used for sauces or other items.

Starch Items and Vegetables. The next items to be planned are usually the starch items and vegetables. Sometimes the starch item is a part of the entrée—sirloin tips in gravy served over rice, for example. At other times, the starch item is separate—a baked potato or a side dish of pasta. In many restaurants a vegetable is served with the entrée. Vegetables can also be offered as side dishes.

Again, the type of operation and its guests determine the variety of starch items and vegetables that are offered. The starch items at many seafood restaurants are limited to baked potatoes or french fries. A restaurant that features fine dining may offer a wide variety of rice, pasta, and potato items; potatoes, for example, may be baked, fried, creamed, mashed, au gratin, etc. Chinese restaurants offer a great variety of vegetables; quick-service operations offer few or none.

Salads. The first decision a planner must make about salads is whether they will be strictly side dishes or whether some salads will be offered as entrées. If they are offered, salad entrées such as chicken salad, shrimp salad, or chef's salad are usually listed separately on the menu. Tossed salad, coleslaw, potato salad, fruit salad, and cottage cheese salad are typical side-dish salads. Salad bars are common in many commercial and noncommercial operations. Today's "fresh is best" philosophy and other concerns about healthy foods have encouraged these offerings.

Diners may order an entrée salad or have a side salad as part of a meal or as an à la carte option.

Desserts. Desserts are typically high-profit items. Possibilities range from cookies in quick-service operations to flamed desserts in upscale restaurants. Some properties feature "homemade" desserts. Others feature signature desserts that are an important part of the marketing effort to attract guests. Low-calorie desserts can be offered for health-conscious guests.

Beverages. Nonalcoholic beverages are often listed at the end of the menu. Coffee, tea, milk, and a selection of carbonated beverages are typical. Upscale restaurants may feature a wide variety of coffees—Colombian, Turkish, espresso, cappuccino, lattes, spiced coffee, and so on—and a number of specialty teas.

If an operation offers alcoholic beverages, a decision must be made about how many types and brands of alcoholic beverages will be available. Should the operation offer a few standard beers, or should it carry a wide variety, including local, international, and the increasingly popular **microbrewery** beers? How many different wines should be offered? Should dessert wines and cordials be included on the wine list? How many different brands of liquor should be available? For chain restaurants and franchise operations, selection decisions are usually made at corporate headquarters. Managers in independent operations must make their own decisions based on guest preferences, the restaurant's image, beverage inventory costs, space, and other factors.

Menu Balance

After all menu items have been selected, the menu should be reviewed for business, aesthetic, and nutritional balance.

What About Salad Bars?

Many food service operations in all segments of the industry offer salad bars for one primary reason: their guests like them! However, they can create special challenges that management must consistently address. Examples include the following:

- Managers must ensure that the costs of "help yourself" service are not excessive. They must select the correct items (for example, small chopped olives are typically better than super-colossal olives on salad bars), and they must routinely calculate food costs.

- Managers must practice portion control as they provide the correct serving utensils at the right places with the correctly sized service items.

- Dedicated labor is required to maintain the salad bar's food products, supplies, and cleanliness.

A wide variety of serving equipment is available for salad bars. See, for example, Restaurant Equipment World (www.rewonline.com) to learn about available items and current costs.

Business balance refers to the relationship between food costs, menu selling prices, the popularity of items, and other financial and marketing considerations. In both commercial and noncommercial operations, the menu must help the operation attain financial goals and should be reviewed with those goals in mind. A process called menu engineering can help managers evaluate current menus or potential revisions and assess revised menus to determine whether profitability goals are being attained. This topic is discussed in a later section of this chapter.

Aesthetic balance refers to the degree to which meals have been constructed with concern about the colors, textures, and flavors of foods. Obviously, balance is more important in a table d'hôte menu than in an à la carte menu, since guests are offered entire meals on a table d'hôte menu, and they have more freedom to choose their own food combinations with an à la carte menu. But aesthetic balance is an issue even with an à la carte menu, since some foods are commonly sold together, such as an entrée with an accompanying starch item and vegetable. À la carte properties may offer salad bars that also must be planned with aesthetic balance in mind.

Color is an important component of a meal's attractiveness. A plate of baked whitefish, steamed cauliflower, and mashed potatoes makes for a boring and unappetizing presentation. Two or three colors on a plate are more interesting than one.

A meal should be composed of foods that vary in texture. Most guests would not like a meal of soup, stew, creamed corn, mashed potatoes, and chocolate pudding. In general, firm entrées should have tender or soft side dishes; soft entrées should have crisp or crunchy side dishes.

Putting compatible flavors together is a matter of experience as well as knowing traditional combinations. Imagine a meal of grape juice, sweet and sour pork, and cherry pie. Such a meal would have too many sweets and sours for most people.

Nutritional balance has historically been more important for noncommercial food service operations than for commercial properties. But managers of commercial properties also should make sure the components of a well-balanced meal are

---

Food Service Seven Miles High

In the not-too-distant past, passengers typically had many complaints about airline meals. Today, the complaints continue because meals are not available, or are available in limited variety for an additional fee in coach-class seats. However, excellent food service is provided to passengers in first-class seats on some airlines as they cruise 35,000 feet (approximately seven miles) high in the sky.

Food served in first-class cabins has become more luxurious and elegant to align with the rest of the first-class experience that attracts high-paying customers. Check out www.airlinemeals.net to learn more about airline meals. For example, you can see photos of the economy, business, and first-class meals offered by your favorite airlines and learn lots of additional information about food services in the skies.

available from among the menu items they offer. Nutritional concerns are important to many guests and must therefore be important to restaurant managers.

Menu Design

Menu items must be organized into a menu that encourages guests to order them. A well-designed menu complements an operation's overall theme, blends in with the interior decor, communicates with guests, and helps sell the operation as well as its menu items.

Menu design depends on the type of operation. The menu in an elegant hotel dining room is far different from a nursing home's menu. In spite of these differences, there are many design and merchandising techniques that are nearly the same for almost all food service operations.

You may manage operations where the menu is designed by the quick-service franchisor or by the corporate headquarters of a restaurant chain. There may be times in your career, however, when you will work at independent restaurants or other operations whose managers will have a complete or partial say in what the menu looks like. A basic knowledge of menu design principles is helpful when you have menu planning responsibilities.

Menus are so crucial to an operation's success that the menu planners of many independent restaurants seek the help of advertising agencies or freelance artists and designers. The menu planner should tell the designer about the restaurant's guests; show the designer the restaurant's interior; and explain the number and complexity of menu items, how often the menu will be changed, what the menu should achieve, and what the budget is for the project. The designer should be able to provide creative layout ideas and explain production costs and options.

Desktop publishing systems are used in many properties, even small ones, to design menus that often have the look and flair of their professionally designed counterparts. (See, for example, www.softcafe.com.)

Copy

After the menu planner has selected the menu items to appear on the menu, copy must be written. Just as with all the other menu design elements, menu copy depends on the operation, its guests, and the meal period. Copy on children's menus should be entertaining, for example; copy on lunch menus should be brief and to the point. Copy on dinner menus may be more descriptive because guests are more likely to have the time to read it and because menu items may be more complex or feature unfamiliar ingredients or preparation methods that require more explanation.

Menu copy can be divided into three elements: headings, descriptive copy for menu items, and supplemental merchandising copy.

Headings. Headings include major heads ("Appetizers," "Soups," "Entrées"), subheads ("Steak," "Seafood," "Today's Specials"), and the names of individual menu items.

Menu item names must be chosen with care. Some operations choose simple descriptive names for their menu items. Others choose more elaborate names. For most operations, it is best to keep menu item names simple and easy to pronounce so guests are not confused.

If menu item names are in a foreign language, a simple description of the item in English will help guests who do not know the language and may increase sales of the item. Pictures of the menu items also may help overcome any language barriers. Pictures are especially important, for example, on room-service menus in hotels frequented by international visitors.

Rules of grammar apply. A good language dictionary can help copywriters spell words correctly and use the correct accent marks. Menu copy in a foreign language works well only if the foreign language is used properly.

Descriptive Copy. Descriptive menu copy informs guests about menu items and helps increase sales. The menu item's main ingredient, important secondary ingredients, and method of preparation are often included in descriptive copy. The description should not be as detailed as a recipe. Flowery language, too many superlatives, technical explanations, and long sentences can turn guests off. Claims should be accurate and made in short, easy-to-read sentences. A few well-chosen words are better than a long-winded paragraph.

Many variables determine when to use descriptive copy. Entrées, which are usually high-profit items, should get the most copy. Specialties of the house deserve extra copy, since they help define an operation's character and appeal. Complex appetizers and desserts, entrée-type salads, and wines are examples of other menu items that need descriptive copy. If an item's name is not very

---

Photos and More Photos of All Types of Menus

A good way to learn about menu design is to see lots of menus, and the Internet makes this easy to do. Type the term "images of" in front of any or all of the following types of menus in your favorite search engine:

- restaurant menus
- children's menus
- airline menus
- poolside menus
- steakhouse menus
- quick-service menus
- resort menus
- family-service-restaurant menus
- buffet menus
- banquet menus
- catering menus
- etc.

descriptive, more copy may be needed to explain the item. There is less need for a description when the item—"steamed asparagus," for example—is self-explanatory.

   Truth-in-menu laws. One of the reasons that descriptive copy should not oversell a menu item is that it leads to disappointed guests. Another reason is that overselling and exaggerated claims and half-truths about menu items may be in violation of **truth-in-menu laws.** Some areas to be careful about include:

- *Grading.* If it is stated on the menu that a steak is USDA prime, the steak served must be of that quality. Or if the copy says sirloin tips, a different cut of meat should not be substituted. Some foods are graded by size, and any size claims must be in line with official standards. If the menu says jumbo shrimp, for example, the item served must be jumbo shrimp, not extra large or large.

- *Freshness claims.* If the menu says an item is fresh, it cannot be canned, frozen, or fresh-frozen.

- *Geographical origin.* Menus cannot make false claims about the geographical origin of a product. Cheese from Wisconsin cannot be sold as "imported Swiss cheese."

- *Preparation.* The copy must be accurate about menu item preparation. For example, if the menu says the item is baked, it cannot be fried instead.

- *Dietary or nutrition claims.* The copy should not make dietary or nutrition claims not supported by scientific data or that the operation cannot produce every time a menu item is prepared.

- *Portion sizes.* A menu showing a picture of a shrimp platter with six shrimp should offer six shrimp on the platter. A description of a six-ounce hamburger patty should yield a six-ounce portion. Note that it may be best to specify "six ounces before cooking" to acknowledge cooking losses that will yield smaller edible portion sizes.

   Supplemental Merchandising Copy. Supplemental merchandising copy is devoted to subjects other than the menu items. It may include such basic information as the property's address, telephone number, days and hours of operation, meals served, and e-mail and website addresses.

   Supplemental merchandising copy can also be entertaining. A history of the restaurant, a statement about management's commitment to guest service, or the restaurant's mission statement may be included. Many food service operations have a special feature, service, history, character, or locale that makes an interesting story to enhance the operation's image or help it stand out from competitors.

   The amount of supplemental merchandising copy used depends on the menu space that is available and management's ideas about whether more copy or something else, such as more artwork, is the way to encourage sales.

Layout

Once menu copy has been written, the menu must be organized into a layout: a rough sketch of how the finished menu will look. Planning a layout includes listing menu items in the right sequence, placing the menu items' names and descriptive copy (if any) on the page(s), determining the menu's format, choosing the correct typeface and paper, and integrating artwork into the menu. Although these steps are presented separately in this section, in reality many layout decisions are made simultaneously because layout elements are so interrelated.

Sequence. A meal has a beginning, a middle, and an end. When there are no separate appetizer and dessert menus, menu items sometimes appear on the menu in the following order: appetizers and soups first, entrées next, and desserts last. The placement of other menu items, such as side orders, salads, sandwiches, beverages, and so on, will depend on the operation and the meal period. Salads may be listed with the entrées at lunch and with the appetizers at dinner. Alcoholic beverages are not listed at all on breakfast menus but may be listed first on dinner menus.

The order in which the various items are placed within their categories is usually determined by popularity and profitability. Based on menu engineering results, the most popular and/or most profitable items are typically placed so guests can find them easily. The least popular and/or least profitable items are usually found in less desirable locations on the menu. There are many ways to draw attention to a menu item: putting it at or near the top of a list, drawing a box around it, placing it in the center of a page, using a photo, positioning eye-catching artwork next to it, or otherwise setting it apart.

Placement. Once menu items have been placed in a tentative order, designers or the menu planning team can make a rough sketch of the menu. This can include boxes or a series of horizontal lines to represent the approximate space the descriptive copy for each menu item will require. Room must also be set aside for supplemental merchandising copy. If artwork has been chosen, space should be allowed for it as well. If the menu is simply being revised, the existing menu's format often helps to decide item placement.

It is important not to make the menu too crowded. A generous use of *white space*, blank areas that help guide the eye toward important content, should be permitted.

If an operation uses a clip-on regularly, blank space should be provided for it on the regular menu because many guests will not lift up a clip-on to see what is printed beneath it.

Format. Format refers to a menu's size, shape, and general makeup. There are many menu formats to choose from (see Exhibit 3), and decision-makers at each operation must decide what is right for them. There are a few general guidelines to keep in mind, however. A menu that is too large may dominate a small table or cause guests to knock over glasses when they pick it up. Menus that are too small are hard to read and often overcrowded. Menus with too many pages may confuse guests.

Some adjustments may be necessary when adjusting the size and format of the menu. If there are too many menu items, adjustments may include: (1) eliminating some menu items, (2) reducing the descriptive copy, (3) shortening the supplemental merchandising copy, or (4) changing to a format with more space. If

Exhibit 3   Menu Formats

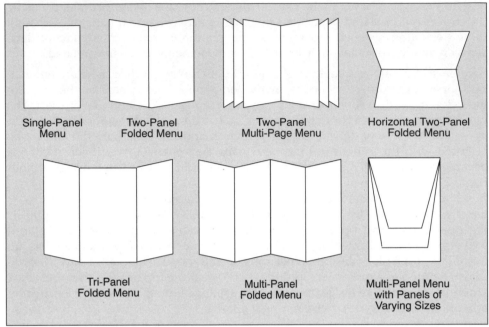

Single-Panel Menu

Two-Panel Folded Menu

Two-Panel Multi-Page Menu

Horizontal Two-Panel Folded Menu

Tri-Panel Folded Menu

Multi-Panel Folded Menu

Multi-Panel Menu with Panels of Varying Sizes

there are not enough menu items to fill the space, options include: (1) adding more menu items, (2) using the extra room for artwork, more extensive descriptions of menu items, or cross-selling of other aspects of the business (for example, describing a Sunday brunch on the property's dinner menu), (3) allowing more white space, or (4) changing to a smaller format or a larger typeface.

Typeface. Some operations that want to project an informal, relaxed image use hand-lettered menus. Most menus, however, are printed. How well guests can read the menu is determined to a large extent by the typeface used. The smaller the type, the harder it is to read. A larger typeface is especially helpful in children's and seniors' menus, and in menus that will be read in subdued lighting. A good general rule is to never set menu copy in anything smaller than twelve-point type. (The size of the copy in this paragraph is ten-point type.)

There should be a comfortable amount of space (called *leading*) between lines of type. In general, words should be a dark color printed on light-colored paper for easy reading. Menu designers would be wise to remember that lighting in restaurant dining rooms is usually much dimmer than in office areas where menus are designed.

It is generally easier to read a combination of uppercase and lowercase letters than all capitals. Headings, menu item names, and other information requiring special emphasis should be the only copy (if any) in all uppercase letters.

Some typeface has a dark, heavy appearance on the page, while other typefaces create an open, light feeling. The typeface chosen should reflect the operation's personality, but the typeface must communicate. If a strange or hard-to-read typeface is used, guests may react negatively and sales may suffer.

Drafts of the menu should be reviewed to see how the type looks and whether more adjustments are necessary. If the menu appears too crowded, for example, planners may choose to enlarge the menu, use a different typeface, or retain the same typeface in a smaller point size. After the changes are made, another careful review is necessary to ensure that the change(s) solved the problems.

Artwork. Artwork includes drawings, photographs, the property's logo, and borders used to attract interest, highlight menu copy, and reinforce the operation's image. If artwork will be included on the menu, it should be compatible with the theme, interior design, and/or overall decorative scheme of the property. Artwork should not be so plentiful or complicated that the guest is overwhelmed or the menu is difficult to read. A cluttered, confusing menu is not inviting to guests and makes ordering difficult and time-consuming.

A freelance artist can create original art for the menu, or the printers can copy graphics and illustrations that are in the public domain. In addition, desktop publishing software provides a seemingly infinite variety of graphic alternatives. (For example, see www.stocklayouts.com; click on "menu" on the site's home page.)

Paper. Most menus are handled by guests. The kind of paper on which the menu is printed communicates something about the operation to guests. An upscale operation's menu may be printed on expensive textured paper. A deli may use an ordinary sheet of paper for its menu.

There are many different kinds of paper, and its texture can vary from coarse to silky smooth. Paper varies in how shiny or reflective it is. Too much reflection causes glare and makes reading the menu difficult. Paper also differs in strength, opacity (the amount of transparency), and ink receptivity. And, of course, paper comes in every color imaginable, so menus do not have to be printed on white paper.

A menu's pages can be foil-stamped, which involves applying a thin foil film onto the paper. The foil can be artwork or copy, such as the name of the restaurant. Paper can be embossed; that is, an image can be stamped in relief on the paper. Paper can be laminated (sealed in thin sheets of plastic) to protect it from stains and tears. Paper can be folded and die-cut for interesting designs. As mentioned earlier, children's menus often come in unusual shapes, and may even include pop-up art.

The right paper depends in part on how often the menu will be handled. If the menu will be disposable, it can be printed on inexpensive paper. However, if the menu will be handled repeatedly over time, a water-resistant paper that can withstand rough usage would be suitable.

The entire menu need not be printed on the same kind of paper. The cover can be a heavier, coated paper stock while the inside pages can be lighter and less expensive.

Cover

Many menu formats feature a cover. A well-designed cover communicates the image, style, cuisine, and even the price range of the operation. It helps set the mood and creates expectations of the dining experience offered.

The name of the restaurant is generally all that is necessary on the cover. Some menus also include such basic information as the operation's address, phone number, and hours of operation. However, covers should not appear cluttered. Basic information can also be printed on the back cover, along with supplemental merchandising copy.

For most restaurants, cover stock should be heavy, durable, and grease-resistant (or laminated). The cover's design must be suitable to the operation. If the restaurant looks like an English pub, the cover should match this decor; a steakhouse's cover may have images of the Old West.

The colors on the cover should either blend in or contrast pleasantly with the color scheme of the restaurant. Colors must be chosen with care, because they produce many conscious and subconscious effects. Colors can make people feel happy, sad, celebratory, and so on. Pastel colors suggest a warm, soothing atmosphere; deep purples and reds suggest richness and opulence. Ethnic menus often have colors appropriate to the culture the food comes from. Bright reds, yellows, and oranges against a sand-colored paper suggest Mexico; black and red suggest Japanese or Chinese food; the colors of the Italian flag—red, white, and green—are often used on menus in Italian restaurants.

Although most of a menu's colors are usually found on the cover, color may also be used on the interior pages, usually on a more limited basis. Color can be used in the background, as trim, or in artwork to create a mood or draw the guest's eye to specific items.

Color gives the menu variety but increases its cost. Using one color, usually black, is the least expensive; four-color printing uses all the colors in the spectrum and is the most expensive.

Common Menu-Design Mistakes

Common menu-design mistakes include the following:

- *Menu is too small.* Crowded menus are usually unappealing and are not effective sales tools because they are harder to read.

- *Type is too small.* Not every guest has 20/20 vision, and lighting in some dining rooms is dim. Guests cannot order what they cannot read.

Look at the Menu Like the Guests See It

The likes and dislikes of the menu planning team should not be a priority concern when menus are planned and designed. It is always better to constantly ask the question "What would our guests like?" as menu decisions are made.

The principle of looking at the menu as the guests do also applies after the menu has been implemented and is in daily use. Is each menu clean, crisp, unwrinkled, and unstained? Does each menu do a good job of representing the food service operation? Too often, these types of details are overlooked in the rush of business. Looking over each menu every day before it is offered to a guest should be a responsibility of every receptionist, server, and dining manager.

- *No or inadequate descriptive copy.* Sometimes the name of the menu item does not describe the item or sufficiently spark guest interest. Good descriptive copy increases sales.

- *Every item is treated the same.* A menu designer should use positioning, boxes, color, decorative borders, larger type, or some other device to call attention to the most profitable and/or best-selling items. If every menu item gets a low-key treatment or if every item is in bold capital letters surrounded by exclamation points, the items you want to sell will not stand out from the others.

- *Some of the operation's food and beverages are not listed.* Some operations do not list all of the wines or specialty drinks they offer, or the menu states "Selected Desserts" rather than listing the available desserts. How can guests order items not on the menu? A better tactic is to note that a wine list is available (if there is an extensive selection) and train service staff to offer it. Likewise, if there are numerous desserts and/or if selections change frequently, the menu designer should add a notation like "Our service staff will tempt you with today's dessert selections," or develop a special dessert menu.

- *Clip-on problems.* Operations that regularly use a clip-on should allow blank space on the menu so the clip-on does not hide important menu items. The clip-on should match the design and quality of the menu. A disorganized clip-on poorly printed on inferior paper can destroy the effect of a well-designed and expensive menu.

- *Basic information about the property is not included.* It is surprising how many restaurants do not include their address, phone number, hours of operation, website address, and payment policies on the menu.

- *Blank pages.* A blank menu page does nothing to sell the restaurant or its menu items. The back cover is the page left blank on many menus. Unless the blank cover adds to the restaurant's image, the restaurant should put additional or supplemental merchandising copy there. For example, a seafood restaurant could devote its back cover to a list of the types of fish it serves and their unique flavor and texture characteristics.

Evaluating Menus

No matter how well planned and designed they are, menus should be evaluated periodically.

General Menu Evaluation Tactics

In order to thoroughly evaluate a menu, management must first set goals that the menu is expected to help meet. For example, a goal for the lunch meal period might be, "The average guest check should be $6." A goal for dinner might be, "Each dinner guest should order something in addition to the entrée—an appetizer, a soup or salad, a glass of wine, or a dessert." If these goals are not met, management must first determine if and to what extent other variables are contributing to the problem. Are food and beverage items meeting the operation's quality standards?

Technology and the Menu

Technology can assist with the on-site display of menus. For example, digital menus or electronic display boards or screens can show a menu with video, audio, and print. These are increasingly displayed in quick-service restaurants but also have applications to other types of properties, including those in other hospitality segments. This technology allows managers to quickly change menus when, for example, prices change or when they add nutritional data.

Some menus can even "talk." Menus That Talk (www.menusthattalk.com) is a book-sized device that allows diners to push buttons to hear about different menu items. The device could be useful for guests with visual impairments and in locations where guests speak and read languages other than that in which the menu is written (menu translation is available in any language).

Guests in many lodging operations can view menus on guestroom TV sets. Guests can often order room service items directly through this interactive medium.

Are food servers doing a good job of trying to sell additional food items through suggestive selling techniques? If these and other variables check out, managers must then take a serious look at the menu.

Menus vary greatly, and each operation must establish its own methods of evaluation. General questions that most food and beverage managers can ask when evaluating a menu include the following:

- Have guests either complained about or praised the menu?

- How does the menu compare with those of competitors?

- Has the guest-check average remained steady or increased?

- Is there enough variety in menu items?

- Are menu items priced correctly?

- Is the right mix of higher- and lower-profit items being sold?

- Is the menu attractive?

- Do the colors and other design elements match the operation's theme and decor?

- Are menu items laid out attractively and logically?

- Is there too much descriptive copy? Not enough? Is the copy easy to understand?

- Is attention called to the items managers most want to sell, through placement, color, description, type size, etc.?

- Is the typeface easy to read and appropriate to the restaurant's theme and decor?

- Does the paper match the restaurant's theme and decor?

- Are menus easy to maintain so that guests always receive a clean, attractive menu?

Operations can create their own menu rating forms with these and other questions listed on the form and grouped into categories such as design, layout, copy, and merchandising. When establishing evaluation factors and creating evaluation forms, managers should keep in mind that an evaluation is worthless unless enough information comes out of it to help menu planners improve the menu.

Menu Engineering

Many production and sales benchmarks can help managers evaluate a menu. Production records and electronic sales history records can indicate how well menu items are selling. **Menu engineering** allows managers to study the impact of two critical variables—popularity and profitability—on each menu item. Menu engineering is not difficult or time-consuming, but it does require the use of precosted standard recipes.

Menu engineering software processes menu mix and contribution margin data for each item on a menu. The resulting information enables managers to evaluate possible changes to a menu's current mix of items and to make sound pricing decisions. A full discussion of menu engineering is beyond the scope of this text.[2] This section presents only a broad overview of the concept.

Menu mix relates the sales of a particular menu item to the total number of menu items sold. A menu mix percentage is calculated by dividing the number sold of a specific menu item by the total number of all menu items sold. Each item on the menu is then categorized as either high or low in popularity.

The contribution margin of a menu item is calculated by subtracting its food costs from its selling price. An item's contribution margin is categorized as either high or low by comparing it with the average contribution margin of all items on the menu. This analysis produces the following classifications:

- Stars—items high in both popularity and contribution margin
- Plowhorses—items high in popularity but low in contribution margin

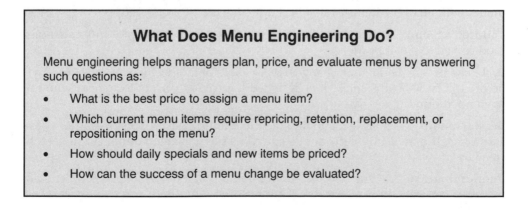

What Does Menu Engineering Do?

Menu engineering helps managers plan, price, and evaluate menus by answering such questions as:

- What is the best price to assign a menu item?
- Which current menu items require repricing, retention, replacement, or repositioning on the menu?
- How should daily specials and new items be priced?
- How can the success of a menu change be evaluated?

- Puzzles—items low in popularity but high in contribution margin
- Dogs—items low in popularity and low in contribution margin

Commercial operations want to increase sales of stars and puzzles. Managers in such nonprofit operations as schools and subsidized business/industry operations can also use menu engineering. Their goal is to maximize the service of popular and low-food-cost items. Menu engineering software identifies practical approaches by which to reengineer the next menu. For example, simple strategies would include retaining stars, repricing plowhorses, repositioning puzzles, and removing dogs.

Endnotes

1. See, for example, Jack D. Ninemeier and David K. Hayes, *Menu Planning, Design, and Evaluation,* 2nd ed. (Richmond, Cal.: McCutchan Publishing Corp., 2008).

2. Menu engineering is discussed at length in Jack D. Ninemeier, *Planning and Control for Food and Beverage Operations,* 8th ed. (Lansing, Mich.: American Hotel & Lodging Educational Institute, 2013).

Key Terms

à la carte menu—A menu in which food and beverage items are listed and priced separately.

aesthetic balance—In menu planning, the degree to which meals have been constructed with an eye to complementary colors, textures, and flavors of foods.

alcoholic beverage menu—A menu that lists cocktails, wines, and other alcoholic beverages an operation offers to guests.

banquet menu—Usually a table d'hôte menu that includes preordered meals with few, if any, choices served to a group of diners.

business balance—In menu planning, the balance among food costs, menu prices, the popularity of items, and other financial and marketing considerations.

California menu—A menu that offers breakfast, lunch, and dinner items on one menu, with all of the items available at any time the property is open.

children's menu—A menu for children featuring familiar, simple, and nutritious food served in small portions.

cycle menu—A menu that changes every day for a specified number of days before the cycle begins again; it is designed to provide variety for guests who eat at an operation frequently.

dessert menu—A separate menu designed to remind guests of the operation's dessert items. It may list desserts not listed on the regular menu and include dessert specials.

doorknob menu—A type of room service menu that a housekeeper or other staff member can leave in a guestroom. Guests select what they want to eat and the time they want the food delivered, then hang the menu outside the door on the doorknob.

ethnic menu—A menu featuring a particular cuisine. Examples include Chinese, Mexican, and Italian menus.

fixed menu—A menu that is used for several months or longer before it is changed. Daily specials may be offered, but a set list of items forms the basic menu.

make-buy analysis—The process of objectively determining quality and cost differences between alternative products that can be made on-site or purchased from one or more suppliers.

menu engineering—A process that helps managers evaluate possible changes in a menu's offerings and make sound pricing decisions based upon popularity and profitability factors.

menu mix—Relates the sales of a menu item to the total number of menu items sold.

microbrewery—A brewery that makes small quantities of specialty beers for consumption on-site or for distribution within a small geographic area.

nutritional balance—In menu planning, the degree to which the menu offers a variety of foods in the basic food groups.

prix fixe menu—A menu that offers a complete meal for one price. Meals on prix fixe (French for *fixed price*) menus are set by the menu planner, and guests are given few, if any, choices. Also referred to as a table d'hôte menu.

room service menu—A menu offered by lodging properties that serve food to guests in their guestrooms, suites, cabins, and so on.

senior citizens' menu—A menu that seeks to accommodate seniors and their special health needs by offering lower-priced items that are low in calories, sodium, fat, or cholesterol.

table d'hôte menu—A menu that offers a complete meal for one price. Meals on table d'hôte menus are set by the menu planner, and guests are given few, if any, choices. Also called a prix fixe menu.

take-out menu—A menu that offers food to guests who want to pick up their food at the restaurant and consume it elsewhere.

truth-in-menu laws—Laws that seek to protect guests by prohibiting inaccurate claims on the menu in such areas as freshness, geographical origin, and food preparation techniques.

Review Questions

1. What are the three basic menu pricing styles?

2. What is a fixed menu? a cycle menu?

3. What are the differences between breakfast, lunch, and dinner menus?

4. What are specialty menus?

5. What are three basic rules in menu planning?

6. What five operational components have a direct impact on the kinds of menu items an operation offers?

7. In what three ways should a menu be balanced?

8. Into what three elements can menu copy be divided?

9. What are some common menu-design mistakes?

10. What are some of the questions food and beverage managers should ask when evaluating a menu?

11. How does menu engineering help menu planners to evaluate menus?

12. How does menu engineering software help managers to plan, price, and evaluate menus?

 **Internet Sites** ⎯⎯⎯⎯⎯⎯⎯⎯⎯⎯⎯⎯⎯⎯⎯⎯⎯⎯⎯⎯⎯⎯⎯⎯⎯

For more information, visit the following Internet sites. Remember that Internet addresses can change without notice. If the site is no longer there, you can use a search engine to look for additional sites.

Menu Planning and Design Resources

Adobe PageMaker
www.adobe.com/products/pagemaker/

CALCMENU
www.eg-software.com

Adobe Photoshop
www.adobe.com/products/photoshop

Resort Software
www.resortsoftware.com

Cafe Creosote Dictionary
www.cafecreosote.com/dictionary.php3

Recipe Sources for Menu Planning

Food Network
www.foodnetwork.com (enter "restaurant recipes" in the site's search box)

Recipe Goldmine
www.recipegoldmine.com/

Sysco Corporation
www.sysco.com (enter "recipes" in the site's search box)

Razzle Dazzle Recipes
www.razzledazzlerecipes.com/
quantity

Online Menus

Most food service operations have websites, many of which feature applicable menus. Use a search engine to look up your favorite restaurants' websites to view their menus.

History of Menus

The Food Timeline
www.foodtimeline.org

New York Public Library Menu
 Collection
http://menus.nypl.org

Chapter 7 Outline

Standard Recipes
    Recipe Management Software
    Developing Standard Recipes
    Adjusting Standard Recipe Yields
Determining Standard Portion Costs for
    Menu Items
    Calculating Standard Portion Costs
    Calculating Total Meal Costs
Determining Total Standard Food Costs
Determining Standard Portion Costs for
    Beverages
Pricing Menu Items
    Desired Food Cost Percentage Markup
    Profit Pricing
    Competition and Pricing

Competencies

1. Discuss the benefits of standard recipes, and explain the procedures involved in using standard recipes. (pp. 155–163)

2. Summarize what is involved in determining standard portion costs for menu items, total standard food costs, and standard portion costs for beverages. (pp. 163–169)

3. Describe the four subjective menu pricing methods, explain the value of the two main objective pricing methods, and describe the role of pricing in managing a successful, competitive food and beverage operation. (pp. 169–172)

7

Managing Food Costs and Menu Pricing Strategies

WHEN PLANNING MENUS, managers must consider guests and the financial goals of the food service operation. It is important to know what the food costs *should* be to produce each item planned for the menu. This chapter explains how these costs can be determined for menu items prepared according to standard recipes. When food cost information is determined for all menu items sold, managers will have a benchmark with which to monitor actual food costs and evaluate how well the operation is meeting its financial objectives.

Final sections of the chapter address various menu pricing methods. These are important to commercial food service operations and many noncommercial food service facilities that, for example, provide some or only à la carte priced items. To ensure that the operation's financial goals are met, managers must be able to determine the most effective selling price for each menu item.

Standard Recipes

A standard recipe is a formula for producing a food (or beverage) item. It specifies the required quantity of each ingredient, preparation procedures, portion size and portioning equipment, garnish, and any other information necessary to prepare the item.

Exhibit 1 shows a sample standard recipe for one menu item, chicken salad. Note that this recipe yields 100 portions, each with a portion size of one cup. The recipe clearly indicates ingredients, weights, measures, and exact procedures for preparing the menu item.

The single most important advantage of using standard recipes is consistency. When standard recipes are followed correctly, items produced will be consistent in quality, flavor, and portion size. This consistency creates satisfied guests and enables a food service operation to build a solid base of repeat business. Also, when food service operations produce consistent products, managers can determine accurate food costs. Managers need consistent information to help ensure that the operation meets its financial goals. If a menu item's food cost changes every time it is made because the staff varies types and quantities of ingredients and portion sizes, managers will have no reliable cost information to help them keep food costs in line with budgeted food costs. Other advantages of using standard recipes include the following:

Exhibit 1   Sample Standard Food Recipe

STANDARD RECIPE FOR CHICKEN SALAD			
YIELD: 100 Portions	Each Portion: 1 Cup		
INGREDIENTS	**WEIGHTS**	**MEASURES**	**PROCEDURES**
Chicken (broiler/fryer)	65 lb		1. Place chicken in steam kettle or stock pot; add water, salt, and bay leaves. Bring to a boil; reduce heat; simmer 2 hours or until tender.
Water		9½ gal	
Salt	7 oz	⅔ cup	
Bay leaves		9 leaves	
Celery, chopped	12 lb	2¼ gal	2. Remove chicken; remove meat from bones. Cut into ½- to 1-inch pieces.
Sweet peppers, chopped	1 lb 8 oz	1 qt	
Onions, chopped	8 oz	1½ cups	3. Add these ingredients; mix thoroughly.
Lemon juice		1 cup	4. Blend these ingredients together. Add to chicken-vegetable mixture. Mix lightly, but thoroughly. Refrigerate until ready to serve.
Salad dressing	3 lb 4 oz	6½ cups	
Salt	4 oz	6 TBSP	
Pepper		1TBSP	

Source: Wisconsin Department of Agriculture, Trade and Consumer Protection—Division of Food Safety.

- More efficient purchasing practices result when managers know the exact amounts of ingredients necessary to produce menu items.

- When managers know that the standard recipe yields a specific number of standard-size portions, it is less likely that too many or too few items will be prepared.

- Less supervision is required since standard recipes tell the employees the quantity and preparation method for each item. Guesswork is eliminated; employees need only follow recipe procedures. Of course, managers should routinely evaluate the quality of items to ensure that standard recipes are followed correctly.

- If the chef is not at work, other employees can still produce food items by following standard recipes. Granted, inexperienced employees will be slow and may make mistakes. However, if the recipe is only known by an absent employee instead of on a standard recipe card or in a computer database, managers will be in an even more awkward position.

Using a standard recipe does not require that the recipe be physically in the work area during production times. After cooks prepare a menu item several times, they will remember ingredients, quantities, and procedures. A standard recipe must always be followed and must always be available, but it does not always need to be read as the item is prepared.

Today, many operations use computerized recipes. Production managers can estimate the quantity of portions required for a future shift, generate a recipe that has been electronically adjusted to yield the required number of portions, print the recipe required for a specific shift, and make it available in the applicable work station. For example, bake shop recipes can be taken to that area; recipes for cold food items can be delivered to the garde-manger work station. A sample computer-generated recipe is shown in Exhibit 2. Note that one ingredient, enchilada sauce, is actually a subrecipe (indicated by "SUBR 2643"). This ingredient is used for a number of menu items and can be produced in large quantities for use with several dishes.[1]

Recipe Management Software

Recipe management software maintains three of the most important files used in an integrated food service computer system: an ingredient file, a standard recipe file, and a menu item file. Most other management software programs must be able to access data contained within these files to produce special reports for management.

Ingredient File. An **ingredient file** contains important data about each purchased ingredient, including the following:

- Purchase unit (for example, 50-lb. case of shrimp; 10 5-lb. boxes per case) and cost per purchase unit

- Issue unit (for example, 5-lb. box of shrimp) and cost per issue unit

- Recipe unit (for example, 3-lb. of shrimp) and cost per recipe unit

Some ingredient files may specify more than one recipe unit. For example, the recipe unit for bread used for French toast is slices; the recipe unit for bread used for stuffing may be ounces.

The initial creation and updating (of purchase prices, for example) of an ingredient file can be challenging. The benefits, however, outweigh the cost of creating and maintaining the file. The best systems allow the ingredient file to be accessed by other management software programs, including inventory software, so ingredient data can easily be transferred (rather than be re-input) to appropriate management software programs. Since other management software programs rely on data from the ingredient file, it is important that the data contained in the file be accurate.

Standard Recipe File. A **standard recipe file** contains recipes for all menu items. Computers simplify and ensure the accuracy of calculations needed to adjust recipes to yield quantities required by sales forecasts. Standard recipe conversion software converts ingredient amounts from purchase units (such as pounds) to production units (such as ounces). It can also calculate nutritional data for a meal or menu item, and it can identify whether ingredients should be issued to a specific workstation within the preparation area.

Exhibit 2   Sample Computer-Generated Recipe

Report #:90	***CBORD Foodservice Management Systems***	
Option: 3.5.8	Menu Management System –V6.23	May 05 XX
Usher # :28	MSU Residence Halls Fall - Lcode 1	1540 Hours
	Production Recipe	

Function Name:

Unit:

Date: Friday   05/05/XX

0084	Burrito Wet Meat (Beef & Turkey)	
		Yield: 1.80 SCP

Portions:	30.00	8.30 oz	Cooking TIme:	25 Min.
Portion Desc:	1 Burrito		Cooking Temp:	350F
Prep Time:			Cooking Equip:	Oven
			Serving Pan:	Shallow Counter Pan
Prepare Main Batch		1 Time(s)	Serving Uten:	Spatula

Ingredient	Main Batch Quantity			Partial Batch Quantity
Revised 12/20/96				
Ground Turkey	2lb	8		oz
Ground Beef	1lb	4		oz
Onions		4	¾	oz
Taco Seasoning		1	¾	oz
Salt		1	¼	oz
Refried Beans	1 qt	3	½	cup
10" Die Cut Tortilla		30		each
Enchilada Sauce SUBR 2643		3	¾	cup
Garnish				
Lettuce Shredded		7	¼	oz
Tomatoes Diced		14	½	oz
Mild Shredded Cheddar		7	¼	oz

1. Brown both ground meats together (be sure they are well mixed) with onions.

2. Drain off fat. Add taco seasoning and salt, mix well. Adjust seasoning if necessary.

3. Add beans to seasoned meat and mix well.

4. Make sauce and hold at a minimum internal temp of 145F.

5. To assemble burritos: place a #12 scoop of filling (4 oz) on lower ⅓ of tortilla. Fold in sides first then roll starting at the bottom to cover filling.

6. Place 16 in each SCP.

7. Cover pans with plastic wrap and foil. Bake in a 350F oven for 25 minutes or until an internal temp of 155F is reached.

8. Uncover and ladle 16 oz of sauce over each pan of burritos.

9. Just before service sprinkle on 4 oz shredded lettuce, 4 oz cheese and 8 oz diced tomatoes.

Note: Heat flour tortillas on a 300F grill for approx. 30 seconds. This will make the tortillas flexible and easy to fold.

Few food service operations purchase all menu items in ready-to-use or pre-portioned form. Some items are made on-site. This means that the ingredients within a standard recipe file may be either inventory items or references to other recipe files (called subrecipes).

Including subrecipes as ingredients for a particular standard recipe is called **chaining recipes**. This enables the computer system to maintain a single record for a particular menu item that includes a number of subrecipes. When ingredient costs change, recipe management software programs automatically update not only the costs of standard recipes, but also the costs of subrecipes that are used as ingredients. (Recall the example of enchilada sauce in Exhibit 2.)

Menu Item File. A menu item file contains information related to the menu items tracked by an integrated **point-of-sale (POS) system**, such as recipe code number, selling price, ingredient quantities for inventory reporting, and sales totals (by unit).

The file also stores historical information about the actual number of items sold. Increasingly, sales data is automatically transferred from an electronic cash register or POS system through an interface to the restaurant's management system. This data can be used to project future unit sales, determine the number of ingredient quantities to purchase, and schedule necessary personnel. It can also produce various sales analysis reports for management.

Developing Standard Recipes

The process of developing standard recipes does not require throwing out existing recipes and starting over. Rather, it requires standardizing existing recipes according to a series of steps.

Managers should select a time period for standard recipe development. For example, they may choose to standardize three recipes at each weekly cooks' meeting. At these meetings, the manager should ask the cook or head bartender to talk through the preparation of the item. What are the ingredients? How much of each ingredient is required? What are the exact procedures? What are cooking/baking temperatures and times? What portion-control tools are, or can be, used? On what plate or bowl is the item served? What garnish is used? Managers should double-check the recipe by closely observing as the cook actually prepares the item.

The recipes should be recorded in a standard format that will be helpful to those preparing the items. For example, managers could do the following:

- Decide on the desirable yield. If 75 portions of a food item are prepared for slow periods and 150 portions are prepared for busy times, recipes can be designed to yield both quantities.

- List all ingredients in the order used.

- Decide whether to use weights or measures or both. Weighing is always more precise than measuring and it is just as practical to weigh liquids and flour as it is to measure them. Exhibit 3 presents some equivalent weights and measures. Avoid confusion by using consistent abbreviations throughout all the standard recipes.

Exhibit 3   Equivalent Weights and Measures

1 pound	=	16 ounces	$^3/_4$ cup	=	12 tablespoons
1 tablespoon	=	3 teaspoons	1 cup	=	16 tablespoons
$^1/_4$ cup	=	4 tablespoons	1 quart	=	4 cups
$^1/_2$ cup	=	8 tablespoons	1 gallon	=	4 quarts
$^1/_3$ cup	=	5$^1/_3$ tablespoons (or 16 teaspoons)	2 pints	=	1 quart
$^2/_3$ cup	=	10$^2/_3$ tablespoons (or 32 teaspoons)	2 cups	=	1 pint

- Whenever possible, express all quantities in amounts that are most practical for those preparing the item. For example, convert all measures into the largest possible units. Change ⅛ cup to ½ cup, four cups to one quart, or three teaspoons to one tablespoon. At this point, make sure that the proper measuring and weighing tools are available. It does little good to specify a three-ounce quantity or two tablespoons of an ingredient if the tools to weigh and measure are not available. Also, when applicable, recipes should use standard-size pans and other equipment.

- Record procedures in detailed, concise, and exact terms. Avoid ambiguous statements. For example, what does "one cup whipping cream" mean? Does it mean one cup of cream that has been whipped or does it mean one cup of cream that must be whipped? When mixing is called for, tell how to mix (by hand or by machine) and provide the exact time and speed if a machine is used. State the size and type of equipment needed and always list exact temperatures, cooking times, and other necessary directions.

- Provide directions for portioning. Indicate the type and size of the serving dish. Also, indicate portioning equipment, such as ladle or scoop, and specify the expected number and size of portions. List any needed garnishes or sauces.

After drafts of the standard recipes have been developed, share them with other production staff. Solicit their ideas about accuracy and possible improvements.

Finally, test the recipes to be certain they yield products of the desired quantity and quality. Some food service operations use a tasting committee or panel. This group may include management staff, cooks, other interested employees, and even guests. A rating scale similar to the one shown in Exhibit 4 can be used to evaluate a menu item on the basis of specific characteristics. For example, baked goods may be evaluated on the basis of external appearance and flavor; meats, on the basis of aroma, tenderness, and juiciness; vegetables, on the basis of color, moisture content, texture, and taste.

After successful testing, the recipe may be considered standardized. Production staff should now be given copies or, if a computerized system is used, the new recipes should be used for recipe calculations. Employees should be trained in their use and supervised to ensure compliance. Pictures of the finished product after portioning may give additional help to production and service staff.

Exhibit 4   Sample Menu Item Rating Scale

Name of
Menu Item: _____

Date: _____
Sample Number: _____

Instructions: Check (✓) your feeling toward
the characteristics specified for the menu
item being evaluated.

Characteristics

Your Rating:	Color	Moisture	Texture	Shape	Taste
Like Very Much					
Like Moderately					
Like Slightly					
Neither Like/Dislike					
Dislike Slightly					
Dislike Moderately					
Dislike Very Much					
Comments					

Despite the advantages of using standard recipes, there may be some difficulties when implementing them. Employees who have never used standard recipes may have negative attitudes about them. Cooks may feel that they can no longer be creative in the kitchen. Other difficulties may relate to concerns about time. It takes time to standardize existing recipes, and it takes time to train production employees to follow them.

These concerns, however, are minor when compared to the points already noted in favor of using standard recipes. Managers can minimize difficulties with implementing standard recipes by explaining to employees why standard recipes are necessary and by involving employees in developing and implementing them.

When standardizing a recipe, ensure that all required ingredients will be available as long as the menu is used. Seafood, certain fruits, or fresh mushrooms may not be available or may become very expensive as they go out of season. Managers may wish to exclude such items from the menu or, to avoid disappointing guests, simply qualify their listing on the menu with phrases such as "when available."

All recipes must be tested. Even minor equipment and temperature variations can make a big difference in the quality of the item produced. Bake shop items are of special concern; altitude and humidity can affect the quantity of liquid, yeast, and other ingredients required. Managers should test the recipe and fine-tune it before adding the item to the menu.

When standardizing recipes from external sources, such as trade magazines, quantity food cookbooks, production staff members, and culinary and recipe websites, it is important to address operating concerns. Production and management staff must agree that the recipe is concise, accurate, and readable with regard to the following:

- Amounts of ingredients
- Types of ingredients
- Production and portioning procedures
- Service procedures

This agreement will ensure efficient use of time and energy and help eliminate human error as much as possible. Once the recipe has been adapted for use, the menu item's popularity with guests and the equipment, skills, and number of labor hours necessary to produce the item should be periodically reviewed.

Adjusting Standard Recipe Yields

The yield from a standard recipe can be easily increased or decreased through the use of an **adjustment factor**, which is determined by dividing the desired yield by the original yield. For example, if a recipe yields 100 portions, and you want 225 portions of the same size, the adjustment factor would be calculated as follows:

$$\text{Adjustment Factor} = \frac{225 \text{ portions (desired yield)}}{100 \text{ portions (original yield)}} = 2.25$$

Each recipe ingredient is then multiplied by the adjustment factor to determine the amount required for the desired yield. For example, if the original recipe required 8 ounces of sugar, the adjusted quantity would be:

$$\text{New Amount} = \underset{\text{(original amount)}}{8 \text{ oz}} \times \underset{\text{(adjustment factor)}}{2.25} = 18 \text{ oz (1 lb, 2 oz)}$$

Note that 18 ounces is equal to 1 pound, 2 ounces. If the kitchen has a scale that weighs only to 16 ounces, the quantity of sugar needed should also be expressed as 1 pound, 2 ounces. If the scale weighs to 2 pounds or more, the amount of sugar can be expressed as 18 ounces.

A similar process can be used to produce the same number of portions with a different portion size. Assume a recipe yields 40 12-ounce portions, and 40 8-ounce portions are required:

$$\frac{\text{Desired Portion}}{\text{Original Portion}} = \text{Adjustment Factor}$$

$$\frac{8 \text{ oz}}{12 \text{ oz}} = 0.67 \text{ (rounded)}$$

Each ingredient in the original recipe can now be multiplied by this factor to determine the quantity of ingredients needed for the required yield. Assume a recipe requires 20 pounds of ground beef to yield 40 12-ounce servings, and 40 8-ounce portions are needed.

$$\text{New Amount} = \underset{\text{(original amount)}}{20 \text{ lb}} \times \underset{\text{(adjustment factor)}}{0.67} = 13.4 \text{ lb}$$

A recipe can also be adjusted when both the number of portions *and* the portion size change. First, determine the total volume of the original and desired amounts, then calculate the adjustment factor. For example, if a recipe yields 50 4-ounce servings and the desired yield is 75 6-ounce servings, the adjustment factor would be:

$$\frac{\text{Total Volume of Desired Yield}}{\text{Total Volume of Original Yield}} = \text{Adjustment Factor}$$

Total Volume of Desired Yield = 75 portions × 6 oz/portion = 450 oz
Total Volume of Original Yield = 50 portions × 4 oz/portion = 200 oz

$$\frac{450 \text{ oz}}{200 \text{ oz}} = 2.25$$

Using an adjustment factor can provide accurate ingredient quantities when the total volume of a recipe's yield does not change significantly. However, an adjustment factor for a recipe in which the yield changes substantially must be used carefully. It is unlikely that a recipe yielding 10 portions of a specific size can merely be multiplied by an adjustment factor of 100 to yield 1,000 portions of the same size.

In such situations, it is best to start with the indicated adjustment factor and then carefully modify it until the recipe yields the desired volume. Another tactic is to adjust the recipe until you have the number of portions required for a specific pan size (a 12" × 20" × 2" counter pan, for example). Then determine the number of pans needed to yield the required portions. Assume, for example, that a recipe yielding 20 portions is adjusted to yield 50 portions, the number of portions in one pan. If 250 portions are needed, the recipe modified for 50 portions can be adjusted (multiplied by 5) to yield the desired amount. Likewise, be careful when calculating revised quantities for spices and herbs. It is often best to add these ingredients on a "to taste" basis until you are certain about the exact quantity needed.

Many recipe software packages automatically adjust standard recipes to increase or decrease the number of portions and/or portion sizes, and they do so quickly and with great accuracy. However, there is one potential disadvantage to electronic recipe adjustments: the weight or volume of each required ingredient may be rounded to a relatively unusable amount, and some slight adjustment may be necessary. For example, a cook is unlikely to be able to accurately weigh "1.63 pounds" or measure "2.17 teaspoons." For most recipes, it is probably appropriate to round up or down to the approximate quantity needed. However, when precise measurements are required, some manual attention to electronic calculations may be necessary.

Determining Standard Portion Costs for Menu Items

After standard recipes and standard portion sizes have been established, **standard portion costs** for individual portions or entire dinners can be calculated. A portion cost is the cost of food incurred by preparing one portion of a menu item according to its standard recipe. By contrast, **total meal costs** are calculated for items that are combined to form meals that are priced and sold as one menu selection. For example, a fish amandine dinner may include salad and dressing, potato, vegetable, and bread and butter in addition to the fish entrée. The standard portion cost of each individual menu item must be calculated and combined to determine the cost for the complete meal.

Calculating Standard Portion Costs

A portion cost is determined by dividing the sum of the recipe's ingredient costs by the number of portions that the standard recipe yields. For example, if the food cost to prepare a recipe is $75.00 and it yields 50 portions, the portion cost for that recipe item is $1.50 ($75.00 ÷ 50 portions). The prices for ingredients listed in standard recipes can be obtained from current invoices.

Exhibit 5 shows an example of computerized **precosting** of a hamburger sandwich. The quantity (unit) for each ingredient is noted, as is the net cost for the quantity of each ingredient used. Other information includes the food cost percentage (food cost divided by selling price: 28.58%) and the gross margin (selling price minus food cost: $2.14).

Calculations made automatically with software have historically been made manually. Consider the hamburger buns in Exhibit 5. The ingredient file for this item indicates that it is purchased ready-made by the dozen for $1.993 per dozen. Electronic precosting, then, yields the bun cost in Exhibit 5:

Exhibit 5   Building the Cost of a Menu Item

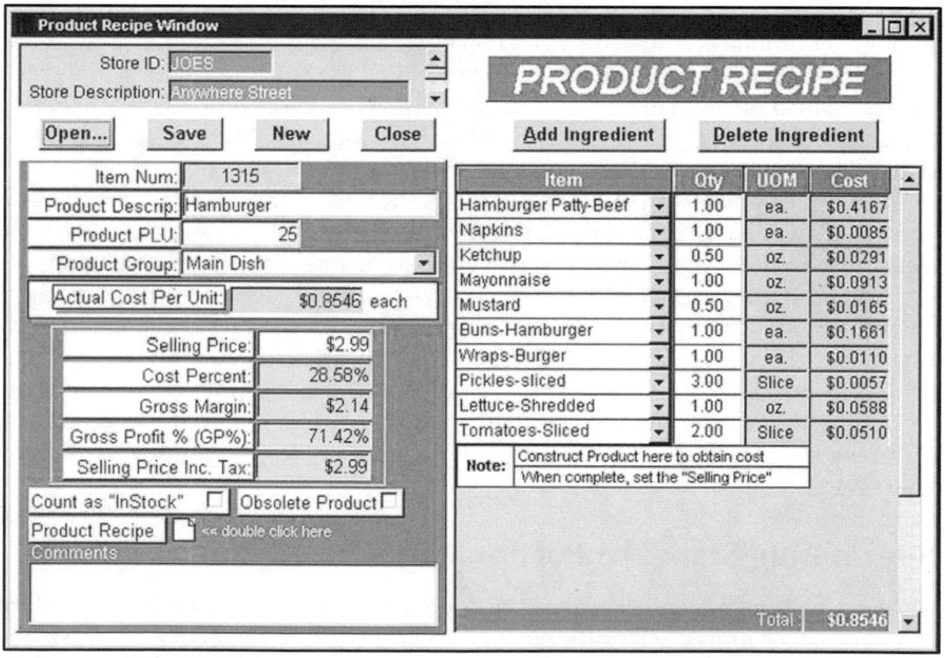

Courtesy of TracRite Software Inc. (www.tracrite.net).

$$\$1.993 \div 12^* = 0.1661$$

*Note: There are 12 buns in a package.

Calculating Total Meal Costs

The worksheet shown in Exhibit 6 provides a format for determining total meal costs for a combination of menu items sold at one price. The cost of each item listed on the worksheet is obtained from a precosted recipe for that item. In the example shown in Exhibit 6, the costs of items offered as part of the fish fillet amandine dinner are added to arrive at the total dinner cost of $4.14.

The vegetable varies from day to day, and guests have choices in the potato, dressing, and juice categories, so it is impractical to determine the total meal cost for all the different possible combinations. For categories in which the guests have a choice, managers might choose the cost of the most popular item in the category to determine the dinner cost. For example, if guests choose baked potatoes most often, the portion cost from the precosted recipe for baked potatoes would be used to calculate the dinner cost. It is also possible to select the item with the highest portion cost in a category and use that high portion-cost item when determining the total meal cost.

What happens when an ingredient cost changes? For example, what if the per-pound cost of ground beef rises from $3.55 to $3.78? All of the standard recipes containing this ingredient will need to be precosted. Food service operations with computerized precosting systems can quickly and accurately revise (recost) all recipes containing a particular ingredient to reflect the new per-portion costs of

Exhibit 6   Standard Total Meal Cost Worksheet

		Date of Precost
Name of Dinner *Fish Fillet Amandine*		*8/1/XX*
	Item	
Entrée	Fish Amandine	$1.99
Vegetable	du Jour	.32
Potato	Choice	.40
Salad	Tossed Green	.60
Dressing	Choice	.15
Juice	Tomato/Pineapple	.25
Bread	Loaf	.15
Butter	Butter	.06
Other		
Garnish	Orange/Lemon/Parsley	.10
Condiment	Cocktail Sauce	.12
		$4.14

the affected menu items. This use of technology makes it fast and simple to have consistently current and accurate information available for menu pricing, food cost control, and related financial purposes.

Determining Total Standard Food Costs

Managers use a control process to determine what the total **standard food cost** *should* be based on actual sales of each menu item and their standard portion costs. They also calculate what their **actual food costs** were based on food cost calculations.[2]

Today, most food service operations use POS systems to record the individual unit sales of specific menu items. It is relatively easy, then, to determine the actual number of each menu item sold. This information can be electronically tallied by hour, shift, or day, and can be added to determine the total number of sales for each menu item over any time period. Printouts typically indicate the food cost that should be incurred to produce all of the items sold during the trial period. Exhibit 7 shows a section of a computerized printout for a day's food sales. Let's take a close look at this printout:

- Column 1 indicates the menu category (in this case, *Dinners*). Other categories (not shown) in this type of report can include appetizers, sandwiches, salads, desserts, beers, and so on.

- Column 2 shows the code numbers used to identify menu items and track their sales.

- Column 3 lists the names of the menu items.

- Column 4 shows the number of each menu item sold during the period covered by the food cost report, such as one hour.

- Column 5 indicates the amount of revenue generated from the sale of each menu item. For example, revenues of $76.13 were generated from the sale of six steaks during the time period covered by this standard food cost report.

Exhibit 7   Standard Food Cost Report

(1) Category	(2) Item Num	(3) Item Name	(4) Num Sold	(5) Revenue	(6) Food Cost	(7) CM	(8) Food Cost %	(9) % Revenue	(10) % Cat Revenue
Dinners	6406	Steak	6	76.13	26.76	49.37	35.15	11.47	22.54
	6412	Chicken\nHalf	6	50.66	17.76	32.90	35.06	7.63	15.00
	6416	Turkey\nBreast	9	71.75	25.29	46.46	35.25	10.81	21.24
	6419	PorkChop	3	21.08	7.38	13.70	35.00	3.18	6.24
	6423	BarbRibs	6	50.66	17.76	32.90	35.06	7.63	15.00
	6426	FishPlatter	3	39.48	13.95	25.53	35.33	5.95	11.69
	20310	DinSalad	6	28.02	9.90	18.12	35.33	4.22	8.29
		Tot Dinners:	39	337.78	118.80	218.98	35.17	50.87	

- Column 6 indicates the food cost associated with producing each menu item. For example, food costs of $26.76 were incurred to sell the six steaks; food costs are calculated by multiplying the number of an item sold by the per-portion food cost identified in the precosted recipe.

- Column 7 shows the contribution margin for each menu item. **Contribution margin** is calculated by subtracting food costs from revenue. In the case of steaks, the revenue of $76.13 (Column 5) minus the food cost of $26.76 (Column 6) yields a contribution margin of $49.37.

- Column 8 shows the food cost percentage for each menu item. Food cost percentage is calculated by dividing the food cost by food revenue. For steaks, $26.76 ÷ $76.13 = 35.15 food cost percentage.

- Column 9 shows the total revenue for each menu item as a percentage of the revenue derived from all food and beverage items. For example, revenue from the sale of steaks was 11.47 percent of the total food and beverage revenue generated by the operation during the time period covered by this report.

- Column 10 shows the percentage of menu category revenue for each menu item. In the case of steaks, the menu category is *Dinners* (see Column 1). Revenue from the sale of steaks was 22.54 percent of all dinner revenue for the time covered by this standard food cost report.

A report similar to the one shown in Exhibit 7 can be printed for each hour, day, week, or other time period desired.

The ideal (theoretical) food cost for all food items sold during an accounting period such as one month can be calculated. For example, in Exhibit 7, the total food cost incurred to produce all dinners during the time period covered by the report was $118.80 (in Column 6). This will suggest what food costs should be for the accounting period. This figure, summed with its counterparts for the entire month or other accounting period, must be compared to actual food costs for the period.

By comparing the ideal (theoretical) food cost with the actual food cost for all items in all categories, managers can assess the performance of the food service operation. If the actual food cost is greater than the total standard food cost, managers need to investigate the cause(s) and, when necessary, take corrective action. This is important, because bottom-line profit is reduced by one dollar for each dollar that food costs are higher than required: Every dollar that can be saved by reducing food costs will drop to the bottom line as profit. If the actual food cost is lower than the total standard food cost, investigation also is called for, even though this may seem like good news. For example, this may indicate that guests are paying more for less food than managers had planned for. If this is the case, adjustments must be made so that this is corrected. Otherwise, guests may stop coming to the property because they are not receiving the value that they should for the money they are spending.

Determining Standard Portion Costs for Beverages ─────

Establishing a standard portion cost for a beverage item is relatively simple because usually the beverage has only a few ingredients. A standard recipe form for a beverage, such as the one for a Manhattan shown in Exhibit 8, can provide space for listing ingredient costs and calculating the standard drink cost.

Ingredients are listed in Column 1 of the standard recipe. The bottle size for each liquor ingredient is noted in Column 2. Most alcoholic beverages are sold by the liter rather than by the ounce. Therefore, if recipes and bar equipment use ounces as a unit of measure, it becomes necessary to convert liters to ounces before making recipe extensions or costing calculations. The cost of the bottle of liquor is recorded in Column 3. The amount of each ingredient is listed in Column 4. Column 5 shows the cost of each ingredient needed to produce one drink.

How are ingredient costs calculated? To determine the cost of the rye whiskey used in the Manhattan, for example, first the price of the bottle of rye whiskey must be divided by the number of ounces in the bottle to obtain the cost per ounce:

Exhibit 8   Sample Standard Beverage Recipe

ITEM: Manhattan

	Date 6/19/—
A) Drink Sales Price	$4.00
B) Drink Cost	.53
C) Drink Cost Percentage	13.3%

		Bottle Data	Drink Data	
		6/19—		
Ingredients	Size	Cost	Size	6/19
1	2	3	4	5
Whiskey, Rye	L (33.8 oz)	9.65	1.50 oz	.43
Vermouth, Sweet	750 ML (25.4 oz)	2.69	.75 oz	.08
Angostura Bitters	16 oz	4.56	dash	.01
Cherry (Stem Maraschino)			1 ea.	.01
Water (Ice)			.75 oz	—
TOTALS			3 oz	.53

PREPARATION PROCEDURE:

Place ingredients into a mixing glass. Add ice and stir long enough to chill. Strain into cocktail glass. Garnish with a stem maraschino cherry.

GLASS USED: 3 ½ oz Line Cocktail

Standard Recipes for Alcoholic Beverages

Standard recipes for alcoholic beverages are required for the same reason that they are needed for food items. They provide consistency in the types and quantities of ingredients used to prepare each beverage item. This, in turn, enables managers to better control product taste, which is of concern to guests; and ingredient costs, which are of concern to managers.

There is one additional reason why standard recipes for alcoholic beverages can be very helpful. Since they indicate the quantity of alcohol used in their preparation, if followed, they will indicate the quantity of alcohol consumed by guests. This helps to protect the property because, with sales records available, managers can determine the quantity of alcohol consumed by a guest at the property if challenges related to the responsible service of alcoholic beverages arise.

$$\text{Cost per Ounce} = \frac{\$9.65 \text{ (price per bottle)}}{33.8 \text{ (ounces per bottle)}} = \$.286 \text{ (rounded)}$$

(When calculating a bottle's cost per ounce, some beverage managers deduct a small amount before dividing to allow for evaporation or spillage. This will increase the cost per ounce.)

Since 1.5 ounces of rye whiskey are used in a Manhattan, the ingredient cost for rye whiskey is $.43: $.286 × 1.5 ounces = $.429, or $.43 (rounded); see Column 5.

The costs of the rye whiskey and the other ingredients in the Manhattan are added together, and the total drink cost ($.53) is recorded at the bottom of column 5. This figure is then transferred to line B at the top of the recipe.

Line C at the top of the recipe indicates the drink cost percentage, which expresses how much of the drink's selling price (recorded on line A) goes toward the drink's cost. The drink cost percentage is calculated by dividing the cost of the drink by the drink's selling price and multiplying by 100. The drink cost percentage for the Manhattan in the sample recipe is calculated as follows:

$$\frac{\text{Drink Cost}}{\text{Percentage}} = \frac{\$.53 \text{ (drink cost)}}{\$4 \text{ (selling price)}} = .133 \text{ (rounded)} \times 100 = 13.3\%$$

The portion cost for a drink is only one factor to consider when determining the drink's selling price. The type of drink—highball, cocktail, or specialty—and the quality of liquor—house, call, or premium—are also taken into account when establishing a drink's selling price.

Pricing Menu Items

Commercial food service operations and many noncommercial facilities must establish selling prices for menu items. Prices affect guests' perceptions of value. A property perceived as offering good value is more likely to generate the sales revenue required to meet its financial goals. Many managers use subjective pricing methods that fail to relate selling prices to profit requirements or even costs.

Many managers speak about the art of pricing and suggest that intuition and special knowledge about the guest's ability to pay are the most important factors. Consider the following pricing methods, and notice that each is based upon the manager's guesses about selling prices:

- *The reasonable-price method.* This method uses a price that the food service manager thinks will represent a value to the guest. The manager presumes to know, from the guest's perspective, what charge is fair and equitable. In other words, the manager asks, "If I were a guest, what price would I pay for this item?"

- *The highest-price method.* The manager sets the highest price that he or she thinks guests are willing to pay. The concept of value (price related to quality and quantity) is stretched to the maximum and is then "backed off" to provide a margin of error in the estimate.

- *The loss-leader price method.* An unusually low price is set for an item (or items). The manager assumes that guests will visit the property to purchase the low-priced item(s) and will then select other items as well. This pricing method is sometimes used for early-bird or senior-citizen discounts to attract specific market segments.

- *The intuitive-price method.* When prices are set by intuition, the manager takes little more than a wild guess about the selling price. Closely related to this approach is a trial-and-error pricing plan: if one price does not work, another is tested. The intuitive-price method differs from the reasonable-price method in that the manager expends less effort in determining what represents value from the guest's perspective.

By contrast, objective pricing methods ensure that costs, the property's profit requirements, and the guest's perceived value of the dining experience are incorporated into the selling price. Two objective pricing methods are desired food cost percentage markup and profit pricing.

Desired Food Cost Percentage Markup

Some managers price menu items by using a desired food cost percentage. For example, when a new food item is to be offered, the manager determines a reasonable food cost percentage for the item. Using intuition, a national average, or a previous acceptable food cost percentage at the property, perhaps the manager decides that a 33 percent food cost is desirable. Assume that the manager then refers to the item's precosted recipe and notes that the standard portion cost for one portion is $1.50. The menu item's selling price is then determined by dividing the item's standard food cost per portion by its desired food cost percentage (as a decimal):

$$\text{Selling Price} = \frac{\$1.50 \text{ (item's standard food cost)}}{.33 \text{ (desired food cost percentage)}} = \$4.55 \text{ (rounded)}$$

If the manager does not like this price, another price of $4.75, $4.95, or even $4.25 can be established. Desired food cost percentages used for this markup method can be obtained from the property's approved operating budget.

Even when an objective cost-based pricing approach like this is used, however, other factors must still be considered, including what the competition charges and the **elasticity of demand** (the relationship between selling price and volume sold), when setting the actual selling price.

Is Lower Food Cost Percentage the Goal? The markup method just discussed seems to suggest that lower food cost percentages are better for the operation because they translate into greater profits. While this theory sounds good, it is not necessarily accurate. Consider the following example:

Menu Item	Food Cost	Menu Selling Price	Food Cost %	Contribution Margin
Chicken	$2.50	$8.25	30.3	$5.75
Steak	$5.50	$14.00	39.3	$8.50

In this example, chicken has the lower food cost percentage (30.3 percent compared to 39.3 percent for steak). Therefore, it would seem that the sale of chicken should help the operation more than the sale of steak. However, as shown by the contribution margin (the menu item's selling price minus the item's food cost), only $5.75 is left from the sale of chicken to pay for all other costs and to make a contribution to profit. In the case of steak, $8.50 remains. Which would you rather have left to pay for nonfood expenses and to contribute to profit: $5.75 or $8.50? You want the $8.50, of course.

With the food cost percentage pricing method, the manager assumes that the markup will cover not only food costs, but nonfood expenses and profit requirements as well. It is possible, however, to use an even more objective pricing method, one that incorporates nonfood expenses and profit requirements into the pricing decision from the very beginning.

Profit Pricing

The **profit pricing** method ensures that profit requirements and nonfood expenses are factored into the pricing decision. This method first considers what an **allowable food cost** for the year would be if nonfood expenses and profit requirements are subtracted from forecasted food revenues.

Assume an operation offers food service only and the budget prepared for the upcoming year forecasts food revenue at $800,000, estimates nonfood expenses at $415,000, and indicates that the owners require a profit of $75,000. Given this information, allowable food costs for the year (food costs "allowed" by the annual operating budget) can be determined as follows:

$$\text{Allowable Food Costs} = \underset{\substack{\text{(forecasted} \\ \text{food revenue)}}}{\$800,000} - \underset{\substack{\text{(nonfood} \\ \text{expenses)}}}{\$415,000} - \underset{\substack{\text{(profit} \\ \text{requirements)}}}{\$75,000} = \$310,000$$

Once allowable food costs are determined, a **budgeted food cost percentage** can be calculated simply by dividing allowable food costs by forecasted food revenues:

$$\text{Budgeted Food Cost Percentage} = \frac{\$310,000 \text{ (allowable food costs)}}{\$800,000 \text{ (forecasted food revenues)}} = .388 \text{ (39\% rounded)}$$

The selling price of a menu item can then be determined by dividing the item's standard food cost by the budgeted food cost percentage. If the menu item's standard food cost is $1.50, the base selling price would be $1.50 ÷ .39, or $3.85. This base price would be adjusted by factors that include the value perceived by guests, competition, price rounding, and the prices currently or traditionally charged by the food service operation.[3]

Competition and Pricing

One of the most important concerns in pricing decisions relates to your competition: those that offer similar menu items and, perhaps, similar service and atmosphere. To price menu items effectively, you must know your competitors' menus, selling prices, and guest preferences.

One way to attract customers from competitors is to lower menu prices. This tactic may bring more people into your operation, but only if they regard your lower-priced items as substitutes for what the competition offers. If there are no significant differences between what your operation offers and what the competition offers, guests may see price as the determining factor in selecting your operation over the competition. However, if there are differences unrelated to price that are important to guests (such as location, atmosphere, and entertainment), this technique may not work.

Raising prices is also a way of responding to pressure from the competition. With higher prices, fewer menu items will need to be sold in order for the operation to maintain its required profit level. Does this technique work? The answer depends on the needs, desires, and preferences of guests. These factors determine whether people will continue to buy a menu item at a higher selling price.

Raising a menu item's price may be an effective strategy only if the increased revenue from the price increase makes up for the revenue lost as demand falls off and current guests begin to buy other menu items as substitutes. In some cases, a more effective strategy for increasing total revenue may be lowering a menu item's price. Lowering prices may increase the volume of unit sales, and this increase may produce an increase in total revenue.

What we are really talking about here is the concept of elasticity of demand. Elasticity is a term economists use to describe how the quantity demanded responds to changes in price. If a certain percentage price change creates a larger percentage change in the quantity demanded, the demand is elastic and the item is considered to be price-sensitive. If, on the other hand, the percentage change in quantity demanded is less than the percentage change in price, the demand is inelastic. Before changing the established price of a menu item, it is important to know the elasticity of demand for that item—the extent to which demand changes as the price changes.

Endnotes

1. Michael L. Kasavana, *Managing Technology in the Hospitality Industry,* 6th ed. (Lansing, Mich.: American Hotel & Lodging Educational Institute, 2011), pp. 169–176.

2. Interested readers can learn about this process in Jack D. Ninemeier, *Planning and Control for Food and Beverage Operations,* 8th ed. (Lansing, Mich.: American Hotel & Lodging Educational Institute, 2013), pp. 311–319.

3. See Chapter 3 in Ninemeier, *Planning and Control,* for objective pricing methods.

 Key Terms ————————————————————————————————————

actual food costs—The combined food costs actually incurred for the production of all menu items sold for a period of time (meal period, day, week, month, etc.).

adjustment factor—The number by which the amount of each ingredient in a standard recipe is multiplied to increase or decrease the recipe's yield: desired yield ÷ original yield.

allowable food cost—A budgeted food cost determined by subtracting nonfood expenses and profit requirements from forecasted food sales.

budgeted food cost percentage—A tool used in the profit pricing method; determined by dividing allowable food costs by forecasted food sales. The resulting percentage is divided into an item's standard food cost to arrive at a selling price.

chaining recipes—Including subrecipes as ingredients for a standard recipe. This enables the food service computer system to maintain a single record for a particular menu item that includes a number of subrecipes.

contribution margin—The menu item's selling price minus the item's standard food cost.

elasticity of demand—A term economists use to describe how demand responds to price changes.

ingredient file—Contains important data on each purchased ingredient, such as ingredient code number, description, purchase unit, purchase unit cost, issue unit, issue unit cost, and recipe unit cost.

point-of-sale (POS) system—A computerized system that records sales information, may print guest checks, and generates information useful in sales history analysis and production estimating.

precosting—The process of determining ingredient costs used in a standard recipe to yield a standard portion cost for one portion produced by the recipe.

profit pricing—A pricing method that ensures that profit requirements and nonfood expenses are factored into the pricing decision.

standard food cost—The total expected food cost based on all of the menu items sold multiplied by their portion costs (see standard portion cost).

standard portion cost—The standard food cost for an item that is sold as a single menu selection. The standard portion cost indicates the cost incurred by preparing one portion of the menu item according to its standard recipe.

standard recipe file—Contains recipes for all menu items. Important data maintained by this file include recipe code number, recipe name, ingredients, preparation instructions, number of portions, portion size, cost of ingredients, menu selling price, and food cost percentage.

total meal cost—The standard food cost for items combined to form dinners or other meals that are priced and sold as one menu selection.

Review Questions

1. How does a food service operation benefit from using standard recipes? How, if at all, do guests benefit when a standard recipe is used?

2. What factors should a food service manager consider when standardizing existing recipes?

3. How can a food service manager convince a head cook of the need to develop standard recipes?

4. How is an adjustment factor used to increase or decrease the yield of a standard recipe?

5. What is the difference between portion costs and total meal costs?

6. Why should standard recipes be used to prepare alcoholic beverages?

7. What is the difference between the standard portion cost of a menu item and its actual food cost?

8. How has technology simplified the recipe precosting process and made it more accurate and less time-consuming?

9. Why is it incorrect to assume that a lower food cost percentage is always better than a higher one?

10. How might lowering menu prices actually produce an increase in total sales revenue?

Internet Sites

For more information, visit the following Internet sites. Remember that Internet addresses can change without notice. If the site is no longer there, you can use a search engine to look for additional sites.

Recipe Management Software

CALCMENU
www.eg-software.com

FoodSoftware.com
www.foodsoftware.com

ChefTec
www.cheftec.com

Optimum Control Software
www.tracrite.net

CostGuard Foodservice Software
www.costguard.com

System Concepts, Inc.
www.foodtrak.com/Default

Eatec Solutions
www.agilysys.com

Recipe Sources (Food)

Gordon Foodservice
www.gfs.com
(enter "recipes" in the site's search box)

Kraft Foodservice
www.kraftfoodservice.com
(click on the site's search box and then
click "recipe search")

RecipeSource
www.recipesource.com

Sysco Corporation
www.sysco.com
(enter "recipes" in the site's search box)

Recipe Sources (Beverages)

idrink.com
www.idrink.com

DrinksMixer.com
www.drinksmixer.com

Recipe Goldmine
www.recipegoldmine.com
(click on "beverages")

Problems

Problem 1

You have learned about the need to express all ingredient quantities in a recipe in the most practical amounts, which are usually in the largest possible units. Use the information in Exhibit 3 to determine how much salad oil to use if recipe adjustment calculations yield the following requirements:

    a. 8 tablespoons

    b. 6 tablespoons

    c. 7 teaspoons

    d. 10 cups

    e. 3 cups

    f. 5 quarts

Problem 2

What is the standard recipe adjustment factor, given the following information?

	ORIGINAL RECIPE		NEW RECIPE (DESIRED YIELD)	
	Number Portions	Portion Size	Number Portions	Portion Size
a.	35	.25 cup	75	.25 cup
b.	75	4 oz.	35	4 oz.
c.	35	.50 cup	35	.25 cup
d.	75	6 oz.	75	10 oz.
e.	35	6 oz.	75	8 oz.
f.	75	.50 cup	35	.25 cup

Problem 3

a. Using information from the chapter's discussion of Exhibits 5 and 6, determine the standard portion (food) cost for a steak platter based upon the following information:

- 4 oz. sirloin steak (pre-cut)—$10.15/lb.
- 1 baked potato—12 potatoes for $3.70
- Sour cream—1 oz. (purchased in 5-lb. jar for $7.15 per jar)
- 4 oz. corn—frozen; 5-lb. pkg. for $5.73/pkg.
- 2 dinner rolls—$3.83/dozen
- Three half-ounce butter patties—$3.84/lb.
- Plate garnish—stuffed cherry tomato garnish for .09

b. Assume the manager desired a .31 food cost percentage from the sale of the steak platter above. What would be its selling price?

Problem 4

Complete the abbreviated standard food cost percentage report below given the following data. (Hint: Review Exhibit 7 and its discussion.)

Item	No. Sold	Revenue	Food Cost	CM	Food Cost %
a	25	187.50	47.75		
b	37	231.25	62.50		
c	41	297.25	92.40		
d	40	340.00	99.50		

Problem 5

a. What is the beverage cost of a gin and tonic given the following?

Gin—1 oz. (liter bottle price = $12.75)

Tonic—4 oz. (32 oz. bottle = 1.70)

Lime—1 slice (12 slices per lime; .45/lime)

b. What is the drink cost percentage if the drink's selling price is $4.75?

Problem 6

What is the budgeted food cost percentage for the Anytown Restaurant when its manager uses the profit-pricing method and the following information?

- Forecasted food revenue $1,250,000
- Profit requirement $140,000
- Non-food expenses $725,000

Part III

Production and Service

Chapter 8 Outline

Purchasing
    Why Is Purchasing Important?
    Goals of a Purchasing Program
    Security Concerns During Purchasing
    Ethical Concerns in Purchasing
Receiving
    Space and Equipment
    The Receiving Process
    Other Receiving Tasks
Storing
    Security
    Quality
    Recordkeeping
    Reducing Inventory Costs
Issuing
Special Beverage Management Concerns
    Purchasing
    Receiving
    Storing
    Issuing
Technology and Operating Controls
    The Internet
    Just-in-Time Inventory Systems
In-House Software Applications
    Purchasing
    Storing and Issuing

Competencies

1. Describe the various roles of purchasing, receiving, storing, and issuing as each function relates to food production. (pp. 179–197)

2. Describe the various roles of purchasing, receiving, storing, and issuing as each function relates to alcoholic beverage service. (pp. 197–200)

3. Discuss how technology helps managers with various preproduction tasks. (pp. 200–203)

8

Preparing for Production

THIS CHAPTER FOCUSES on the flow of food and beverage products through a food service operation. First it describes the basics of purchasing, and then reviews guidelines for receiving, storing, and issuing food and beverages.[1] The final sections of the chapter review technology and operating controls, and in-house software applications.

Purchasing

Many activities make up the purchasing process. (See the numbered activities in Exhibit 1, which correspond to the numbered activities discussed in this section.) When food and beverage production employees need food, beverages, and other supplies to prepare menu items, they (1) send **requisitions** (written orders to withdraw items from storage) to storeroom personnel, who then (2) issue the requested products. Note: requisitions can be hard copy or, increasingly, electronic copies.

At some point, storeroom **inventory** (the amount of food, beverages, and other supplies on hand) will have to be replenished. To reorder supplies, storeroom personnel (3) send **purchase requisitions** to the purchasing department. Purchase requisitions are forms that specify the products to be reordered, the quantity needed, and when they are needed. The purchasing department (4) orders these products from suppliers, through either a formal **purchase order** system or an informal **purchase record** system. Copies of the orders (5) are given to receiving and accounting personnel. Steps 3–5 can involve hard copy or electronic forms.

Suppliers (6) deliver the ordered products to the receiving area and give receiving personnel a **delivery invoice**, the supplier's bill indicating the products that were delivered, their quantity and prices, and the total amount owed. Receiving personnel check the delivery against their copy of the purchase order or purchase record, and also check for such things as quality and damage.

After the delivered products have been checked and accepted, receiving employees (7) transfer the products to the proper storage areas, and (8) send the delivery invoice to the accounting department. This alerts accounting staff members that the supplier has delivered the products, so they (9) can process the necessary documents and pay the supplier.

While purchasing procedures vary from operation to operation, these basic steps generally apply, even when electronic data replaces some or all of the

Exhibit 1   The Purchasing Process

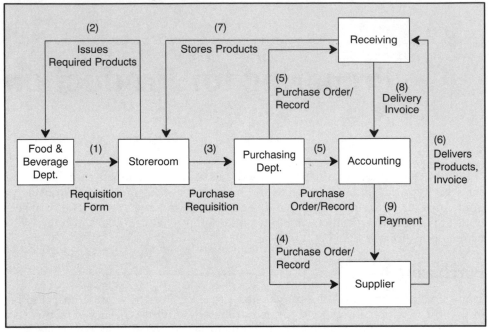

paperwork mentioned in Exhibit 1. (The chapter later reviews the role of technology in preproduction tasks.)

Why Is Purchasing Important?

Purchasing is important because a food and beverage operation must have the required food, beverages, and other supplies on hand to produce and sell food and beverage items. It is also important because an operation can save or lose money based on how effective its purchasing process is. That is, if too few items are purchased and stockouts occur, the operation will lose sales and guests will be disappointed. If the operation purchases too many items, money is tied up in unnecessary inventory and is unavailable to meet other obligations. Also, product quality can deteriorate.

The importance of purchasing can be summed up in one simple phrase: purchasing directly affects the bottom line. Every dollar saved through effective purchasing increases a property's profit by one dollar. Only the best possible purchasing program can help food service managers achieve the best possible economic results.

Goals of a Purchasing Program

Whether purchasing is done by a staff specialist in the purchasing department of a large operation or by a line manager at a small operation, the goals of a purchasing program include the following:

- Buy the right product.

- Obtain the right quantity.

- Pay the right price.

- Deal with the right supplier.

Buy the Right Product. The menu dictates the products to be purchased. If green beans are required for some menu items, the operation must purchase green beans. Questions about the type, the quantities, and the quality of green beans to purchase then become important. What type of green bean is right for the operation?

To answer this question, managers must develop purchase specifications that reflect the operation's required standards. A **purchase specification** is a detailed description defining the quality, size, weight, and other factors desired for a particular item. Exhibit 2 shows one purchase specification format. Managers should develop a purchase specification for each expensive item and others for which quality variations can create production challenges. Once developed, purchase specifications should be provided to suppliers to let them know exactly what products the operation wants and to help them meet the operation's product expectations. Specifications also provide quality benchmarks against which receivers can evaluate incoming products as they are received.

The desired quality for each product is an important part of purchase specifications. Some price-conscious operations want the least expensive items available, while other operations want only the highest-quality products because they know their guests will pay for them. Most operations fall between these two extremes. Therefore, in most operations, managers must make decisions about the level of quality that is acceptable for each product.

The quality level necessary for a particular product is determined in part by the product's intended use. If the operation wants to use olives as salad garnishes, colossal olives may be appropriate. If the operation wants olives to chop up for a salad bar topping, colossal olives are of a higher-than-necessary quality, and lower-priced, smaller olives or olive pieces might be acceptable.

At independent restaurants, product quality decisions are usually made by the food service manager, the chef (for food products), and the beverage manager (for beverage products). At restaurant chains, most quality decisions are made at corporate headquarters.

Convenience foods. In some cases, convenience foods may meet the operation's quality standards. **Convenience foods** are foods that have been manufactured or processed to some extent so that less on-site labor is necessary to prepare them. Convenience foods may be less costly to prepare and usually are easier to purchase, receive, store, and issue. For example, purchasing and preparing a frozen beef stew entrée takes less time, labor, and equipment than purchasing and preparing the beef, potatoes, carrots, broth, and other ingredients that make up a beef stew.

Some food service managers have negative attitudes about convenience foods, even though many high-quality convenience foods are available. If convenience foods can meet the operation's quality standards, managers should seriously investigate the possibility of purchasing and using them.

Exhibit 2   Sample Purchase Specification Format

(name of food and beverage operation)

1. Product name: _____

2. Product used for:

> Clearly indicate product use (such as olive garnish for beverage or hamburger patty for grill frying for sandwich).

3. Product general description:

> Provide general quality information about desired product. For example, "iceberg lettuce; heads to be green, firm without spoilage, excessive dirt or damage. No more than 10 outer leaves; packed 24 heads per case."

4. Detailed description:

> Purchaser should state other factors that help to clearly identify desired product. Examples of specific factors, which vary by product being described, may include:
>
> | | | |
> |---|---|---|
> | • Geographic origin | • Product size | • Medium of pack |
> | • Variety | • Portion size | • Specific gravity |
> | • Type | • Brand name | • Container size |
> | • Style | • Density | • Edible yield, trim |
> | • Grade | | |

5. Product test procedures:

> Test procedures occur at time product is received and as/after product is prepared/used. For example, products to be at a refrigerated temperature upon delivery can be tested with a thermometer. Portion-cut meat patties can be randomly weighed. Lettuce packed 24 heads per case can be counted.

6. Special instructions and requirements:

> Any additional information needed to clearly indicate quality expectations can be included here. Examples include bidding procedures, if applicable, labeling and/or packaging requirements and special delivery and service requirements.

Source: Jack D. Ninemeier, *Planning and Control for Food and Beverage Operations*, 8th ed. (Lansing, Mich.: American Hotel & Lodging Educational Institute, 2013), p. 190.

Make-or-buy decisions. How can managers determine if a food product should be purchased as a convenience food or be prepared on-site? They should carefully consider the quality and cost considerations of product alternatives. For example, perhaps dinner rolls can be baked at the property rather than be purchased. Making them on-site could have several advantages. For instance, production of the rolls might be integrated with other work tasks, so managers can make better use of equipment and labor. Quality standards can be better maintained if the property makes the rolls. In addition, it may be less likely that the property would run out of a product if it is made on-site.

Perhaps the most important possible advantage is that products prepared on-site may be less expensive. A **make-or-buy analysis** can help determine whether it is less expensive to prepare a product on-site than to purchase it ready-made. For example, suppose managers at an operation that has always prepared its own Bloody Mary mix discover a commercially prepared mix that meets the operation's quality (taste) standards. Should the managers purchase it?

Assume the commercial mix costs $42 per case of 12 quart bottles. There is a 5 percent price reduction when the mix is purchased in five-case lots. The operation can purchase in this quantity; therefore, the cost per quart bottle would be: $42/case − 5% of $42 = $39.90; $39.90 ÷ 12 bottles = $3.33 per qt. (rounded).

The costs of making the Bloody Mary mix on-site are:

- Product cost: The current cost of ingredients used in the standard recipe, which yields two gallons (or eight quarts), is $17.45. Therefore, the product cost per quart is $2.18: $17.45 ÷ 8 quarts = $2.18 (rounded).

- Labor cost: The bartender who prepares the mix is paid $15 per hour (including fringe benefits). It takes 15 minutes (¼ hour) to prepare the mix. Therefore, the labor cost to prepare the eight quarts of mix is $3.75: $15 × ¼ = $3.75. The labor cost per quart is $.47: $3.75 ÷ 8 quarts = $.47 (rounded).

The total estimated cost to prepare one quart of Bloody Mary mix on-site is $2.65: $2.18 (product cost) + $.47 (labor cost) = $2.65.

The final step in the make-or-buy analysis is to compare the cost of preparing the product on-site with the cost of the commercial mix:

Cost of commercial mix	$3.33 per quart
Cost of on-site production	$2.65 per quart
Savings per quart by preparing the mix on-site	$.68 per quart

This make-or-buy analysis suggests that the operation can save 68 cents per quart if it continues to prepare its own Bloody Mary mix. While the per-quart savings may seem small, the operation saves $5.44 on mix each day, since the operation uses eight quarts per day ($.68 per quart × 8 quarts). This is equal to a weekly savings of $38.08 ($5.44 × 7 days) or an annual savings of $1,980.16: $38.08 per week × 52 weeks.

Obtain the Right Quantity. Cash flow is adversely affected if inventory levels are too high; stockouts, lost sales, and guest dissatisfaction may result if inventory levels are too low. That is why it is so important to purchase food and beverage products in the right quantities.

Some operations use a **minimum/maximum ordering system** to make sure inventories are kept at optimal levels. Under this system, a par level (the minimum amount of a product that should always be in inventory) is established for most products in inventory. Par level equals the lead-time quantity plus the safety stock level of any given product. The **lead-time quantity** is the number of units of a particular product that will be withdrawn from inventory and used between the time the product is reordered and the time it is delivered. The **safety stock** level is the number of purchase units of a product needed in case of emergencies, spoilage, or unexpected delays in delivery. When the inventory level of a product reaches the minimum quantity, additional supplies of that product must be ordered.

Maximum quantity is the greatest number or amount of a product that should be in stock at any given time. Every product in inventory with an established minimum level also has a maximum level. Maximum levels are established so that cash is not tied up in unnecessary inventory. The shelf life of a product also affects the maximum quantity that can be stored.

Factors other than a property's minimum/maximum levels may affect the quantity of products purchased, including the following:

- *Changing prices.* Rising or falling prices may affect how much a property buys.
- *Available storage facilities.*
- *Storage and handling costs.*
- *Waste and spoilage concerns.*
- *Theft and pilferage concerns.*
- *Market conditions.* For example, some products may be in limited supply.
- *Quantity discounts, if any.*
- *Minimum order requirements imposed by suppliers.* Some suppliers will not break cases (sell partial cases). If they charge an excessive price to do so, it may be necessary to purchase in case-lot quantities only, which may be more than the optimal quantity desired.
- *Transportation and delivery problems.*
- *Order costs.* Costs to place and process an order can be high, making it better to place larger, less frequent orders.

Such perishable products as fresh produce, bakery goods, and dairy items must be purchased for immediate use and are usually purchased several times a week. Since they are ordered frequently, managers generally know the usage rates for these products and will not assign formal minimum/maximum levels to them. The quantity of perishable products to purchase can be assessed by counting the number already on hand and subtracting this number from the amount managers know from experience they will need.

Exhibit 3 is an example of a quotation/call sheet managers can use to prepare a perishable product order and select the supplier. (Note: the process may involve calling suppliers for their current prices or using an electronic system.) The top

Exhibit 3   Sample Quotation/Call Sheet

Item	Needed	On Hand	Order	A & B Co.	Green Produce	Local Supplier
		Amount			Supplier	
1	2	3	4	5	6	7
Spinach	6 cs	2 1/2 cs	4 cs	$22^{00}/cs = \$88.00$	$14^{85}/cs = \$59.40$	$21^{70}/cs = \$86.80$
Ice Lettuce	8 cs	1 cs	7 cs	$17^{00}/cs = \$119.00$	$16^{75}/cs = \$117.25$	$18^{10}/cs = \$126.70$
Carrots	3-20#	1-20#	2-20#	$14^{70}/bag = \$29.40$	$13^{90}/bag = \$27.80$	$13^{80}/bag = \$27.60$
Tomatoes	2 lugs	1/2 lug	2 lugs	$18^{60}/lug = \$37.20$	$18^{00}/lug = \$36.00$	$18^{10}/lug = \$36.20$
			Totals	$861.40	$799.25	$842.15

line shows that six cases of spinach are required for the period covered by the order. An inventory count reveals that two-and-a-half cases are on hand. Ordering three-and-a-half cases would bring the inventory level up to six cases; four cases, however, may need to be ordered if the supplier will not sell a partial case, if the partial case is too expensive, or if the manager does not want restaurant personnel to have to handle partial case quantities. After the perishable products on hand are counted and the needed quantities determined, three suppliers are contacted and asked to quote a current price for the items. Each supplier has copies of the operation's purchase specifications for these products so each supplier can quote a price for the same quality of product.

After all suppliers are contacted, the manager has two choices. He or she can give the order to the supplier with the lowest total price for all products, or the order can be awarded on an item-by-item basis. Suppliers often place minimum dollar restrictions on orders. Therefore, it is not usually possible to award only one item to a supplier.

Pay the Right Price. Perhaps the most important purchasing objective is to obtain products and services at the right price. This is not necessarily the lowest price. With bargain prices, there is often a risk that the product might not be delivered or might not be of the proper quality.

Several techniques can help reduce purchasing costs, including the following:

- *Negotiate.* Bargaining over the price is a well-established practice. However, for each product there is a price below which a supplier will not go. This price is determined in part by prices charged by other suppliers, the supplier's operating costs, and the extent to which the supplier controls the market.

- *Consider purchasing lower-quality products.* Products must be suitable for their intended use, but are not necessarily the highest-quality (and most expensive) products available.

- *Determine whether the operation actually must buy a particular product.* As already explained, it may cost less to make the product on-site than to purchase it.

- *Discontinue some supplier services.* Product price includes delivery costs, extension of credit, and technical assistance. If some of these (or other) services are not needed, prices might be lowered.

- *Combine orders.* If the operation uses fewer suppliers and each gets more of the purchaser's orders, prices may be decreased through volume purchases.

- *Reevaluate the need for high-cost items.* If prices increase for certain garnishes, for example, the purchaser could order less expensive garnishes instead.

- *Pay cash.* Some suppliers may offer a lower price for cash transactions.

- *Speculate about price trends.* If prices are decreasing, the purchaser could order smaller quantities until the price stabilizes at a lower rate. If prices are rising, the purchaser may want to order more now.

- *Change the purchase unit size.* Product cost per unit may decrease as larger purchase units are ordered. For example, one pound of flour will likely cost less when a fifty-pound sack is purchased rather than a ten-pound sack.

- *Be innovative.* Cooperative purchasing or competitive bidding procedures may reduce prices. With reciprocal purchasing, food service managers may trade prepared meals and beverages (that is, provide complimentary lunches to suppliers) for food supplies.

- *Take advantage of suppliers' promotional discounts.*

- *Bypass the supplier.* Purchase directly from a distributor, manufacturer, or grower.

Product prices are also affected by the method of payment. If the supplier offers a discount for prompt payment, the operation should consider paying promptly. Generally, payment terms should be negotiated after an agreement is reached on the price.

Deal with the Right Supplier. Experienced purchasers realize they should consider additional factors when selecting a supplier, not just prices. These factors include the following:

- *Supplier's location.* A close location shortens delivery time. Many food service purchasers like to buy from local businesses because they believe it fosters goodwill and improves community relations.

- *Supplier's facilities.* A visit can help the purchaser determine sanitation levels, processing procedures, and how interested the supplier's staff members are in providing good service.

- *Financial stability.* Purchasers should investigate the financial soundness of potential suppliers.

- *Technical ability of supplier's staff.* Good suppliers do more than just take orders. They know their products and can help customers understand how best to use them.

- *Honesty and fairness.* The supplier's reputation and business practices can reveal these qualities.

- *Dependability.* Many purchasers pay higher prices to suppliers who consistently meet the operation's quality standards and delivery schedules.

In short, food service buyers not only want reasonable prices, they also want prompt delivery, adequate quality, helpful information, and good service. Purchasers should evaluate each potential supplier on all these points before placing an order.

Security Concerns During Purchasing

Theft during purchasing is less of a concern in small properties, since the owner/manager is responsible for purchasing. In larger operations, however, more people are involved in purchasing, so the chances of theft increase.

For example, purchasers at large operations might buy items for their own use or for other employees. They might take kickbacks or set up fictitious companies. Kickbacks result from collusion between the purchaser and an employee from the supplier's company. Products are seemingly purchased at higher-than-usual prices, with the difference in cost divided between the purchaser and supply company employee. Setting up a fictitious supplier company enables a purchaser to steal by submitting invoices from the fake supplier and collecting money for products the food operation never receives.

Ethical Concerns in Purchasing

Purchasers must meet high ethical standards to preserve one of their most valuable business assets: their personal and professional integrity. Purchasers are obligated to their operation, to colleagues, to suppliers, and to themselves to deal with suppliers fairly and honestly. Ethical dealings safeguard the operation's reputation, help avoid legal problems, and encourage suppliers to compete for the operation's business.

Each operation should adopt purchasing policies and procedures reflecting ethical and professional standards. The policies should address various issues, such as whether purchasers should be allowed to accept gifts or meals from suppliers, and how the operation should handle travel and other expenses incurred in visiting a supplier. Policies addressing such ethical issues vary from operation to operation. Exhibit 4 offers some ethical guidelines for professional purchasers.

Exhibit 4   Sample Code of Ethics for Purchasers

As a professional purchaser, I accept the following obligations and have the following responsibilities:

- To give primary concern to the best interests of my company

- To try to obtain maximum value for each dollar I spend

- To be active in professional groups to improve my own knowledge

- To desire and accept advice from colleagues, top management, and suppliers

- To be fair and honest in all my dealings with managers, employees, and supplier representatives

- To practice effective, ethical procedures that enhance relations with suppliers

- To learn as much as possible about all products and services that are needed

- To honor my obligations and ensure that all commitments are consistent with good business practices

Receiving

In some operations, the employee closest to the back door when products arrive is the one who receives them. However, receiving is so important that it should be performed by a knowledgeable employee who follows specific and proper receiving procedures.

In small operations, a single person—generally a manager, if not the owner— may be responsible for purchasing and receiving. When this person is the owner, there is little reason to worry about theft. If another employee assumes both tasks, however, the possibility of theft increases. As operations grow, purchasing and receiving duties are split: purchasing may be handled by a separate purchasing department, while receiving and storage become the responsibilities of the accounting department.

Space and Equipment

In some operations, the receiving area is little more than a wide space in a hallway. Even then, sufficient space should be set aside so the receiver can properly review all incoming products. When possible, the receiving area should be located near the delivery door to restrict the access of delivery persons to other areas.

Every product should be weighed, counted, and/or measured. In addition to an accurate scale, the receiver needs transport equipment to move products to storage, a desk or file cabinet to house receiving documents, a calculator to check order calculations, and small items such as a thermometer, a clipboard, and supplies for marking incoming products.

The Receiving Process

The receiving process involves six steps.

Step One. Inspect incoming products against a purchase order (at large properties) or a purchase record (at small properties).

Purchasing staff members prepare purchase orders for food or other supplies and submit them to suppliers (see Exhibit 5). The purchasing department retains copies of the orders. These documents identify the product, quantity, unit cost, and total cost of the order. In addition, a purchase order may include contractual information such as guarantees, warranties, payment requirements, and inspection rights.

Rather than use written or electronic purchase orders, the purchaser for a small operation may telephone suppliers to place orders. Alternatively, the supplier's representative may make a personal sales call to obtain order information from

Exhibit 5 Sample Purchase Order

Purchase Order Number: _____	Order Date: _____
	Payment Terms: _____
To: _____ (supplier)	From/ Ship to: _____ (name of food service operation)
_____ (address)	_____ (address)
	Delivery Date: _____
Please Ship:	

Quantity Ordered	Description	✓	Units Shipped	Unit Cost	Total Cost

Total Cost _____

Important: This purchase order expressly limits acceptance to the terms and conditions stated above, noted on the reverse side hereof, and any additional terms and conditions affixed hereto or otherwise referenced. Any additional terms and conditions proposed by seller are objected to and rejected.

_____
Authorized Signature

the purchaser or, increasingly, the purchaser may place an online order through the supplier's website. The purchaser fills out a purchase record (Exhibit 6) so the operation can keep track of what it has ordered. The purchase record is not submitted to suppliers.

Receiving employees are provided with copies of the purchase order or purchase record so they know what products (and their quality requirements) should be delivered and can refuse items that were not ordered.

Step Two. Inspect incoming products against purchase specifications to confirm that the quality of the incoming products meets the operation's standards.

This critical step is often overlooked. How does the receiving clerk know if *fresh* fish actually is fresh or if it is frozen fish that was thawed before delivery? How can the clerk tell that meat labeled *choice* really is choice? For some products, tests can be run to verify quality. For other products, the only way to know is to learn what the right product looks, smells, and feels like. Then the receiver can carefully inspect delivered products with these subjective factors in mind. As receiving personnel gain experience, they learn what to look for.

Traditionally, many industry observers have believed that one effective way to help ensure that the quality of product ordered is in fact the quality of product received is to deal with *honest* suppliers. In theory, this is an excellent suggestion. In practice, it is difficult to determine whether suppliers and their employees are honest.

Sometimes suppliers themselves are deceived about the products they secure from their own vendors for sale to their food service accounts. Food service managers paying premium prices for swordfish might instead receive much-less-expensive mako shark, or they might order red snapper, scallops, and tuna but have lesser-quality products substituted at delivery. Dishonest suppliers or their vendors might cut the flesh from the wing of a skate fish (related to the stingray) with cookie cutter–like implements and label the resulting product *scallops*. Buyers of fresh tuna are increasingly discovering that the cherry-red flesh traditionally used to identify top-quality tuna might instead exhibit the proper color because it has been sprayed

Exhibit 6   Sample Purchase Record

			(supplier)				
Date Ordered	Item Description	Unit	Price	No. of Units	Total Cost	Invoice No.	Comments

with carbon monoxide. This process is not harmful and does not make the product unfit for human consumption; however, it allows products that are relatively old to look very fresh. Wise receiving personnel should know that color is no longer representative of the product's quality.

Can experienced suppliers tell if these substitutions and quality-enhancing practices are affecting the seafood they provide to food service operations? Can receiving personnel in food service operations tell the difference? It is increasingly important that all parties in the food purchasing chain become more knowledgeable about the products they buy and sell.

Step Three. Inspect incoming products against the delivery invoice. If the invoice states that seventy-five pounds of ground beef have been shipped and delivered, the receiver should weigh the ground beef to confirm that seventy-five pounds were delivered. The receiving staff might verify the price per unit and the arithmetic extensions, or accounting and purchasing department managers or employees might assume these tasks. Verification is important because the dollar amount indicated on the delivery invoice is what the property owes the supplier once the invoice has been signed.

If a product is not delivered for any reason—if the supplier is temporarily out of it or if a product is accepted but the quantity or quality of the delivered product is different from the quantity or quality stated on the invoice—the receiver should complete a **request-for-credit memo** to adjust the amount of money due to the supplier (see Exhibit 7). This memo should be signed by the delivery person and a copy attached to the delivery invoice for routing to the accounting office. The accounting department should be sure to pay the adjusted amount on the delivery invoice, not the original amount.

Step Four. Accept the products. The receiving clerk accepts the products for the operation by signing the delivery invoice. Beyond this point, the responsibility for the products rests with the food and beverage operation, not the supplier.

Step Five. Move products to storage for quality and security reasons. It is poor practice to allow the supplier's delivery person to place items in storage. The delivery person should deliver products to the receiving area, where they are checked. After the delivery person leaves, the receiving clerk or another employee of the property can move items to the correct storage areas.

Step Six. Complete daily receiving reports or other forms as required to keep track of the suppliers who made deliveries that day and what they delivered. The specific records kept vary from operation to operation.

Other Receiving Tasks

Other receiving tasks include marking and rejecting products.

Marking Products. Marking helps facilitate proper stock rotation and inventory evaluation. Marking the date of delivery and price directly on the shipping or storage container before placing the product in storage makes it easier to withdraw the oldest products from inventory first. When inventory values must be

Exhibit 7   Sample Request-for-Credit Memo

Request-for-Credit Memo

(prepare in duplicate)   Number: _____

From: _____   To: _____
                                                        (supplier)
        _____   _____

        _____   _____

        _____   _____

Credit should be given on the following:

Invoice Number: _____   Invoice Date: _____

Product	Unit	Number	Price/Unit	Total Price

Reason: _____   Total: _____

_____   _____
(delivery person)   (authorizing signature)

calculated, having the cost of items written on product containers may make the task easier, depending on the inventory valuation method used.

Rejecting Products. Sometimes receiving personnel must reject incoming products because they were not ordered or delivered on time, their quality is inadequate, or their price is incorrect. The receiving clerk who notes potential problems generally contacts the purchaser, chef, or other property official for a second opinion. If only a partial order is delivered or products are on back order, the receiving clerk may need to contact a manager who can reevaluate production plans.

Storing

After items are purchased and received, they must be stored. In some operations, storing means little more than putting items in storage areas and letting employees fetch products whenever they need them. This is not a secure strategy, however. Effective storage procedures must address security, quality, and recordkeeping issues.

Security

Think of storerooms as bank vaults and the food and beverage products within them as money. Many operations keep products collectively worth thousands of dollars in storage areas. Ask yourself, "If I had a roomful of money, how would I safeguard it?" Your answer will suggest how products in storage areas should be controlled.

Storage security measures include the following:

- *Lockable storage areas.* Walk-in refrigerators and freezers, dry storage areas, and liquor storage areas should be lockable. It may be impractical to lock walk-in or reach-in refrigerators if employees need to enter them frequently. In such cases, expensive items requiring refrigerated storage, such as fresh meats, seafood, and wines being chilled, can be locked in special cages within walk-in refrigerators, or selected compartments of reach-in refrigerators can be kept locked. Production personnel usually need to enter walk-in freezers less often than walk-in refrigerators. If it is impractical to keep walk-in freezers locked, it may be wise to purchase or construct lockable storage compartments for them as well.

- *Precious storage.* Very expensive items should be kept locked in special cabinets or in compartments within locked storage areas.

- *Limited access.* Managers should allow only authorized personnel to enter storage areas. When practical, keep storage areas locked except when issuing products.

- *Effective inventory control procedures.* The operation should control expensive and theft-prone items through the use of a perpetual inventory system (discussed later in the chapter).

- *Central inventory control.* At the end of a shift, items in work station storage areas should be returned to central storage areas for better inventory control.

- *Secure design.* Managers should design storage areas with security in mind. Walls should extend to the ceiling, and doors should be properly constructed and lockable. It should be impossible to enter the storeroom through the ceiling. The storeroom should have no windows.

- *Lighting and monitoring.* Adequate lighting is necessary in storage areas. Some operations use closed-circuit television systems to monitor storage areas.

Quality

Efforts made to develop purchase specifications and to check incoming products against them will be wasted if managers do not safeguard product quality during storage.

This means more than just ensuring that food will not spoil. Spoiled items must be discarded, of course, but products that deteriorate even slightly in quality can cause problems. For example, what happens when fruit is just a little too ripe? Using such products might help reduce food costs but doing so risks guest dissatisfaction.

Basic storage procedures that safeguard quality include the following:

- *Rotate food stocks.* Items that have been in storage the longest should be used first. This concept is referred to as **first-in, first-out (FIFO)**. The FIFO rule is easier to follow when incoming products are placed in back of or underneath products that are already there. Marking delivery dates on products before they are stored is also helpful in ensuring that stock is properly rotated.

- *Store foods at the proper temperatures.* Use accurate thermometers in storage areas to ensure that refrigerated storage temperatures are kept at 41°F (5°C) or lower and dry storage areas are kept between 50°F and 70°F (10°C and 21°C). The appropriate temperature for frozen food storage varies among products, but a temperature of 0°F (–18°C) is usually an acceptable benchmark.

- *Clean storage areas.* Routine cleaning of all storage areas helps protect product quality.

- *Ensure proper ventilation and air circulation.* Keep items off the floor and away from walls to permit air circulation. Normally, items should be stored in their original packing containers. Items that absorb odors (such as flour) should be kept away from items that give off odors (such as onions). Store food in airtight or covered containers.

Recordkeeping

Food service managers must track the quantity and value of products in storage. They must know what is already in inventory to know what they need to order. Accounting managers use the value of products in inventory to calculate food costs when developing income statements. They determine food costs, in part, by assessing the value of products taken from storage. They cannot do this accurately without inventory records.

Recordkeeping is also important in controlling theft because it allows managers to note differences between what should be in storage and what actually is.

The two basic systems for tracking inventory are the perpetual inventory system and the physical inventory system.

Perpetual Inventory System. A perpetual inventory system allows managers to track items in storage on an ongoing basis (see Exhibit 8) in much the same way a checkbook record is maintained. As money (food) enters the checking account (storeroom), the running balance increases and is noted in the checkbook register (inventory form). As checks are written (employees present requisitions and food is withdrawn), the running balance decreases and is subtracted from the running total in the checkbook register (inventory form). At all times, managers know the amount of money (food) in the checking account (storeroom). This is useful when managers want to calculate the cost of food used to produce menu items over a given period of time.

Perpetual inventory records tell managers the quantity of each product that *should* be in storage. This amount must be confirmed at regular intervals (usually monthly) through a physical count. Any discrepancy between what should be in inventory and what is actually there can be investigated to determine whether theft, poor recordkeeping, or another problem is involved.

Exhibit 8   Sample Perpetual Inventory Form

Perpetual Inventory								
Product Name: _P.D.Q. Shrimp_				**Purchase Unit Size:** _5 lb bag_				
Date	**In** **Carried Forward**	**Out**	**Balance** 15	**Date**	**In** **Carried Forward**	**Out**	**Balance**	
Col. 1	Col. 2	Col. 3	Col. 4	Col. 1	Col. 2	Col. 3	Col. 4	
5/16		3	12					
5/17		3	9					
5/18	6		15					
5/19		2	13					

For control purposes, the person who conducts the physical inventory should not be the same person who maintains the perpetual inventory records. Often it is easier if two people take the physical inventory. One person can call out the count of inventory units while another person records the count on the form. For example, a manager and the chef (for food) or the head bartender (for beverages) could take the physical inventory.

Physical Inventory System. An operation that uses a physical inventory system does not track what is added and subtracted from inventory on an ongoing basis. Rather, it counts what is in storage on a periodic basis, usually at the end of each month (see Exhibit 9).

An advantage of the physical inventory system is that it avoids the time and cost associated with the perpetual inventory system. A disadvantage is that food cost information is calculated only once each month. With a perpetual inventory system, food costs can be calculated for each day or any combination of days. Comparatively, then, the measurement of inventory and the accounting and operating information that can be calculated is much less accurate when an operation uses a physical inventory system.

A Practical Approach. Since there are advantages to each inventory system, managers at many operations use both to keep track of inventory. They use the perpetual inventory system to keep track of expensive and theft-prone products in inventory, because keeping close track of them is worth the trouble and cost involved. Managers track inexpensive inventory items quickly and easily, on the other hand, by physically counting them on a regular basis, typically at the end of each month.

Reducing Inventory Costs

The following procedures can help managers effectively manage inventory:

Exhibit 9   Sample Periodic Inventory Form

		Physical Inventory					
		Month _____			Month _____		
Product	Unit	Amount in Storage	Purchase Price	Total Price	Amount in Storage	Purchase Price	Total Price
Col. 1	Col. 2	Col. 3	Col. 4	Col. 5	Col. 6	Col. 7	Col. 8
Applesauce	6 #10	4 ⅓	$15.85	$68.63			
Green Beans	6 #10	3 ⅚	18.95	72.58			
Flour	25# bag	3	4.85	14.55			
Rice	50# bag	1	12.50	12.50			
			Total	$486.55			

- *Carry a smaller amount of inventory.* This may be possible if managers can obtain more frequent deliveries and purchase smaller quantities of products.

- *Be sure that required levels of inventory are correct.* Periodically examine minimum/maximum inventory levels to make sure they are set properly.

- *Decrease the number of product types the operation carries.* For example, perhaps the operation needs only one or two different types of shrimp rather than four or five.

- *Refuse to accept early deliveries.* The operation will have to pay for early products sooner than it would if the products were delivered as originally scheduled.

Issuing

Issuing involves distributing food and beverages from storage areas to authorized individuals who requisition them. Large food and beverage operations may have one or more full-time storeroom employees who issue products.

Issuing procedures depend in part on the recordkeeping system the operation uses. If it uses the perpetual inventory system for every item in storage, a requisition must be used to withdraw products from inventory. A requisition is an order identifying the type, amount, and value of items needed from storage (see Exhibit 10). Requisitions should be signed or initialed by an authorized person such as the chef (for food products) or bartender (for beverage products).

Exhibit 10 Sample Requisition Form

Food Requisition

Storage Type (check one):
☐ Refrigerated
☐ Frozen
☑ Dry

Date: _____

Work Unit: _____

Approved for Withdrawal: _____

					Employee Initials	
Item	Purchase Unit	No. of Units	Unit Price	Total Cost	Received By	Withdrawn By
Col. 1	Col. 2	Col. 3	Col. 4	Col. 5	Col. 6	Col. 7
Tomato Paste	CS-6 #10	2 ½	$28.50	$ 71.25	JC	Ken
Green Beans	CS-6 #10	1 ½	22.75	34.13	JC	Ken
			Total	$596.17		

At the end of each day (or on another regular basis), the storeroom clerk or another employee can use the requisitions they have collected to update perpetual inventory records. The requisition forms can then be forwarded to a manager or to the secretary or bookkeeper for review and calculation of daily food and beverage cost information.

As you can imagine, issuing every product using the perpetual inventory system requires much time and trouble. That is why many operations simplify inventory recordkeeping, and therefore issuing procedures, by using the perpetual inventory system for selected products only. Note that automated systems discussed later in this chapter can ease the task of taking and valuing inventory.

Another way to simplify issuing is to have employees obtain all the products they need for production at one time. Not only does this help control, it also increases employee productivity since employees do not have to repeatedly leave production areas to retrieve items from storage.

Special Beverage Management Concerns

Many control procedures for alcoholic beverages are the same as those for food. However, there are some differences. This section looks at special control concerns for beverages.

Purchasing

Managers are less likely to use purchase specifications for alcoholic beverages, since they purchase many of them by brand name.

In many states, laws and other restrictions regulate the purchase of alcoholic beverages. Some states operate *state stores* from which all alcoholic beverages must be purchased, and prices for many beverages may be set by law, making it pointless to negotiate and shop for better values. Even in less-regulated states, calling suppliers in search of the best price may not work, since there is likely only one wholesaler in the area who carries a particular brand of alcohol.

A **house brand** is a beverage brand served when the guest requests no special brand. How do beverage managers determine which house brands to purchase? Their attitudes can range from "Don't use anything you wouldn't be proud to display on the back bar" to "Use the least expensive, and let the guest pay extra for a premium brand." In practice, managers often use middle-range brands—neither the least nor the most expensive—for house brands.

Call brands are specific beverage brands that guests request by name when they place an order. Deciding what kinds of call brands to carry is a marketing decision. Sometimes beverage managers make the mistake of trying to please everyone. They offer many brands, each of which must be ordered, stored, issued, and controlled. Beverage operations would be more efficient if they had a selection of brands available to meet the needs of most regular guests instead of trying to satisfy everyone's tastes. If one call brand is not available, usually a reasonable substitute can be offered.

From time to time, beverage suppliers in some states may offer special deals, such as a per-bottle or per-case discount when a specified quantity is purchased. However, before making a large-volume purchase to take advantage of a discount, managers should consider the following questions:

- How much cash will be tied up in inventory?

- Will cash flow be affected?

- Does a greater risk of theft warrant the purchase?

- If deals are for brands the operation does not normally carry, will guests accept the change?

Also, **inventory turnover rates** are generally lower for beverages than for foods because foods are more perishable. For example, a property's food inventory may turn over an average of twenty-six times per year, meaning that the value of goods on hand at any point equals the approximate amount of foods used during a two-week period. By contrast, a property's beverage inventory may turn over only twelve times per year, meaning that the amount of beverage inventory on hand approximately equals the cost of beverages purchased for one month's use. Any extra beverages purchased to take advantage of a volume discount might be in storage for a long time, therefore tying up cash unproductively in inventory.

Receiving

Alcoholic beverages are more prone to theft than most food products. Therefore, some of the receiving principles for food noted earlier in the chapter should be reemphasized here:

- Cases should be opened and bottles checked to make sure all incoming beverages noted on the delivery invoice were, in fact, delivered.

- After beverages are received, they should be moved immediately to secure storage areas. The longer beverages remain unlocked in receiving areas, the greater the chance of theft.

- Purchasing and receiving tasks for beverages should be separated, unless the owner/manager in a small operation assumes both tasks. Even when these tasks are separated, collusion between purchasing and receiving employees is still possible and should be guarded against.

Storing

Prevention of unauthorized physical access, the need to keep effective records, and sanitary storage are as important for beverages as they are for food.

In addition to a central beverage storage area, many operations have behind-the-bar storage. This storage area should be locked when the food and beverage operation is closed. Generally, quantities of beverages kept in a behind-the-bar or other non-central storage area should be minimized, since security controls are less effective in these areas. The main concern is to establish correct *bar pars*, the number of bottles that should be on hand behind the bar.

When possible, wines, beer, and other refrigerated beverages should be stored away from refrigerated food items. If this is not possible, a locked storage area for beverages should be provided.

It is critical to closely monitor the beverage inventory. Normally, all alcoholic beverages can be kept under a perpetual inventory system; quantities should be verified by physical count at least monthly.

Issuing

Beverages should normally be issued on a bottle-for-bottle basis to replenish bar pars. If the bar par for house scotch is five bottles, and two are empty at the end of the shift, two bottles must be issued to maintain the bar par. The empty bottles should be given to whoever is in charge of issuing beverages from inventory (usually a manager), so that he or she can issue full replacement bottles. The empty bottles must then be broken or disposed of in compliance with local or state ordinances and the operation's policies.

Normally, beverages should be issued once each shift, preferably at the end. If bartenders frequently run out of a certain beverage before a shift ends, the operation should reexamine the shift's par level.

As beverages are issued, bottles should be marked to:

- Identify a bottle as coming from the property's central storage.

- Indicate the date of issue. Managers might question why a bottle of fast-selling liquor is at the bar for a long time.

- Identify to which bar, if applicable, a bottle has been issued.

Managers also may wish to inconspicuously note the bottle's purchase price on the bottle's label so that employees can easily find the price when completing requisitions for the beverages. However, this practice may be impractical if guests can see the price on bottles of liquor used for tableside flaming of food or on bottles of wine served at the table.

Some managers believe that the key to the locked beverage storage area should be kept at the bar, since there may be times when a manager with a key is not on duty. However, this practice decreases management's control over issuing. When possible, it is usually better to set bar par levels high enough to avoid stockouts.

Technology and Operating Controls

Technology provides many exciting ways to help food service managers control purchasing, receiving, storing, and issuing activities. The systems described in this section are in use today in many operations and will become increasingly common in the future. The basic systems described are useful for both noncommercial and commercial operations.

The Internet

The Internet has become an essential part of business for today's food service managers, who increasingly use it to conduct business transactions. The development of **e-commerce** has significantly changed the way business is conducted in the food service industry.

Purchasing activities provide one example. Food service organizations can electronically link to suppliers to share product information, purchase specifications, pricing, and so on. Food service operations gain real-time access to suppliers and current product-availability information that cannot be provided in a printed paper catalog (or in a face-to-face conversation with a supplier representative who is using a catalog with outdated data). In addition, online purchasing allows suppliers to customize product offerings for a select clientele, and it can dramatically reduce food service companies' search time. If desired, inventory levels can be automatically tracked, and, when a preestablished order point is reached, an order to replenish stock can be electronically placed with the appropriate supplier. Such efforts lower costs while streamlining inventory, accounting, and receiving processes.

Just-in-Time Inventory Systems

Just-in-time (JIT) inventory systems will enable food operations to keep just a small quantity of food items on-site for emergency purposes. The majority of all items will be delivered daily, perhaps early in the morning for that day's use, or, alternatively, late in the evening for the next day's use.

Central to the JIT system is the use of a prime supplier. The food service manager will estimate the total quantity of ingredients (inventory items) needed for a specified time period and will solicit price quotations from approved suppliers who determine their best prices for items that meet the operation's purchase specifications. Since it is often impossible to quote prices over an extended time period, suppliers might quote on the basis of an upcharge from the current market price, such as a specified percentage above the market price for the product at the time it is delivered. The supplier quoting the lowest upcharge for the time period covered by the bid will then be awarded the contract for the time covered by the agreement.

Let's see how JIT works. Suppose a food service manager uses a computer to forecast basic production requirements. He or she also uses judgment to evaluate the forecasted needs and to adjust them as necessary (for example, by considering the quantities of portions already available). Then two things occur:

- Recipes that yield the exact number of portions to be prepared will be printed or sent electronically to terminals in each applicable work station. For example, the bake shop will receive all recipes for pastry items; cooks will receive recipes for items they will produce in their work stations.

- The type and quantity of major ingredients required to prepare all recipes will be calculated and electronically transmitted to the prime supplier, who will assemble and deliver all necessary products to the food and beverage operation.

A delivery invoice accompanies the shipment. The receiver forwards the invoice to the operation's accounting office so it can match it up with the original invoice submitted by the supplier. Payment will be made when any discrepancies are corrected. In larger operations, the prime supplier might establish a mini-warehouse that it staffs with supplier personnel. Shipments of ordered products will be delivered to the food service operation and will be billed to it when items are issued from the mini-warehouse directly to production units.

With a prime-supplier system in place, a food operation has a lessened need for a formal issuing system, since almost all products delivered on a specific date will be used on that date (or the next day). Of course the operation needs space for workstation storage and/or broken-case rooms to hold some products, since suppliers ship only in purchase units (for example, a case of six #10 cans, a fifty-pound sack, and so on).

In-House Software Applications

Inexpensive, cost-effective software can help managers with many preproduction activities that until recently had to be performed manually. As such, some tasks were not done or were done infrequently because they were too time-consuming and/or outputs contained inaccuracies that affected subsequent operations. Use of software does not substitute for the manager's knowledge, experience, and common sense, but it does yield output that provides a benchmark for management assessment and decision-making.

Let's look at software applications that help food service operators with pre-production planning.[2]

Purchasing

The following is a partial list of purchasing tasks that can be included in a comprehensive automated system.

- Quantities of ingredients to be purchased can be estimated by systems that consider sales forecasts applicable to the order period and then calculate the amount of ingredients necessary to produce the required number of items for that period.

- Suppliers' price quotes can be compared to determine the lowest prices and price changes since the last purchase. If the per unit (such as case) change exceeds a specified amount for a product of the same quality, an "exception" is noted and a purchaser or manager can investigate.

- The supplier selected to supply a product can be contacted, and a purchase order can be automatically generated.

- Managers can use a tablet or other personal-sized computer to place orders with suppliers directly from the storeroom when physical inventory counts verify that order points have been reached.

- Shopping lists for special events and banquets can be generated based upon recipes, event guarantees, and other guest count estimates.

- Inventory count and value information can be moved between production and profit/cost centers in multi-unit operations.

Storing and Issuing

Inventory programs track inventory items by unit and cost. Conversion tables within the software track ingredients by unit and cost as they pass through purchasing, storing, and production control points.

Assume an ingredient such as canned green beans is purchased, issued, and used by an operation. When a shipment of canned green beans arrives, the inventory record can be updated by entering the number of purchase units (cases of #10 cans) received. The computer system can then convert this entry into issue units (#10 cans). At the end of a meal period, systems can update inventory records by entering the standard recipe units used to prepare the menu items sold.

Similarly, one can track costs associated with these various units. For example, assume that bottled ketchup is purchased by the case (twenty-four twelve-ounce bottles), issued from the storeroom to the kitchen by the bottle, and used in recipes by the ounce. Given information about the purchase unit's net weight and cost, inventory software can extend costs for issue units and recipe units. A fully integrated computer system can perform these calculations in fractions of a second.

Managers should know how the operation's inventory software tracks usage: by unit, by cost, or by both unit and cost. A system that tracks items by unit may be able to report changes in stock levels, but may not be able to provide financial data necessary for food costing. A system that tracks items primarily by product cost may not facilitate spot-checks of items in storage or maintain perpetual inventory data. The most effective inventory programs are those that track items in terms of both unit and cost.

Items that are in storage, including alcoholic beverages, can be easily tracked with high-tech assistance. Universal product bar codes are now available on almost all packaging so that incoming products can be scanned into the operation's inventory system. If they are not on packaging when products are received, bar codes can be added with in-house systems. As items are issued from storage, they can be scanned out of inventory in a system similar to that used in supermarkets: when a customer checks out, products are electronically scanned to determine the amount owed and to reduce the storage inventory by the quantity that has been purchased. With this method, it is fast and easy to accurately determine the quantity and cost (value) of all items in storage and the quantity and cost of items used in daily (shift) production.

Behind-bar beverage inventories are also fast and easy to access: each type and bottle of beverage can be assigned a specific identification number. To determine inventory cost, each bottle can be placed on a computerized scale. Alternatively, new systems allow inventory-takers to touch the screen of a handheld device indicating the appropriate amount of product remaining in an open bottle. The scale or handheld system can then deduct the weight of the bottle from the total unit weight, calculate the quantity and cost of remaining liquid, and estimate the sales value based upon the quantity that has been used. This information can be carried forward for all behind-bar bottles to determine actual beverage costs and estimated bottle sales for each bar during each shift.

Endnotes

1. For more information about purchasing, receiving, storing, and issuing, see Jack D. Ninemeier, *Planning and Control for Food and Beverage Operations*, 8th ed. (Lansing, Mich.: American Hotel & Lodging Educational Institute, 2013).

2. Readers desiring detailed information about the use of technology for preproduction planning activities are referred to Ninemeier, *Planning and Control*, and Michael L. Kasavana, *Managing Technology in the Hospitality Industry*, 7th ed. (Lansing, Mich.: American Hotel & Lodging Educational Institute, 2015).

Key Terms

call brand—A specific beverage brand that guests request by name when they place an order.

convenience food—A food item that has some or all of the labor costs for processing built in so less on-site labor is required for preparation.

delivery invoice—A supplier's bill indicating the products that were delivered, their quantities and prices, and the total amount owed to the supplier.

e-commerce—The buying and selling of products and services over the Internet.

first-in, first-out (FIFO)—An inventory system of rotating and issuing stored food in which items that have been in storage longest are used first.

house brand—A beverage brand served when a guest does not request a special brand.

inventory—The amount of food, beverages, and other supplies on hand.

inventory turnover rate—The number of times in a given period that inventory is converted into (turned into) revenue.

issuing—The movement of food and beverages from the storeroom to authorized individuals who requisition these items.

just-in-time (JIT) inventory—The process of keeping only emergency quantities of products on hand and ordering and receiving the majority of food and beverages "just in time" to issue and use them. This system can reduce the need for extensive storage space, decrease loss due to spoilage and pilferage, and free funds from being tied up in storing unnecessary inventory.

lead-time quantity—The number of units of a product that will be withdrawn from inventory and used between the time the product is re-ordered and when it is delivered.

make-or-buy analysis—A study done to determine if it is less expensive to prepare products on-site or to purchase products of the same quality from suppliers.

minimum/maximum ordering system—A system that helps managers determine when and how many products to purchase. The process involves assessing the minimum quantity below which inventory levels should not fall and the maximum quantity above which inventory levels should not rise.

purchase order—A paper or electronic form used to order food or other supplies from suppliers.

purchase record—A paper or electronic record of all incoming shipments from suppliers, typically used in small food service operations.

purchase requisition—A paper or electronic form used by storeroom personnel to alert the purchasing department that products need to be reordered from suppliers. The form specifies the needed products, quantity needed, and when they are needed.

purchase specification—A detailed description of the quality, size, weight, and other characteristics desired for a particular item.

request-for-credit memo—A form completed by the property's receiving clerk that lists products on the supplier's invoice that were not delivered or were not accepted.

requisition—A written or electronic order used by production personnel identifying the type, amount, and value of items needed from storage.

safety stock (inventory level)—The number of purchase units of a product kept on hand in case of emergency, spoilage, or unexpected delivery delays.

? Review Questions

1. What one phrase summarizes the importance of purchasing?
2. How can quality requirements be incorporated into the purchasing process?
3. What does the term *make-or-buy decision* mean?
4. What factors affect purchase quantities?
5. How can buyers attempt to get reduced prices while maintaining quality?
6. When selecting a supplier, what factors should purchasers consider?
7. What steps make up the receiving process?
8. What is the meaning of *FIFO*?
9. How does a perpetual inventory system differ from a physical inventory system?
10. How can the issuing process be simplified?
11. How do the procedures for purchasing, receiving, storing, and issuing beverages differ from the procedures used to control food products?
12. In what ways can computerized systems simplify procedures used in purchasing, receiving, storing, and issuing?

Internet Sites

For more information, visit the following Internet sites. Remember that Internet addresses can change without notice. If the site is no longer there, you can use a search engine to look for additional sites.

Hospitality Software Companies

ChefTec
www.cheftec.com

Hospitality Control Systems
www.aloharadiant.com

CostGuard Foodservice Software
www.costguard.com

MICROS Systems, Inc.
www.micros.com

Eatec Solutions
www.agilysis.com

System Concepts, Inc.
www.foodtrak.com

Electronic Purchasing

Adaco
www.adaco.com

Sysco
www.sysco.com

Purchase Specifications

CooksInfo.com
www.cooksinfo.com (enter "food purchase specifications" into the site's search box)

U.S. Department of Agriculture
www.usda.gov (enter "purchase specifications" in search box)

Receiving

HiEndSecurity.com
www.hiendsecurity.com

(For general information about receiving, enter "restaurant receiving procedures" in your favorite search engine.)

Restaurant Report
www.restaurantreport.com (enter "receiving" in search box)

Storing

Food Management
www.food-management.com (enter "storage procedure" in search box)

Traulsen (commercial refrigeration equipment)
www.traulsen.com

Problems

Problem 1

The manager of the Anytown Restaurant wants to conduct a make-or-buy analysis to determine whether she should continue to purchase bulk ground beef or instead buy portion-controlled (four-oz. serving AP) patties.

The two ground beef patty alternatives are of equal quality. The following are the specifics:

1. Making patties from bulk ground beef:

    *   10# poly bag of beef costs $32.08.
    *   Labor required to portion 10# of patties is 35 minutes; the cook is paid $11.25 per hour with an additional 17 percent in fringe benefits.

2. Using pre-portioned patties:

    *   Patties cost $87.50 for a 20# box.

Which product should the Anytown manager purchase?

Problem 2

a. Complete the following abbreviated quotation/call sheet by calculating the total costs for each item and supplier.

Item	To Order	Supplier #1	Supplier #2	Supplier #3
A	3 cases	18.50/case =	19.20/case =	17.50/case =
B	2 cases	12.25/case =	11.20/case =	13.10/case =
C	5 gallons	6.00/gallon =	6.55/gallon =	7.00/gallon =
D	4 lugs	39.50/lug =	39.75/lug =	38.75/lug =

b. If you wanted to purchase the items on the basis of the lowest cost per item, from which supplier (1, 2, or 3) would you purchase each item? (Use the information provided in the table in Problem 2a.)

Item A _____

Item B _____

Item C _____

Item D _____

c. If you wanted to purchase all items from the supplier quoting the lowest total price, from which supplier (1, 2, or 3) would you purchase the four items? (Use the information provided in the table in Problem 2a.)

Problem 3

Complete the Balance column on the following Perpetual Inventory Form:

Date	In	Out	Balance
Beg.			12
7/14	3	2	
7/15		3	
7/16	4	3	
7/17		5	
7/18	7	4	

Problem 4

Calculate the physical inventory value for the following items in inventory at the Anytown Restaurant.

Item	Unit	Amount in Storage	Purchase Price	Total Price
A	6# 10	3 ⅔	23.75	
B	25# bag	2	41.12	
C	50# bag	2	38.10	
D	gallon	4	16.50	

Problem 5

What is the total cost of the items withdrawn from inventory, as listed on the following requisition form?

Item	Price Unit	No. Units	Unit Price	Total Cost
A	case (6/10)	3⅓	26.75	
B	gallon	2	28.50	
C	25# bag	1	31.00	
D	case (25#)	3	33.00	

Chapter 9 Outline

Competencies

1. Explain how production planning can help food service operations to meet and exceed guest expectations. (pp. 211–214)

2. Identify the major functions and basic principles of food production. (pp. 215–217)

3. Describe proper preparation and cooking methods for fruits and vegetables. (pp. 217–222)

4. Identify and describe the four common characteristics of meat and poultry, and summarize their cooking considerations and methods. (pp. 222–225)

5. Describe cooking considerations when preparing fish, eggs, and dairy products. (pp. 225–228)

6. List common ingredients used when preparing baked products, and explain the effects each has on the finished product. (pp. 229–230)

7. Describe how to meet or exceed guest expectations when making and serving coffee and tea. (pp. 230–231)

8. Describe what food operations can do to help protect the environment, and outline managers' primary concerns during food and beverage production, including various control activities used to address these concerns. (pp. 231–234)

9

Production

THE FOOD AND BEVERAGE PRODUCTS produced at a food service operation must conform to quality standards. Excellent service, an inviting ambience, and clean surroundings cannot overcome the negative effects of improper or ineffective production procedures. Quality, the consistent delivery of products according to standards, is a constant concern. Managers must define quality standards for each food and beverage product, and they must then incorporate the standards into purchase specifications. Managers must also supervise and evaluate employees to ensure that they meet quality standards. This requires that managers first train employees to follow standard procedures. Quality standards must be incorporated into production activities through standard recipes and use of the proper tools, equipment, and supplies. These quality-enhancing resources must be used consistently.

Countless books and articles have been written about food and beverage production. Since this chapter is an introduction to food and beverage operations, it does not attempt to provide extensive details about preparation. Instead, it presents basic information for students and new or prospective food and beverage managers and other personnel who must understand fundamental principles and procedures of food preparation.

Production Planning

Production planning is the first step toward providing dining experiences that meet or exceed guest expectations. Operations of all sizes must plan for production so that food and beverage products, personnel, and equipment are available when necessary.

Production planning should be tailored to the needs of the specific operation. In small operations, the manager, who may also be the owner and/or chef, may have all planning responsibilities. In larger operations, production planning is a formal task undertaken during regularly scheduled meetings attended by various personnel that may include managers, chefs, meeting and convention services personnel, purchasing staff, and others.

The primary task of production planning is to determine the quantity of menu items to prepare. Many operations use sales history records to estimate production needs for the upcoming week or other time period. These records indicate for each date the total meals served, the number of portions of some or all menu items served, the weather, and special events or activities. Exhibit 1 shows one type of sales history record. It is generated by a point-of-sale system, and recaps sales of appetizers for one week. It can report data from a longer or shorter period of time,

Exhibit 1   Consolidated System Menu Item Sales Summary

Weekly Consolidated System Menu Item Sales Summary
Subtotal By Family Group
Mike Rose Cafe - Beltsville, MD

Sunday   Friday   NEAL.MAHAFFEY
From : 09/22/   To : 09/27/

	Sales Qty	% of Ttl	Net Sales	% of Ttl		Sales Qty	% of Ttl	Net Sales	% of Ttl
					1012 CRAB DIP	151	14.49%	1,019.25	15.07%
1002 BROC/CHEESE	40	3.84%	186.00	2.75%					
					1013 BBQ SHRIMP APP	42	4.03%	287.70	4.25%
1003 QUESADILLA	13	1.25%	74.75	1.11%					
					1014 LOADED SKINS	75	7.20%	446.25	6.60%
1004 CHIX FINGER APP	111	10.65%	704.85	10.42%					
					1015 TAQUITOS	18	1.73%	107.10	1.58%
1005 WHITE PIZZA	20	1.92%	139.00	2.06%					
					1016 WINGS	238	22.65%	1,404.20	20.76%
1007 ULTIMATE NACHO	29	2.78%	172.55	2.55%					
					1017 DOUBLE WINGS	45	4.32%	492.75	7.29%
1008 SUPER COMBO	80	7.68%	716.00	10.59%	**Total APPS**	**1,042**	**100.00%**	**6,763.40**	**100.00%**
					Grand Total	1,042		6,763.40	
1009 FRIED MOZZ	87	8.35%	430.65	6.37%	- Other Disc			-1192.14	
					Net Sales Total			5,571.26	
1010 CHIX NACHOS	38	3.65%	226.10	3.34%					
1011 SPINACH DIP	57	5.47%	356.25	5.27%					

MI_S102.RPT   Page 1

Courtesy of MICROS Systems, Inc., Columbia, Maryland.

as desired, and can include data for other periods (the current week or month or the previous year, for example) for comparison purposes. This type of information can be helpful as managers estimate the total number of food items needed for the time period being planned. Lodging operators often use occupancy levels to help estimate the number of guests that hotel dining rooms might expect. The forecast of hotel guests is combined with other estimates, including reservations and estimates of nonhotel guests, to determine the dining room sales potentials.

Many large food service operations take information generated from sales history records and expand it into master food production planning worksheets. An example showing the types of information collected for representative items is shown in Exhibit 2. The worksheet tells production personnel the estimated number of portions needed each day and also provides requisitioning, leftover, and actual sales information that the operation can use in future planning.

Production planning meetings also help managers anticipate the need for other resources. For example, having an estimate of the number of meals to prepare makes it possible to schedule labor and equipment.[1] If special events such as banquets, holiday get-togethers, or other catered functions are scheduled for the upcoming week, managers will need to plan, communicate, and coordinate to ensure that no problems arise.

With proper planning, it is less likely that resources will be overused or underused as various departments undertake their respective activities. Effective planning minimizes potential problems.

Exhibit 2　Sample Master Food Production Planning Worksheet

Day ___Tuesday___　　Master Food Production Planning Worksheet　　Local Weather Forecast ___Cloudy & mild___

Date ___8/1/XX___

Items	Standard Portion Size	Estimated Portions	Requisitioning Guide Data		Remarks	Number of Portions Left Over	Actual Number Served
			Raw Materials Requested	State of Preparation			
Appetizers							
Shrimp Cocktail	5 ea	51	12 lbs of 21–25 count	RTC		—	53
Fruit Cup	5 oz	20	See Recipe for 20 Portions			—	19
Marinated Herring	2½ oz	16	2½ lbs	RTE		—	14
Half Grapefruit	½ ea	8	4 Grapefruit			—	9
Soup	6 oz	36	Prepare 2 Gallons			5	32
Entrées							
Sirloin Steak	14 oz	29	29 Sirloin Steaks (Btchr.)	RTC		—	28
Prime Ribs	9 oz	64	3 Ribs of Beef	RTC	Use Re-heat if necessary	out at 10:45 P.M.	62
Lobster	1½ lb	28	28 Lobsters (check stock)			—	26
Ragout of Lamb	4 oz	26	12 lbs lamb fore (¾" pcs)		Recipe No. E.402	1+	25
Half Chicken	½ ea	38	38 halves (check stock)			—	39
Vegetables & Salads							
Whipped Potatoes	3 oz	58	13 lbs	AP		2–3	56
Baked Potatoes	1 ea	120	120 Idahos			out at 11:10 P.M.	120
Asparagus Spears	3 ea	113	8 No. 2 cans			2	110
Half Tomato	½ ea	54	27 Tomatoes			2	52
Tossed Salad	2½ oz	112	See Recipe No. S.302			—	114
Hearts of Lettuce	¼ hd	67	18 heads			—	69
Desserts							
Brownie w/ice cream	1 sq./1½ oz	26	1 pan brownies			—	24
Fresh Fruits	3 oz	11	See Recipe No. D.113			—	10
Ice Cream	2½ oz	40	Check stock			out at 10:50 P.M.	43
Apple Pie	⅐ cut	21	3 Pies				21
Devils Food Cake	⅛ cut	8	1 cake			1	7
Total No. of Persons		185					180

Abbreviations: AP —as purchased; RTC —ready-to-cook; RTE —ready-to-eat

Beverage operations usually require very little production planning if adequate bar par inventory levels have been established and if an effective minimum/maximum inventory system is used in central storage areas. Beverage planning typically focuses on scheduling employees and maintaining a constant supply of required brands of liquors, wines, and beers.

Technology Helps with Production Planning

As is true with manual systems used to forecast production requirements, automated planning systems begin by generating and analyzing sales history information. Point-of-sale systems can collect unit sales information on any historical period, such as by day of the week for the past six weeks, last year's college homecoming weekend, or the last three months. Information can also be summed for any length of time within that historical period, such as by the hour, meal period, day, or week. Data for the historical period can be separated by outlet (such as a hotel with several dining venues) or by unit (as in the case of a multi-unit organization). Sales data can be based on total units sold or on average number of units sold during the time period.

After the historical sales data is reviewed, a forecast of future sales based on the historical benchmark can be made. This will yield the estimated number of portions of each menu item to be sold during the period for which plans are being developed. Some systems use spreadsheet technology that enables the planner to easily modify the estimated number of portions to be sold and, therefore, the estimated revenue to be generated. For example, a property may be gearing up for a Saturday night prime rib promotion, and the number of sales of this item is expected to be well above the average for the previous periods analyzed. Some systems allow managers to modify sales forecasts by additional factors such as quantities of items needed for off-site catering and on-site operations.

As a result of such data manipulation, managers can finalize their sales forecasts. It is then possible to consider the profitability of each item for the planning period. Kitchen management software can easily and quickly calculate profitability on a by-menu-item and total-sales basis by multiplying the estimated number of items to be sold by the item's food cost determined from precosted standard recipes. It also calculates estimated revenues by multiplying the number of items sold by each item's selling price. The difference between total selling price and total food cost represents the estimated **contribution margin** from the sale of each item and from the sales of all items. Some software programs even conduct a pre-sale menu engineering analysis that, based on forecasted sales, reflects the profitability/popularity status of each item. This type of analysis can help planners identify, before the planning period even begins, those items requiring special attention if planning is on target.

When sales forecasts are completed, production planners know the total number of items to be produced and, therefore, the quantities of ingredients that will need to be requisitioned and purchased; those quantities can be electronically calculated. For example, the quantity of ground beef required to produce all menu items using ground beef can be determined by considering ingredient quantities needed per portion based upon standard recipes. This amount can be compared to quantities currently available in storage, and additional quantities needed, if any, will be known. A shopping list of ingredients to purchase can be generated and the ingredients can be ordered using manual or computerized purchasing systems.

Food Production Functions

Food production involves several functions that may be performed in one or more types of kitchens. Some managers find it helpful to consider three separate activities in the food production process (see Exhibit 3). As you review the exhibit, note that the first step in food production is preparing. Examples include rinsing fresh produce and trimming excess fat from meat products. Many, but not all, products must be prepared, although such items as frozen pre-portioned meat patties involve no preparation and can immediately undergo cooking, the second food production activity. In cooking, heat is applied to make items more palatable. After cooking, menu items that are prepared in batches must often be held (the third food production activity) at the proper serving temperature until they are served.

Exhibit 3 also shows that some items are not cooked. After preparation, they are held for service. Examples include lettuce and other salad ingredients and fresh fruits used for desserts.

The number of production activities depends on the characteristics of the specific operation—large or small, cafeteria or table service, limited menu or extensive menu, and so on—and on the specific items to be produced based upon menu needs.

Typical major functions include preparing cold foods, cooking, baking, and preparing beverages. Each of these major functions encompasses other functions and has many applications. For example, there are many types of cooking methods for many types of foods. Cooking methods can be broadly categorized as moist heat and dry heat, as shown in Exhibit 4. **Moist-heat cooking methods** require water or another liquid. **Dry-heat cooking methods** require hot air or hot fat.

This chapter addresses major preparation functions for fresh fruits and vegetables; meats and poultry; fish; eggs and dairy products; baked goods; and coffee and tea. First, though, the chapter reviews important food production principles that food preparation personnel must remember whenever they undertake food production activities.

Exhibit 3   Three Food Production Activities

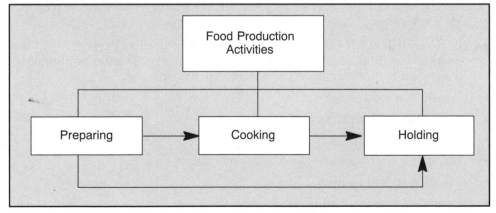

Exhibit 4   Examples of Moist-Heat and Dry-Heat Cooking Methods

> **Moist-Heat Cooking Methods**
>
> **Boiling**—cooking food in 212°F (100°C) water. Blanching and parboiling are types of boiling in which foods are partially cooked for a short time.
>
> **Poaching**—cooking food in liquid below the boiling point of water. The food may or may not be covered with liquid.
>
> **Simmering**—cooking food in a liquid that is below its boiling point.
>
> **Steaming**—using water converted to an invisible vapor or gas by heating it to the boiling point. Cooking with steam helps retain nutrients.
>
> **Stewing**—simmering small cuts of poultry or meat in a thickened liquid.
>
> **Dry-Heat Cooking Methods**
>
> **Baking**—cooking with dry heat in an oven.
>
> **Roasting**—using baking principles applicable to meat and poultry as opposed to other foods.
>
> **Broiling**—cooking food at a high temperature on a rack that is located above, below, or between heat sources.
>
> **Barbecuing**—broiling, grilling, or roasting while basting with a sauce.
>
> **Grilling**—cooking on an open grid over gas, charcoal, or electric heat.
>
> **Griddling**—cooking on a solid heated surface, usually with a small amount of fat.
>
> **Frying**—cooking quickly in fat. Frying includes pan-frying, stir-frying, sautéing, deep-frying, and pressure-frying. All but deep-frying and pressure-frying use a small amount of fat.

Food Production Principles

Food is cooked or otherwise prepared for these reasons: (1) to develop, enhance, or alter flavor; (2) to improve digestibility; and (3) to destroy harmful organisms. Too much cooking or other improper preparation destroys vitamins, affects the potency of proteins, and can unfavorably change the color, texture, and flavor of food. Therefore, foods should be prepared according to basic principles that include the following:

- Begin with quality food (which is not necessarily the most expensive). In this context, quality food is food that meets purchase specification requirements developed to meet or exceed the guests' expectations.

- Ensure that food is clean.

- Make sure food is properly handled.

- Use proper seasonings.

- Use the right preparation techniques and equipment.

- Follow standard recipes.

- Do not cook larger-than-necessary quantities.

- Serve food as soon as possible after preparation (that is, minimize holding times).

- Serve hot food hot and cold food cold.

- Make every presentation something special.

- Never be satisfied with a less-than-excellent product. Always try to make it perfect.

Preparing Fresh Fruits and Vegetables

Increased nutritional awareness is leading Americans to consume a larger quantity and variety of fresh fruits and vegetables. The quality of these products is constantly improving. Excellent choices of fresh fruits and vegetables are often available year-round because of the diverse climates in the United States and because technology has improved storage and transportation systems. However, there are still times when fruits and vegetables are in limited supply, with lower quality and higher prices. Wise managers attempt to compensate for this by eliminating the items from nonessential preparations such as garnishes, or by substituting other foods, such as endive or escarole for iceberg lettuce, for example.

Fresh Fruits

The term **fruit** refers to the matured ovary of a plant, including the seeds and adjacent parts. It is the reproductive body of the seed plant. Fruits are high in carbohydrates and water and are excellent sources of minerals and vitamins.

Normally, only ripe fruit is used for food production. When fruit is ripe, it is at full size, its tissue is soft and tender, its color is good, it tastes better because the starch has turned to sugar, and its aroma has developed.

Fruit costs are affected by:

- Perishability
- Pesticides

You Get What You Pay For?

Have you ever heard the old saying, "You get what you pay for"? Many people, including some food service managers, believe this to be true: when you pay more for a product, you receive a better product. "Better" can mean higher quality, greater quantity, and/or a recognized brand.

Unfortunately, there are many times when this old saying is not true, especially when purchasing fruits and vegetables. It is a regrettable reality that, when specific types of produce are in limited supply because of weather conditions or transportation and access challenges, the products often are of low quality at very high prices. Savvy food service managers know that, unless these items are extremely important to the menu, their purchase should be curtailed until more normal quality and cost conditions arise. If appropriate, a different item may be substituted.

- Weather conditions

- Consumer preferences

- Packaging

- Processing

There are many precautions to take and procedures to follow when working with fresh fruit. Careful washing is a must. Fresh fruit should be handled as little as possible to avoid bruising. Citrus fruit is easier to peel after it has been steamed, which can be done efficiently in a compartment steamer. To prevent darkening of low-acid fruits after cutting, the cut fruit should be placed in orange or lemon juice to slow the browning process. The cut fruit could also be covered with a sugar solution to prevent contact with oxygen, which causes the color change.

Remember that fresh fruits are often more palatable and nutritious than cooked fruit. Try to find innovative ways to serve fresh fruits.

Usually, fresh fruits are best stored at refrigerated temperatures. Bananas are an exception and should be purchased for immediate use because they are highly perishable.

Fresh Vegetables

The term **vegetable** refers to any plant grown for an edible part other than the ovary. Generally, vegetables have less sugar and more starch than fruits. The structure of a vegetable is formed by cellulose and can be maintained only when water remains in the cell. Vegetables shrink and wilt as they dry.

Vegetables are classified by the part of the plant from which they come. Examples include:

- Roots—sweet potatoes, beets, carrots, parsnips, and turnips

- Tubers or underground stems—potatoes

- Bulbs—onions, garlic, and leeks

- Stems—celery, rhubarb, and asparagus

- Leaves—lettuce, spinach, and cabbage

- Flowers—cauliflower, broccoli, and artichokes

- Pods and seeds—green beans, peas, and lima beans

- Sprouts—soybeans and alfalfa

- **Vegetable fruits**—tomatoes, eggplants, squash, pumpkin, okra, peppers, and cucumbers (vegetables that technically are classified as fruits because they contain the ovary of the plant).

Vegetables are rich in minerals and vitamins. They generally cost less when they are in season because they are abundantly available.

Careful washing is important when preparing fresh vegetables. Wilted vegetables can be soaked in cold water or covered with ice to help regain crispness, but this does not restore lost nutrients. To avoid unnecessary waste, do not throw away usable leaves of lettuce and outer stalks of celery. Pare potatoes and other vegetables thinly to reduce nutrient and product loss.

Fresh vegetables should be purchased only for immediate consumption. They should be stored in a cool, well-ventilated space. Most vegetables other than roots or tubers require refrigeration.

Fruit and Vegetable Salads

Fruits and vegetables for salads should be fresh and have fine flavor and color. Salads may be served as accompaniments to entrées or as meals by themselves. The following guidelines are helpful in salad-making:

- Use fresh, ripe products.

- Use a variety of colors.

- Use varied textures. Crisp, soft, and smooth combinations work well. Mushiness is unacceptable.

- Use the right cleaning, cutting, and chopping tools such as a clean vegetable brush, sharp knives, and a cutting board used only for preparing salads.

- Freshen washed vegetables in very cold water just until they are crisp. Drain well before using.

- Chop or cut salad ingredients in pieces of uniform size; avoid crushing.

- Handle prepared salad ingredients gently. Toss mixed salads together lightly.

- If salad dressings are added to salads rather than served on the side, add them just before serving to avoid wilting the salad.

- Keep salad ingredients, finished salads, and salad dressings refrigerated until serving time.

There appear to be no limits to the types of hot or cold salads that can be prepared. Some common types include tossed salads, cabbage slaws, pasta salads, molded salads, fruit salads, hot vegetable salads, and protein salads. Note that many of these types overlap; that is, fruit salads can be tossed, layered, frozen with whipped cream, molded in gelatin, can have a cream or cottage cheese base, or can be arranged in any number of ways. Fruits can be diced and served with complementary foods or served as halves or sections. (Want to learn some great ideas about unusual salads and their often very creative presentations? Just enter "images of uncommon salads" in your favorite search engine.)

Tossed salads are made with one or more kinds of salad greens. Salad greens include escarole, endive, and chicory, and iceberg, romaine, Boston, and Bibb lettuces. Parsley and spinach also are frequently used in tossed salads. Slaws are made with chopped or shredded green and/or red cabbage mixed with other shredded vegetables or, perhaps, mixed fruit, marshmallows, nuts, cheese, or onions.

Molded salads generally have a plain gelatin or dessert gelatin base. They can be layered with fruit, vegetables (cooked or raw), meat, fish, cheese, or cream. Salads made with meats, poultry, fish, or dairy products (especially cheeses) are common entrées.

Salad Dressings and Marinades. Salad dressings and **marinades** are special enhancements that are typically coupled with vegetables and fruits. Marinades are also used in preparing meat, poultry, and fish.

There are probably as many types of salad dressings as there are types of salads, but many have certain characteristics and ingredients in common. Most salad dressings are either stable or unstable emulsions. An **emulsion** is a mixture of two ordinarily unmixable liquids. Stable emulsions are those that do not separate, such as mayonnaise. Unstable emulsions are those that separate when left standing, such as oil and vinegar. Unstable emulsions must be shaken to remain evenly mixed. Other types of dressings include those that are cooked or boiled and those with yogurt or sour cream bases.

Marinades are seasoned liquids that are usually made with vegetable or olive oil and an acid such as wine, vinegar, or fruit juice. Herbs, spices, or vegetables are often added for flavoring. Marinated foods are those that have been soaked in a marinade. The marinade may be used to tenderize as well as to enhance the flavor of the food item. Marinades can also be used as a cooking medium and as a sauce for the cooked food.

Fruit and Vegetable Garnishes

Fruits and vegetables are frequently used as **garnishes** to decorate plates and platters of food. Garnishes should contribute form, color, and texture to the foods with which they are served. There is an endless variety of fruit and vegetable garnishes ranging from lemon slices to exotic truffles.

Actually, the range of garnishes is limited only by one's imagination and the general rule that the garnishes be edible. Fruits and vegetables are not the only foods used as garnishes. Other examples are sieved egg whites, chocolate curls, stuffed anchovies, croutons and toast points, and edible flowers.

Fruit and Vegetable Cookery

Preparation principles for cooking fresh vegetables and fruits are basically the same as those for cold vegetables and fruits: the produce must be washed and sometimes trimmed, cut, torn, or soaked. Fresh produce should be properly stored as soon as possible after delivery, and should be used as quickly as possible. (Typically, food operators purchase fresh produce in relatively small quantities for several-times-weekly delivery.) Vegetables such as potatoes and carrots require scrubbing, while greens and others require soaking. Water used to clean vegetables should not be reused.

General principles for cooking fruits and vegetables are simple to learn and practice. Preparation goals are to retain nutrients, to yield a high level of flavor, and to produce a food item that is tender, firm, and colorful. Normally, fruits and vegetables are cooked in just a small amount of water until tender and firm but not soft.

As noted earlier, overcooking destroys many valuable nutrients and distorts color, flavor, texture, and shape. Preparation should be scheduled as close to serving time as possible. Most vegetables should be cooked in covered cooking vessels. Green vegetables, however, should be cooked without a cover. Baking soda (or any other alkaline chemical) deepens the green color of vegetables, but it can also cause a loss of vitamin C and, therefore, should not be used.

When heating canned vegetables, remember that they have already been fully cooked. Only a very short heating time is necessary, and should be scheduled as close to serving time as possible. Canned vegetables lend themselves to batch cooking methods. Batch cooking is a method in which small quantities of products are prepared immediately before serving. For example, if seventy-five portions of cooked carrots are needed over a two-hour period, the chef might prepare twenty-five portions at a time. While more effort is required to prepare three batches instead of one, the advantage of higher quality at the time of service often makes the effort worthwhile.

Cooking Methods. Fruit and vegetable cooking methods include steaming, baking, frying, microwaving, and boiling.

Steaming. Steaming, one of the best cooking methods for fruits and vegetables, uses water that has been converted to an invisible vapor or gas. Compartment steamers have low-, high-, or room-pressure compartments into which steam is injected. The direct application of steam quickly cooks the food while maintaining high quality and nutritional levels. The instructions from the steam equipment manufacturer should always be followed closely. Steamed vegetables normally should be salted and seasoned *after* they are cooked.

Baking. Baking is a dry-heat cooking method using hot air. It is appropriate for fruits and vegetables such as potatoes, squash, eggplants, apples, and tomatoes because they contain enough water to form steam.

Frying. One frying method particularly popular for fruits and vegetables is stir-frying. Stir-frying requires high heat, a small amount of oil in an open skillet or wok, and a short amount of cooking time. Stir-fry vegetables should be diced or cut into same-sized pieces and crisp-cooked. Sautéing—cooking quickly in a small amount of hot fat—is similar to stir-frying.

Deep-frying is appropriate for such vegetables as potatoes, eggplants, and onions. Deep-frying uses a large amount of fat and requires that vegetables be rinsed and dried before frying. Tempura is a method of deep-frying in which products are parboiled, dried, and breaded, usually in a flour and water batter, before they are deep-fried in fat.

Microwaving. Vegetables to be cooked in a microwave oven should be placed in a covered microwave-safe dish with a very small amount of liquid. Since vegetables cook quickly, timing is critical to prevent overcooking.

Boiling. Boiling involves cooking food in water or other liquid at a temperature of 212°F (100°C). When boiling, bring water to a full boil, add vegetables, cover the cooking container (if applicable), lower the temperature, and continue cooking at a gentle boil. Cooking in water can destroy water-soluble vitamins. The problem worsens when the water used in cooking is discarded rather than used to prepare the product.

Blanching is a form of boiling. When foods are blanched, they are submerged in boiling water for a short time. Peaches and tomatoes may be blanched so their skins are easier to remove when peeling. Blanching is also used when preparing fruits and vegetables for freezing. Vegetables are often blanched as a preliminary

---

What About "Al Dente" Vegetables?

"Al dente" is an Italian term often associated with pasta that also describes vegetables that are only cooked until they reach the "tender crisp" phase: they still offer resistance as one bites into them but are not soft or overdone, nor do they have a hard center.

The difference between "undercooked" and al dente can sometimes be subjective, based on the perceptions of the customer (who is always right!). Some cooks are concerned about cooking vegetables too long, and others are challenged to consistently cook vegetables only until they are tender but fresh.

Many people who enjoy al dente vegetables do so because of their fresh and natural taste and/or because they want to maximize the nutritional contributions of vegetables cooked this way.

---

process in cooking. Just before serving, blanched vegetables may be cooked by another process. Vegetables can also be parboiled, which is similar to blanching. This process involves immersing them in boiling water until they are partly cooked in preparation for roasting.

Vacuum processing. Vacuum processing produces partially cooked or prepared food. Fruits and vegetables can be partially cooked and vacuum-packed in plastic pouches. The pouches are then refrigerated (not frozen). To reheat, pouches may be dropped in boiling water or steamed in a special oven. If they have been processed by the *sous vide* method, they may require steaming in a special oven. Operations can purchase vacuum-packed commercially processed foods or they can use vacuum-processing techniques on-site. Advantages of the latter include potential labor savings, increased shelf life of food, and higher-quality products. A potential disadvantage involves sanitation problems if packaging is done improperly.

Preparing Meats and Poultry

Meats and poultry are often the most expensive and important items on a menu. Great care should be taken in purchasing, preparing, and serving these entrées. Popular meats include beef, pork, veal, and lamb (see Exhibit 5); chicken and turkey are the most popular types of poultry. Meats and poultry have many common characteristics, including their four primary components:

- *Muscle fiber.* Muscle is made of fibers held together by connective tissue. The thickness of the fibers, the size of fiber bundles, and the amount of connective tissue determines the grain of the meat.

- *Connective tissue.* Connective tissue holds muscles together and determines the tenderness of the meat. This tissue covers the walls of muscle fibers, binds fibers into bundles, and surrounds the muscles. Tendons and ligaments that attach the muscle to the bone are composed of connective tissue. Less-tender meat cuts have more connective tissue.

Exhibit 5   Meat Cuts: Beef, Pork, Veal, and Lamb

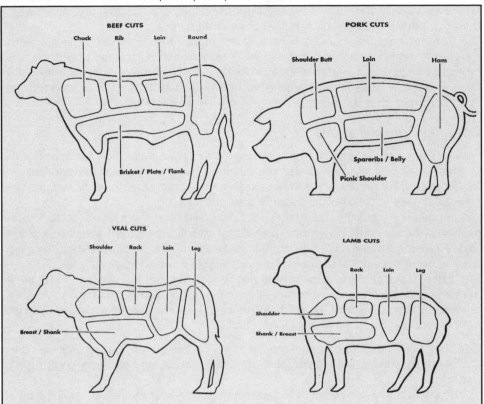

Source: Jerald W. Chesser, *The Art and Science of Culinary Preparation: A Culinarian's Manual* (St. Augustine, Florida: Educational Institute of the American Culinary Federation, 1999), pp. 249, 251, 252, 253.

There are two types of connective tissue: collagen (white), which breaks down into gelatin when heat is applied; and elastin (yellow), which does not break down when heated. Tender meat contains collagen instead of elastin. The type of connective tissue within the meat determines the cooking method.

- *Fat.* Fat is distributed inside meat in small layers called marbling. Fat contributes to tenderness and flavor. Exterior layers of fat cover the muscle.

- *Bone.* Bone is not edible. A high proportion of meat to bone is favorable because there is a lower cost per edible unit. The shape of bone helps identify the meat cut. Bones are used in soup stocks to add flavor.

Tenderness

Tenderness is important in selecting, preparing, and serving meats and poultry. As just noted, tenderness is influenced by the type and amount of connective tissue that is present. Fat and age also affect tenderness. Tender meat has more fat, and young animals yield tender meat. The location of the muscle on the animal also affects tenderness. The least-used muscles (loin and rib cuts) are more tender than fully developed muscles such as chuck and round.

Temperature influences tenderness: the higher the cooking temperature, the tougher the meat, especially if the meat is overcooked. Grinding, pounding, and other techniques can tenderize meat. Aged meat (that hung in a refrigerator during the time of after-death changes) will be more tender. Enzymes injected into meat before or after the slaughtering process are also tenderizers.

Cooking Considerations

Goals of meat cooking include improving flavor, changing color, tenderizing the product, and destroying harmful organisms. Cooking at a low temperature for longer periods of time is better than using a high temperature for a shorter cooking time, because there will be less weight and nutrient loss.

Some meats (portion-cut items) can be cooked from their frozen state. If done properly, there is little difference in tenderness, juiciness, and flavor of frozen or thawed meats. Frozen meats should be processed at a lower temperature for a longer period of time while incorporating applicable food safety principles.

Microwave cooking generally is not useful for cooking meats. While cooking time is faster, the product often is drier (tougher) and shrinks more. Another drawback is that, unless special heating elements are used, the meat surface is not browned.

Cooking Methods. Popular cooking methods for meat and poultry include roasting, broiling, pan broiling, frying, braising, simmering, and pressure cooking and steaming.

Roasting. Roasting in an oven is a common dry-heat method of cooking meat. Meat to be roasted should be placed on a rack in a roasting pan with the fat side up so the meat can baste itself. A meat thermometer should always be used, often inserted in the thickest part of the muscle away from bone. Do not rely on charts that list minutes per pound or other roasting factors. While these can serve as general guides, careful use of a meat thermometer is always best.

Guests have preferences about how their meat is prepared. Some people prefer meat that is well done (no pink color; gray throughout). Others like rare meat (browned surface with a red interior). Still others like their meat between these stages (a thicker layer of gray surface with a pink interior). Popular cooking references vary in the recommended interior temperatures necessary to attain different stages of doneness, and experienced cooks have their own standards. Food service managers should work with chefs to develop cooking procedures that meet the operation's food quality and safety standards, especially considering health department and public concerns that consumers could contract foodborne illness from eating undercooked meat.

Meat continues to cook after it is removed from the oven. Therefore, it should be removed when the internal temperature of the product is a few degrees cooler than the desired temperature.

Pork should always be cooked until it is well done with an internal temperature of at least 145°F (63°C) followed by a three-minute rest time. This prevents trichinosis, a disease caused by a roundworm that may be present in the meat because of improper care of the animal before slaughter or poor sanitary practices after slaughter.

Broiling. Broiling uses direct radiant heat. Meats should be approximately half-cooked when turned with tongs or a spatula. Normally, high temperatures should be used when broiling meat, poultry, and other food.

Pan broiling. With this technique, meat is broiled in a heavy fry pan and cooked slowly. The pan should not be covered and water or fat is seldom added. Fat from cooking should be poured off as it accumulates.

Frying. There are many frying techniques, as noted earlier. All use a small amount of fat except deep-frying, which uses a large amount of fat.

Braising. Braising is a process in which meat is first browned in a small amount of fat, then cooked slowly in a small amount of liquid in a covered cooking container.

Simmering. When simmered, meat is cooked in a small amount of water or broth in a covered pan until tender. The temperature of the water should be below the boiling point.

Pressure cooking and steaming. Meat can be cooked under pressure in a compartment steamer or steamed in an oven. Meat steamed in an oven should be covered with aluminum foil to prevent moisture loss. Trapped moisture becomes steam, which helps cook the meat.

Other Cooking Procedures. Meat stocks are used in preparing many meats and other products. Stocks are made from cracked bones, cut meat pieces, and other ingredients that are covered with water and simmered for several hours, when vegetables and spices are added. After cooking, the stock is strained, chilled, and degreased by removal of fat that congeals on the surface. Further processing can then be done. If a brown stock is desired, bones are roasted before simmering. Bones are not roasted for a white stock. Bouillon is a brown stock that has been clarified by the addition of egg whites.

Preparing Fish

There are two types of edible fish: finfish that have bony skeletons and come from salt water or fresh water, and shellfish without bony skeletons that come mainly from salt water. There are two types of shellfish: mollusks have hard-hinged shells (oysters, clams, scallops, mussels), and crustaceans have segmented shells (lobsters, shrimp, crabs).

The fat content of fish ranges from less than one percent (cod and haddock) to more than 25 percent (salmon, mackerel, and lake trout). The fat content is an important factor in determining the cooking method. The nutrient value of fish is generally quite high. Fish is a good source of minerals and protein and a good alternative to meat protein. Fish with a high fat content is a good source of vitamins.

Cooking Considerations

Fish has relatively little connective tissue compared to meat and poultry, and therefore requires shorter cooking times. Fish should be cooked at a moderate

How to Reduce Food Waste

It may seem obvious to say that food service managers should not purchase food they will not produce and sell. However, many do so frequently, and food waste is a significant reason for higher-than-planned food costs in numerous food service operations. Some commonsense tactics can help to ensure that all food purchased is used to generate revenue:

- Adjust inventory levels for perishable products to closely match production and sales needs. If product is losing quality while in storage, you have a problem!

- Use hourly or shift production schedules to reduce over-prepping and review production schedules at the end of the shift or day to learn if future adjustments might be helpful.

- When prepping fruits and vegetables, trim off only what is needed. Standard recipes should state ingredient quantities (example: number of usable ounces per pound) based on trim levels.

- Ask that all trimmings be put in a holding container for review before disposal. If excess trimming is observed, retrain and supervise preparation personnel or consider purchasing the product as a convenience food.

- Use vegetable and meat trimmings for soup stock, if applicable.

- Evaluate and adjust the size of portions if items are consistently being returned unfinished (check garbage cans or observe dishwashers). Offer guests smaller portions and price menu items accordingly.

- Place hot foods in shallow containers and pre-cool them in an ice bath before placing them in the refrigerator. This faster cool-down helps to reduce spoilage during storage for future use.

temperature long enough for flavor to develop, connective tissue to break down, and protein to coagulate.

Fish should not be overcooked because it becomes tough. The flesh is cooked sufficiently when it falls into clumps or flakes when tested with a fork. If cooked beyond this point, the product will become tough, dry, and flavorless. Fish that is properly cooked breaks up easily, so careful handling is necessary during cooking and serving.

Fish can be prepared without heat, using a marinade with acids like lemon or lime juice. The acid in the marinade speeds the coagulation of the fish protein, causing it to turn white. Marinated products such as pickled herring are favorites with many guests. Fish is also served raw with sushi (rice with vinegar) in some establishments featuring Japanese cuisine.

Popular cooking methods include such dry-heat techniques as broiling, baking, and frying. Moist-heat methods such as poaching and steaming also can be used. Low-fat fish may require some fat in the cooking process. However, cooks normally do not need to add fat while cooking high-fat fish products.

Shellfish can be cooked by placing the product in simmering water. Shrimp is usually steamed, baked, charbroiled, or deep-fried.

Preparing Eggs and Dairy Products

Eggs

Eggs are a good source of vitamins and minerals. They can be prepared in various ways or used as an ingredient in other menu items. There is no relationship between the color of the eggshell (brown or white) and the quality and taste of egg products.

Cooking Considerations. Food preparation staff should follow these guidelines when cooking eggs:

- Use eggs as soon as possible after purchasing. Flavor and appearance deteriorate with age.
- Boiling causes eggs to become rubbery. When cooking eggs in the shell, place the eggs in boiling water, then turn down the heat to a simmering temperature or remove the eggs from the heat.
- Hard-cooked eggs should be cooked no more than fifteen minutes.
- Eggs cooked soft in the shell should be cooked for no longer than one to three minutes.
- After removing eggs cooked in the shell from the water, immerse them in cold water and peel them immediately to prevent yolks from turning green.
- To poach eggs, bring water to a simmer before adding the eggs. Eggs should be broken into a separate dish before they are added to the poaching container.
- Cook eggs at the lowest possible temperature.

Cooking Uses. There are many different ways to use eggs in cooking. When eggs are heated, the protein in the yolk coagulates. This makes eggs useful as thickening agents and for coating other foods. When heat is applied to the egg white, it changes from transparent to a soft white color. When sugar is added to an egg mixture, higher heat is necessary for coagulation; when salt is added, a lower temperature is needed. When an acid such as lemon juice is added, the temperature for coagulation is lowered and a fine gel is produced.

　　Binding and coating. Eggs help make ingredients stick together in products such as meat loaf and in batters for deep-fried products.

　　Leavening agent. Leavening involves incorporating gases into a product to increase the product's volume and make it lighter. Beaten egg whites turn into a foam made of air bubbles surrounded by thin layers of egg-white film. When this foam is incorporated into a mixture and heated, the air bubbles expand and the film hardens. This process is used to make omelets, soufflés, and sponge cakes. Egg whites should be beaten only until the peaks that form stand straight. If the whites are overbeaten, the volume of the foam will be reduced. If sugar is added while egg whites are being beaten, the resulting foam will be more stable.

Egg yolks can also be used as a leavening agent: when heated, they increase in size. However, because of the presence of fat, yolks are less effective leavening agents than egg whites.

Emulsifying agent. Oil and vinegar separate unless the oil droplets are coated with egg or some other emulsifier to prevent the separation. Egg yolks are used as an emulsifier in mayonnaise, ice cream, and cake.

Interfering substance. Eggs prevent ice crystals from combining to create a larger mass. They are used in this way to make sherbets.

Clarifying agent. When egg protein coagulates, it traps particles in the substance so they can be removed. This makes liquids clear and free of impurities. Broths, for example, can be clarified with egg whites.

Dairy Products

Milk is a naturally nutritious product. It is usually pasteurized and homogenized. **Pasteurization** is a process of controlled heating that destroys bacteria to make milk safe to consume. **Homogenization** is a process that breaks up fat particles so they will remain suspended in the milk. This prevents milk from separating into fat and liquid parts.

Milk has many cooking uses, but it is delicate. Milk curdles, scorches easily, and is highly perishable. While many types of milk are available, basic cooking procedures are the same regardless of which milk product is used.

Cooking with Milk. Acids such as lemon juice, tomato juice, and vinegar can cause milk to curdle. This is a frequent problem. To prevent curdling, heat should be kept as low as possible during cooking, and salt should be withheld until the product is served. Warming the milk first, or blending a small amount of the acid mixture at a time with the milk, helps prevent curdling.

To prevent scorching, milk should be heated in a double boiler, a steam-jacketed kettle, or a steamer. Milk's flavor and odor can be affected by prolonged cooking, or a surface skin can form. The latter can be prevented by covering the milk, stirring it, or placing a small amount of fat such as butter on the surface of the milk. Low heat and frequent stirring are two important preparation principles to follow when cooking with milk.

Cooking with Cheese. The basic cooking procedures for milk are also important when cooking with cheese. There are many cheese varieties and, like milk, cheese is a very nutritious food. Expensive cheeses are not necessarily higher in food value. The extra expense is due to the cost of popular flavoring techniques and the supply and demand characteristics of the marketplace.

Remember that protein coagulates with heat. Cheese can become tough and rubbery when it is overheated. This can occur when it is heated too long or at too high a temperature. Fat in cheese is solid at room temperature. As it warms, it softens. When cheese is heated, it melts.

Cream cheese is frequently used in cooking since it is easy to blend. Cheddar is the most popular cheese used in cooking and should be chopped or grated before being added to a sauce or cooked dish. This increases the cheese's surface area and hastens the melting process.

Preparing Baked Products

Some food service operations bake some or all of their bread and dessert products. Bakeshop production is both an art and a science. Sometimes it is difficult to develop quality bakery products, even with the best recipes. Altitude, humidity, and moisture content of the specific flour used affect baking times and temperatures and the amount of ingredients that must be added to some baked products.

Common Baking Ingredients

Flour. Flour is made when wheat, rye, barley, or corn are ground and sifted. It also can be made from rice, potato, or soy products. Wheat is the most popular flour and is classified by *hardness*. *Hard* wheat flour has a higher protein content and produces a larger volume and finer texture of bread product. *Soft* wheat flour is lower in protein and is used in cakes, pastries, and cookies. Durum wheat has the highest protein content, and is used to make macaroni and similar products. There are many types of wheat flour; some of the most popular are noted in Exhibit 6.

Leavening Agents. Leavening agents are used to make dough light and porous. Dough products can be leavened by incorporating air or by forming gas.

Air can be incorporated into dough by beating eggs or by creaming fat and sugar. Gas can be formed in dough when water in the dough turns into steam (a gas), which then expands the dough. Popovers and cream puffs are examples of products leavened entirely by steam.

Carbon dioxide (CO_2) gas is created as yeast interacts with sugar. The types of yeast most commonly used for baking purposes are pressed yeast and dry yeast. Pressed yeast (live yeast cells pressed into a cake) and dry yeast (yeast dried in granular form) are packaged in metal foil or jars to avoid contact with the air. Carbon dioxide can also be produced by using baking soda with water. Baking powder (made from dry acid, baking soda, and starch or flour) is another popular leavening chemical. Whenever baking powder or baking soda is used, it should always be added with the dry ingredients so that the gas-forming reaction can be delayed until the water is added as one of the final steps in the preparation process.

Fat. Fat creates a tenderizing effect by coating flour particles and preventing them from coming together. The term *plasticity* refers to a fat's ability to be molded. Fats that are more *plastic*—those with a waxy texture—tend to hold their shape in a batter or dough, have a high melting temperature, and have greater *shortening power,* the ability of shortenings to surround flour particles and other ingredients, lubricating them so they cannot stick together.

Liquids. Liquids are used for several purposes in baking. They can hydrate (add water to) starch and gluten. Liquids can dissolve salt, sugar, and baking powders. In addition, liquids moisturize baking powders and sodas to start carbon dioxide production.

Eggs. Eggs incorporate air into batter and add flavor and color. Since egg proteins coagulate, eggs add rigidity to the structure of baked products.

Exhibit 6 Types of Wheat Flour

Whole wheat (graham) flour—This wheat flour contains the entire wheat kernel ground into the flour.

Bread flour—High in protein content, this flour is used for yeast breads. The protein ingredients develop into gluten, which gives the bread structure, elasticity, and strength.

All-purpose flour—This flour is made of blended wheats with a lower protein content than bread flour. It has less strength and elasticity and is used for pastry, cookies, and homemade bread.

Pastry flour—This type of flour has a lower protein content than all-purpose flour and is used in the commercial baking industry for pastries and cookies.

Cake flour—Cake flour has a very low protein content and is very finely ground. It is bleached white and, as the name suggests, is used in cake production.

Instant flour (quick mixing)—This type of flour does not need to be sifted and creates no flour "dust."

Self-rising flour—A leavening agent such as baking soda is added to self-rising flour.

Gluten flour—This flour is very high in protein content (approximately 41 percent) and is used for special bakery purposes.

Enriched flour—Enriched flour has B vitamins, iron, and other ingredients added.

Sugar. Sugar adds sweetness, creates a browning effect, and serves as a yeast food. Sugar also tenderizes by interfering with development of the gluten in the flour and helps contribute to the fine texture of bakery products.

Mixing Batter and Dough

Flour mixtures can be classified as either dough or batter. Dough for pie or bread is thick enough to be rolled or kneaded. By contrast, batter can be poured, as in cake-making, or dropped, as in cookie preparation.

There are several methods of mixing batter and dough. With the muffin method, dry ingredients are sifted together first. Then eggs are beaten, and liquid and fat are added to them. This mixture is then blended with dry ingredients. With the pastry method, dry ingredients are sifted together, and fat is blended with the dry ingredients. The liquid is added last. With the conventional cake method, fat and sugar are first creamed together and then eggs are added. Dry and liquid ingredients are alternately blended with the fat/sugar/egg mixture.

Preparing Coffee and Tea

Coffee and tea are two of America's most popular beverages. Some guests judge their entire meal by the quality of these beverages. Food service professionals must ensure that the flavor and consistency of the coffee and tea they serve meet or exceed their guests' expectations.

Coffee

Blends of coffee used in food service operations are specially designed to maintain quality for relatively long periods of time. Coffee normally is made in an urn or in an automatic coffeemaker.

When made in an urn, ground coffee is carefully measured and placed in a container lined with a filter. Fresh cold water is poured into the container, and the coffee is brewed at the proper temperature. Temperatures, times, and recipes vary depending on the type of coffeemaker, the manufacturer, the type of coffee, and the operation's recipe. It is important to follow manufacturers' directions. When the coffee is brewed, grounds should be removed immediately. Then, half of the coffee should be drawn and poured back into the urn to mix the stronger, bottom-of-the-urn liquid with the rest of the coffee.

Procedures for using an automatic coffeemaker are similar. Coffee should be held at approximately 185°F (85°C), should *never* be allowed to boil, and should not be held longer than one hour. Coffeemakers should be rinsed after each use and cleaned regularly according to manufacturers' instructions.

Coffee used for iced coffee is often made double strength to allow for dilution from ice.

Tea

Tea is made with loose tea or tea bags. Water for making tea should be at the boiling point when it is poured over the loose tea or the tea bag. The teapot or cup should be kept hot, and the tea should be allowed to steep for no more than five minutes. It should be served immediately.

Iced tea is often prepared with one-ounce tea bags immersed in water that has reached the boiling point. The normal proportion is two ounces of tea to one gallon of water. Like hot tea, iced tea should steep for no more than five minutes and then be poured into a glass with ice. When this is impractical, tea should be precooled, and ice should be added to the glass when the tea is served. Ice will dilute the tea, so it should be made stronger than hot tea.

Green Restaurants

One of today's most significant and popular trends is the emphasis on **green restaurants**. Food service operations of all types recognize that environmental initiatives are important. The public is increasingly interested in these issues, operating costs can be reduced with subsequent increases in profitability, and many people feel a societal obligation to help protect the environment. Food service operations have taken measures that range from the simple to the complex, from substituting paper-based cups for polystyrene disposables (paper decomposes more quickly in landfills) to constructing energy-efficient buildings and adopting operating procedures that emphasize environmental concerns without sacrificing quality standards.

Food service operations can protect the environment during food production in numerous ways. For example, many restaurants serve water to guests only upon request. Production staff can thaw frozen food in the refrigerator instead of under running water in a sink, and can wash vegetables in a basin of water rather than under running water. Operators can repair leaking kitchen sinks, reduce hot-water temperatures (why heat water to such a high temperature when it must be cooled to make it comfortable and safe for employee use?), and install low-flow faucet spray valves.

Food operations can reduce energy usage in the kitchen in various ways. Routine preventive maintenance and daily cleaning make equipment operate more efficiently, and incandescent kitchen lighting is less expensive than other types of lighting. Kitchen equipment, including hoods, should be turned off when not in use, and the operation can purchase equipment with Energy Star ratings when applicable. (Energy Star, a joint program of the U.S. Environmental Protection Agency and the U.S. Department of Energy, promotes environmental protection through the use of energy-efficient products and practices.)

Operators can install energy curtains in walk-in refrigeration areas to reduce energy usage, use high-efficiency refrigeration equipment, and keep refrigerators and freezers full when possible. It may be feasible to empty or combine the contents of refrigeration units and disconnect those that are not in use. Dispenser coils for refrigerators and freezers should be cleaned according to the manufacturers' recommendations, and door gaskets and hinges should be inspected regularly and repaired or replaced as necessary. Products to be frozen should be wrapped in the proper freezing material (such as freezer paper or aluminum foil), and the date should be noted on the label. Perishable products should be rotated (placed in front of or on top of those recently delivered) to minimize spoilage.

Food production employees should be trained to use energy, water, and waste reduction strategies. Ongoing supervision can help ensure that environmental procedures are in use. In addition, food production personnel, especially those with experience, may have suggestions about useful green procedures and should be encouraged to make them.

Environmental concerns also apply to foods being produced. For example, operators can purchase food grown or manufactured locally to reduce

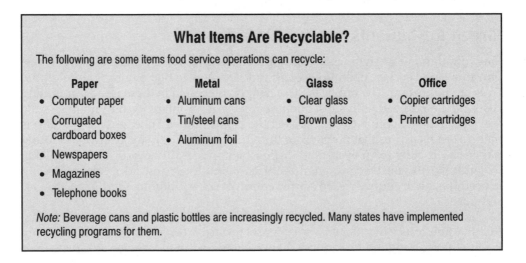

What Items Are Recyclable?

The following are some items food service operations can recycle:

Paper	Metal	Glass	Office
• Computer paper	• Aluminum cans	• Clear glass	• Copier cartridges
• Corrugated cardboard boxes	• Tin/steel cans	• Brown glass	• Printer cartridges
• Newspapers	• Aluminum foil		
• Magazines			
• Telephone books			

Note: Beverage cans and plastic bottles are increasingly recycled. Many states have implemented recycling programs for them.

transportation costs and the environmental impacts of transportation. Organic or naturally raised ingredients offer another possibility. For example, operators may wish to purchase grass-fed beef, since grazed pasture removes more atmospheric carbon dioxide than many other land uses, and grass-fed cattle produce up to 20 percent less methane gas than their grain-fed counterparts.

Operators can use bio-friendly, chemical-free cleaning products and even chlorine-free paper products for production and clean-up purposes. It is also important that operations correctly mix cleaning chemicals. Container labels and Material Safety Data Sheets (MSDSs) provide proper mixing instructions.

Food service operations can recycle cardboard, aluminum, plastic, glass, and newspaper. The two basic steps in recycling efforts are (1) to reduce the amount of waste initially generated, and (2) to reuse materials whenever possible. Examples of ways to reduce initial waste include purchasing food in the correct amount and rotating food in inventory. Restaurants can also serve smaller portions and dispense condiments in bulk rather than in individual packets. Many food service operations (and consumers!) recognize that bottled water is expensive (consider the transportation, marketing, and container costs alone) and serve tap water when guests request water. (Note: at the opposite extreme, other properties have bottled water lists similar to wine lists!) Daily production sheets help to minimize excessive preparation and unnecessary waste.

Operations can use recycled paper products, reusable serviceware, and reusable coffee filters to minimize waste. Some properties donate leftover food to community food banks for the homeless and hungry, a practice that could yield public

---

Waste Minimization in Food Service Operations

Waste minimization is an environmentally friendly practice that involves reducing, reusing, and recycling waste to lessen the amount of waste food service operations produce and the amount of money that must be spent to dispose of it. The ultimate goal is to ensure that disposal is done in an approved and environmentally suitable manner. The potential economic benefits of waste minimization can be significant, because waste haulage expenses can consume a large portion of a property's operation and maintenance budget.

Waste minimization begins at purchase. For example, buying products in bulk and using products made from recycled materials minimizes waste. Two other tactics are to control product usage and to work with suppliers to reduce product packaging.

To reduce waste through recycling, managers can allocate space for a program that accepts materials like glass, metal, plastic, paper, and cardboard. When planning this space, remember that the space and necessary containers should be as close to the point of use as possible, so it is easy and fast to dispose of recyclable items. Also, storage and pick-up spaces should be sufficient to contain the bulk recyclables collected from point-of-use locations.

Source: Adapted from material found in Chapter 13 of Joe Perdue and Jason Koenigsfeld, editors, *Contemporary Club Management,* 3rd ed. (Lansing, Mich.: American Hotel & Lodging Educational Institute, 2013).

relations benefits within the community. Also, it may be possible to work with suppliers to recycle shipping containers that transport products to the property.

Control During Food and Beverage Production

The primary concerns of managers during food and beverage production are: (1) to make quality-enhancing ingredients available for food and beverage production, and (2) to ensure that the operation consistently attains its quality standards.

Control activities to preserve quality and maximize food production efficiency include the following:

- Require that all standard cost control tools, such as standard recipes and standard portion sizes, be consistently used.

- Ensure that weighing and measuring tools are available, accurate, and always used.

- Ensure that only the amount of food actually needed for production is issued.

- Train personnel to comply with required food production procedures.

- Minimize wasted food.

- Monitor and control employee eating/drinking practices.

- Make sure that items removed from storage but not used are returned to secure storage areas, if applicable.

- Inspect and approve items that have spoiled in storage or were not properly prepared before they are discarded.

- Maintain production records and use them for revising quantities of items to be produced in the future.

- Analyze sales and production records to determine how much revenue each menu item is generating.

- Study and resolve production bottlenecks.

- Study systems for managing equipment, layout and design, and energy usage. Implement procedures for reducing costs without lowering quality standards.

- Confirm that labor-saving convenience foods or equipment items do, in fact, reduce labor costs.

- Recruit, train, and schedule personnel who are genuinely concerned about preparing and offering high-quality products that meet the property's standards.

Endnote

1. Details about scheduling are available in Jack D. Ninemeier, *Planning and Control for Food and Beverage Operations*, 8th ed. (Lansing, Mich.: American Hotel & Lodging Educational Institute, 2013).

Key Terms

contribution margin—Food revenue minus food cost.

dry-heat cooking methods—Cooking methods that require hot air or hot fat.

emulsion—A mixture of two ordinarily unmixable liquids. Unstable emulsions (such as oil and vinegar) separate when left standing; stable emulsions (like mayonnaise) do not separate.

fruit—The matured ovary of a plant, including the seeds and accessory parts; the reproductive body of the seed plant. Fruit is high in carbohydrates and water and is an excellent source of vitamins and minerals.

garnish—(1) Decorative edible items used to ornament or enhance the eye appeal of another food item. (2) Adding such a decorative item to food.

green restaurants—Restaurants that implement practices that help protect the environment by controlling water and energy usage and by creating less waste.

homogenization—A process that breaks up fat particles so they will remain suspended.

leavening—Incorporating gases into a product to increase the product's volume and make it lighter.

marinade—A seasoned liquid, usually containing vegetable or olive oil and an acid such as wine, vinegar, or fruit juice. Herbs, spices, or vegetables are often added for flavoring.

moist-heat cooking methods—Cooking methods that require water or some other liquid.

pasteurization—A process of controlled heating that destroys bacteria in milk and other food products.

sous vide—A French term meaning *under vacuum*. Food items are slowly cooked in sealed pouches from which air has been removed. Items are then quickly cooked for storage and are reheated for service in a water bath or microwave oven.

vegetable—Any plant grown for an edible part other than the ovary.

vegetable fruit—A vegetable (a tomato, for example) technically classified as a fruit because it contains the ovary of the plant.

Review Questions

1. What is the main purpose of production planning?
2. How can technology help food service managers and/or chefs with production planning activities?
3. What are the two basic classifications of cooking methods?
4. Why should fruits and vegetables be pared as thinly as possible?
5. What guidelines should be followed in making salads?

6. What are the effects of overcooking?

7. What factors influence the tenderness of meats and poultry?

8. Why does fish generally require shorter cooking times than meat and poultry?

9. What causes eggs to become rubbery?

10. When cooking with milk, what precautions should be taken?

11. What steps can be taken to control foods and beverages products during production?

Internet Sites

For more information, visit the following Internet sites. Remember that Internet addresses can change without notice. If the site is no longer there, you can use a search engine to look for additional sites.

Food Products

American Egg Board
www.aeb.org

American Meat Institute
www.meatami.org

CoffeeResearch.org
www.coffeeresearch.org

DairyGood
www.ilovecheese.com

Fleischmann's Yeast
www.breadworld.com

International Dairy Foods Association
www.idfa.org

National Food Service Management
  Institute
www.nfsmi.org (enter "produce" in
the site's search box)

North American Meat Association
www.meatassociation.com

Pretty Food
www.prettyfood.com

Produce Marketing Association
www.pma.com

Produce Oasis
www.produceoasis.com

Seafood Network Information Center
seafood.oregonstate.edu

TeaGenius
www.teagenius.com

United States Department of
  Agriculture (USDA)
www.usda.gov

Green Restaurants and Sustainability

Conserve: Solutions for Sustainability
www.conserve.restaurant.org

The Daily Green
www.nrdc.com

Green Restaurant Association
www.dinegreen.com

Pizza Fusion
www.pizzafusion.com

Restaurant Point-of-Sale Systems

ChefTec
www.cheftec.com

Eatec Solutions
www.agilysys.com

MICROS Systems, Inc.
www.micros.com

System Concepts, Inc.
www.foodtrak.com

Squirrel Systems
www.squirrelsystems.com

Problem

Problem 1

Complete the following Consolidated System Menu Item Sales Summary.

Item	Sales Quantity	% of Total	Net Sales	% of Total
A	28		107.00	
B	31		120.00	
C	105		375.00	
D	74		290.00	
E	67		240.00	

Chapter 10 Outline

Types of Service
    Table Service
    Buffet Service
    Cafeteria Service
    Other Types of Service
Providing an Enjoyable Experience for
    Guests
    Standard Operating Procedures
    Guest Service Training
    Teamwork
Preopening Concerns and Activities
    Inspecting Facilities
    Following Reservation Procedures
    Assigning Food Server Stations
    Sidework
    Food Server Meetings
Providing Guest Service
    Service Sequence
    Special Situations
Technology and the Guest Service Process
    Order Entry Devices
    Output Devices (Printers)
    Software and Reports
    Technology and Guest Ordering
    Technology and Account Settlement
Food and Beverage Revenue Control
    Procedures
    Revenue Control and Servers
    Revenue Control and Beverage
        Personnel
Increasing Food and Beverage Sales
    Suggestive Selling
    Selling Beverages

Competencies

1. Identify and describe four types of table service and at least two other food service categories, as well as the ingredients of an enjoyable dining experience for guests. (pp. 239–246)

2. Summarize preopening concerns and activities. (pp. 246–249)

3. Describe what goes into providing good service to guests, and describe a sample service sequence, including procedures for serving alcoholic beverages with care. (pp. 249–257)

4. Identify computer hardware and software used in the service process, describe proper usage procedures, explain how technology is changing the way guests place orders, and discuss how technology has affected account settlement. (pp. 257–267)

5. Explain revenue control procedures for food servers and beverage personnel. (pp. 267–270)

6. Explain the use of suggestive selling and beverage selling techniques. (pp. 270–271)

10

Food and Beverage Service

FOOD AND BEVERAGE SERVICE is the culmination of the planning and production processes and centers on providing a consistently enjoyable experience for guests. It is a complex subject comprising a wide range of factors, activities, and procedures. Factors include the type and size of the operation, the kind of service it offers, and its ambience or atmosphere. Activities may include setting the table or preparing a self-service counter, transferring food and beverage products from production personnel to serving personnel, serving guests, clearing tables, and so on. Procedures to carry out each activity should be standardized when possible so that the operation can consistently meet or exceed the guests' expectations that have been identified.

Food and beverage servers are key personnel because they represent the operation to the guests. Servers interact more frequently with guests than do other employees, so the responsibility of providing an enjoyable experience for the guest rests in large part with them. In many ways, an operation's reputation and financial success depend on its service staff.

Because service varies among types of operations, this chapter first addresses different approaches to service. It then explains why standard operating procedures are important in providing an enjoyable experience for guests. It goes on to describe principles and procedures that are typical of many table-service dining rooms. The focus is on table service because it is more service oriented and guest centered than other approaches to service.

Types of Service

There are many different approaches to serving food. An operation should use the service style, or combination of styles, that best satisfies its guests' wants and needs.

Table Service

Traditional **table service** provides service for guests seated at tables. Servers bring food and beverages to the guests, and also clear and reset tables. The four common styles of table service are plate, family-style, cart, and platter.

Plate. Plate service (also called American service) comes in many variations but usually has several steps: (1) servers take guests' orders after the guests are seated; (2) servers give the orders to production staff, who prepare food and portion it onto plates; and (3) servers bring the plates to the table and present them to guests.

A variation of plate service is often used for banquets, group events at which everyone is served a preplanned meal at the same time. There are many ways to handle banquet service, depending on the occasion, the type of menu planned, and the type of service desired.[1]

Family-Style. Family-style service (also called English service) is much like service at home. Quantities of food are placed in bowls or on platters and brought to the table by servers who present it to the guests. The guests then pass the food around the table, helping themselves to the amounts they desire. Some operations use family-style service when featuring family-oriented themes. Other operations, including private clubs and retirement centers, may use family-style service on holiday occasions when families dine away from home.

Cart. Cart service (also called French service) is used in some dining rooms featuring gourmet foods and an elegant atmosphere. A characteristic of cart service is that food items are partly or completely prepared at tableside. Food for preparation may be brought tableside on a cart with some type of heating unit. Steak Diane, flaming desserts and drinks, and Caesar salads are some popular items prepared in this manner. Cart service requires experienced service employees. Some operations use cart service in combination with plate service; that is, they feature some specialties served in the French tradition along with their regular fare.

Platter. With **platter service** (also called Russian service), food production employees portion and arrange foods attractively on platters. Servers then carry the platters directly to the table and, after presenting the food to guests, serve portions onto the guests' plates. Platter service can be as elegant as cart service, but it is faster and more practical. This style can be used for banquets.

Buffet Service

For **buffet service**, foods are attractively arranged on platters that are placed on large serving tables or counters so guests can serve themselves. There may also be carving stations where a food production employee carves, for example, prime rib or ham slices according to the guests' requests. Sometimes each course is set up on a separate table. Plates, flatware, and other necessary items are conveniently located.

Some restaurants offer only buffet service, while other restaurants and hotels offer buffets part of the time; table-service operations may have special buffets on weekends and holidays, for example. Others offer a combination of table and buffet service all the time. Soup, salad, and dessert bars are examples of buffet service

Service Style Is Not "All or Nothing"

The bride wants Caesar salad prepared tableside for the wedding reception. However, that cannot be done for all 150 guests at the event. (Can you imagine the number of carts, space between tables, and skilled service personnel required?) The solution: prepare the salad tableside at the head table and serve pre-plated salads to the rest of the guests.

combined with table service. Many hotels offer buffet service or a banquet option for guests desiring this service style.

Cafeteria Service

In most cafeterias, guests move through serving lines, selecting their food items as they go. The most expensive or difficult-to-serve food items are usually portioned by service staff. In some operations, however, **cafeteria service** is similar to buffet service; guests help themselves to items on display. Traditionally, cafeterias have required guests to enter the serving area, move along a straight-line serving counter, and pay for their meals at the end of the counter or as they exit the dining room. In contrast, *scramble* layouts allow guests to enter a cafeteria area and pass one another while going to separate serving stations, each with a different type of food. There may be a salad bar, a soup station, a hot and cold sandwich area, an entrée center, a beverage center, and a dessert bar, among many other possible combinations. With a scramble system, guests wait in line less and service is usually faster. These systems are popular in business/industry and post-secondary school food service operations.

Other Types of Service

Table service, buffet service, and cafeteria service are just a few of the most common approaches to food service today. Quick service, deli service, counter service, and tray service are among the others.

Quick-service operations generally offer seating as well as drive-through and take-out services; some offer carry-out service in which servers deliver meals to guests who consume them in the operation's parking area. As much as 70 percent of a quick-service property's total revenue is generated from drive-through sales. Many properties offer late-night drive-through-only service. Some businesses offer only drive-through service and have no (or very limited) indoor seating. Service is limited to taking the guests' orders and giving the food to the guests on trays or in carry-out sacks or cartons.

Delis feature take-out service and also may offer limited seating at tables or counters. Some restaurants have limited deli service. For example, fresh-baked breads and desserts may be available for guests to purchase when leaving the restaurant.

Counter service is often offered in bars, lounges, snack shops, and coffee shops.

Tray service traditionally has been associated with noncommercial food service. Meals are plated, placed on trays, kept hot or cold in special transport carts, and moved from preparation/plating areas to service areas as needed. A variation of tray service has been used in the airline industry. All items except the hot entrée are placed on individual trays and kept chilled. After the entrée is heated, it is added to the tray and served.

Today, many casual-service restaurants generate significant revenue from take-out service. Operators may design buildings with separate entrances and/or may provide dedicated parking near the entrance for those ordering take-out food. Some restaurants take orders from guests who use their phones to place orders as they approach the parking lot. Service employees take the preordered food to the guest's car and can even complete payment card transactions from outside the restaurant.

Hotels and healthcare operations, including acute-care and long-term facilities, offer another type of food service: room service. Even with careful planning and specialized transport equipment, room service can be challenging because of the increased possibility of quality deterioration and difficulty in controlling costs. However, some guests seek out lodging properties that offer room service, and the Michelin and AAA hotel-rating systems grant their highest ratings only to properties that provide this amenity.

Hospitals strive to serve patients meals that are nutritious, attractively presented, and carefully prepared. Today, many healthcare facilities offer menu choices just as their restaurant counterparts do. Retirement center administrators prefer that their residents eat in group dining rooms even if they require assistance. However, some residents cannot access these locations and must eat meals served in their rooms.

Providing an Enjoyable Experience for Guests

Standard Operating Procedures

A primary goal of any type of food or beverage service is to provide an enjoyable experience for guests by meeting or exceeding their expectations. This goal requires effective standard operating procedures (SOPs) that are consistently performed by all employees. Each operation should set its own policies and SOPs.

Many Other Service Alternatives

A complete list of methods used to deliver (provide) food and beverage products to guests is difficult (and may be impossible) to compile. Consider food trucks on streets and parking lots and restaurant order counters fronting walkways where consumers stand in line to place orders. They might then consume their purchases as they stand around the location or as they walk around the area.

Pop-up restaurants are temporary eateries that may operate for only a few days, weeks, or months. Perhaps a famous chef opens a restaurant while on a business "vacation," or a local cook with very limited financial resources opens a temporary facility to see what the business is like.

How about grab-n-go kiosks in hotel lobbies where guests purchase items for consumption in their guestrooms? At least one company (Savioke—www.savioke.com) is developing robots to provide room service in hotels.

An increasing number of food service operations deliver ordered products to guests' homes or places of work. These deliveries can be made by the property's employees or by services such as Grub Hub (www.grubhub.com).

What's in the future? How about the use of drones for home delivery of pizzas or other products, or even for the delivery of plated items to guests seated at tables in table service restaurants?

Consistently producing and serving quality products is a must for sustained success in the food and beverage business. SOPs help provide consistency because they detail exactly what must be done and how it should be done. Tasks must be identified in **job breakdowns**, and procedures to perform the tasks should be spelled out clearly, step by step. Exhibit 1 is a sample job breakdown for a service task that incorporates SOPs.

Performance standards that are measurable and observable should be tied to each operating procedure. These help managers and employees determine whether procedures are being performed correctly. Exhibit 2 shows an example of performance standards developed for a food server at a table service restaurant.

Guest Service Training

Every reasonable concern that a guest might have should be addressed in training sessions for food service personnel. The old saying, "The guest is always right," embodies the attitude that servers should convey to guests. What many operations need to improve service is not expensive equipment or an elaborate atmosphere, but a genuine concern for guests and the use of consistent service procedures.

Training service staff to properly welcome and serve guests is a primary responsibility of dining room or food and beverage managers. Each component of the meal, beginning with before-meal beverages and appetizers and ending with after-dinner beverages or desserts, should be served according to SOPs. Service staff must be polite, properly groomed, and genuinely interested in helping guests enjoy the dining experience.

Servers must be able to identify properly plated entrées and other menu items. They need to know what these items should look like and what garnishes to use with them. If an item does not look right, if a salad is made with brown-tinged lettuce, for example, servers need to know what procedures to use to correct the problem.

Training should include food safety concerns because they go hand in hand with service. Supervision throughout the shift is necessary to prevent or solve problems, ensure timely service, and evaluate training efforts.

Teamwork

Cooperation and good communication between kitchen, bar, and dining room personnel are essential to the success of every food service operation. Making the guest's experience an enjoyable one is not the responsibility of just one person. It requires the combined efforts of the chef, his or her assistants, food and beverage servers, buspersons, and others.

Teamwork among service and production employees is necessary. Servers should submit guest orders to the kitchen in proper form and at the right time. Orders should be readied in the kitchen in reasonable time for all servers. Everyone must work together to obtain the best results.

Teamwork builds morale and esprit de corps, a spirit of cooperation that guests recognize and appreciate, and one that makes everyone's job easier and more enjoyable. Developing this spirit and maintaining it from preopening to end-of-shift activities is every food service manager's challenge.

Exhibit 1   Sample Job Breakdown

Task: *Take Beverage Orders*

Materials needed: A pen and an order pad or guest checks.

STEPS	HOW-TO'S
1. Offer beverages.	❑ Always know how much alcohol your guests are drinking. ❑ Do not suggest alcohol if your guests appear intoxicated or close to becoming intoxicated. ❑ At dinner, ask if guests desire to start their meal with a cocktail and an appetizer. ❑ Take the wine order after the food order unless guests choose otherwise. ❑ During the breakfast period, offer coffee and orange juice immediately after seating the guest. ❑ Know available drinks and the customary way of serving them.
2. Ask for appropriate identification from any guest appearing to be younger than thirty years old.	❑ See job breakdown: "Check IDs of Guests Ordering Alcohol."
3. Follow the order-taking system.	❑ Take orders from women first. ❑ Write orders on the order pad or guest check according to how the guests are seated. Follow a clockwise direction.

Exhibit 1   *(continued)*

Task: *Take Beverage Orders*	
STEPS	**HOW-TO'S**
	❏ See job breakdown: "Take Food Orders" for the order-taking system.
	❏ Use standard food and drink abbreviations.
	❏ Listen carefully to each guest's order; repeat the order.
	❏ Note special requests on the order pad or guest check.
	❏ Determine the guest's preference for beverage service such as "on the rocks" or "straight up."
	❏ Suggest the most popular call brands when a guest does not specify the brand.
	❏ Suggest a specialty drink or bottled water if a guest is not sure what to order.
	❏ When offering cocktails, ask guests who do not want a cocktail if they would like a glass of wine or a nonalcoholic drink.
	❏ Always suggest specific alcoholic and nonalcoholic drinks, such as Beefeater gin and tonic, sparkling water, or a strawberry daiquiri.

Today, food and beverage managers increasingly facilitate self-directed work teams and empower team members to plan and manage their own work. Members of a work team can help develop their department's mission statement or provide input about how to reach operational goals. Self-directed service teams also may help develop work processes, allocate duties, schedule and evaluate team members, and perform other activities that traditionally were performed by food service managers. The goal of giving more freedom and responsibilities to work teams is to make it easier for them to provide excellent service to guests.

Exhibit 2   Sample Performance Standards

Job Performance Standards: Food Server (Lunch Shift)

An effective food server performs the following duties according to the procedures documented in job breakdowns addressed during training:

1. Arrives in the dining room by 10:30 A.M., ready for work in a complete, clean uniform.

2. Has all assigned tables fully set with tablecloths, napkins, glass, silverware, and condiment sets by 11:15 A.M.

3. Greets guests cordially. Approaches the table as soon as guests are seated.

4. Requests a beverage order while guests decide on food selections.

5. Engages in positive communications with the guests concerning daily specials and other menu selections; suggestively sells food and beverages.

6 Writes orders on guest checks legibly and correctly.

7. Enters orders into point-of-sale system following all revenue control procedures.

8. Picks up and delivers orders promptly; serves orders to all guests at a table at one time.

9. Serves food plates from guest's left side with left hand when possible.

10. Serves beverages from guest's right side with right hand when possible.

11. Serves standard condiments with food orders; serves special condiment requests quickly and pleasantly.

12. Checks on each guest for refills of beverages and to ensure that guest requests are quickly filled.

13. Clears china, glassware, and silver from tables as guests complete courses; clears quietly from guest's right with right hand, removing serviceware to a tray on a sidestand nearby.

14. Offers desserts to all guests.

15. Offers coffee service at the end of the meal for all guests.

16. Presents the guest check promptly after the final course is served.

17. Thanks guests for coming and invites them to return.

18. Immediately clears and resets table when guests leave.

Preopening Concerns and Activities

Basic concerns common to all dining rooms, and certain tasks that typically are completed before any dining room is opened to guests, include:

- Inspecting facilities
- Following reservation procedures

- Assigning food server stations
- Performing sidework
- Holding food server meetings

Those responsible for these tasks vary. A dining room manager might be responsible for making inspections, assigning food server stations, and holding food server meetings. A host or receptionist might be responsible for taking reservations. Servers and buspersons generally perform sidework.

Inspecting Facilities

Facilities should be inspected before the dining room is open to ensure that any problems, including those affecting room temperature and lighting, are identified and resolved. Safety hazards such as rips in carpeting, loose banisters, wobbly tables, and wall decorations not securely fastened should be corrected. Managers can use a pre-opening list as a reminder to check these and other potential problems. Additional inspection is necessary for sanitation purposes: to confirm that the dining and public areas have been properly cleaned, that tables are set correctly, and that chairs are clean.

Some dining areas can be viewed from the street. Managers should go outside, look at the dining room from that perspective, and ask themselves, "If I were a potential guest, would I think the dining room and adjacent areas are attractive?"

Following Reservation Procedures

Some operations do not take guest reservations. Others have systems that allow guests to reserve seating at a specified time. Reservations are important to some guests, and reservations can benefit the operation as well, since they help managers better estimate staffing needs and production volumes.

One type of reservation system offers reserved seating only at certain times, such as 7:00 P.M. and 9:00 P.M. A more typical system offers reservations at staggered intervals during the meal period.

Many properties accept telephone reservations. To avoid confusion, only a few employees trained in taking reservations should be permitted to accept them. It is important that employees obtain all necessary information from callers making reservations. A relatively recent innovation allows guests to make reservations through the hotel or restaurant's website.

Guests obviously want to minimize the time they spend waiting to be seated. Restaurants that do not accept reservations might allow guests to call ahead to be placed on a wait list with the idea that the list will shorten as the guests travel to the property. Still other restaurants do not normally take reservations, but require them for parties in excess of a specified size.

The average wait time for tables at casual-dining chains is a statistic some restaurants use to measure sales. As wait times increase, guest counts typically increase; the reverse is also true.

Since accepting a reservation commits the restaurant to having a table ready at a specified time, managers must plan carefully. They should know what to do when guests fail to show up, arrive early or late, change the number in the party, or request a table other than the one reserved. Managers must anticipate these issues so they can develop equitable, consistent procedures before problems arise.

Assigning Food Server Stations

Food server stations are assigned before the dining room opens. A **food server station** is a specified number of tables in a specified location for which a server is responsible. In some operations, servers do not have assigned stations; instead, they are assigned tables by turns as guests are seated. This means that food servers might wait on tables scattered throughout the dining room. This procedure is generally not recommended, especially when the dining area is large, because servers must spend more time walking longer distances between tables, and thus have less time to attend to guests.

The number of tables assigned to a food server depends on various factors, including the following:

- Number of seats
- Type of service style used
- Expected guest turnover
- The server's experience
- Whether any servers are being trained during the shift
- Distance to the kitchen and bar
- Variety of menu items
- Number of food servers scheduled for a specific meal period

Each operation has unique needs. A food server in a busy coffee shop where tables turn over several times in a short interval may not be able to serve the same number of tables as a server in a hotel dining room featuring leisurely dining with a low seat turnover.

Sidework

Setup and cleanup work must be done before dining rooms are opened. This work, called **sidework**, includes such activities as refilling salt and pepper shakers, filling bun warmers, watering dining room plants, polishing tabletops, and replenishing server supply stations. Food service employees know this work must be done, but they may be reluctant to do it. Sidework tasks can be rotated among service personnel so that no employee consistently gets the easy or hard assignments.

Managers must emphasize the importance of doing sidework to prepare the dining room for service. If the work is not done, supplies will likely run out at busy times when service employees are not available, and safety and sanitation problems will arise. Managers can teach new employees that sidework is an important part of the job. With proper supervision, managers can reduce or eliminate problems that many operations have in keeping up with sidework.

Food Server Meetings

A brief food server meeting before the dining room opens can be helpful. Server stations should be reviewed, daily specials explained, questions answered, and menu prices noted. Servers can also taste new dishes and learn how menu items are made. Food server supply stations should be checked to ensure that they are properly stocked. A final discussion with the chef and opening service staff will confirm that everything is ready and that the dining room can be opened.

Providing Guest Service

A host, maître d', receptionist, or other employee should cordially welcome guests as they enter the dining room. If the dining room accepts reservations, guests should be asked whether they have made one.

The person who welcomes guests often also seats them. The operation should satisfy guest requests for special tables, if possible, and provide assistance to individuals with disabilities if they ask for it. No-smoking sections are typically required by law, and, in many states and localities, the entire dining area must be smoke-free. Some food service managers establish no-smoking dining rooms even if not legally required to do so. Managers in many operations often discover that guests appreciate the amenity, and revenue frequently increases.

Employees should always seat guests at the best available table. Tables in traffic aisles, next to kitchen doors, or near server supply stations are less desirable and should be left until no better tables remain. The employee responsible for seating should work closely with food servers to ensure that the workload is evenly distributed. There should be a fine balance between rotating tables so servers get a fair chance at tips and providing quality service to guests.

No industry standard specifies how service should be provided.[2] Each operation has its own way of serving guests. To simplify discussion, this section looks at one example of a dinner service sequence in a table-service restaurant using plate service and offering alcoholic beverages. More details about serving alcoholic beverages will follow in the next section.

Service Sequence

Activities in the following service sequence generally apply to full-service dining operations, and are typically performed by servers, though some of these activities may be handled by buspersons or other personnel. The sequence begins after guests have been seated.

- *Welcome the guests.* Extend a personal welcome, be friendly, and make guests feel comfortable.

- *Serve or pour water.* Use tongs or a scoop for ice.

- *Present the menu and the wine list.* Whether open or closed, they should be right side up.

- *Take the beverage order.* Carefully note how the guests wish their beverages to be served.

- *Serve the beverages.* Generally, beverages are served from the guest's right with the server's right hand.

- *Ask the guests if they wish to order appetizers.* They also may wish to order another drink.

- *Serve the appetizers.* Food is generally served from the guest's left with the server's left hand.

- *Take the food order.* Suggest any daily specials. Answer questions, making sure to remember what each guest ordered.

- *Take the wine order.* Offer suggestions if appropriate or if asked to do so by guests.

- *Remove appetizer dishes.* The server usually removes dishes from the guest's right with the right hand.

- *Follow order-placing procedures for food items.* Write orders carefully and use correct abbreviations.

- *Serve the wine.* See the section on wine service that follows.

- *Serve salad and bread.* Salads should be chilled. Soft bread is usually served warm; hard rolls are usually served at room temperature.

- *Remove salad dishes.* First make sure that guests are finished with them. Some guests continue eating their salads after their entrées arrive.

- *Serve the entrée and its accompaniments.* Place the entrée plate so the main item is closest to the guest. Place side dishes to the left of the guest.

- *Ask if everything is prepared satisfactorily.* Know what to do if something is not satisfactory.

- *Clear the table.* Make sure that guests are finished before clearing.

- *Take the dessert order.* After-dinner drinks might be included in suggestions.

- *Serve dessert and/or after-dinner drinks.* Guests may want water and/or coffee with dessert.

- *Present the guest check.* This is a critical point. Do not make the guests wait. Present the check as soon as possible after determining that they do not wish to order anything else.

The list just presented is just one possible sequence. It is meant only to suggest what must be done to meet guests' basic expectations in some dining rooms. What it takes to exceed guests' expectations is often unique to each operation and its servers. Servers can help make the experience pleasant and memorable by putting themselves in the guests' position and thinking about how they would like to be treated if they were guests. Exhibit 3 offers advice that dining room managers can give to servers to educate and motivate them.

Special Situations

Servers may be concerned about what to do when a guest is in a hurry, when a guest complains or is difficult, and so on. Exhibit 4 suggests ways to address

Exhibit 3   Advice for Servers

Serving is an honorable occupation dating back many centuries. Knowing your craft and the standards your restaurant expects is the most important starting point. Here are some other hints:

1. Always have a positive attitude. Never give off "negative vibes."

2. Make sure your personal appearance—from your hair, to your nails, to your shoes—is the best it can be. Always look neat and clean. Avoid using overpowering colognes or perfumes.

3. Always be aware of what your guests may need. Pay attention and use common sense to predict what your guests need before they need it.

4. Use the Golden Rule. If you treat your guests the way you want to be treated when you dine out, you will likely have happy people at your tables.

5. Remember that you are in charge of your tables. *Everything* that goes on at your tables reflects on you. Make sure those who help you know that you will serve only the best. You *must* have high standards and maintain them.

6. Two important service skills are timing and organization. Without them, waiting on any table can be a problem.

7. Always make time for your guests. Make sure you're there mentally as well as physically; don't be thinking about what you need to get for the next table. No matter how busy you are, slow down when you are at tableside serving guests. Most guests don't mind waiting a few minutes if you give them the proper attention when you are with them.

8. Always check the condition of your tables and chairs at the beginning of your shift, and as often as possible during the shift. This may be the first time your guests have dined with you, and you want them to be impressed.

9. Be *very* knowledgeable about the food you serve. Know how *everything* is prepared. Be aware of what you are able to do for guests on special diets.

10. Be knowledgeable about where you work. Guests will always ask questions, and it's important to know the correct answers.

11. Stay with your tables. Don't talk with another employee or do unnecessary sidework while your guests need you.

12. Make suggestions about food and wine. Always have suggestions ready. The importance of knowing what you serve can't be overstated.

13. Take a real interest in what your guest says to you; most people appreciate a good listener. Manners are also very important. Make sure you always behave in a proper way.

14. Realize when your guests want to be left alone. Romantic couples and many businesspeople don't want you to hover over them. "Read" your guests; you must be able to know when they need or want you around and when you are in the way.

(continued)

Exhibit 3 *(continued)*

15. Don't let unfortunate incidents like dropping a tray of food or not receiving a tip from a guest interfere with your work. These things happen to every server, and the best thing to do is to recover and keep going.

16. Always be professional. Treating your work seriously and learning all you can about serving can make you feel better about yourself and your job, and will lead to higher tips from more satisfied guests.

Courtesy of Gaylord Opryland Hotel & Convention Center, Food & Beverage Training Department, Nashville, Tennessee.

Exhibit 4 Handling Guest Complaints

Suggestions for handling guest complaints include the following:

- Know when to involve your supervisor and when to handle the situation yourself.
- Remember that you are dealing with a person and his or her feelings, not just a problem.
- Look at the situation from the guest's perspective. Consider how you would feel and how you would want to be treated if you were the guest.
- Listen with concern and give the guest your undivided attention.
- Maintain eye contact and avoid interruptions.
- Stay calm and in control of the situation.
- Apologize for the problem. Even when you disagree with guests, apologies may make them feel better.
- Empathize to show guests you know how they feel. Be sensitive to the problem and communicate this to them.
- Ask questions and be prepared to take notes. Learn details about the problem so that you can determine the best solution.
- Offer solutions. Tell the guests what you can do and offer several options if possible. Do not make promises you cannot fulfill.
- Act on the problem. Follow your property's standard procedures and do exactly what you promise the guest. Tell the guest how long it will take to resolve the problem.
- Monitor progress. If another employee or department is involved, stay in touch to help ensure the problem gets corrected.
- Follow up. If you feel it won't disturb the guest, check back to make sure he or she is satisfied once the problem has been corrected.

guest complaints. However, managers should establish policies and procedures for dealing with special situations.

Some special situations and concerns relate to the serving of alcoholic beverages.

Serving Alcoholic Beverages. Bartenders and beverage servers must be trained so they know what their job involves and how to perform it properly. On-the-job training programs and using bar backs (assistant bartenders who perform backup tasks while learning bartending procedures) are two training options. After bartenders and beverage servers are trained, managers must supervise them to ensure that service procedures are followed.

Effective procedures for serving beverages should fit the specific operation's needs. Those serving alcoholic beverages should remember these important tips:

- The guest's exact order should be noted and served. This includes requests for "on the rocks" (with ice), "up" (no ice), a specific brand, a particular garnish, and so on.

- Drinks should be delivered on a cocktail tray, which the server should carry in one hand while serving the drinks with the other. The server should never place the tray on the table.

- Drinks are typically served from the guest's right with the server's right hand.

- Glasses should be cleared from the table as soon as they are empty (from the guest's right with the right hand), and guests should be asked if they wish to order another drink.

Serving wine. Many guests are knowledgeable about wine. It is important that servers know some basics about wine and wine service.

The quality of a wine is determined by the grapes used to make it and the skill of the winemaker, among other factors. The color of a wine depends partly on how the grapes are handled and partly on their color. Color is extracted from the skin, not the juice, so red grape skins are carefully removed from red grapes being fermented for white wine. Red wine can be made only from grapes with red skins, and fermentation takes place "in the skins." The alcohol content of most wines ranges from 11 to 13 percent.[3]

Many operations sell house wines by the glass or carafe. For house wines, service is simple: servers merely use the property's ordering procedures to obtain the wine and serviceware from the bartender, and serve the wine properly. Service is more complicated when bottled wines and wine lists are offered. The following are guidelines servers can follow when guests order wine by the bottle.

- Bring the bottle to the table before opening it. The bottle should rest on a white napkin or towel while the label is shown to the guest who ordered the wine and who is considered the host.

- When the host approves the wine, open the wine following the correct procedure: hold the bottle, cut the foil top and peel it away, wipe the cork and the bottle rim with the napkin or towel, insert the corkscrew and twist until it holds, then pull the cork out and place it at the host's right side. The host may wish to examine the cork.

- After the cork has been removed, wipe the rim again.

- Allow the host to sample a small amount of the wine.

- After the host approves, fill the wine glasses of all the guests. The proper amount per glass differs among operations. Usually a "full" glass is no more than two-thirds or one-half full.

- Know what to do if the host does not approve of the wine.

- The wine bottle should be placed at the right of the host's wine glass. If the wine is red, no ice bucket is necessary since red wine is normally served at room temperature. However, white wine should be placed in an ice bucket draped with a clean napkin.

Serving alcohol with care. Managers have a personal, professional, and social responsibility to serve alcohol with care. Drunk drivers are responsible for numerous driving fatalities in the United States each year. Alcohol is also a factor in many drowning deaths and suicides.[4]

Many states have passed legislation establishing third-party liability for accidents involving intoxicated drivers. **Dram shop acts** state that bartenders, servers, and owners can be held jointly liable if they unlawfully sell alcoholic beverages to a minor or an obviously intoxicated person who causes injury to others.

In some states without a specific dram shop act, operations and servers have been held liable for damages under common law. The factor behind this liability is server negligence. **Negligence** is "failure to exercise the care that a reasonably prudent person would exercise under like or similar circumstances."

Legislation regarding third-party liability can change. Regardless of the specific third-party liability in the operation's location, good sense dictates that the operation serve alcoholic beverages responsibly. No one should sell beverages to minors or to those who are intoxicated. Service staff should be taught to identify minors by recognizing false identification and observing characteristics and actions frequently exhibited by minors, such as nervousness, sticking closely to a group, and pooling money and giving it to another person to buy drinks.

Employees should understand that a 12-ounce glass of beer, a 4-ounce glass of wine, and a 1-ounce serving of 100-proof liquor all have approximately the same ½ ounce of pure alcohol (see Exhibit 5). Employees should know the legal definition of **intoxication**. While this varies, in most states someone is legally intoxicated when the blood-alcohol concentration (BAC) in his or her blood reaches .08 gram of alcohol or higher per 100 milliliters of blood.

How many drinks can someone consume before becoming intoxicated? There is no precise answer to this question because many factors influence the effects of alcohol on a particular person. However, one approach relates the weight of an individual to the number of drinks that may be consumed before reaching a specific BAC (see Exhibit 6). A large, heavy person experiences fewer effects with the same amount of alcohol than does a smaller, lighter person. However, the chart considers only weight and number of drinks consumed. Fatigue and many common illnesses also affect how the body responds to alcohol. When someone in a weakened condition consumes alcohol, the result is quicker intoxication.

Several behavioral warning signs can help service employees recognize that a guest is becoming intoxicated. These include the following:

Exhibit 5   Alcohol Equivalencies

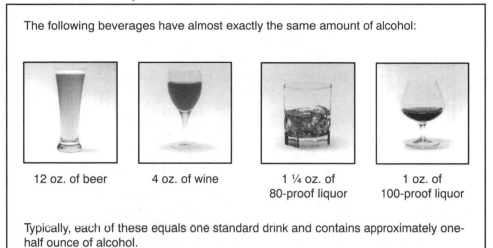

The following beverages have almost exactly the same amount of alcohol:

12 oz. of beer	4 oz. of wine	1 ¼ oz. of 80-proof liquor	1 oz. of 100-proof liquor

Typically, each of these equals one standard drink and contains approximately one-half ounce of alcohol.

- Relaxed inhibitions
- Impaired judgment
- Slow reactions
- Decreased coordination

Remember, however, that it is a *change* in a person's behavior, not necessarily the behavior itself, that may be the most telling to an observant server.

The operation can use the traffic light rating system (see Exhibit 7) to help determine if guests should continue to be served alcoholic beverages. Monitoring alcohol consumption begins in the green zone, when servers first observe guests and look for behavioral warning signs of intoxication. Each time a guest orders another drink it's important to reevaluate the guest's rating. As guests rated green become more relaxed and less inhibited, the rating may change to yellow. A person in the yellow zone will exhibit relaxed inhibitions and impaired judgment. Slow reaction time and loss of coordination will be exhibited by a drinker in the red zone. No person in the red zone should ever be allowed to drive. Servers should not try to physically take car keys away from intoxicated guests; rather, they should inform the guests that they (the servers) will call the police if the guests insist on driving.

It is important for service employees to communicate their observations about guests to other servers, bartenders, and managers. The server or manager should intervene when necessary to "cut off" intoxicated guests. The following procedures can help reduce the possibility of a troublesome confrontation:

- Alert a backup.
- Remove alcohol from the guest's sight and reach.

256 *Chapter 10*

Exhibit 6 A BAC Chart Based on Weight

KNOW YOUR LIMITS

CHART FOR RESPONSIBLE PEOPLE WHO MAY SOMETIMES DRIVE AFTER DRINKING!

Approximate Blood Alcohol Percentage

Body Weight in Pounds / DRINKS	1	2	3	4	5	6	7	8
100	.04	.09	.13	.18	.22	.26	.31	.35
120	.04	.07	.11	.15	.18	.22	.26	.29
140	.03	.06	.09	.13	.16	.19	.22	.25
160	.03	.06	.08	.11	.14	.17	.19	.22
180	.02	.05	.07	.10	.12	.15	.17	.20
200	.02	.04	.07	.09	.11	.13	.15	.18
220	.02	.04	.06	.08	.10	.12	.14	.16
240	.02	.04	.06	.07	.09	.11	.13	.15

Influenced Rarely   Possibly   Definitely

Subtract .01% for each 40 minutes or .03% for each 2 hours of drinking.
One drink is 1 ¼ oz. of 80-proof liquor, 12 oz. of beer, or 4 oz. of table wine.

SUREST POLICY IS...
DON'T DRIVE AFTER DRINKING!

Source: Distilled Spirits Council of the United States.

*This chart is provided for information only. Nothing contained in this chart shall constitute an endorsement by the American Hotel & Lodging Educational Institute (the Institute) or the American Hotel & Lodging Association (AH&LA) of any information, opinion, procedure, or product mentioned, and the Institute and AH&LA disclaim any liability with respect to the use of such information, procedure, or product, or reliance thereon.

- Be nonjudgmental; do not refer to the person as being "drunk."
- Be firm.
- Minimize the confrontation.
- Remind intoxicated guests that driving while intoxicated is dangerous and against the law, and suggest an alternate form of transportation.
- Keep a personal record of the incident.

Exhibit 7   Traffic Light Rating System

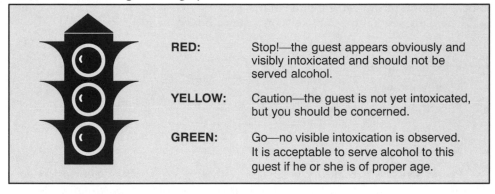

RED: Stop!—the guest appears obviously and visibly intoxicated and should not be served alcohol.

YELLOW: Caution—the guest is not yet intoxicated, but you should be concerned.

GREEN: Go—no visible intoxication is observed. It is acceptable to serve alcohol to this guest if he or she is of proper age.

Technology and the Guest Service Process

Automated systems allow managers to achieve control over the production-to-serving-to-service link and receive timely information about sales results that can help them plan more efficient and effective service and revenue collection.[5]

Point-of-sale (POS) terminals are the basic hardware components of food service computer systems. A POS terminal contains its own input/output units and may have a small storage (memory) capacity, but it does not have its own central processing unit (CPU). To process POS transactions, the terminal must be connected to a CPU located outside the terminal unit. Since the CPU is the most expensive component of a computer system, food service organizations reduce costs by connecting (interfacing) several POS terminals located throughout dining and bar areas to one large CPU.

POS terminals or registers are generally modular units, and other items (such as a cash drawer) are optional equipment. Managers may select no cash drawer, or have several cash drawers connected to a single register. Multiple cash drawers enhance the cash control system when several cashiers work at the same register during the same shift. Each cashier can be assigned a separate cash drawer so managers can reconcile the receipts for each cashier's drawer at the end of the shift.

Precheck terminals have no cash drawers. They are used to enter orders but not to settle accounts. Servers can use them in the dining room to send orders to the kitchen or bar. A POS unit with a cash drawer can usually perform precheck and cashier functions.

In addition to terminals, food service computer systems generally require hardware components for order entry and output devices for printing.

Order Entry Devices

Order entry devices include keyboards, touchscreen terminals, magnetic strip readers, and handheld terminals.

Keyboards. The most common order entry device has traditionally been the keyboard, although touchscreen terminals are now common even in small operations. Micromotion keyboard surfaces are flat and resistant to spills. Reed-style keyboards have waterproof keys raised above the surface. Both designs are usually capable of supporting interchangeable menu boards.

There are several types of keys on a **menu board**, including:

- Preset keys
- Price look-up keys or screen icons
- Modifier keys
- Function keys
- Settlement keys
- Numeric keypad

Preset keys. A **preset key** is labeled with a name (such as *hamburger*) or a drawing of an item. The key accesses the price, descriptor, department code, tax, and inventory status for the menu item shown on the key. Automatic menu pricing makes faster guest service possible and eliminates servers' price and tax errors.

Once a preset key is pressed, a description of the item and its price appear on the operator's display unit, and this data may be sent to the appropriate production station or printed on a guest check. The revenue data generated from this transaction is retained for revenue reporting and tracking inventory levels.

Price look-up keys. Price look-up keys supplement preset keys and require the user to identify a menu item by its reference code number rather than by its name or descriptor. For example, if a server wants to record the sale of a cheeseburger and there is no preset key for that item, the code number for cheeseburgers (706, for example) would be entered and the price look-up key would be pressed.

Modifier keys. Modifier keys allow servers to relay preparation instructions (such as rare or well-done for a steak) to remote work station printers or video display screens in food production areas. Modifier keys can also be used to legitimately alter menu item prices. For example, if a restaurant sells house wine by the carafe and half-carafe, a single preset key can be designated for house wine by the carafe and a modifier key can be programmed as a half-portion modifier. When a half-carafe is sold, the server presses the carafe preset key and half-portion modifier key to register a half-carafe sale.

Function keys. Function keys help process transactions. Sample function keys include clear, discount, void, and no-sale. These keys are important for error correction (clear and void), legitimate price alteration (discount), and proper cash handling (no-sale).

Settlement keys. Settlement keys record the methods by which accounts are settled, including cash, payment card, house account, or charge transfer to the guest's folio (in a hotel).

Numeric keypad. Keys in the **numeric keypad** ring up menu items by price, access price look-up data by menu item code number, access open guest check accounts by serial number, and perform other data entry operations. For example, if the register or terminal is used to record and store payroll data, the numeric keypad can be used to enter employee identification numbers as employees begin and end their work shifts. The numeric keypad may also be used to enter report codes that initiate production of management reports.

Touchscreen Terminals. Touchscreen terminals simplify data entry procedures and are increasingly used in place of traditional keyboards. In fact, they dominate the marketplace across all types of food service operations. A special microprocessor within the terminal is programmed to display data on areas of the screen that are sensitive to touch. Touching one of the sensitized areas produces an electronic charge that is translated into signals processed by the terminal.

Touchscreen terminals require much less counterspace than traditional POS terminals. They simplify data entry by prompting servers through order entry and settlement procedures. For example, when a server enters an order for a steak, the screen shifts to display modifiers such as "rare" or "medium." Identification of required information is necessary before the server can proceed to the next item.

Wireless Handheld Server Terminals. Handheld server terminals are remote order entry devices that are increasingly replacing traditional server order pads and precheck terminals. Also called *portable server terminals*, they perform most of the functions of precheck terminals and enable servers to enter orders while at guest tables. This can be a major advantage for large establishments with long distances between server stations and outdoor dining areas or for very busy lounges where it is difficult to reach a precheck terminal. Service may be faster since servers do not have to wait in line to use one during peak business periods, as they do with precheck terminals. In some cases, appetizers and drinks may be ready to serve just seconds after a server has finished entering the orders and has left the table.

A two-way communications capability allows servers to communicate special instructions to production areas (*no salt*, for example) when keying in the order. Production employees can also communicate with servers. For example, they can immediately notify servers if an item is out of stock. Typically, when an order is ready for pickup, a production employee can alert the server via a signal sent to the server's handheld terminal.

Self-Service Order Entry. Kiosks are computer terminals on a podium, counter, or table used by guests for self-ordering of food and beverage products. Attractive graphics simplify order entry. Photographs can be used with logos to specify beverage choices. For example, a rope lasso can indicate ranch dressing; the Eiffel Tower can represent French dressing.

Guests activate the system by touching a start feature on the screen, and the screen display asks if the order will be for on-site or take-out consumption. Menu options are then displayed and the guest touches the graphics of desired items. A video receipt appears that maintains a running balance of the amount of the order. When the order is complete, the customer touches a "Finished" box and a suggestive selling display may appear asking if additional items are desired. A final display shows the total amount due along with settlement options and instructions.

Output Devices (Printers)

Output devices are available in several types.

Guest Check Printers. Guest check printers are standard POS output devices. Most guest check printers have **automatic form number reader** capability to facilitate order entry. Instead of accessing a guest check by manually inputting a guest check's serial number, a bar code imprinted on the guest check presents the check's serial number in a machine-readable format. The server slips the guest check into the terminal's automatic form number reader unit, and the bar code provides rapid access to the correct guest check account.

Work Station Printers. Work station printers are usually placed at kitchen preparation areas and service bars. Orders entered at precheck or cashier terminals are sent to a designated remote work station printer to initiate production. This enables servers to spend more time meeting guest needs and significantly reduces traffic in kitchen and bar areas.

If hard-copy output in production areas is not critical to an operation's internal control system, the operation might instead install video display units (**kitchen monitors**). Since these units can display several orders on a single screen, kitchen employees need not handle numerous pieces of paper. The units are commonly used in quick-service operations in view of guests ordering at the counter.

Receipt Printers. Receipt printers produce hard copy on narrow and flimsy register tape. They help control the production of menu items that are prepared in departments that do not have work station printers or video display units. Operators can ensure proper order entry by requiring a server picking up a dessert to deliver a receipt tape as proof that the dessert has been properly posted to the guest check.

Software and Reports

The hardware just described does nothing by itself. Software programs must tell the system what to do, how to do it, and when to do it.

The major files used in POS systems include a menu item file, an open check file, and a labor master file.

Menu Item File. A **menu item file** contains data for all meal periods and menu items sold. Data may include the menu item's identification number, description, recipe code number, and selling price. This file also stores historical information about the actual number of items sold. This data can be accessed directly by managers or forecasting programs to project future sales and to help schedule personnel.

Open Check File. The **open check file** maintains current data for all open guest checks (those for which guests have not yet paid). This file is accessed to monitor items on a particular guest check, to add items to a guest check after the initial order has been entered, and to close the guest check at the time of settlement. Data contained in an open check file can usually be printed at any time.

Labor Master File. The **labor master file** contains one record for each employee and maintains data required to produce labor reports. Each record in the labor master file may include employee name, employee number, Social Security number, job codes, hours worked, total hourly wages, wages declared, credits for employee meals, number of guests served per meal period, and gross sales per meal period.

Consolidated Reports. POS systems may access data contained in several files to produce consolidated reports for management. While the kinds of reports produced vary with the system used, reports often include sales summaries (items sold and revenue generated), open check reports, server productivity reports, and daily labor reports.

Exhibit 8 shows a report that summarizes menu item sales, applicable revenue totals, and related data for all servers for one shift (meal period). Item-level detail is shown only for appetizers.

An open check report lists all guest checks that have not been settled and may report such items as the serial number of a guest check, the server number, the time the guest check was opened, the time elapsed since the guest check was opened, the number of guests, the table number, and the amount currently owed. If individual server check-out reports are printed before servers leave the property, managers can ensure that all checks assigned to servers have been properly settled. If not, the open check report lists the guest checks for which the server is accountable.

After servers close each guest check when guests settle their accounts, accurate server productivity reports can be produced. Daily productivity reports may be generated for each server and cashier to indicate guest count, total sales, and average sales. In addition, a weekly productivity report may be generated, showing the average sales amount per guest for each server. Exhibit 9 shows a sample server productivity report for one day (shift).

POS systems may access data in several files to produce a daily revenue report, which managers use to determine sales trends, identify product needs, and monitor advertising and sales promotional efforts.

Modern POS systems produce an extensive variety of sales analysis reports that can meet the needs of almost any food service manager. A common sales analysis report enables managers to measure the sales performance of individual menu items by department or product category within certain time intervals. These time intervals are commonly referred to as *day parts* and vary with the type of food service operation. Quick-service restaurants may want sales analysis reports segmented by fifteen-minute intervals, table service restaurants by the hour, and non-commercial food service operations by meal period.

Technology and Guest Ordering

Traditionally, guests have placed their orders in person at a table, bar, drive-up window, or counter. Today's technology provides numerous, increasingly popular alternatives for guests wanting to order food and beverages from their favorite restaurants.

Online Ordering Systems. Many casual-service restaurants generate significant revenues from carry-out/take-home food services. Guests can visit the restaurant to place these orders, or order by telephone, e-mail, or an online ordering system. When guests place orders at the restaurant, employees generally enter order information into the restaurant's POS system. However, operations require special software to process orders placed over the Internet. The operation's website can feature high-quality marketing information and no-cost advertising messages to encourage more sales. In addition, reductions in incorrect or lost orders can yield increased business and greater levels of guest satisfaction.

Exhibit 8   Sample Detailed Revenue Center Menu Item Report

Daily Revenue Center Menu Item Sales Detail
Subtotal By Family Group
Kellogg Center-Kellogg Center
Period From: 05/06/20XX To: 05/06/20XX

Friday 5/6/20XX		MLVL	Price	Sales Qty	% of Ttl	Rtn Qty	% of Ttl	Gross Sales	% of Ttl	Item Disc
1-State Room										
11004	Shrimp Cktl	Lunch	8.00	2	6.67%	0	0.00%	16.00	5.61%	0.00
11005	Maple Salmon	Lunch	8.00	2	6.67%	0	0.00%	16.00	5.61%	0.00
11009	Spinich Dip	Lunch	6.00	2	6.67%	0	0.00%	12.00	4.21%	0.00
16007	Oysters	Dinner	8.00	9	30.00%	0	0.00%	72.00	25.26%	0.00
16010	Citrn Shrmp Cktl	Dinner	8.00	8	26.67%	0	0.00%	64.00	22.46%	0.00
16018	Grad Cheese Pltr	Dinner	15.00	3	10.00%	0	0.00%	45.00	15.79%	0.00
16019	Grad Antpsta Plt	Dinner	15.00	1	3.33%	0	0.00%	15.00	5.26%	0.00
16021	Grad Rangoon Plt	Dinner	15.00	3	10.00%	0	0.00%	45.00	15.79%	0.00
Total Appetizer				30	1.93%	0	0.00%	285.00	2.43%	0.00
Total Soup				83	5.35%	0	0.00%	264.00	2.25%	0.00
Total Salad				144	9.28%	0	0.00%	800.50	6.82%	0.00
Total Sandwich				78	5.03%	0	0.00%	656.25	5.59%	0.00
Total Side Item				29	1.87%	0	0.00%	73.50	0.63%	0.00
Total Breakfast Entrée				105	6.77%	0	0.00%	808.65	6.89%	0.00
Total Lunch/Dinner Entrée				291	18.76%	0	0.00%	5,354.30	45.60%	0.00
Total Special				4	0.26%	0	0.00%	39.85	0.34%	0.00
Total Desserts				120	7.74%	0	0.00%	424.50	3.62%	0.00
Total NA Beverage				323	20.83%	0	0.00%	643.75	5.48%	0.00
Total Kids Menu				7	0.45%	0	0.00%	34.65	0.30%	0.00
Total Breakfast				61	3.93%	0	0.00%	823.50	7.01%	0.00

Exhibit 8 *(continued)*

Friday 5/6/20XX	MLVL	Price	Sales Qty	% of Ttl	Rtn Qty	% of Ttl	Gross Sales	% of Ttl	Item Disc
Total Dinner			4	0.26%	0	0.00%	86.00	0.73%	0.00
Total Liquor			1	0.06%	0	0.00%	9.00	0.08%	0.00
Total Beer			27	1.74%	0	0.00%	100.75	0.86%	0.00
Total Bottled Wine			15	0.97%	0	0.00%	388.00	3.30%	0.00
Total Wine Flights			88	5.67%	0	0.00%	625.00	5.32%	0.00
Total Vodka			19	1.23%	0	0.00%	33.75	0.29%	0.00
Total Gin			2	0.13%	0	0.00%	4.25	0.04%	0.00
Total Rum			3	0.19%	0	0.00%	8.50	0.07%	0.00
Total Tequila			3	0.19%	0	0.00%	0.00	0.00%	0.00
Total Whiskey			11	0.71%	0	0.00%	0.00	0.00%	0.00
Total Scotch			10	0.64%	0	0.00%	50.50	0.43%	0.00
Total Bourbon			2	0.13%	0	0.00%	8.50	0.07%	0.00
Total Cordials			1	0.06%	0	0.00%	8.50	0.07%	0.00
Total Cocktails			37	2.39%	0	0.00%	187.75	1.60%	0.00
Total Non Price Fd Prep			48	3.09%	0	0.00%	0.00	0.00%	0.00
Total Priced Food Preps			3	0.19%	0	0.00%	1.50	0.01%	0.00
State Room Total			1,551	100.00%	0	0.00%	11,742.45	100.00%	0.00

Courtesy of MICROS Systems, Inc., Columbia, Maryland and The State Room, Michigan State University, East Lansing, Michigan.

Exhibit 9   Sample Daily Employee Productivity Report

Daily Employee Detail
Mike Rose Cafe - Beltsville, MD

NEAL MAHAFFEY
Printed on Tuesday, October 15, 20XX - 9:32 AM

Shift 6 - From 09/22 - 2:36am - To 09/23 - 1:12am

1002 - BEV NELSON

		Returns	0	0.00				Gross Receipts	446.27
Net Sales	444.02	Voids	0	0.00	Carried Over	0	0.00	Charged Receipts	49.40
+Service Charge	29.64	Credit Total		0.00	+Checks Begun	12	495.89		
+Tax Collected	22.23	Change Grand Ttl		501.86	-Checks Paid	12	502.05	Service Charges	27.80
=Total Revenue	495.89	Rounding Total		0.00	+Transferred IN	0	0.00	+Charged Tips	8.00
		Training Total		0.00	-Transferred OUT	0	0.00	+Tips Declared	0.00
Item Discount	0.00				=Outstanding	0	-6.16	=Total Tip 8.02%	35.80
+Subtotal Discoun	-5.97	Mgr Voids	0	0.00					
=Total Discounts	-5.97	Error Corrects	12	28.10	No Sale	0		Tips Paid	35.80
		Cancel	0	0.00				Tips Due	0.00

Order Type	Net Sales	% of Ttl	Guests	% of Ttl	Avg/Guest	Checks	% of Ttl	Avg/Chk	Tables	% of Ttl	Avg/Tbl	Turn Time
1 - Dine In	444.02	100.00%	31	100.00%	14.32	12	100.00%	37.00	0	0.00%	0.00	0.00
Total	444.02		31		14.32	12		37.00	0		0.00	

3 - Employee Tracking

.Insuf Bev	0	0.00	60% Emp Meal	1	-5.97	Visa	1	59.87
.Bev Added	0	0.00	40% Emp Meal	0	0.00	MasterCard	0	0.00
Food Cold	0	0.00		0	0.00	Discover/Bravo	0	0.00
Took Too Long	0	0.00	40% Emp Comp	0	0.00	Diners/CB	0	0.00
Did not want	0	0.00	20% Coupon	0	0.00	=TTL CREDIT	0	0.00
OverCooked	0	0.00	Dead Food	0	0.00	G/C 21 Customer	0	0.00
Foreign Object	0	0.00	Dead Liquor	0	0.00	G/C 22 Employee	0	0.00
Tough	0	0.00	20% Teacher	0	0.00	G/C 23 Charity	0	0.00
Too Spicy	0	0.00	=Ttl Disc	0	0.00	G/C 24 Advertising	0	0.00
Server Error	0	0.00	$ Charged Tips	1	8.00	G/C 25 Special	0	0.00
Bar Error	0	0.00	Non Rev Svc Chg	0	0.00	G/C 26 Compliment	0	0.00
Kitchen Error	0	0.00	15% Auto Tip	1	21.64	=Gift Certificate	0	0.00
=Ttl Voids	0	0.00	=TTL Srv Chrg	0	0.00	.House Accounts	0	0.00
100% Discount	0	0.00	Amex	0	0.00	.COMPS	0	0.00
Subtotal	**0**	**0.00**	**Subtotal**	**3**	**23.67**	**Subtotal**	**1**	**59.87**

Courtesy of MICROS Systems, Inc., Columbia, Maryland.

Customers enjoy advantages provided by online ordering systems, including reduced waiting time and greater convenience. Online ordering is simple. Customers can look at the menu on the restaurant's website, select items to order, and enter their name, address, and other required information, which is automatically sent to the property. Online ordering systems can validate the customers' payment card, allow customers to order several (or more) days in advance of the preparation date, and let customers place orders at any time of day. Systems display images of menu items, and also allow for easy duplication of previous orders.

Systems automatically post price differences for items available at both lunch and dinner, and display food options and choices, such as types of salad dressing. They can also show food items available for additional charges. The systems may provide a text area that lets customers add special ordering instructions.

Some restaurants provide curbside cashier service. Guests who have placed online orders drive to a designated area at the restaurant where a server delivers their order to them. Guests pay with a payment card via a handheld terminal carried by the server.

Call Centers. Technology is increasingly involved in another method of customer ordering: the use of call centers. Large food service organizations may operate centralized call centers that serve as many as hundreds of restaurant units. Some operators set up call centers in which employees enter customer orders via the restaurant's website. While most call centers are staffed with employees, some use voice-recognition technology to reduce labor costs. Food operators could also hire independent home-based agents to manage customer calls, and technology can reduce logistical communication problems. For example, some quick-service restaurant orders placed from a vehicle in a drive-through lane are processed at call centers hundreds or even thousands of miles away, and are then routed back to the restaurant for preparation and customer pick-up after payment.

Digital Signage. Digital menus feature display boards or screens that are programmed to display and change content at preset times. High resolution, moving images, and high-definition video provide graphics to catch customers' attention. Innovative programmers find numerous ways to suggestively sell menu items on their display boards that have proven to be most profitable from use of menu engineering or other evaluation tactics. Managers can quickly change an item, a photo, or a price on the display without having to change the entire menu board on, probably, multiple menu displays. Multi-unit operations can make specific changes at central locations.

Smartphone Ordering. Mobile web-ordering allows users to view entire menus, make selections, and place orders. Links to Google maps take users to addresses of specific locations, and also provide directions. Customers can use *plan-ahead ordering* several weeks in advance of their pick-up, can order 24/7 (24 hours daily, seven days a week), and can use a *favorites wizard* that remembers their favorite selections.

More Ways to Use Technology for Ordering

There are numerous other ways that guests can or soon will be able to order their favorite menu items. Examples include the following:

- The Ford Motor Company's SYNC in-car connectivity system enables drivers to use voice commands to place food orders hands-free while driving.

- One quick-service restaurant chain is testing a mobile app ordering system that allows guests to place orders and pay for them via their mobile devices before the guests enter the restaurant.

- Live Deal (www.livedeal.com) enables restaurant managers to post deals specific to a day and time; customers can view these deals and take advantage of them (place their orders) in real time.

- New technology enables guests seated at their table to review a menu and order menu items from a menu that is projected onto the table's surface (www.e-table-interactive.com).

- One full-service restaurant chain (Stacked—www.stacked.com) requires its guests to order food and beverage products via an iPad. While some restaurants use iPads as menus or wine lists, with several iPads being shared around the restaurant, the Stacked concept involves placing iPads permanently on tables.

    The availability of these and other technologies requires restaurant managers to accurately determine what their guests want as they consider service-related decisions.

Other Digital-Ordering Applications. People can order pizza while on Facebook (a social-networking website), and via TiVo while in front of their televisions.

The ordering process ends when guests pay for their meals. Restaurants may use pay-at-the-table systems, in which servers take handheld terminals to dining tables to process guest charges made with payment cards.

Technology and Account Settlement

Technology has provided various methods to collect revenue from guests; examples of this technology are described in the following sections.[6]

Magnetic Strip Readers. A **magnetic strip reader** connects to a cashier terminal and collects data stored on a magnetized filmstrip typically located on the back of a payment card. This technology enables payment cards to be handled directly by the POS system. (Note: terminals equipped with magnetic strip readers can also be used by employees with an applicable identification card to sign into the system.)

Power Platforms. Processing payment and gift card transactions is simplified when a **power platform** consolidates electronic communication between the food service operation and a remote authorization application. All POS terminals at a location can be connected to a single processor for transaction reconciliation. Swift data retrieval results and helps reduce the time, cost, and risk that can be related to deferred settlement.

Smart Cards. A **smart card** is usually the same shape and size as a credit card; microchips are embedded within them that can be accessed by a specially designed reader. Smart cards contain the necessary information to complete electronic purchases and a specially designed reader can process a transaction and reduce the cash value on the card's microchip by a corresponding amount.

Debit Cards. Holders of **debit cards** must have money deposited in a linked bank account or ATM to establish settlement value. As the cardholder makes a purchase, the value of the bank account balance decreases to reflect the amount of funds used. In on-line debit transactions, the cardholder uses a PIN to authorize the transaction. When an off-line debit transaction occurs, the cardholder provides a signature to complete the transaction.

Cashless Payments. Cashless payments can use an open-loop system to accept bank-sponsored credit and debit cards such as Visa. This requires external authorization, processing, and settlement through an automated clearing house. When a closed-loop system is used, the entire transaction is handled internally at specific POS locations supported by the user. For example, a food service operation can issue a branded gift card and the entire transaction is handled internally.

Contactless Payments. This payment process involves a cashless transaction initiated and completed without physical contact between the payment media and a payment reader. These transactions can be conducted with a wave or tap of a radio frequency identification (RFID) chip embedded in a plastic card or other device; a magnetic strip reader is not used. For mobile devices such as cell phones and personal digital assistants, near field communications (NFC) are used instead of

RFID. NFC offers the user an interface that provides rapid transaction settlements with the option to require entry of a PIN number to authorize transactions.

Food and Beverage Revenue Control Procedures

Managers of commercial food service operations must control revenue generated from food and beverage sales. They must implement and enforce procedures to help ensure that the operation receives revenue for all items served.[7]

Dishonest employees can find many ways to try to "beat the house." Managers should ask themselves, "If I were an employee who wanted to steal, how would I do it?" To the extent that managers can answer this question, they can identify potential problems and try to prevent them. Managers must not assume that employees will be honest and never steal. While the majority of employees are honest, some unfortunately are not.

Revenue Control and Servers

With Guest Check Systems. Guest check systems are not nearly as popular today as they were in the past; however, some operations, especially small ones, still use them.

With a guest check system, no guest order for a food or beverage product should be taken without listing each item on a guest check. No food or beverage order should be prepared if it is not written on a guest check. Numbered guest checks are issued to food servers and become the servers' responsibility. Managers can determine the amount of revenue a food server should have collected by adding the totals on all of his or her guest checks after the checks have been accounted for.

When an operation uses duplicate guest checks, a copy is given to food or beverage production employees. At a later time, managers can compare these copies with the originals given to guests and retained by the cashier.

With Precheck Registers. When the operation uses a precheck register, the server takes the guest's order, writes it on a guest check, and goes to the precheck register. The server inserts the check into the register, presses a clerk key (identifying which server is using the machine), and enters the guest's order into the register. Use of the precheck register authorizes the order on the guest check to be prepared. The order is taken to the kitchen (or is sent to a remote printer) and prepared. Before the server leaves at the end of the shift, the orders he or she entered into the precheck register are totaled to assess the amount of revenue due from the guest checks the server wrote. The actual guest checks are also totaled, and this amount is compared with the server's total as indicated by the precheck register.

Revenue Control and Beverage Personnel

The bartender is unique within a food and beverage operation. No other position is responsible for taking and preparing guest orders, determining the amount of money that should be collected, collecting revenue, and ringing up orders into the revenue management system. Bartenders serve guests at the bar and at tables when service personnel are absent. Bartenders may also be responsible for serving food. Frequently, there is no practical way to separate all of these tasks.

Bartenders must be given a cash bank at the beginning of their shifts. They are responsible for the amount of cash in the bank until the bank is returned at the end of the shift.

Certain revenue control tasks should be performed at the end of each bartender's shift.[8] The bartender must account for all beverage guest checks (if they are used). The amount of money in the cash register must be verified with tallies of guest checks, precheck register totals, or a review/verification of sales rung on his or her code or key. Use of modern electronic equipment that provides sales journal tapes and/or electronic information within the POS terminal allows a manager to verify the amount of revenue for which the bartender is responsible. Issuing procedures are also an important part of the bartender's closing procedures. Management should ensure that the amount of liquor at the bar at the beginning of the bartender's shift is accounted for at the end of the shift. This includes keeping track of empty bottles.

Supervising a bartender is difficult, especially when the operation is busy. Common theft methods include working from the tip jar instead of the register, and not ringing up drinks that are served. A dishonest bartender might use the "no sale" key to deposit money collected from guests into the cash drawer. Because it was entered into the register as a "no sale," this money is not recorded or accounted for on the register tapes. Swizzle sticks, maraschino cherries, bent matches, or a slip of paper with several tears are common items dishonest bartenders might use to track the number of unrecorded drinks representing cash they are "owed" from the cash drawer. Managers should occasionally go behind the bar, read the amount of revenue rung on the register, and replace the first cash drawer with a new one. The amount of money in the first drawer should equal the original cash balance plus the amount of revenue rung up on the register since the beginning of the shift. More money than this may represent income deposited as "no sales" that the bartender intends to steal.

Other methods of theft and precautions that can be taken to protect against them are listed in Exhibit 10.

Shopper Services for Bartender Control. Sometimes operations hire a shopper service to check bartenders. The *shopper* poses as a guest to observe the beverage operation. An operation may use shopper services primarily for detecting bartender theft, but an operation intending to make improvements might use the services to look at the entire operation.

All bartenders should be routinely shopped. Bartenders should be told when hired that shoppers may be used. New bartenders or persons the managers have reason to suspect are stealing might be shopped more frequently. Obviously, the bartenders must not know or recognize the shopper.

Shoppers should meet with management staff before visiting the property to learn about required procedures and systems. If there are special problems, the shopper can be told about them during the meeting.

When shoppers visit the bar, they should order a drink and carefully observe as the bartender takes the order, prepares the drink, serves it, and collects cash for it. Shoppers should note how the bartender rings up the drink on the register. The shopper can remain at the bar and casually observe various transactions and

Exhibit 10   Bartender Control Techniques

Common Types of Bartender Theft	Precautions
Violating procedures for POS operation, including bunching sales, no rings, and working out of the tip jar.	• Develop specific POS operating procedures. • Place the tip jar away from the POS. • Supervision is necessary to ensure that all required procedures are followed consistently.
Underpouring or diluting drinks and pocketing cash from the sale of the "extra drink."	• Require that bartenders use a portion tool when preparing all drinks.
Bringing in personal bottles of liquor, preparing drinks from these bottles, and keeping the money.	• Mark bottles and check them often.
Selling drinks for cash and recording drinks as spilled, returned, or complimentary.	• No drinks should be served without charge unless approved by the manager. • Returned drinks should not be discarded without the manager's approval.
Bartender working in collusion with beverage server(s) so drinks are served but revenue is not received.	• Use a rotating schedule for employees. • Be aware of gossip about employee relationships. • Monitor beverage cost percentages.
Writing a lower beverage charge on the guest check and ringing it into the POS (undercharging).	• Make routine audits of guest checks and/or POS sales data to uncover pricing errors.
Trading liquor with the cook for food products.	• Enforce all employee eating and drinking policies. • Be aware of signs of employee eating and drinking, such as plates and glasses left in workstations or restrooms.
Using stolen checks to replace cash.	• No personal checks should be accepted without the manager's approval.
Using counterfeit guest checks to collect revenue.	• Use unique, hard-to-duplicate guest checks.
Taking cash from the cash drawer.	• Use a basic revenue control system to determine how much money should be in the cash drawer. • Make the bartender liable for all cash shortages (if legal in your locality).
Giving away drinks to promote a bigger tip, or giving drinks to friends.	• No complimentary drinks should be given without the manager's approval. • Guest checks must be in front of each guest at all times.

interactions. However, the shopper should also visit the restroom, look at other public areas, and react as a guest to the total experience.

After the visit, the shopper reports all findings to the manager. The shopper may have observed signs of dishonesty, such as misuse of the register, a bartender pouring free drinks, or suspicious conversations between the bartender and employees or guests. Armed with this information, the manager can take steps to deal with any problems.

Increasing Food and Beverage Sales

Maximizing financial objectives while meeting the needs of guests is a goal common to all food and beverage managers. To do so, managers must ensure that servers know how to effectively sell food and beverages.

Suggestive Selling

Suggestive selling includes a variety of techniques that servers can use to encourage guests to buy certain menu items. When guests know what they want, servers should make no effort to change their minds. However, some guests may not know what they want and might appreciate assistance as they order.

Two objectives of suggestive selling are to (1) increase sales of the most profitable items, and (2) increase the **check average** (the total food and beverage revenue divided by the total number of guests consuming meals).

Let's look first at suggestive selling designed to increase sales of the most profitable menu items. The food server can draw the guest's attention to these items and make recommendations when presenting the menu. This technique works especially well when the operation has planned its menu around the items it wants to sell. For example, items on a menu that head a list, are boxed, or have written descriptions often sell with greater frequency than other items.

To increase the check average, food servers should ask questions that guests cannot answer with a "no," such as, "Our strawberry shortcake is fantastic and the chef's own special cherry pie just came out of the oven; which would you like?" and "Would you like a white or a red wine with dinner?"

"You've probably noticed all the desserts we've prepared tableside this evening. Everyone raves about our cherries jubilee and flaming crepes. Which would you prefer?" is an example that illustrates another important idea behind suggestive selling: people are influenced by what they see others eating. If guests see a Caesar salad being prepared tableside, they may be strongly inclined to order the salad.

Suggestive selling can be applied to cafeteria service as well as table-service operations. A server can make suggestions to guests passing through the cafeteria serving line. Suggestive selling also has implications for buffet service. The way items are placed on the buffet line and the use of garnishes can affect guests' desires to take portions of the menu items.

Selling Beverages

The sale of alcoholic beverages can increase a food and beverage operation's profitability because contribution margins are high. After product cost is subtracted from revenue, a significant amount is left over to contribute to profit.

Traditionally, many food service managers made special efforts to sell alcoholic beverages. Today, however, there is an ongoing emphasis on serving alcohol with care. While many observers feared significant losses in profitability as social concerns about alcohol evolved, these fears have proven unfounded. Operators have been able to enhance dining experiences for their guests and increase profits while still being socially responsible.

To effectively sell beverages, employees should know:

- What drinks are available

- Drink ingredients and preparation methods

- How to make suggestions

- Which wines to suggest with menu items

- How to present, open, and serve wine and champagne

To increase beverage revenues most effectively, service staff must be trained.

A well-rounded wine list is very important, and much has been written on the topic. A good list should include dry and sweet wines, white and red wines, and champagne (sparkling wine) at low, medium, and high prices.

The wine list is an important marketing tool. A description of the wine, even if it is only several words, can be of great help. Recommended wines can be listed next to appropriate items on the food menu. Wine displays set up around the dining room, wine-tasting stations where guests can sample alternative selections, table tent cards, and menu inserts may also help sell wine. Some properties employ a wine steward (also called a sommelier) who is very knowledgeable about wines and can suggest them to discriminating guests.

Some operations specialize in preparing and serving exotic tropical or flaming drinks. It is important that the manager provide drink menus, table tent cards, and other merchandising items to make guests aware of the special drinks. The service staff must reinforce these messages. The manager can help motivate the staff by noting that, as more beverages are sold, check averages increase, and so should tips.

Seasonal drinks are relatively easy to sell. Tom and Jerry drinks during the Christmas season, green beer on St. Patrick's Day, and special fruit punch drinks during summer months are examples.

Many merchandising techniques used to sell alcoholic beverages can also effectively sell nonalcoholic beverages. Nonalcoholic beverages are easier to sell when they are expertly prepared and attractively presented. Using standard recipes is an important first step. It also helps to serve the beverages in distinctive glassware and to garnish the drinks appropriately.

Contests among employees can also help boost beverage sales. A free meal for a service employee and his or her guest is an example of the type of incentive the operation can use to inspire service staff to sell beverages.

The bottom line is that managers must always try to fulfill the guests' wants with the type of products, service, and atmosphere the operation provides. The operation that finds a way to distinguish its beverage products from the competition's, or from those the guest can make at home, is more likely to increase beverage revenues.

Endnotes

1. For details about banquet service, see Ronald F. Cichy and Philip J. Hickey, Jr., *Managing Service in Food and Beverage Operations*, 4th ed. (Lansing, Mich.: American Hotel & Lodging Educational Institute, 2012).

2. For details about dining room service, see Cichy and Hickey.

3. Ronald F. Cichy and Lendal H. Kotschevar, *Managing Beverage Operations*, 2nd ed. (Lansing, Mich.: American Hotel & Lodging Educational Institute, 2010).

4. This discussion is adapted from *Controlling Alcohol Risks Effectively*, an industry-taught seminar offered through the American Hotel & Lodging Educational Institute.

5. For more information about technology applications for food and beverage service, see Michael L. Kasavana, *Managing Technology in the Hospitality Industry*, 6th ed. (Lansing, Mich.: American Hotel & Lodging Educational Institute, 2011); and Jack D. Ninemeier, *Planning and Control for Food and Beverage Operations*, 8th ed. (Lansing, Mich.: American Hotel & Lodging Educational Institute, 2013).

6. Michael L. Kasavana, *Managing Technology in the Hospitality Industry*, 6th ed. (Lansing, Mich.: American Hotel & Lodging Educational Institute, 2011), Chapter 6.

7. For more information, see Ninemeier (endnote 5).

8. Details of bartender closing procedures are beyond the scope of this chapter. For more information, see Ninemeier (endnote 5).

Key Terms

automatic form number reader—A feature of a guest check printer that facilitates order entry procedures. Instead of a server manually entering a guest check's serial number to access the account, a bar code imprinted on the guest check enables the machine to read the serial number.

buffet service—Traditional buffet service involves arranging food on platters that are then placed on large serving tables or counters.

cafeteria service—A type of service in which guests pass through serving lines and receive food items from service staff. Scramble cafeteria layouts provide separate serving stations for different types of food.

cart service—A table-service style in which specially trained staff members prepare menu items on a cart beside the guest's table, then serve the guest. Also called *French service*.

check average—Total food and beverage revenue divided by the total number of guests.

debit card—Debit cards differ from credit cards in that the cardholder must deposit money in order to give the card value. The cardholder deposits money in advance of purchases through a debit card center or an electronic debit posting machine; as purchases are made, the balance on the debit card falls.

dram shop act—Legislation establishing third-party liability for accidents involving intoxicated drivers that may hold bartenders, servers, and owners jointly liable if they unlawfully sell alcoholic beverages to a minor or an intoxicated person who then injures others.

family-style service—A table-service style in which servers deliver food on large platters or in large bowls to guest tables. The guests at each table then pass the food around their table, serving themselves. Also called *English service.*

food server station—A specific section or number of tables in the dining room for which a server is responsible.

function keys—Part of an electronic cash register/point-of-sale system terminal. Function keys assist the user in processing transactions; they are important for error correction (clear and void), legitimate price alteration (discount), and proper cash handling (no-sale).

guest check printer—A sophisticated printer that may be equipped with an automatic form number reader and/or automatic slip feed capabilities.

intoxication (legal definition)—In most states, a blood-alcohol concentration (BAC) of .08 grams or more of alcohol per 100 milliliters of blood.

job breakdown—A description of the steps (procedures) required to successfully complete one task that is part of a job.

kiosk—A computer terminal on a podium, counter, or table that guests use for self-ordering of food and beverage items.

kitchen monitor—A video display unit capable of showing several orders on a single screen.

labor master file—A file containing one record for each staff member, usually with data including name, employee and Social Security numbers, job codes, hours worked, total hourly wages, wages declared, and credits for meals.

magnetic strip reader—Optional input device that connects to a POS system register or terminal capable of collecting data stored on a magnetized film strip typically located on the back of a credit card or house account card.

menu board—A keyboard overlay for an electronic cash register/point-of-sale system terminal that identifies the function performed by each key.

menu item file—A file containing data for all meal periods and menu items sold, including identification number, description, recipe code number, selling price, ingredient quantities for inventory reporting, and sales totals.

modifier key—Part of an electronic cash register/point-of-sale system keyboard used with preset and price look-up keys to detail preparation instructions for food production areas or to alter prices based on designated portion sizes.

negligence—Failure to exercise the care a reasonably prudent person would exercise under like or similar circumstances.

numeric keypad—Part of an electronic cash register/point-of-sale system keyboard. It is the set of keys used to ring up menu items by price, access price look-up data by menu item code number, access open guest check accounts by serial number, and perform other data entry operations.

open check file—A file that maintains current data for all open guest checks and is accessed to monitor items on a particular guest check, add items to a guest check after initial order entry, and close a guest check when it is settled.

plate service—A table-service style in which menu items are individually produced, portioned, plated, and garnished in the kitchen, then carried to each guest directly. Also called *American service*.

platter service—A table-service style in which servers present platters of fully cooked food to guests for approval. Servers then set hot plates in front of each guest and place food from the platters onto the plates. Also called *Russian service*.

point-of-sale (POS) terminal—An electronic unit that contains its own input/output component and possibly a small storage (memory) capacity, but usually not its own central processing unit.

power platform—Consolidates electronic communications between a hospitality establishment and a credit card authorization center. Power platforms can capture credit card authorizations in three seconds or less. A POS power platform connects all POS terminals to a single processor for transaction settlement.

precheck terminal—An electronic cash register/point-of-sale system terminal with no cash drawer; used to enter orders but not to settle accounts.

preset key—Part of an electronic cash register/point-of-sale system keyboard programmed to maintain the price, description, department, tax, and inventory status of a designated menu item.

price look-up key—Part of an electronic cash register/point-of-sale system keyboard that operates like a preset key except that it requires the user to identify a menu item by its reference code number.

receipt printer—A printing device that produces hard copy on narrow register tape.

settlement key—Part of an electronic cash register/point-of-sale system keyboard, used to record the methods by which accounts are settled: cash, credit card, house account, charge transfer to the guest's folio (in a hotel), or other payment method.

sidework—Setup and cleanup work, such as restocking server supply stations, that must be done before and after dining rooms are opened.

smart card—Smart cards are made of plastic and are about the same size as credit cards. Microchips embedded in them store information that can be accessed by a specially designed card reader. Smart cards can store information in several files that are accessed for different functions, such as a person's vital health statistics, dietary restrictions, credit card number, and bank balance. Information stored in smart cards is secured by a personal identification number (PIN) that must be used to access files.

suggestive selling—Techniques used to encourage guests to buy certain menu items to increase sales of the most profitable items and increase the check average.

table service—A type of service in which guests are seated at a table and food servers wait on them. Four basic styles of table service are cart (French), family-style (English), plate (American), and platter (Russian).

work station printer—A printing device usually placed in kitchen preparation areas and service bar locations.

Review Questions

1. How does cart service differ from platter service?

2. How does family-style service differ from plate service?

3. What is the primary goal of most table-service operations?

4. Why are standard operating procedures important for service?

5. What factors should managers consider when determining the number of tables to assign to food servers?

6. What are some important points servers should know to properly and legally serve alcoholic beverages with care?

7. What are some guidelines food service managers and servers can follow to help reduce the possibility of a troublesome confrontation with an intoxicated guest?

8. What factors should managers consider when determining what type of hardware and software would best meet the operation's dining service needs?

9. What are examples of POS outputs (reports) that would help you run your hotel or restaurant's food services?

10. How does a server banking system differ from a cashier banking system?

11. What precautions can managers take to protect the operation from theft by bartenders?

12. From the manager's perspective, what are the two primary objectives of suggestive selling?

Internet Sites

For more information, visit the following Internet sites. Remember that Internet addresses can change without notice. If the site is no longer there, you can use a search engine to look for additional sites.

Point-of-Sale Systems

Comtrex Systems Corporation
www.comtrex.com

Elo Touch Systems
www.elotouch.com

Digital Dining
www.digitaldining.com

Maitre'D POS
www.maitredpos.com/home.aspx

MICROS Systems, Inc.
www.micros.com

POSitouch
www.positouch.com

NCR Corporation
www.ncr.com

Squirrel Systems
www.squirrelsystems.com

Reservations/Seating Systems

Dine Plan
www.dineplan.com

My Seat
www.openmyseat.com

iMagic Software
www.imagicrestaurantsoftware.com

OpenTable, Inc.
www.opentable.com

Chapter 11 Outline

Competencies

1. Explain and identify the causes of unsafe food, and list the basic types of foodborne illnesses. (pp. 279–284)

2. Discuss the effects that personal cleanliness can have on food quality and service. (pp. 284–286)

3. Outline proper food handling and cleaning procedures. (pp. 286–303)

4. Describe the role OSHA plays in keeping the workplace safe. (pp. 303–304)

5. Identify common food service accidents and some important ways to prevent them. (pp. 304–310)

6. Outline management's role in sanitation and safety programs, including first aid requirements. (pp. 310–312)

11

Sanitation and Safety

Sanitation and safety are two topics food and beverage managers cannot ignore. If an outbreak of **foodborne illness** is traced to an operation, the costs in human suffering, productivity (if employees become ill), medical and hospital expenses, legal expenses (including claims settlement), negative publicity, and lost business can be devastating. The costs in human suffering and the monetary costs to the operation can also be significant if a worker or guest is injured on the property because of unsafe conditions.

Sanitation must be addressed at every stage of the food-handling process. Serious illness and even death can be caused by the failure to follow simple, basic food handling procedures. Safety concerns are just as vital. Food service managers have a personal, professional, and legal responsibility to provide safe conditions for employees and guests.

Sanitation

Food products must be purchased, received, stored, prepared, and served under sanitary conditions. Clean equipment must be used and sanitary work habits must be practiced. One of a food service manager's most important duties is to make sure that the food served to guests is safe and wholesome.[1]

Guests are concerned about sanitation. Cleanliness along with food quality and service are integral parts of the "product" being purchased by guests.

The U.S. Food and Drug Administration's 2001 Food Code, upon which some of the recommendations in this chapter are based, contains sanitation guidelines designed to safeguard public health.[2] Food service operations must comply with their own state and local recommendations, even when state and local regulations differ from the federal recommendations contained in the Food Code.

What Causes Unsafe Food?

Two causes of unsafe food are chemical poisoning and microorganisms.

Chemical Poisoning. Chemical poisoning occurs when toxic substances contaminate foods or beverages. Chemicals may be added before the food reaches the food service operation (apples may have pesticide residues on their skins, for example) or after the food arrives there. For example, an employee who is not trained, has reading problems, or for whom English is a second language may mistakenly substitute harmful cleaning chemicals for cooking ingredients. Or improperly manufactured cooking containers or utensils may react with foods (especially those containing acids) to cause a relatively common type of chemical poisoning.

Managers can take many commonsense precautions to minimize the possibility of chemical poisoning. One is to buy food only from dependable sources. This means not purchasing food from "backdoor salespersons" who offer special buys on food that was grown, slaughtered, or caught (example: fish) locally. Another simple precaution is to carefully wash fruits and vegetables to remove any pesticide residues or other chemicals.

Managers should use caution when spreading chemicals for mice and rodents and spraying for flies, cockroaches, and other insects. Pesticides should be handled by a professional trained in their use. Personnel should be careful with chemicals used to clean kitchen equipment. These cleaners must be approved for use around food and should be applied according to the manufacturer's instructions. All chemicals should be stored in appropriate containers away from areas where food is kept.

Microorganisms. Microorganisms are small living organisms all around us that are too small to see without a microscope. They vary in length, but it takes 2,500 to 13,000 of them, placed end to end, to make one inch.

Not all microorganisms are harmful. Some are required to produce such foods as cheese, sauerkraut, and bread. Others help manufacture drugs and useful chemicals. Still others are in our bodies and help us digest and absorb vitamin K.

Unfortunately, some microorganisms are dangerous. This chapter will refer to them as *germs*. They cause illness and disease if they are allowed to multiply and spread to humans through food or some other means.

Several types of harmful germs can make food unsafe. Examples include bacteria, molds, parasites, and viruses. Unfortunately, the germs most harmful to

---

Cleaning Chemicals Can Contaminate Food

It should be easy to understand that items such as cleaning chemicals should not be stored in food preparation or service areas because they can be mistaken for a recipe ingredient and used in food production. One would hope that this would be obvious to everyone. However, it is not!

During the week this chapter was revised, national news reported two instances of chemical food poisonings in restaurants that affected numerous guests. In one, an employee of an independently owned and operated restaurant mistook a cleaning chemical in the food preparation area for a recipe ingredient. The second instance occurred at a property affiliated with one of the largest multi-unit food chains in the country. In this case, an employee inadequately rinsed an empty cleaning chemical container and used it to store vanilla, which was an ingredient in several recipes.

The "obvious" food safety principle was not obvious to the managers and employees of these two operations! Empty cleaning, pesticide, and other chemical bottles should be discarded. They should never be rinsed, washed, sanitized, or sterilized (if that is even possible in a restaurant) for re-use!

people also like many foods we do: nonacidic, high-protein foods such as meat, fish, poultry, eggs, milk, and baked goods with cream fillings. High-protein foods are most susceptible to germ growth and are classified as potentially hazardous. While all foods must be handled with care, **potentially hazardous foods** should be given special attention.

Germs need certain conditions in order to multiply. First, they need moisture. Freezing or drying foods will not necessarily kill germs. Rather, since moisture is removed (in drying) or changed into another form (ice crystals in freezing), germs may become dormant—but begin multiplying when moisture is again available, such as when moisture is added to dry products or when frozen products are thawed.

Germs thrive in comfortable temperatures. The **food temperature danger zone** is 41°F (5°C) to 135°F (57°C). Germs will multiply rapidly in foods that are within this temperature range. Food production and service personnel should do everything possible to minimize the time that foods are in this danger zone.

Acidity also affects the ability of germs to grow. Some germs can live in very acidic foods such as citrus fruits, but most germs grow best in neutral foods that do not contain large amounts of acids. Unfortunately, many foods high in protein (for example, meats, seafood, eggs, and milk) are in the neutral acid range. This reinforces the need to give special food handling attention to protein foods.

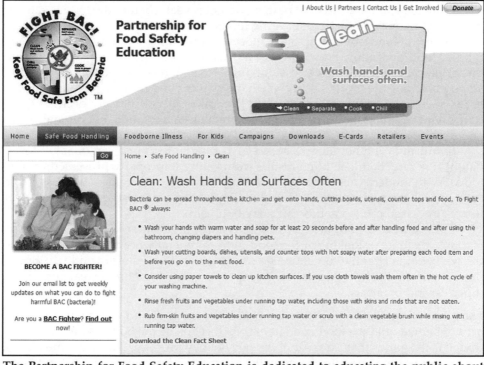

The Partnership for Food Safety Education is dedicated to educating the public about safe food handling to help reduce the occurrence of foodborne illness outbreaks. Fight BAC! (www.fightbac.org) is its campaign to help consumers keep food safe from harmful bacteria.

Other factors affect the optimal growth of germs. Managers who know how to make the environment inhospitable for germs can help create a safe, sanitary food service operation. Later, the chapter discusses germ-fighting strategies managers and employees can use when purchasing, receiving, storing, preparing, and serving food.

Foodborne Illnesses

Harmful germs in food can cause people who consume them to become ill. An overview of some common foodborne illnesses is shown in Exhibit 1. There are two basic types of foodborne illnesses:

- *Food poisoning*, an illness caused by germ-produced toxins (poisons)

- *Food infection*, an illness caused by germs in food

Food Poisoning. Food poisoning occurs when germs get into food and produce wastes. With food poisoning, it is the poison that causes the illness, not the germs themselves.

Once a food is poisoned by germs, there is nothing anyone can do to make it safe for consumption. For example, heat applied to the food will kill germs, but will not eliminate any poisons in the food. Also, the poison often has no taste, odor, or color, so the common practice of smelling or tasting the food to determine if it is safe to eat is ineffective. At best, it will not reveal whether the food is safe. At worst, people may get sick from tasting foods that contain poison.

Types of food poisoning. Staphylococcal poisoning, or staph, is a common type of food poisoning. Staph germs are found on the skin and in the nose and throat of people with colds and sinus infections. Foods most often involved in staph poisoning are meats—especially ham, poultry, and meat salads—and cream foods such as cream puffs and cream-filled cakes. Illness usually occurs within four hours of eating the food. Symptoms are nausea, vomiting, abdominal pains, and diarrhea.

Botulism is another illness caused by poison in food and can be fatal; fortunately, it is rare. Botulism often results from eating improperly processed canned foods. With modern canning and processing methods, outbreaks of botulism from commercial sources are rare. However, improperly processed homegrown or home-processed canned goods can carry botulism.

The presence of botulin (the toxin that causes botulism) cannot be detected by tasting, smelling, or looking at the food. Illness generally occurs within twelve to thirty-six hours after the contaminated food is eaten. Symptoms include dizziness; double vision; difficulty in swallowing, speaking, and breathing; weakness in the muscles; and paralysis.

Food Infection. Food infections are caused by bacteria and viruses in food that are consumed with the food and later reproduce inside the body. With food infection, it is the germs themselves, not the poison they produce, that cause the illness.

Types of food infection. Salmonellosis, or sam, is a common form of food infection. Sam germs live in the intestinal tract of people and some animals, including hogs and chickens. Foods especially susceptible to salmonellosis include ground beef, pork, and poultry; fish; eggs and egg products; and baked goods containing

Exhibit 1   Overview of Common Foodborne Illnesses

Type of Illness	How People Become Infected	Food Commonly Associated with This Illness	How This Illness Can Be Prevented

Staph poisoning (staphylococcus)	Eating food infected by careless food handlers:
	  Germs from cuts
	  Coughing or sneezing around food
		Potentially hazardous food high in protein content:
		  Custard and cream dishes
		  Meat dishes (especially ham, poultry, and meat salads)
			Careful food-handling habits
			Employees free of infections
			Thorough cooking of food followed by immediate serving or refrigeration

Botulism	Eating food containing poison from the bacteria	Canned goods improperly processed, such as beans, corn, meat, and fish	Careful processing of canned foods Do not use home-processed canned goods in food service operations

Sam poisoning (salmonella)	Eating improperly cooked foods contaminated by:
	  The organism
	  Contact with fecal material (often from rodents)
		Foods high in protein content:
		  Meats
		  Poultry
		  Eggs and egg products
		  Baked products with cream fillings
			Good personal habits of food handlers
			Thorough cooking and immediate serving or refrigeration of foods
			Good food-storage practices

Clostridium perfringens	Eating food contaminated by:
	  Food handlers
	  Insects
		Foods high in protein content:
		  Meats
		  Poultry
		  Sauces, soups, and gravies made with meat and poultry
			Thorough cooking and immediate serving or refrigeration of foods
			Good food-storage practices
			Good personal habits of food handlers

E. coli (*Escherichia coli*)	Eating food contaminated with the organism	Raw and undercooked beef Unpasterurized milk and apple juice Improperly processed salami Lettuce Bean sprouts	Thorough cooking of beef Proper food-handling practices Proper personal hygiene Use of pasteurized milk and juices
Trichinosis	Eating pork products that are contaminated	Pork and pork products	Thorough cooking of pork and pork products Local, state, and federal pork inspection
Tuberculosis	Eating food infected by food handlers who carry the disease	Foods high in milk or milk products	Milk pasteurization Proper sanitation of all eating, drinking, and cooking utensils Careful food handling Routine health exams for employees

Remember:	1. Handle foods properly:
	  a. Follow good personal hygiene habits.
	  b. Be careful with all foods high in protein content.
		2. Keep foods at proper temperature:
		  a. Minimize the time that foods are in the temperature range of 41°F (5°C)–135°F (57°C).
		  b. Keep hot foods hot and keep cold foods cold (out of the food temperature danger zone) or do not keep the food at all.

Adapted from U.S. Department of Agriculture, Food and Nutrition Services, *Principles and Practices of Sanitation and Safety in Child Nutrition Programs*, Washington, D.C., undated.

cream fillings. Illness usually occurs within twelve to forty-eight hours. Symptoms include abdominal pains, diarrhea, fever, vomiting, and chills.

Clostridium perfringens is a germ found almost everywhere: in the soil, in the intestinal tracts of people and animals, and in dust. Food sources include soups, gravies, and stews kept lukewarm in deep containers for long periods of time. Illness usually occurs within eight to twelve hours after eating the contaminated food; symptoms are abdominal pains and diarrhea.

While the specific foods, symptoms, and appropriate food-handling practices differ somewhat between each type of foodborne illness, there is some good news: managers and food handlers can use a basic set of procedures that will help to eliminate the opportunity for any type of food-related illness to occur.

Exhibit 2 outlines basic procedures that a manager may follow when a guest complains of foodborne illness. Procedures will vary from operation to operation.

Exhibit 2   Sample Procedures for Investigating Alleged Foodborne Illnesses

What should a food service manager do if a guest complains about a foodborne illness? Managers should follow their own operation's policies, which may involve contacting upper management, the operation's attorney, and/or insurance representatives before any other action is taken.

1. Obtain the name, address, and phone numbers of the guest.

2. Ask for specific signs and symptoms of the illness.

3. Obtain details about what foods the guest consumed and when they were consumed, when the guest became ill, the duration of the illness, any medication taken for it, known allergies, and any medication taken or inoculation received before the illness.

4. Obtain the name of the physician consulted and/or the hospital visited by the guest. If the guest has not seen a physician, encourage him or her to do so for a proper diagnosis.

5. If the property has a doctor on retainer, alert him or her to the problem. Do not call the doctor at night unless the guest wants to speak with the doctor.

6. Notify the local board of health authorities if food poisoning is diagnosed by a physician. Comply with any instructions provided.

7. A committee comprising the food and beverage manager, chef, and key kitchen personnel should be notified *immediately* to analyze the entire production process and determine where and how the menu item(s) could have been contaminated.

8. Find out how many portions of the menu item(s) responsible for the food poisoning were served. If possible, collect samples and specimens and send to a lab for analysis.

9. Determine which employee(s) prepared the suspected menu item(s). Send the employee(s) to a physician for a medical examination to determine if the employee(s) is(are) ill or carrying germs.

10. Reexamine cleaning standards in the areas where the suspected menu items were prepared and served. Take swabs from the equipment and send them to a lab for analysis.

11. Review sanitation inspection forms/checklists covering the production areas involved in the incident. Evaluate the need for more strict sanitation measures in these areas, and, if needed, train affected employees to follow the new or revised procedures.

Personal Cleanliness and Health

Many foodborne illnesses are traced to employees who handle foods. They should not cough or sneeze into their hands, smoke, scratch their heads, touch their faces, or do other things that will contaminate their hands and the food with which they work. Exhibit 3 lists sample personal cleanliness guidelines.

All food service employees should have regular physical examinations. Local laws may require blood tests, chest X-rays, and examinations when a food service worker is hired and on a regular basis thereafter.

Food service employees who are sick should not report to work. An employee with a cold, cough, open sore, or boil could easily contaminate food. An employee who has been exposed to an infectious disease should consult a doctor before returning to work.

Exhibit 3   Sample Personal Cleanliness Guidelines for Food Service Employees

1. Bathe daily and use deodorant and antiperspirant.
2. Shampoo your hair as often as necessary to keep it healthy and clean, and maintain a simple, easy-to-manage style.
3. Wear clean clothes or uniforms.
4. Keep your fingernails clean, well-trimmed, and free of nail polish.
5. Do not wear excessive makeup and perfume.
6. Do not wear jewelry other than unadorned wedding bands. This guideline is primarily for sanitary reasons, but it also helps protect you and your jewelry.
7. Wear clean, low-heeled, properly fitting shoes with nonskid soles. The heel and toe should be completely enclosed. Do not wear tennis shoes, slippers, or sandals.
8. Always wash your hands with soap and warm water before beginning work and before beginning a new food-handling procedure. Your hands should also be washed before returning from the restroom, after touching your face or hair, and after handling soiled articles, including money.
9. Wash hands in handwashing basins, not preparation or dish- or pot-washing sinks.
10. Use disposable towels to dry your hands, not dish towels, aprons, or your clothes or uniform.
11. Wear hair restraints; do not use hairspray as a substitute. Avoid hairpins and barrettes because they can slip out.
12. Do not comb your hair, use hair spray, file your nails, or apply makeup in food service areas.
13. Do not smoke or chew gum in any food production areas.
14. Do not cough or sneeze near food. It is unsanitary to carry used handkerchiefs in your pocket. If needed, disposable tissues should be used and then discarded. Wash your hands before continuing to work.

Employee eating habits have an impact on sanitation. Managers should establish and enforce rules about where and when employees can eat. They should designate specific areas for employee use and permit eating only in those areas. Employees should be required to wash their hands after eating.

Procedures for Safe Food Handling

Proper food handling involves developing the correct attitude—not memorizing an extensive list of do's and don'ts. If managers and employees understand the need to be careful with food and also know basic sanitation principles, many of the specific rules become a matter of common sense. The first step in proper food handling is confirming, by observation and a review of food-handling procedures, that sanitation is a priority when purchasing, receiving, storing, preparing, and serving foods.

Purchasing. Buyers should always purchase food that is wholesome and suitable to eat. Food should be obtained from commercial sources that comply with all applicable local, state, and federal sanitation laws.[3]

Generally, U.S. laws require that meat and poultry products shipped between states be inspected by agents from the U.S. Department of Agriculture (USDA) to make sure the products are suitable for human consumption. Inspection is done at the processing plants to make sure that (1) meat and poultry products have the proper quality, (2) the plant is clean, and (3) proper handling procedures are used by the plant's employees.

Government agencies other than the USDA are also involved in food inspection. For example, the U.S. Public Health Service helps ensure the wholesomeness of milk; the U.S. Department of the Interior's Bureau of Commercial Fisheries administers an inspection program for many types of processed fish products.

A wise purchaser buys only federally inspected meat and poultry products or makes sure that state or local inspection programs are acceptable substitutes for federal inspection before buying local products. Eggs and egg products such as frozen egg whites and yolks and pressed egg yolks are also generally inspected for wholesomeness by the USDA. Inspection of cheese and fresh and processed fruits and vegetables is not required by law and is done for producers and growers who request (and pay for) the service.

Purchasers should know the difference between inspection and grading. **Food inspection** refers to a mandatory examination of food to determine whether it is wholesome (fit to eat). **Food grading** involves analyzing foods relative to specific, defined standards to assess quality (see Exhibit 4). Inspection may be required by law, but grading is optional. Many purchasers buy graded products because the products have met specific quality standards; that is one reason producers are willing to pay to have their fruits, vegetables, cheese, and other products graded. However, purchasers should be aware that products are graded at the processing plants; subsequent improper handling during transport or by restaurant personnel after foods are received can still adversely affect quality.

Receiving. All incoming foods should be checked to make sure they meet quality standards stated in applicable purchase specifications. Receiving personnel must

Exhibit 4   Inspection and Grading: What Is the Difference?

The inspection and grading of meat and poultry are two separate programs within the United States Department of Agriculture (USDA). Inspection for wholesomeness is mandatory and paid for with tax dollars. Grading for quality is voluntary and is paid for by meat and poultry producers/processors who request the service for their customers.

Inspection

The Food Safety and Inspection Service (FSIS), the USDA's public health agency, inspects all raw meat and poultry sold in interstate and foreign commerce. The agency monitors meat and poultry products after they leave federally inspected plants. In addition, the FSIS monitors state inspection programs that inspect meat and poultry products sold only within the state. These state inspection programs must be "at least equal to" the federal program.

Meat that has been federally inspected and passed for wholesomeness is stamped with a round purple mark.

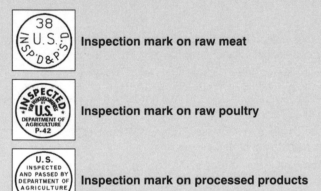

Inspection mark on raw meat

Inspection mark on raw poultry

Inspection mark on processed products

Grading

Grading for quality means evaluating traits related to tenderness, juiciness, and flavor of meat, and, for poultry, a normal shape that is fully fleshed, meaty, and free of defects.

Beef

Beef is graded as whole carcasses for quality (tenderness, juiciness, and flavor) and yield (the amount of usable lean meat on the carcass based on the amount of marbling, color, and maturity).

Quality Grades

- Prime grade is produced from young, well-fed beef cattle. It has abundant marbling, and prime roasts and steaks are excellent for dry-heat cooking.

(continued)

Exhibit 4 *(continued)*

- Choice grade is high quality with less marbling than prime grade. Choice roasts and steaks from the loin and rib will be very tender, juicy, and flavorful. They are, like prime cuts, suited to dry-heat cooking. Many of the less-tender cuts, such as those from the rump, round, and blade chuck, can also be cooked with dry heat.

- Select grade is very uniform in quality and is normally leaner than higher grades. It is fairly tender but may lack some of the juiciness and flavor of the higher grades. Only the tender cuts (loin, rib, or sirloin) should be cooked with dry heat. Other cuts should be marinated before cooking or cooked with moisture.

Yield Grades

Yield grades range from 1 to 5 and indicate the amount of usable meat from a carcass. Yield grade 1 is the highest (lean and heavily muscled) and Grade 5 is the lowest (fat and lightly muscled).

Veal and Calf

There are five grades for veal and calf: prime, choice, good, standard, and utility. Prime and choice grades are juicier and more flavorful than the lower grades.

Lamb

There are five grades for lamb. Normally, only two grades—prime and choice—are found at the retail level.

- Prime grade is very high in tenderness, juiciness, and flavor. Its marbling enhances both flavor and juiciness.

- Choice grade has slightly less marbling than prime, but is still of very high quality.

Pork

Inspection of pork is mandatory, but grading for quality is voluntary. USDA grades reflect only two levels: "acceptable" (the only pork sold in grocery stores) and "utility" (used mainly in processed food and not available in grocery stores).

Poultry

The USDA grades for poultry are A, B, and C.

- Grade A is the highest quality and the only grade likely to be available at the retail level.

- Grades B and C poultry are usually used in further processed products where the poultry meat is cut up, chopped, or ground. If sold at retail, it is not usually identified by grade.

be trained to recognize whether these standards are attained. Employees who receive meats and poultry for the operation should look for the USDA "Inspected and Passed" labels.

The following are examples of sanitation guidelines for receiving:

- Look at the condition of the delivery vehicle. Does the interior look clean? Are refrigerated trucks transporting dairy products, meat, and produce?

- Carefully inspect the contents of every case that appears damaged.

- Check all deliveries for evidence of insect or rodent contamination.

- Check incoming products for unusual or foul odors. They generally mean a problem exists.

- Do not accept frozen foods from vendors that feel partially or completely thawed or appear to be spoiled.

- Use an accurate thermometer to check the temperatures of refrigerated items.

Storing and Issuing. Food should be stored as soon as possible after receiving. Keep stored foods covered so they do not dry out or absorb odors, and to prevent debris or other objects from falling into uncovered food from storage shelves above. Store frozen foods in their original containers because they are usually moisture- and vapor-proof. Store such staples as flour, cornmeal, and rice in rust-proof and corrosion-resistant containers with tight-fitting lids. Do not use metal containers; they are hard to clean, sanitize, and maintain.

Keep stored food away from walls and dripping pipes. Place food on slotted shelves that are at least two inches (5.1 cm) away from the wall and six inches (15.2 cm) off the floor to facilitate air circulation and floor cleaning. Do not line shelves with paper or other materials because that can block airflow. All shelves must be cleaned according to an established schedule.

Food that cannot be stored on shelves because of size or bulk should be stored on easily movable dollies or skids, not directly on the floor. Even if it is in containers, food should never be stored on the floor because, after issuing, containers may be placed on kitchen counters to be opened and emptied. That would allow soil on the bottom of the containers to contaminate the counter.

Ideal temperatures in refrigerated storage areas vary with the type of food being stored. Managers should minimize the time products spend in refrigerators, which should maintain an internal temperature of food at 41°F (5°C), with a relative humidity of 80 to 90 percent. Freezer temperatures should be at a temperature that keeps products frozen. While this temperature varies for specific items, as a rule of thumb, the temperature should be 0°F (−18°C) or below. Food products not requiring refrigeration or freezing should be stored in clean, cool, and moisture-free areas that are well-ventilated and free from rodents and insects. Temperatures for dry food products should be between 50°F (10°C) and 70°F (21°C); relative humidity should range from 50 to 60 percent.

Food should be issued to preparation or service areas on a first-in, first-out (FIFO) basis. In other words, products that are in storage the longest should be used first. When products are received, they should be marked with the receiving dates on the packages or containers in which they will be stored. Products that seem spoiled or unusable should be thrown away, but employees should notify a manager first.

Inspect storage areas often. Do not keep poisons, toxic substances, or cleaning materials in food storage areas. Exhibit 5 lists receiving and storing practices that address sanitation concerns.

Preparing. Food preparers should always follow basic sanitation procedures when working with and around food (see Exhibit 6). Keeping hands clean during food preparation is a must. The use of disposable gloves is often recommended.

Clean food preparation tools and other equipment properly. Sanitize contact surfaces between every food-processing task.

Wash the tops of cans before opening them. Do not use cans that have swelling at the tops or bottoms, or those with dents along the side seams. Swelling could mean that germs have contaminated the product; dents along the side seam may indicate that the can's seal is broken. If canned products have unusual or unfamiliar odors, or if the contents seem foamy or milky, do not use them.

Wash all raw fruits and vegetables thoroughly before preparation or serving. Be especially careful when handling and preparing meat, eggs, fish, shellfish, and other high-protein foods. Do not use meats that smell strange or have slimy surfaces. Generally, any type of food that appears moldy or cloudy or that has a strange smell should be discarded. Do not taste foods, since this "test" proves nothing and can make you ill.

Never leave food out overnight to thaw. Potentially hazardous foods should be thawed in one of the following ways:

- In refrigerators; frozen items can be issued from the freezer to the refrigerator on a timely basis so they will be ready for food production when needed.

- Under *running* water at a temperature of 70°F (21°C) or below.

- In a microwave oven if the product will be immediately transferred to another cooking process.

- As part of the cooking process—for example, when steaks are charbroiled from their frozen state.

Do not refreeze thawed products. Freezing, thawing, and refreezing can create sanitation problems and destroy food quality.

Prepare perishable foods as close to serving time as possible. To kill any germs that may be present, all foods should normally be heated to at least 140°F (60°C) in the center of the food mass. Some foods require a higher temperature. The center of poultry, poultry stuffings, stuffed meats, and stuffings containing meat should be heated to 165°F (74°C), and pork should be heated to 145°F (63°C). New strains of very dangerous bacteria have been discovered that have prompted chefs to reconsider preparing rare meats (those that are heated only to 130°F (54°C) or slightly above) for guests. Many managers include a safety warning about consumption of rare and undercooked items on their menus. Meat and poultry temperatures should be checked with a cooking thermometer.

Keep cold foods refrigerated until serving begins (or during service, in cafeteria and buffet operations). Many kitchens have refrigerators in work stations to keep prepared foods until service.

Exhibit 5 Sanitation Practices for Receiving and Storing

Receiving

- Inventory items should be checked to ensure they meet purchase specification requirements.
- The internal temperatures and sensory-tested qualities of products should be evaluated.
- The supplier's invoice should be checked for accuracy in quality descriptions, quantities, and prices.
- Products should be moved to storage in the following order:
  1. Most perishable products (frozen foods).
  2. Moderately perishable products (refrigerated foods).
  3. Least perishable products (dry and nonfood items).

Storing

- Food products should be stored on shelves at least six inches (15.2 cm) off the floor and two inches (5.1 cm) away from walls.
- Storage temperatures and relative humidities should be maintained as follows:
  - Dry storage—50°F to 70°F (10°C to 21°C); 50 to 60 percent relative humidity.
  - Refrigerated storage—41°F (5°C) or less; 80 to 90 percent humidity.
  - Freezer storage—generally 0°F (–18°C) or less.
- Newly arrived products should be placed behind old inventory as part of a first-in, first-out (FIFO) system.
- Storage time and temperature combinations should be closely monitored.
- Refrigerated leftovers should be marked with the date they are first stored.
- Perishable and potentially hazardous leftovers should be refrigerated in pans no more than four inches (10.2 cm) deep, and should be served or discarded within twenty-four hours.
- Inventory items should be stored to prevent cross-contamination.
- Packaged food should not be stored in contact with water or undrained ice.
- Toxic chemicals, such as cleaners, sanitizers, and pesticides, should be stored away from food products in physically separate areas.
- All damaged products, including those with abnormal odors or colors, should be discarded.
- Records of all spoiled food should be maintained, so problem areas can be identified and deficiencies corrected.
- One's senses (smell, sight, and touch) should be used during storing to monitor product quality.
- Potentially hazardous foods should not be stored in contact with other foods.
- Cooked foods should be stored above raw foods.
- All foods in storage should be dated and wrapped or covered.
- Freezers should be used to store already frozen foods, not to freeze or refreeze them.

Adapted from Ronald F. Cichy, *Quality Sanitation Management* (Lansing, Mich.: American Hotel & Lodging Educational Institute, 1994), pp. 239–242.

Exhibit 6   Basic Food Sanitation Practices

	Sanitation Practice	Reason for Practice	Suggestion
1.	Do not leave inventory on the loading dock.	Avoids spoilage of perishable goods.	Count inventory immediately and store in proper area (refrigerators, freezers, and dry storage).
2.	Do not store food on the floor.	Food is easily contaminated by dirt on floor.	
3.	Do not store food against walls.	Prevents air circulation.	Food should be two inches (5.1 cm) away from the wall to ensure circulation.
4.	Do not leave leftover food at room temperature.	To avoid contamination.	Refrigerate food as soon as possible.
5.	Do not hold food in temperatures of 41°F–135°F (5°C–57°C).	To avoid contamination.	
6.	Do not refreeze food.	Quality decreases and bacterial count can increase.	Use completely or store after product is cooked.
7.	Do not cook food incompletely.	To avoid contamination.	Heat food without interruption.
8.	Do not taste suspicious-looking food.	Preservation of employee's health.	If it looks suspicious, throw it out.
9.	Do not serve unwashed fruits or vegetables or food from opened cans with unwashed tops.	To avoid contamination.	
10.	Do not leave food particles on equipment, glasses, flatware, or dishware.	To avoid contamination.	Clean all equipment after use and inspect glasses, flatware, and dishware before service.
11.	Do not use cracked or chipped glasses or dishware.	Bacteria can grow in the cracks, and the damaged item can cause cuts.	
12.	Never handle glasses by the rim, utensils by the eating portion, or tops of plates.	Avoids transfer of bacteria from hands to dishware.	Touch dishes only by the edge, cups by handles, glasses near the base, and utensils by the handles.
13.	Never place soiled dishes on the same tray with food to be served.	Avoids contamination.	Use buspersons or clear the table with a separate tray.
14.	Do not allow food to stand on the service counter.	Cooling food increases chances of bacterial growth.	Serve it at once.
15.	Never sit on counters or tables; do not lean on tables.	Contaminants on clothing are transferred to tables.	
16.	Do not fail to use a hair restraint.	Hair can fall in food and cause contamination. It is also not appetizing.	Wear hairnets or hats.
17.	Keep your hands away from your face and hair and out of your pockets; do not touch money unless necessary.	Possible contamination.	If you must do any of these things, wash hands thoroughly when finished.
18.	Never chew gum or anything of a similar nature.	It can spread infection.	
19.	Never carry guest checks or pencils in your mouth. Do not put pencils in your hair.	Bacteria can be spread.	Checks should be carried in your hand, pencils in your pocket.
20.	Avoid sneezing, yawning, or coughing.	Spreads infection.	If unavoidable, be sure to turn away from food or guests and cover your mouth, and then wash hands thoroughly.
21.	Do not spit.	Spreads infection.	
22.	Do not eat while working; never eat from bus trays or soiled dishes.	Disease can spread.	Eat at designated break times and wash hands thoroughly when finished.

Exhibit 6 *(continued)*

Sanitation Practice	Reason for Practice	Suggestion
23. Never smoke on duty.	Germs are spread from one's mouth to one's hands.	Smoke in designated areas during breaks; wash hands thoroughly after smoking.
24. Never use your apron as a towel.	Clean hands are contaminated on a dirty apron.	Use disposable towels.
25. Never handle food with dirty hands.	Possible contamination.	Wash hands using warm, soapy water. Lather well and rinse with clear water. Dry hands with disposable towels.
26. Never handle clean dishes if hands have not been cleaned after touching soiled dishes.	Possible contamination from soiled dishes.	Wash hands thoroughly between these two stages. This is for all personnel, including dishwashers, servers, and buspersons.
27. Never touch or pick up food with hands.	Spread of infection from the skin.	Use the proper serving tool or gloves.
28. Do not report to work in soiled clothes.	Soil contains germs.	Always wear a clean uniform and apron.
29. Avoid excessive jewelry.	Food particles can collect and cause contamination.	Wear minimal jewelry.
30. Do not arrive at work needing a bath.	To avoid bacterial contamination.	Bathe and use deodorant daily.
31. Never use the same knife and cutting board for meats and vegetables without washing.	Microorganisms can spread.	Use a different knife and board, or wash board and use a sanitizer.
32. Do not report to work if sick.	Increases the chances of spreading the illness.	Call in so a replacement can be found.
33. Do not work with exposed wounds.	Increases risk of infecting the wound and spreading infection.	Always keep wounds covered with the proper type of bandage.
34. Do not report to work if your health card has expired.	Prevents the spread of communicable disease.	Keep track of the expiration date and renew it when necessary.
35. Never wash hands in sinks used to prepare food.	Contamination of food.	Use designated handwashing sink.
36. Never taste food with your finger.	Contamination of food by saliva.	Use a clean tasting spoon and return it to the dishwashing area after use.
37. Never re-use food that has been served to guests.	Handling of the food by guests can spread disease.	Throw food away; avoid serving excessive portion size.
38. Never serve pork rare.	To prevent trichinosis.	Cook pork until done.
39. Never leave racks of glasses right-side up.	Airborne organisms can collect.	Store glassware inverted.
40. Never store food in an open container.	Airborne particles can contaminate foods.	Always store food in sealed containers.
41. Do not leave prepared food at room temperature.	Possible contamination.	Prepare just before cooking or serving.
42. Never dry dishware, glasses, utensils, or cooking equipment with a towel.	Possible bacterial contamination.	Let air dry or dry in dishwashing machine's cycle.
43. Do not store garbage with food.	Increases chances of infection.	Have the proper places for each.

A common problem in many food service operations involves holding hot foods that are prepared in advance of service. Casseroles, stews, gravies, and other products high in protein are often kept in a hot water bath at lukewarm temperatures for long periods of time. If germs contaminate these products, conditions are ideal for food poisoning or infection. Protein foods must be kept above 140°F (60°C) or below 41°F (5°C), or they should not be kept at all.

Rapid cooling is important for potentially hazardous foods that are left over after service or are cooked for use during later work shifts. Preparation staff must minimize the time that these foods are within the food temperature danger zone. They should be concerned about the temperature in the center of the food mass, not just the temperature on the food's surface. Stirring frequently, using ice water baths, refrigerating hot foods as soon as possible after cooking, placing hot food in shallow pans, and ensuring effective air circulation are examples of good sanitation procedures to hasten cooling.

Leftovers must be handled carefully. After removing them from the production or service areas, place leftovers in proper containers and quickly refrigerate or freeze them for use as soon as possible. Exhibit 7 reviews sanitation concerns that are important when food is produced and held for service.

HACCP and food preparation. All food service managers must reduce sanitation risks. The Hazard Analysis Critical Control Point (HACCP) process helps them do this by identifying specific hazards at each point where they may occur. A HACCP plan is a written document that outlines formal procedures to help reduce health risks at any point in a food service system where loss of control may result in a health risk.[4]

A properly developed HACCP system identifies and monitors specific foodborne hazards. An analysis process establishes **critical control points (CCPs)** and identifies steps in the process that must be most controlled to ensure food safety. Properly used, HACCP is an important tool for protecting food. The key to its success rests with staff training. Employees must know which control points are critical and what production and handling procedures are necessary at each step to keep food products safe.

The seven HACCP principles should be incorporated in the process:

- *Principle 1—Hazard analysis.* Identify significant hazards and develop preventive measures for a process or product to ensure safety. A thorough analysis includes a review of ingredients, processing, distribution, and intended product use.

- *Principle 2—Identify critical control points (CCPs).* Steps including cooking, chilling, recipe control, and prevention of **cross-contamination** are CCPs that might apply to a specific recipe.

- *Principle 3—Establish critical limits/preventive measures.* Proper cooking, holding, and storage temperatures are examples of standards that must be incorporated into food-handling procedures.

- *Principle 4—Establish procedures to monitor CCPs.* These procedures help identify problems, assess the results of corrective actions, and provide written documentation for HACCP plans.

- *Principle 5—Establish necessary corrective action(s).* This helps to identify reasons for deviations from HACCP plans and helps to ensure that critical CCPs are controlled.

Exhibit 7   Sanitation Practices for Producing and Holding Food

Food Production

- Food should be cooked with as little hand contact as possible; the correct utensils should always be used to handle food.

- Food-production surfaces should be cleaned and sanitized before use to avoid cross-contamination of food products.

- Potentially hazardous foods should be cooked to a minimum internal temperature of 145°F (63°C) for fifteen seconds *except*:

   - Field-dressed wild game animals, poultry, stuffed fish, stuffed meats, stuffed pasta, stuffed poultry, and stuffing containing fish, meat, or poultry. These items should be cooked to a minimum internal temperature of 165°F (74°C) for fifteen seconds.

   - All potentially hazardous foods cooked in a microwave oven. These foods should be cooked to a minimum internal temperature of 165°F (74°C) and allowed to stand covered for two minutes after cooking.

- Potentially hazardous foods should be reheated to an internal temperature of 165°F (74°C) within two hours.

- Internal temperatures should be monitored with accurate thermometers.

- Potentially hazardous foods should be thawed safely.

- Sensory tests should be used in combination with temperature checks.

Holding Food

- When leftovers remain after the meal period, they should be cooled quickly and safely in small batches; leftover egg- and cream-based foods should be discarded immediately after the meal period.

- Leftovers should be cooled from 135°F (57°C) to 70°F (21°C) or less within two hours and from 70°F (21°C) to 41°F (5°C) or less within the next four hours.

- Leftovers should be covered, labeled, and dated before refrigerating.

- Leftovers should not be refrozen.

- Sensory tests should be used in combination with temperature checks.

Source: *ServSafe Coursebook*, 5th ed. (Chicago: National Restaurant Association Educational Foundation, 2008).

- *Principle 6—Establish an effective recordkeeping system.* Plans must detail hazards at each CCP, specify monitoring and recordkeeping procedures, and outline implementation strategies.

- *Principle 7—Establish procedures to verify that the HACCP system is working.* Plans must be reviewed and verified, CCP records must be studied, and managers must determine that risk management decisions have been effectively made when production deviations occur.

High-Tech Food Safety

The implementation of a consistently effective food safety program requires a significant amount of training, compliance with procedures, and ongoing vigilance to ensure that all required procedures are correctly used all the time.

One company, ParTech, has developed a white paper that notes five basic steps in a coordinated food safety program:

- Go back to the food safety basics

- Share knowledge with entire team

- Develop and use efficient checklists

- Install an effective follow-up program

- Bring it all together through technology

For more information, go to the ParTech website at www.partech.com.

Exhibit 8 shows a recipe that identifies CCPs and recommended procedures to reduce risk at each step. Note that the recipe in Exhibit 8 was developed for a product prepared in a central commissary and transported for later service at a satellite center. Risks, including food transport and increased time between product preparation and service, make the sanitation precautions identified in the recipe especially necessary.

Serving. The need for sanitary work procedures does not end after food is prepared. Food must be safely handled as it is portioned and served to guests.

For food quality and sanitation reasons, employees in table service operations should plate food when it is needed for pickup for service—not before. Employees should not touch food with their hands when portioning it. Instead, they should use tongs, scoops, spatulas, or other tools that are cleaned properly between uses. It is improper, for example, that a ladle used to portion a protein-rich casserole be placed in a container of lukewarm (and quickly soiled) water between uses and then used to portion another dish. The food safety and food quality concerns related to this all-too-often-practiced procedure should be obvious.

Employees serving beverages should use a scoop to dispense ice, not their hands or a drinking glass, because hands can spread germs, and a glass can break, requiring that the entire ice bin be emptied and cleaned.

Most operations that serve food in salad bars or buffet or cafeteria lines are required by law to use sneeze-guards or breath protectors. These panels, often made of transparent plastic, minimize the possibility of guests or servers coughing, sneezing, or breathing on displayed food items. Guests should be alerted and required to use clean serviceware if they return to the self-service line for additional food.

Food servers and buspersons must be especially careful with dishes and flatware when serving guests. They should pick up flatware by the handles and dishes by the edges, and never touch the eating surfaces. Following the operation's

Exhibit 8   HACCP Recipe for Chicken Salad

HACCP RECIPE FOR CHICKEN SALAD			
YIELD: 100 Portions		Each Portion: 1 Cup	
SANITATION INSTRUCTIONS:		Sanitize All Equipment & Utensils; Wash Hands Frequently	
INGREDIENTS	**WEIGHTS**	**MEASURES**	**PROCEDURES**
Chicken (canned)		43 cans	1. Open cans and drain. (Juice may be saved if used within 24 hours and immediately cooled to 40°F.)
Water		9½ gal	
Salt	7 oz	⅔ cup	
Bay leaves		9 leaves	
Celery, chopped	12 lb	2¼ gal	2. Prewash onion and celery in chilled water. (50 ppm chlorine solution may be used.)
Sweet peppers, chopped	1lb 8 oz	1 qt	
Onions, chopped	8 oz	1½ cups	
			3. Chop celery, peppers, and onions on sanitized cutting board with sanitized knife. (Gloves are recommended.)
Lemon juice		1 cup	
Salad dressing	3 lb 4 oz	6½ cups	
Salt	4 oz	6 TBSP	
Pepper		1 TBSP	4. Add all remaining ingredients except salad dressing to sanitized mixing bowl(s).
NOTE: Proper hygiene practices including frequent handwashing and use of single-service gloves are necessary at each step. Production process should not be interrupted for more than 30 minutes, and should be completed within 1 hour.			5. Add prechilled salad dressing and blend manually using sanitized utensils. (Gloves are recommended.)
			6. Serve immediately; hold at 40°F or less for no more than 2 hours.
			7. Transfer leftovers to shallow pans and cool to less than 40°F within 4 hours. Record time to cool to 40°F.

Source: Wisconsin Department of Agriculture, Trade and Consumer Protection—Division of Food Safety.

procedures for wiping down tables is also a responsibility of servers or buspersons. Service staff should not use a food service towel to wipe away water spots on chairs, tabletops, or flatware because cross-contamination can occur. Many guests place flatware and food such as rolls on the table's surface. If the table is not clean, it can easily contaminate the flatware and food placed on it.

Servers should discard rolls, butter, or cream in pitchers if guests do not consume them. No food items should be reused unless they are individually wrapped items such as small packages of cream, crackers, butter, margarine, or jelly.

Servers and buspersons should not eat food that has been served to guests but not eaten, and kitchen employees should never reuse food that has been served to guests but returned to the kitchen uneaten.

Food Safety and Terrorism

Unfortunately, food service operators and their counterparts who handle food for retail purchase and consumption away from home must address a relatively recent threat: terrorism. The goal is to minimize the risk that food under their control will be subject to tampering or other criminal or terrorist actions. Numerous guidelines have been developed to suggest measures that food service operators and others can take, including the following:

- Assigning responsibility for security to knowledgeable individuals who should conduct an initial assessment of food security procedures and operations.

- Providing an appropriate level of supervision to all staff, including contract workers and new employees, and investigating threats or information about signs of tampering or other related activities.

Food Safety in the News

Unfortunately, food safety problems can arise in any type of food service operation at any time, often despite prevention tactics utilized by food service managers. When these foodborne illness outbreaks occur, the results can be devastating for victims and food service operations.

Foodborne illness outbreaks linked to contaminated produce have occurred in several locations. Hepatitis A was linked to green onions and *E.coli* was found in lettuce. Note that tainted produce can be contaminated in fields, packing plants, and/or delivery trucks. Parasites have been found on imported cranberries, and salmonella has contaminated cantaloupes.

Many food service operators are concerned about mad cow disease (scientific name: bovine spongiform encephalopathy), the origins of which have been traced to livestock feed. Changes in requirements regarding the content of animal feed, increased inspections, and import standards are among the tactics used by the USDA to help ensure that this disease does not occur in the United States.

National and local news media personnel may review public health department food establishment inspection records and then produce television shows highlighting problems they have noted. These "dirty dining" claims can have a significant negative impact on operations. Managers typically take critical violations seriously and work hard and quickly to resolve them. They want the public to understand their genuine commitment to safety. Sometimes, however, operators believe that issues are sensationalized, taken out of context, and/or misinterpreted. Food service operators must use these instances to make a public statement about their ongoing concern with sanitation and food safety.

- Examining the background of all staff regardless of race, national origin, religion, and citizenship or immigration status.

- Knowing which employees should be on-site for each work shift and establishing a system of positive identification and recognition.

- Identifying staff that require unlimited access to all areas of the facility and managing the types of personal items allowed in nonpublic areas of the facility.

- Training staff about ways to prevent, detect, and respond to tampering or terrorist activities or threats and watching for unusual or suspicious behavior.

- Preventing access of nonemployees to nonpublic areas of the facility, including loading docks, receiving areas, and storage rooms.

- Protecting nonpublic perimeter access, minimizing the number of entrances to nonpublic areas, and implementing a system to control vehicles authorized to park in nonpublic parking areas.

- Limiting poisonous chemicals to those required for the operation and maintenance of the facility, and providing proper storage for them.

- Using only known and appropriately licensed or permitted sources for all products purchased, and inspecting incoming products for signs of tampering, contamination, or damage.

- Notifying the FDA's twenty-four-hour emergency number and local law enforcement and public health authorities about any suspicions regarding products that may have been subject to tampering or other terrorism-related actions.

- Ensuring that water systems are equipped with backflow prevention.

- Implementing procedures to ensure the security of incoming mail and packages.[5]

Most of these tactics are important for the effective management of a food service operation regardless of the possibility of terrorism. However, food service professionals must recognize their important responsibility to protect the health and well-being of their employees and guests. This includes increased vigilance to reduce terrorism.

Cleaning Up

Cleaning and sanitizing dishes, flatware, pots, pans, and the facility itself is a very important responsibility.

Ware Washing. Dishes and other small wares can be cleaned manually or with a dishwashing machine.

Manual cleaning. Local ordinances typically specify equipment and procedures to be used for manual cleaning of dishes, flatware, pots, and pans. General guidelines are included in Exhibit 9.

There are two ways to properly sanitize dishware washed manually:

Exhibit 9   General Guidelines for Manually Cleaning Small Wares

1. Remove large quantities of soiled food from dishware with a spatula, brush, or other utensil before washing. Inspect dishware during washing and discard cracked, chipped, or unusable items. Presoaking is often required to properly wash heavily soiled dishware.

2. Wash dishware in a sink that has at least three compartments. If a three-compartment sink is used sequentially, procedures will involve washing, rinsing, and sanitizing. If a four-compartment sink is used, the normal process will involve prewashing, washing, rinsing, and sanitizing.

3. Use the proper type and quantity of dishwashing soap based on information provided by the manufacturer or supplier. Provide employees with the proper measuring equipment.

4. Use plastic brushes with firm bristles to wash dishware. Do not use dishcloths, dish mops, or soft sponges—they are very difficult to keep clean. Do not use metal cleaning brushes because they can leave metal slivers in or on items being washed. Wash glasses with a glassware brush.

5. The normal order of washing is: glassware, flatware, dishes, trays, and then pots and pans.

6. Frequently drain wash water sinks and refill them with clean, fresh, hot water.

7. After washing them, glasses, cups, and bowls should be loosely placed upside down in rinse racks so rinse water will reach all surfaces. For the same reason, dishes, trays, and pots and pans should not be crowded on the rinsing racks.

8. After washing, place flatware in the rinse baskets with handles up.

9. Remove all detergent from dishes before placing them in the rinse sink.

10. Fill rinsing sink with clean water at a temperature of 170°F (77°C) or above if sanitizing with hot water. Water at this temperature will scald one's hands, and utensils being washed (sanitized) will need to be handled with tongs. For this reason, it is typically best to sanitize with approved chemicals in the approved concentrations. If sanitizing with chemicals, it's possible to sanitize with water at a much lower temperature. (Different chemicals require different temperatures—always check the manufacturer's instructions.)

11. Change rinse water frequently.

12. Always follow all local and other applicable health code rules when manually cleaning small wares.

- *Hot water.* Water must be at least 170°F (77°C) to sanitize dishware in a rinse sink using a manual process. Raising water to that temperature requires the use of a booster heater or an electrical heating element that can be immersed directly in the water. Since employees cannot remove items from water this hot with their hands, they must use tongs or other devices. This practice is typically unsafe, and energy costs are increased because of the need to heat and maintain rinse water at this high temperature.

- *Chemicals.* It is generally more practical to use a chemical sanitizing agent to sanitize dishes, since the water does not need to be excessively hot and safety concerns are lessened. Proper chemical sanitizing agents should be used in the correct amount. Managers should determine the correct quantities, provide appropriate training and measuring utensils to employees, and supervise employees on an ongoing basis.

Dishwashing machines. The following guidelines apply when a dishwashing machine is used to clean dishes and small wares:

- Dishwashing machines should be operated according to the manufacturer's instructions. Carefully follow procedures for using automatic detergent dispensers, wetting agents and other chemicals, and attachments.

- Inspect the machine before using. Remove bits of food, broken glass, or other foreign objects. Ensure that spray arms are clean and working properly.

- Make sure temperature gauges for wash and rinse water cycles are functioning accurately.

- Rinse dishes and flatware before running them through the machine. Rack them properly so all surfaces are exposed to wash and rinse water.

- Air-dry dishware and other items after washing; never use towels. Towel-drying can recontaminate sanitized dishes.

- Handle clean dishes and flatware with plastic gloves or clean hands.

Wash water temperature for dishwashing machines must normally be between 150°F (66°C) and 165°F (74°C). Most machines sanitize with hot water that must be above 180°F (82°C) for the time specified by local sanitation codes. A booster heater will be required to raise the water temperature to the proper level. If sanitizing with chemicals, it is important to follow the manufacturer's recommendations about water and chemical concentrations and proper water temperature. Local regulations may also specify requirements.

Cleaning Kitchen and Dining Areas. All floors, walls, ceilings, and equipment within kitchen and dining areas must be kept clean and in good repair. Generally, cleaning should be done when the least amount of food is exposed. Dustless methods such as wet mopping or vacuuming are recommended for floor cleaning in back-of-house areas.

Properly constructed facilities and equipment are more easily cleaned than those constructed without regard for recommended construction and maintenance guidelines. Wall coverings should be smooth and nonabsorbent. Smooth, durable floor materials such as sealed concrete, terrazzo, or ceramic tile are best in most food service areas and will likely be specified in food safety and construction codes.

A cleaning schedule for all kitchen and dining areas is important to help ensure that the property's sanitation goals are met. Typical cleaning schedules list the equipment or area to be cleaned, the employee or position that is responsible, when the cleaning should be done, and the appropriate cleaning manuals and written cleaning procedures that should be consulted. It is very important to have

formal cleaning procedures that can be written or generated electronically according to predetermined schedules that coincide with cleaning needs. For each equipment item and area to be cleaned, there should be a description of the cleaning
task, steps needed to complete the job, and the correct materials and tools to be
used. Every piece of equipment can have its cleaning procedures posted next to
it. These same cleaning procedures should be used in on-the-job training sessions.
Managers must follow up to make sure all areas and equipment are cleaned effectively. See Exhibit 10 for a sample cleaning schedule.

Handling Garbage and Refuse. Food service operations may use their own garbage and refuse handling procedures, but some guidelines are universal. Cover
all garbage containers in food preparation areas. Use easily cleanable containers
and thoroughly scour and disinfect them on a routine basis to prevent odors and

Exhibit 10   Sample Cleaning Schedule

Equipment or Area to Be Cleaned	Person Responsible	Cleaning Frequency	Cleaning Manual Page Reference*
Can Opener	Dishwasher	Daily	
Ceilings	Maintenance Staff	Monthly	
Charbroiler	Station Cook	Daily Weekly	
Coffee Urn	Server	After Each Brew Daily	
Compartment Steamer	Station Cook Dishwasher	Daily Weekly	
Convection Oven	Station Cook	Daily Weekly	
Walk-In Freezer	Sous Chef Maintenance Staff	Daily Weekly Monthly	
Walk-In Refrigerator	Sous Chef Maintenance Staff	Daily Weekly Monthly	
Walls	Dishwasher Pot and Pan Washer Maintenance Staff	Daily Weekly Monthly	
Work Tables	Station Cook	As Needed Daily	
*Refers to page numbers in the property's standard operating procedures manual.			

Source: Ronald F. Cichy, *Quality Sanitation Management* (Lansing, Mich.: American Hotel &
Lodging Educational Institute, 1994), p. 333.

protect against rodents, insects, and germs. Provide a suitable area to perform the cleaning process.

Take indoor garbage containers outside and empty them regularly throughout the day or as soon as they are full. Outdoor garbage areas and containers can attract rodents and insects that may enter and infest the operation's building(s), so these areas and containers must be clean. Keep all garbage stored outside in closed containers and have it collected regularly. Normally, refuse pick-ups should be scheduled several times weekly; more frequent service will be required for high-volume properties and/or during warm weather when spoilage and odors are more likely.

Safety

Safety relates to the prevention of accidents that can harm guests, employees, and others. Most accidents are caused by someone's carelessness and can be prevented. The most important issue addresses what food service managers can do to help protect others from danger or injury while at the property. Managers also wish to prevent damage to or loss of equipment and other physical assets.

All employees should be trained in what to do in case of an accident. If one occurs at the property, managers should learn from it to help ensure that a similar problem does not arise.

This section discusses the Occupational Safety & Health Administration and its impact on safety in the workplace. It also reviews types of food service accidents and lists safety principles that, when followed, can help prevent accidents. Finally, the section discusses first aid procedures and accident reports.

OSHA

The **Occupational Safety & Health Administration (OSHA)** is an agency of the U.S. Department of Labor created to improve the safety of working conditions for U.S. employees. OSHA:

- Requires employers to furnish employees with jobs and places of employment that are free from recognized safety hazards.

- Establishes mandatory job safety and health standards.

- Develops enforcement programs.

- Designs reporting procedures relating to job injuries, illnesses, and fatalities.

- Creates and implements many procedures to help improve working conditions.

- Implements programs to encourage employers and employees to reduce workplace hazards.

OSHA regulations usually apply to every U.S. employer with one or more employees, so food service operations of all types are generally covered.

OSHA permits states to develop their own programs for occupational safety and health, but state programs must be at least as stringent as federal programs. OSHA standards then become benchmarks that state plans must meet or exceed.

Major components of OSHA laws that affect food service operations relate to:

- *Recordkeeping requirements.* OSHA requires employers to maintain certain records. These range from a daily inspection report on employer vehicles used to transport guests to reports dealing with employee injuries and illnesses.

- *Inspections.* OSHA inspectors may visit an operation to look for potential safety hazards. After an inspection, OSHA officials may hold a meeting with the operation's representatives to discuss and review any violations and to address remedial actions. Follow-up inspections may be scheduled.

- *Fines.* If a food service operation does not comply with OSHA requirements and fails to take remedial actions suggested by OSHA officials, fines are possible.

OSHA has developed information to educate food service managers and employees about safety concerns. Also, its representatives can provide creative suggestions to resolve safety-related problems. OSHA officials are more than just inspectors; they are consultants who work with food service establishments to identify and resolve problems that, left undetected and uncorrected, could cause injury or death to the property's employees or guests.

Material safety data sheets (MSDSs) provided by chemical manufacturers are valuable tools that help ensure employee safety. These documents present information about safe handling, storage, and use of potentially hazardous chemical substances. Exhibit 11 shows a sample MSDS. Note that it contains important information about bleach, a potentially dangerous chemical that can be used to sanitize dishes and clean food service facilities. The MSDS provides employees with information about precautions to take when handling bleach, and also provides instructions to follow when a spill or leak occurs. Employers must make MSDSs easily accessible in appropriate languages to applicable employees, so many food service operations will need copies in several languages. It is then the employees' responsibility to become familiar with the information and to follow the instructions given for the potentially hazardous products handled in the food service operation.

Food service operations of all sizes benefit from the routine use of MSDSs. For example, they should be reviewed with new employees during orientation and can form the basis for ongoing training. Managers will find the information helpful when developing emergency plans.

Food Service Accidents

This section looks at common types of food service accidents and suggests ways to protect employees and others.

Burns. Many accidents in food service operations result in burns. The following measures can help prevent burns:

- Follow recommended procedures when using any cooking equipment and when lighting gas equipment.

- Plan ahead. Always have a place prepared for hot pans before removing them from a range or oven.

Exhibit 11   Sample Material Safety Data Sheet (MSDS)

			Clorox-HMIS	
CLOROX	**The Clorox Company** 7200 Johnson Drive Pleasanton, California 94566 Tel. 94150 847-6100	**Material Safety Data Sheet**	HEALTH FLAMMABILITY REACTIVITY Personal Protection	2* 0 1 8

I   Chemical Identification

NAME:	REGULAR CLOROX BLEACH	**CAS no.**	7681-52-9
DESCRIPTION:	CLEAR, LIGHT YELLOW LIQUID WITH CHLORINE ODOR	**RTECS no.**	NH 3486300

Other Designations	**Manufacturer**	**Emergency Procedure**
EPA Reg. No. 5813-1 Sodium Hypochloride Solution Liquid Chlorine Bleach	The Clorox Company 1221 Broadway Oakland, CA. 94612	Notify your Supervisor Call your local poison control center or Rocky Mountain Poison Center (303) 573-1014

II   Health Hazard Data

* Causes severe but temporary eye injury. May irritate skin. May cause nausea and vomiting if ingested. Exposure to vapor or mist may irritate nose, throat and lungs. The following medical conditions may be aggravated by exposure to high concentrations of vapor or mist: heart conditions or chronic respiratory problems such as asthma, chronic bronchitis, or obstructive lung disease. Under normal consumer use conditions the likelihood of any adverse health effects are low. FIRST AID: EYE CONTACT: Immediately flush eyes with plenty of water. Remove contact lenses first. If irritation persists, see a doctor. SKIN CONTACT: Remove contaminated clothing. Wash area with water. INGESTION: Drink a glassful of water and call a physician. INHALATION: If breathing problems develop remove to fresh air.

III   Hazardous Ingredients

Ingredients	Concentration	Worker Exposure Limit
Sodium Hypochlorite CAS# 7681-52-9	5.25%	not established

None of the ingredients in this product are on the IARC, NIP or OSHA carcinogen list.

IV   Fire and Explosion Data

Not flammable or explosive. In a fire, cool containers to prevent rupture and release of sodium chlorate.

V   Special Protection Information

Hygienic Practices: Wear safety glasses. With repeated or prolonged use, wear gloves.

Engineering Controls: Use general ventilation to minimize exposure to vapor or mist.

Work Practices: Avoid eye and skin contact and inhalation of vapor mist.

VI   Spill or Leak Procedures

Small quantities of less than 5 gallons may be flushed down drain. For larger quantities wipe up with an absorbent material or mop and dispose of in accordance with local, state and federal regulations. Dilute with water to minimize oxidizing effect on spilled surface.

VII   Reactivity Data

Stable under normal use and storage conditions. Strong oxidizing agent. Reacts with other household chemicals such as toilet bowl cleaners, rust removers, vinegar, acids or ammonia containing products to produce hazardous gases, such as chlorine and other chlorinated species. Prolonged contact with metal may cause pitting or discoloration.

VIII   Special Precautions

Keep out of reach of children. Do not get in eyes or on skin. Wash thoroughly with soap and water after handling. Do not mix with other household chemicals such as toilet bowl cleaners, rust removers, vinegar, acid or ammonia containing products. Store in a cool, dry place. Do not reuse empty container; rinse container and put in trash container.

IX   Physical Data

Boiling Point . . . . 212°F/100°C
(Decomposes)
Specific Gravity $H_2O = 1$ 1.085
Solubility in Water . . . . Complete
pH 11.4

- Use dry potholders to handle hot pots and pans; a wet or damp potholder can cause a steam burn. Never use an apron, towel, or dishcloth.

- Never use pans with loose handles (they can break off) or rounded bottoms (the pans may tip).

- Do not overfill pots, pans, or kettles. Open pots carefully by raising the back of their lids away from you so steam can escape from the back of the vessel.

- Stir food carefully with long-handled spoons or paddles; avoid spattering and splashing.

- Do not reach into hot ovens; use a puller or other proper tool.

- Allow equipment to cool before cleaning it.

- Know how to put out fires. If food catches on fire, spread salt or baking soda on the flame; do not use water. Know the location of fire extinguishers and other safety equipment, and know how to use them.

- Prohibit horseplay.

- Be careful when pouring coffee and other hot liquids.

- Use caution around heat lamps.

Muscle Strains and Falls. To avoid muscle strains, always have a firm footing before lifting heavy objects. Keep your back straight; do not bend forward or sideways. Bend your knees to pick up low objects and lift with your legs, not your back. Do not try to carry too many items at one time or items that are too heavy. When carrying a heavy load, ask for help or use a cart.

Most falls in food service operations are slips or trips at floor level. Precautions to prevent falls include the following:

- Keep floors clean and dry at all times. Wipe up spills immediately. Use slip-resistant floor waxes and "Caution" or "Wet Floor" signs when appropriate.

- Keep hazardous objects such as boxes, mops, and brooms off floors. Replace loose or upturned floor tiles as soon as they are noticed.

- Repair cracked or worn stair treads.

- Wear properly fitting shoes with low heels and non-skid soles. Never wear worn-out or thin-soled shoes, slippers, high heels, tennis shoes, or sandals. The heel and toe of the shoe should be completely enclosed. Keep shoestrings tied to prevent tripping.

- Walk—do not run—and use caution when going through swinging doors. "Keep to the right" is the policy in many operations with side-by-side, in-and-out doors.

- Use a sturdy stepladder when reaching for objects in high places.

- Make sure that entrances and exits are clean and safe. Remove snow and ice if this is a potential problem in winter. Keep floor mats or other protective devices clean and in good condition.

- Keep all work and walk areas well-lighted. Pay special attention to exterior areas and steps.

Cuts. Cuts are constant hazards for food preparation employees. Employees must be alert when using knives, slicers, or similar equipment.

When using knives, place the food to be cut on a table or a cutting board. Cut away from your body; the food item should be firmly grasped and sliced by cutting downward. When chopping food with a knife, hold the food with your free hand and keep the point of the chopping knife on the block. Dull knives cause more problems than sharp knives because they require employees to exert more pressure, and slippage problems are more likely to occur.

Discard or repair knives with loose handles. Do not leave knives on the edge of a counter—push them back so they cannot fall on the floor or on someone's foot. Do not try to catch a falling knife. Never play with knives or use them as substitutes for screwdrivers or can openers. Do not use knives to open cardboard cartons; use the proper container-opening tool.

Employees can also cut themselves when washing knives or other sharp tools, so all sharp tools should be washed separately. Never place knives or other sharp tools in sinks filled with water. People reaching into the sink might not see them and could cut themselves. A small pan placed on the soiled counter of the pot and pan sink can hold knives until they are washed. Clean all sharp tools with caution. Use a folded heavy cloth and work slowly and carefully from the center of the blade to the outside cutting edge. When cleaning a slicer, make sure its blade is in the position recommended for cleaning. Unplug the unit and refer to the manufacturer's operating and maintenance manual for specific cleaning instructions.

Minimizing glass in the kitchen can help prevent cuts. Broken glass should be cleaned up immediately with a broom and dustpan, not by hand. If glass or china breaks in a dishwasher, drain the dishwasher and pick up the pieces with a damp cloth. Always place broken pieces in a separate, marked refuse container.

The following are some additional precautions for preventing cuts:

- Keep knives, cleavers, saws, and other sharp tools in racks or special drawers when not in use.

- Use the correct-size cutting tools and make sure they have the proper blade.

- Use safety guards and any other safety items provided on equipment.

- Be careful with grinders. Use the feeder/tamper.

- Use caution when operating slicers and other electric cutting tools.

- When using sharpening steels, be sure there is a finger guard between the handles and the steel.

Equipment Accidents. Safety precautions should be used whenever employees work with equipment. Do not take shortcuts when operating potentially hazardous food service equipment; always follow the manufacturer's instructions carefully. Place the instructions on or near equipment so that employees can refer to them.

Train employees to use, maintain, and clean equipment. Carefully supervise new employees to ensure that they consistently follow proper procedures. Whenever possible, disconnect equipment from power sources before cleaning.

Properly maintain equipment. Improper maintenance can lead to unsafe working conditions. Conduct regular and detailed equipment inspections with

Top Four Restaurant Injuries

One in twenty on-the-job injuries and illnesses worldwide occur at eating and drinking establishments. OSHA estimates that for every $1 spent in safety programs, businesses can save between $4 and $6 from injury- and fatality-related costs. After identifying the injuries that occur most often, managers can plan training programs to reduce and, ideally, eliminate them. The top injuries are:

- *Lacerations/punctures.* Restaurant staff members can incur lacerations or puncture wounds from frequent contact with knives, slicers, and broken dishes and glasses.

- *Burns.* From boiling water to fryers and hot stovetops, heat and water burns create potential hazards for restaurant workers, and as many as one-third of occupational burns occur in restaurants.

- *Sprains/strains.* Misplaced or hard-to-reach items can cause worker injury due to overreaching or trips; employees also suffer from strains due to improper lifting.

- *Eye injuries.* Splashes from grease or sanitizing chemicals can result in eye injuries.

  Several steps can help prepare food service operations for common injuries:

1. Install an on-site first aid cabinet in a location where all employees have easy access to it.

2. Stock the cabinet with the supplies needed for common food service injuries.

3. Ensure the cabinet is restocked regularly.

4. Train employees about the proper use of first aid items and how to handle emergency situations.

5. Supplement first aid initiatives with other safety initiatives such as fire drills and ongoing training.

Source: Adapted from "Top Four Restaurant Injuries," *QSR*, September 9, 2011.

maintenance personnel or representatives from the equipment supply company. Make sure all gas connections conform to applicable regulations. Gas equipment in the United States should bear the seal of approval of the American Gas Association.

Special precautions for working with electrical equipment include the following:

- Ensure that all electrical equipment and connections conform to national, state, and local electrical code requirements. Where applicable, electrical equipment should bear the Underwriters Laboratories seal of approval.

- Carefully follow the manufacturer's instructions whenever operating electrical equipment.

- Always unplug electrical equipment before cleaning it. Never touch metal sockets and electrical equipment when your hands are wet or when you are standing on a wet floor.

- Practice preventive maintenance. A qualified electrician or maintenance person should regularly inspect all electrical equipment, including wiring and switches.

Fire. The following precautions will lessen the danger of fire:

- Properly clean and maintain cooking equipment and exhaust hoods/filters.

- Limit smoking to restricted areas.

- Be sure there is adequate fire extinguishing equipment available. Personnel should know where it is located and how to use it. Consult local fire authorities about the purchase, use, and inspection of fire extinguishing equipment.

- Consider using specialized detection devices that can detect smoke, flames, and/or heat.

- Consider using automatic sprinkler systems. They are a very effective way to control fires.

Sprinkler systems are generally required by local fire ordinances, but even if they are not, they may be a wise investment. Special fire extinguishing systems under kitchen-equipment ventilation filters are normally required by local ordinances. Regardless of the type (dry chemical, carbon dioxide, or chemicals in special solutions), this equipment can be effective only if it is professionally designed, installed, and maintained.

Employees should know where all emergency exits are located, and fire drills should be conducted regularly. Contact the local fire department for specific help in designing emergency procedures. Make sure all doors to the property open out and that fire exits are kept clear at all times. Fire department telephone numbers should be located near telephones.

First Aid

Immediately after an accident occurs, first aid is the primary concern. Someone trained in first aid should apply treatment. People without first aid training normally should undertake only commonsense procedures. In the case of a serious injury, make the person as comfortable as possible without risking further injury, and call for medical help. For minor injuries, give the person whatever aid is necessary from the property's first aid kit, fill out an accident report, and urge the victim to see a physician if it seems appropriate.

Encourage employees to receive first aid training. The American Red Cross provides excellent training throughout the United States. If possible, training should be provided to several employees to increase the likelihood that someone with first aid training will always be available on-site.

First aid equipment and supplies should be kept in a convenient area. OSHA and some state labor departments, municipal regulatory agencies, and insurance companies have first aid equipment requirements. Large operations, particularly those with more than one floor, should keep a first aid kit in each of several locations.

Display first aid information. Display various types of medical and first aid posters in appropriate places throughout the food service operation. To see numerous examples of such posters, use your favorite search engine and enter "images of workplace safety posters" in the search bar.

Accident Reports

OSHA regulations and state workers' compensation laws require that accidents occurring in the workplace be reported. Exhibit 12 illustrates information required for workers' compensation purposes in one state. As a result of this report and, perhaps, investigations by state labor officers or insurance company representatives, a settlement consistent with the applicable state compensation laws will normally be made.

An accident investigation should: (1) assess exactly what happened, (2) determine why the accident occurred, (3) suggest what should be done to prevent recurrences, and (4) follow up. It is important that managers see all accident reports and follow up to ensure that preventive action has been taken.

Management's Role in Sanitation and Safety Programs

All members of the food service staff should take an active role in the operation's sanitation and safety program. However, managers have the ultimate responsibility for developing, implementing, and monitoring the property's sanitation and safety efforts. Their role includes:

- Incorporating sanitation and safety practices into operating procedures
- Ensuring that sanitation and safety concerns take priority over convenience
- Training employees in sanitary and safe work procedures
- Conducting sanitation and safety inspections
- Completing accident reports, assisting in investigations, and doing whatever is necessary to ensure that problems are quickly corrected
- Assisting in treatment and seeking medical assistance for injured employees or guests when necessary
- Reporting necessary repairs or maintenance, changes in work procedures, or other conditions that are potential problems
- Conducting sanitation and safety meetings
- Urging the active participation of all staff members in solving sanitation and safety problems

Inspections

Inspections are usually at the heart of management's effort to ensure that sanitation and safety procedures are consistently followed. Managers can develop

Exhibit 12 Sample Accident Report Form

EMPLOYER'S BASIC REPORT OF INJURY
Michigan Department of Labor & Economic Growth
Workers' Compensation Agency
PO Box 30016, Lansing, MI 48909

An employer shall report immediately to the agency on Form WC-100 all injuries, including diseases, which arise out of and in the course of the employment, or on which a claim is made and result in any of the following: (a) Disability extending beyond seven (7) consecutive days, not including the date of injury; (b) Death; (c) Specific losses. In case of death, an employer shall also immediately file an additional report on WC-106. See instructions on reverse side for filing/mailing procedures.

I. EMPLOYEE DATA

1. Social Security Number	2. Date of injury	3. Employee name (Last, First, MI)		
4. Address (Number & Street)		5. City	6. State	7. Zip Code
8. Date of birth (MM/DD/YYYY)	9. Sex ☐ Male ☐ Female	10. Number of dependents	11. Telephone number	
12. Tax filing status: ☐ A. Single ☐ B. Single, Head of Household ☐ C. Married, Filing Joint ☐ D. Married, Filing Separate				

II. EMPLOYER/CARRIER DATA

13. Employer name	14. Federal ID Number		
15. Injury location code	16. Mailing location code	17. UI number	18. Type of business (SIC/NAICS)
19. Employer street address	20. City	21. State	22. Zip code
23. Insurance company name (if employer not self-insured)	24. Insurance company telephone number (if known)		

III. INJURY/MEDICAL DATA

25. Last day worked	26. Date employee returned to work (if applicable)	27. Did employee die? ☐ Yes ☐ No	28. If yes, date of death
29. Injury city	30. Injury state	31. Injury county	32. Did injury occur on employer's premises? ☐ Yes ☐ No (If no, see item 53)
33. Case number from OSHA/MIOSHA log	34. Time employee began work ☐ a.m. ☐ p.m.	35. Time of event ☐ a.m. ☐ p.m.	If time cannot be determined, check here ☐

36. What was the employee doing just before the incident occurred? Describe the activity, as well as the tools, equipment, or material the employee was using. Be specific.

37. How did the injury occur? Examples: "When ladder slipped on wet floor, worker fell 20 feet;" "Worker was sprayed with chlorine when gasket broke during replacement"

38. Describe the nature of injury or illness	39. Part of body directly affected by the injury or illness

40. What object or substance directly harmed the employee? Examples: concrete floor, chlorine, radial arm saw. If this question does not apply to the incident, leave it blank.

41. Name of physician or other health care professional	42. Was employee treated in an emergency room? ☐ Yes ☐ No	43. Was employee hospitalized overnight as an in-patient? ☐ Yes ☐ No

44. If treatment was given away from the worksite, where was it given? (Include name, address, city, state and zip code of facility)

IV. OCCUPATION AND WAGE DATA

45. Date hired	46. Total gross weekly wage (highest 39 of 52)	47. Number of weeks used	48. Value of discontinued fringes
49. Occupation (Be specific)	50. Was employee a volunteer worker? ☐ Yes ☐ No	51. Was employee certified as vocationally handicapped? ☐ Yes ☐ No	
52. Date employer notified by employee	53. If temporary service agency, provide name/address of employer where injury occurred.		

V. PREPARER DATA   I CERTIFY THAT A COPY OF THIS REPORT HAS BEEN GIVEN TO THE EMPLOYEE

Making a false or fraudulent statement for the purpose of obtaining or denying benefits can result in criminal or civil prosecution, or both, and denial of benefits.

54. Preparer's name (Please print or type)	55. Preparer's signature	56. Telephone number	57. Date prepared

Notice to employee: Questions or errors should be reported immediately to the individual listed above in space 54

WC-100 (Rev. 10/05) Front

Source: Michigan Department of Labor & Economic Growth.

inspection forms or checklists that focus attention on equipment, facilities, food-handling practices, and/or food service employees. Persons with special knowledge, including insurance representatives and state or local fire inspectors, can help managers create these checklists. A sample safety checklist is shown in the appendix to this chapter.

The frequency of sanitation and safety inspections depends, in part, on how well the property measures up during the first inspection. A complete inspection should be made at least monthly. However, if necessary, managers should also conduct daily inspections of specific work station areas or equipment.

Sanitation and safety inspections should reveal potentially dangerous conditions. Corrective measures should be taken promptly. If problems cannot be corrected for some time, employees should be informed of the possible hazards. Employees should also be trained to alert managers to problems that they find, and steps should be taken to correct them in a timely manner.

After an inspection is completed, inspection forms and checklists should be filed for later reference. Review of earlier documents can give managers an indication of the long-range effectiveness of their sanitation and safety programs. Also, if inquiries are made by OSHA, insurance companies, or other agencies, the forms provide evidence of management's efforts to maintain a sanitary and safe food and beverage operation.

Endnotes

1. Readers desiring more detailed information about sanitation are referred to National Restaurant Association Educational Foundation, *ServSafe Coursebook*, 6th ed. (Chicago: National Restaurant Association Educational Foundation, 2012).

2. U.S. Department of Health and Human Services, Public Health Service, Food and Drug Administration, *2013 Food Code* (Washington, D.C., 2013).

3. Details about purchasing procedures are available in Ronald F. Cichy and Jeffery D Elsworth, *Purchasing for Food Service Operations* (Lansing, Mich.: American Hotel & Lodging Educational Institute, 2007).

4. National Restaurant Association Educational Foundation, *ServSafe Coursebook*, 6th ed. (Chicago: National Restaurant Association Educational Foundation, 2012). See Chapter 9.

5. U.S. Department of Health and Human Services, Food and Drug Administration Center for Food Safety and Applied Nutrition, *Retail Food Stores and Food Service Establishments: Food Security Preventive Measures Guidance* (Washington, D.C., 2003; revised 2007).

Key Terms

chemical poisoning—Occurs when toxic substances contaminate foods or beverages.

cross-contamination—The contamination of a food product through contact with a bacteria-carrying nonfood source (knives, cutting boards, and other equipment).

critical control points—Places in a specific food system where loss of control may result in an unacceptable health risk.

foodborne illness—An infection of the gastrointestinal (GI) tract caused by food or beverages that contain harmful organisms or chemicals.

food grading—The process of analyzing food relative to specific, defined standards in order to assess its quality. Food grading is optional.

food infection—A type of foodborne illness caused by eating food contaminated by bacteria and viruses that later reproduce inside the body. With food infection, it is the germs, not the toxins they produce, that cause the illness.

food inspection—An official examination of food to ensure wholesomeness. Inspection of certain foods is required by law.

food poisoning—Occurs when germs get into food and produce toxic waste products. With food poisoning, it is the toxin, not the germs themselves, that produces the illness.

food temperature danger zone—A temperature zone between 41°F (5°C) and 135°F (57°C) in which many kinds of harmful germs multiply rapidly.

material safety data sheets (MSDSs)—Documents (provided by chemical manufacturers) that impart information about safe handling, storage, and use of potentially hazardous chemical substances.

Occupational Safety & Health Administration (OSHA)—An agency of the U.S. Department of Labor created to help make working conditions safer for employees.

potentially hazardous food—Nonacidic, high-protein food (such as meat, fish, poultry, eggs, and milk) that is most susceptible to germ growth.

Review Questions

1. What basic precautions can prevent the chemical poisoning of food?

2. What conditions must be present for germs to multiply?

3. How is food poisoning different from food infection?

4. How can food service managers help ensure that incoming products are wholesome?

5. What are some guidelines for preparing food in a sanitary way?

6. What procedures can service personnel follow to help ensure that guests are served wholesome food?

7. What major components of OSHA laws affect food service operations?

8. What common types of accidents occur in food service operations? How can each be prevented?

9. What is the purpose of accident investigations? How should they be conducted?

10. What is management's role in sanitation and safety programs?

11. How can safety checklists be used to better ensure safe operations and work areas?

Internet Sites

For more information, visit the following Internet sites. Remember that Internet addresses can change without notice. If the site is no longer there, you can use a search engine to look for additional sites.

Safety-Related Sites

American Gas Association
www.aga.org (click on "Knowledge Center")

National Fire Protection Association
www.nfpa.com (enter "restaurant fires" in the site's search box)

National Institute for Occupational Safety and Health
www.cdc.gov/niosh (enter "restaurant safety" in the site's search box)

Occupational Safety & Health Administration
www.osha.gov (enter "restaurant safety" in the site's search box)

Safety Today, Inc.
www.safetytoday.com

Underwriters Laboratories Inc.
www.ul.com (enter "restaurant safety" in the site's search box)

Sanitation-Related Sites

Bad Bug Book
www.cfsan.fda.gov (enter "bad bug book" in the site's search box)

FDA Food Code
www.fda.gov (enter "FDA Food Code" in the site's search box)

FoodSafety.gov
www.foodsafety.gov

Food Safety and Inspection Service (FSIS)
www.fsis.usda.gov

International Food Information Council (IFIC) Foundation
www.ific.org

Partnership for Food Safety Education
www.fightbac.org

Local Restaurant Inspection Results

Using your favorite search engine, enter "restaurant inspections for Your County Your State" in the search bar.

Appendix:

Sample Safety Checklist

The following checklist covers physical factors in the property and work practices of your personnel. During your inspection be as aware of unsafe acts as you are of unsafe conditions.

Area	Yes	No	Comments
Receiving Area:			
Are floors in safe condition? (Are they free from broken and defective floor boards? Are they covered with nonskid material?)			
Are employees instructed in correct handling methods for various shipping containers that are received?			
Are garbage cans washed daily in hot water?			
Are garbage cans always covered?			
If the garbage disposal area is close to or part of the general receiving area, are floors and/or dock areas kept clear of refuse?			
Are garbage containers properly stored? Are garbage containers on dollies or other wheel units to eliminate lifting by employees?			
Are adequate tools available for opening crates, cartons, and other containers?			
Are containers opened away from open containers of food?			
Storage Area:			
Are shelves adequate to bear weight of items stored?			
Are employees instructed to store heavy items on lower shelves and lighter materials above?			
Is a safe ladder provided for reaching high storage areas?			
Are cartons or other flammable materials stored at least two feet away from light bulbs?			
Are light bulbs provided with a screen guard?			
Is a fire extinguisher located at the door?			
Are employees carefully instructed in the use of chemicals?			
Do you have a process for disposal of broken glass or china?			
Where electrical controls are in a passageway, are they recessed or guarded to prevent breakage or accidental starting?			
Are dish racks in safe condition (free of sharp corners that could cause cuts)? Are these racks kept off the floor to prevent tripping?			

Source: Adapted from the National Safety Council, Chicago, undated.

Area	Yes	No	Comments
Serving Area:			
Are steam tables cleaned daily and maintained regularly, and are they checked regularly by a competent serviceperson?			
Is safety valve equipment operative?			
Are serving counters and tables free of broken parts and wooden or metal slivers and burrs?			
Do you have regular inspections of: Glassware? China? Silverware? Plastic equipment?			
If anything breaks near the food service area, do you discard all food adjacent to the breakage?			
Are tray rails adequate to prevent trays from slipping or falling off at the end or corners?			
Are floors and/or ramps in good condition (covered with nonskid material, free from broken tile and defective floorboards)?			
Are these areas mopped at least daily, and waxed with nonskid wax when necessary?			
Is there effective traffic flow so guests do not collide while carrying trays or obtaining foods?			
Dining Area:			
Are floors free from broken tile and defective floor boards? Are they covered with nonskid wax?			
Are pictures securely fastened to walls?			
Are drapes, blinds, or curtains securely fastened?			
Are chairs free from splinters, metal burrs, and broken or loose parts?			
Are floors "policed" for cleaning up spillage and other materials?			
Is special attention given to floors adjacent to water, ice cream, or milk stations?			
Are vending machines properly grounded?			
If guests clear their own trays before the trays return to dishwashing area, are the floors kept clean of garbage, dropped silver, and/or broken glass and china?			
If dishes are removed from the dining area on portable racks or bus trucks, are these units in safe operating condition (for example, are all casters working? all shelves firm?)?			
Soiled Dish Processing Area:			
Are floors reasonably free of excessive water and spillage?			
Are floor boards or mats properly maintained and in safe condition?			
Are all electrical units properly grounded?			

Area	Yes	No	Comments
Are switches conveniently located to permit rapid shutdown in emergencies?			
Can employees easily reach switches?			
Pots and Pans Area:			
Are duckboards or mats in safe condition?			
Are employees properly instructed in the use of correct amounts of detergent and/or other cleaning agents?			
Are adequate rubber or other gloves provided?			
Is there an adequate drainboard or other drying area so that employees do not have to pile pots and pans on the floor before and after washing them?			
Do drain plugs permit draining without the employee placing hands in hot water?			
Walk-in Coolers and Freezers:			
Are floors in the units in good condition and covered with slip-proof material? Are they mopped at least once a week, and whenever spills occur?			
Are portable and stationary storage racks in safe condition (free from broken or bent shelves and set on solid legs)?			
Are blower fans properly guarded?			
Is there a bypass device on the door to permit exit if an employee is locked in (or is there an alarm bell?)?			
Is adequate aisle space provided?			
Are heavy items stored on lower shelves and lighter items on higher shelves?			
Is the refrigerant in the refrigerator nontoxic? (Check with your refrigerator service person.)			
Food Preparation Area:			
Is electrical equipment properly grounded?			
Is electrical equipment inspected regularly by an electrician or qualified maintenance person?			
Are electrical switches located so that they can be reached readily in the event of an emergency?			
Are the switches located so that employees do not have to lean on or against metal equipment when reaching for them?			
Are floors regularly and adequately maintained (mopped at least daily and waxed with nonskid wax when necessary? Are defective mats and tiles replaced when necessary?)?			
Are employees instructed to immediately pick up or clean up all dropped items and spillage?			
Are employees properly instructed in the operation of all machines?			
Are employees forbidden to use equipment unless specifically trained in its use?			
Are machines properly grounded?			

Area	Yes	No	Comments
Stairways and Ramps:			
Are they adequately lighted?			
Are the angles of ramps set to provide maximum safety?			
If stairs are metal, wood, or marble, have abrasive materials been used to provide protection against slips and falls?			
Are pieces broken out of the casing or front edge of the steps?			
Are clean and securely fastened handrails available?			
If the stairs are wide, has a center rail been provided?			
Do Not Overlook:			
Lighting—is it adequate in the: Receiving Area? Storage Area? Pots and Pans Area? Walk-in Coolers and Freezers? Food Preparation Area? Cooking Area? Serving Area? Dining Area? Soiled Dish Processing Area? Outdoor Areas?			
Doors—do they open into passageways where they could cause an accident? (List any such locations.)			
Are fire exits clearly marked and passages kept clear of equipment and materials? (List any violations.)			
Ventilation—is it adequate in the: Receiving Area? Storage Area? Pots and Pans Area? Walk-in Coolers and Freezers? Food Preparation Area? Cooking Area? Serving Area? Dining Area? Soiled Dish Processing Area?			
Other Safety Concerns:			
Do employees wear proper shoes to protect their feet against injury from articles that are dropped, spilled, or pushed against their feet?			
Is employee clothing free of parts that could get caught in mixers, cutters, grinders, or other equipment?			
Are fire extinguishers guarded so they will not be knocked from the wall?			
If doors are provided with a lock, is there an emergency bell or a bypass device that will permit exit from the room should the door be accidentally locked while an employee is in the room?			

Area	Yes	No	Comments
Is there a pusher or tamper provided for use with grinders?			
Are mixers in safe operating condition?			
Are the mixer beaters properly maintained to avoid injury from broken metal parts and foreign particles in food?			
Are material safety data sheets (MSDSs) for all chemicals available for employee use? Is their location well known to all employees?			

Part IV

Design and Finances

Chapter 12 Outline

The Planning Process
    Preliminary Considerations
Redesigning the Kitchen
    Design Factors
    Layouts
Redesigning Other Areas
    Receiving and Storage Areas
    Dining Room Areas
    Lounge Areas
Green Restaurant Design
Food and Beverage Equipment
    Factors in Equipment Selection
    Types of Food Service Equipment
    Types of Beverage Equipment

Competencies

1. Outline and describe the layout and design planning process. (pp. 323–325)

2. List and briefly discuss kitchen design factors, explaining how different kitchen layouts affect work flow. (pp. 325–330)

3. Summarize considerations that are important in redesigning receiving and storage areas, dining areas, and lounge areas. (pp. 330–334)

4. Identify environmental or "green" construction strategies that will help restaurants address sustainability concerns. (pp. 334–335)

5. Identify factors in food and beverage equipment selection, and describe different types of equipment necessary for cooking food and serving beverages. (pp. 335–353)

12

Facility Design, Layout, and Equipment

A FOOD SERVICE FACILITY'S design and layout have a great impact on its appeal to guests and on the productivity of employees. If facilities are poorly designed, guests may be inconvenienced and receive slow service. Production employees will incur extra walking and wasted motions when preparing food; service employees might walk farther between food pickup areas and guest tables or between production and cafeteria areas. Wasted time means staff will have less time to interact with guests. Like good design and layout, the right equipment improves employee productivity and food quality, while the wrong equipment leads to problems.

An operation's design, layout, and equipment influences its profitability, so owners are concerned with these factors. Design and layout affect **capital costs**. If more space is designed into the facility than necessary, capital and labor costs will be greater than necessary. Unnecessary operating costs for servicing the extra space (heating, ventilating, air-conditioning, cleaning and maintenance, and so on) will be incurred.

Government agencies play a role in facility design for many reasons—one example is because of regulations about occupancy levels relative to space available.

Food service facilities will likely be used a long time. What if a menu change requires new and different types of equipment? Are there ways to design flexibility into the facility? The best designs and layouts are flexible.

Managers may not have helped to design the facility in which they work. However, they may be involved in remodeling projects. Even simple rearrangements of production equipment or dining room tables should be based on some very basic principles. Therefore, regardless of the manager's role, some knowledge of design and layout is helpful.

There has never been more interest in making hospitality operations more environmentally friendly. This is typically much easier and less expensive to do when green concerns are incorporated into initial construction rather than into later remodeling plans and activities. Also, today's production equipment often comes with energy-saving advantages. These benefit the operation by reducing utility consumption and by providing the operation with opportunities to be a good community citizen. There are, indeed, many topics to cover in this chapter, so let's begin.

The Planning Process

A facility's construction or remodeling should address the following goals:

- The best price possible will be negotiated for contracted labor, building materials, furniture, fixtures, and equipment, given quality requirements.

- The facility will appeal to guests and employees.

- There will be a maximum **return on investment**.

- There will be an efficient flow of people and products within the facility, and equipment will be well placed.

- The facility will provide safe working space for employees and public access space to guests.

- Design and layout will consider food safety concerns and regulations.

- The facility will contribute to employee efficiency, and fewer employees will be needed to meet quality standards; labor costs will be lower.

- Facility maintenance costs will be low. Since energy costs are a concern, buildings and equipment should be energy efficient.

- Facility design will make employee supervision and other management activities easier.

Effective planning takes time and generally requires the specialized knowledge of contractors, food service design consultants, food service suppliers, and interior designers.

Preliminary Considerations

Many steps and people are involved in planning new construction or remodeling. The commitment of capital funds is likely to be significant, and planning to help ensure that project goals are met without surprises involves a substantial time commitment. The most important principles apply to both new construction and remodeling. For the sake of simplicity, the following discussion focuses on a remodeling project.

The Planning Team. The first step is to form a planning team. The general manager and the owner must be team members, and an architect is typically necessary. Unless managers are thoroughly familiar with the complex task of interior layout design, a food service facility consultant may also join the team.

The planning team must develop concepts and ideas for the facility. Does the remodeling project involve the exterior and/or the interior of the facility? Does it include the entire kitchen or just one area? The team must review such factors as the type of facility (commercial or noncommercial); its size and hours of operation; the menu; and quality requirements of production, service, and atmosphere.

It is important to think through exactly what activities are performed in an area before redesigning it. While it is not possible to look ahead many years, it is still important to think about general work activities and provide some design flexibility.

Equipment and Space Needs. The menu is a primary factor in dictating equipment and space needs. Other factors include employee skills and the variety and volume of food and beverages the operation produces. Consider a restaurant serving extensive menus for three meal periods daily; a diner open for breakfast only; and a hospital's central kitchen responsible for patient meals, a cash cafeteria operation, a physicians' dining room, satellite job facilities, and numerous banquets and other group functions.

Those planning a food service operation first consider individual work stations. A **work station** is a place where one employee works or where one menu item is made. Work stations are put together to form work sections that are then organized into a larger work area. For example, the work station for one bartender may be designed first. It can then be matched with similar bartender work stations to form a work section: the bar. This work section must be appropriately placed in a still-larger work area: the lounge.

Preliminary layout and equipment plans help with space allocation; floor plans can show the general arrangement of equipment, work aisles, and the relationship of one work area to another. Cost estimates can be based on these plans. If estimated costs are greater than the amount budgeted for redesign and renovation, adjusting the plans will be necessary.

Redesign Goals. Managers must determine what they want the redesign to accomplish. Managers of an elegant facility may want the dining room to project an atmosphere of luxury, while managers of a quick-service establishment desiring high guest turnover may use bright, hot colors in its dining area to discourage guests from lingering over their meals.

Managers must also keep government safety regulations in mind. Laws may restrict equipment placement and require expensive ventilation equipment in the kitchen and passenger elevators in public areas. Regulations may also restrict the number of guests that can be seated in the dining room, dictate the number and placement of emergency-lighting fixtures, detail the placement and number of exits, and so on.

Blueprints and Specifications. When preliminary information has been reviewed and approved, final blueprints can be drawn and equipment specifications prepared. These are used to solicit price quotations and make decisions about hiring contractors and suppliers. Construction and installation tasks follow. Contractors, equipment suppliers, and the operation's planning or management team should agree on a schedule and stick to it.

Redesigning the Kitchen

Kitchen redesign plans should address several concerns, including the following:

- *Physical fatigue.* Employees work hard in the kitchen. Everything practical to reduce physical fatigue should be built into the kitchen's design. Examples are reducing distances that employees must walk, adjusting heights of work areas to best suit employees, and providing comfortable locker, restroom, and employee dining facilities.

Regulatory Agency Building Codes Can Be Substantial

Local building codes address many aspects of the design and construction of commercial and noncommercial food service operations. You may wish to review building codes for your community. Enter "building codes" for "name of your city and state" in your favorite search engine. Then type "restaurant" or "commercial kitchen" in the site's search bar. Note: you may need to skim through several alternate websites to discover the information.

- *Noise.* Excessive noise makes employees uncomfortable and can distract employees and guests. Noise can be minimized with soundproofing materials and quiet equipment.

- *Lighting.* Much detail work is done in kitchen preparation areas. Adequate lighting helps employees work safely without eyestrain.

- *Temperature.* Kitchen areas can be hot. Cooking and cleaning equipment that generates heat and steam can make working conditions uncomfortable. Heating, ventilating, and air conditioning plans must deal with these problems.

- *Government safety codes.* Government safety codes designed to safeguard workers typically regulate the design, size, and placement of kitchen ventilation systems. Construction materials, exits, plumbing and electrical systems, and locations of fire extinguishers also may be regulated by local, state, and/or federal laws.

Design Factors

Kitchen design factors include cost, the menu, food quantity, food quality, equipment, utilities, space, sanitation and safety, and type of service.

Cost. Limited funds typically restrict kitchen remodeling. If preliminary planning reveals that the project cannot be completed with available funds, the planning team can: (1) defer the project until funds are available, (2) adjust the plans to match the money budgeted, (3) attempt to generate additional funds by borrowing or reducing stockholder dividends, or (4) cancel the project. Experienced managers, contractors, and others on the planning team will know which option is best for the specific project.

The Menu. The menu is one of the most important factors in kitchen design because menu items help drive kitchen space and equipment needs. Convenience foods also influence kitchen design; an operation that uses many convenience foods requires less space, less equipment, and fewer employees. However, the menu will likely change numerous times over the life of the kitchen. The first kitchen design planners must consider the menu when planning equipment, while subsequent menu planners will have to consider the equipment when planning the menu!

Food Quantity. The quantity of food the operation produces must be considered. If a large volume of food is purchased, received, stored, issued, produced, and served, more kitchen equipment and production space will be needed. Additional storage space will also be necessary unless frequent deliveries are expected.

Food Quality. Food quality is enhanced when food is prepared as close as possible to the time of service. However, batch cooking (preparing food in small batches as needed during the meal period) has space, cost, and equipment implications. Batch cooking requires less production equipment, and capital costs may be decreased. On the other hand, batch cooking may result in higher labor costs. The restaurant's managers must decide what level of quality is acceptable for food items, and then purchase the type and amount of equipment to deliver that quality.

Equipment. A wide variety of equipment is available to meet almost any storage, production, or service requirement. Many equipment items are mobile and can be moved easily for quick installation in new work stations or areas. It is often wiser to purchase such multipurpose equipment as tilting braising pans and vertical cutter-mixers than one-purpose specialty equipment.

Utilities. Utility concerns are closely aligned with equipment needs. It is time-consuming and expensive to install equipment in areas without convenient access to utilities (plumbing, electricity, and gas, for example). The availability and cost of utilities during the life of the equipment must also be estimated.

Space. When facilities are remodeled, kitchen and dining area spaces have already been allocated. Unfortunately, original designers often minimize kitchen space to provide more room for guests or facility needs. Making room for more guests may not necessarily lead to more guests. Usually, when kitchen space is limited, so is the quantity and, often, variety of food that can be produced, which may lead to dissatisfied guests. If the kitchen is cramped, part of the redesign might be to enlarge it.

Sanitation and Safety. Sanitation and safety concerns should be incorporated into kitchen design. Food service managers must provide a sanitary and safe operation for guests and employees. As already noted, some sanitation and safety precautions are required by law. Operations must include areas for washing and sanitizing nondisposable dishware and flatware. Sanitary storing and holding facilities are also important. For safety reasons, kitchen lighting should be good, and work aisles near production equipment should be wide enough to accommodate wheeled carts.

Type of Service. The type of service provided to guests is another factor to consider when redesigning the kitchen. For example, banquet service may require large quantities of food to be prepared and portioned quickly. This calls for a type of kitchen different from that in a coffee shop offering counter service.

Layouts

The process of redesigning a kitchen is complex. **Work flow**—the traffic patterns employees create as they go about their work—is another factor that must be considered. The sample layouts shown in this section are designed to minimize employee backtracking.

L-Shaped Layout. The L-shaped layout shown in Exhibit 1 illustrates a work area found in some food service kitchens: a bakeshop. This layout is good for the tasks performed in a bakeshop. Consider the task of making dinner rolls; an L-shaped layout makes this easy for the worker. Dinner rolls, like many other baking recipes, require water. Therefore, time can be saved if a sink (see number 1 on the exhibit) is located next to the mixer (2). Because bread products such as dinner rolls must be kneaded, portioned, and shaped, a bakery table (3) is positioned close to the mixer, and flour can be stored in mobile bins under the bakery table. Dinner rolls can be quickly shaped with a bun divider/rounder (4) located close to the table. When proportioned and shaped rolls come out of the divider, they must be put onto pans; a table (5) makes this easier. After the rolls are panned, they must be proofed and transported to ovens. A mobile proofing cabinet (6) helps with this task. Since bakeshops use ovens, they should be located close to the bakery area (7).

Straight-Line Layout. The straight-line layout in Exhibit 2 shows how pots and pans may be washed. First, they are brought to the soiled pot counter (1). Remaining food can be scraped and sprayed into a garbage disposer trough (2 and 3) before washing. Depending on local sanitation codes, sinks for washing, rinsing, and sanitizing (4, 5, and 6)—in that sequence—are needed. After sanitizing, space is necessary for clean pots and pans to air dry; a clean pot counter (7) serves this purpose. Items must be stored after drying; a mobile pot rack (8) can be used for storing and transporting pots and pans to work areas for their next use.

U-Shaped Layout. Exhibit 3 depicts a U-shaped layout for a dishwashing work area. The process begins at the refuse container (1) where service staff place tubs and trays of soiled dishes. Shelves inverted to a forty-five-degree angle above the soiled dish counter (2) can hold racks of glasses and cups. The shelf below the soiled dish counter can hold stacks of soiled dishes until they are washed. The next counter (3)

Exhibit 1   L-Shaped Layout for Bakeshop Area

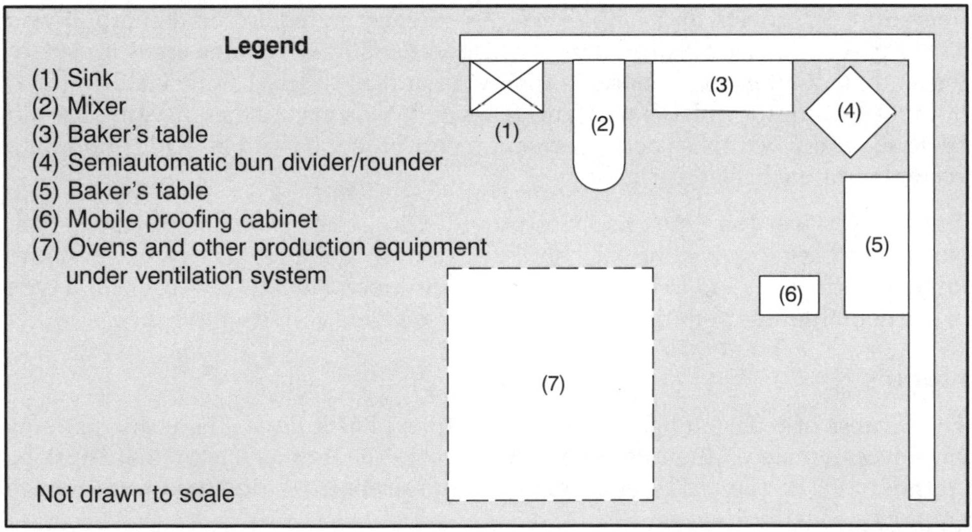

Legend
(1) Sink
(2) Mixer
(3) Baker's table
(4) Semiautomatic bun divider/rounder
(5) Baker's table
(6) Mobile proofing cabinet
(7) Ovens and other production equipment under ventilation system

Not drawn to scale

Exhibit 2   Straight-Line Layout in Pot/Pan Wash Area

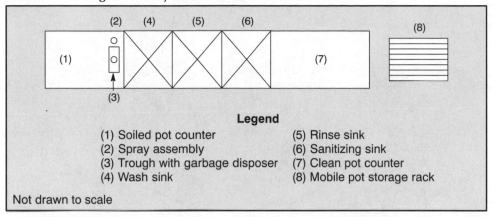

Legend

(1) Soiled pot counter   (5) Rinse sink
(2) Spray assembly   (6) Sanitizing sink
(3) Trough with garbage disposer   (7) Clean pot counter
(4) Wash sink   (8) Mobile pot storage rack

Not drawn to scale

Exhibit 3   U-Shaped Layout in Dishwashing Area

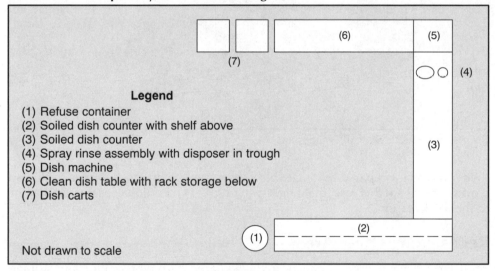

Legend

(1) Refuse container
(2) Soiled dish counter with shelf above
(3) Soiled dish counter
(4) Spray rinse assembly with disposer in trough
(5) Dish machine
(6) Clean dish table with rack storage below
(7) Dish carts

Not drawn to scale

is used to rack soiled dishes before prerinsing (4) and running through the dish-washing machine (5). As with pots and pans, clean dishes must be air dried, so a clean dish table (6) is necessary. After dishes are dry, they must be stacked and transported to the serving counter or food service stand on mobile dish carts (7).

Exhibit 4 shows employee work flow in a modified U-shaped layout for a dishwashing area.

Parallel Layout. Exhibit 5 illustrates a parallel layout for a frying station. A work counter with refrigerated storage below (1) can store items to be fried. Food items can be battered on the work counter and placed in the deep fryer (2). After frying, they can be placed on the work counter (3) for plating. The cook can then turn to the work counter/pickup station (5) and give the items to food servers or place

Exhibit 4   Modified U-Shaped Layout in Dishwashing Area

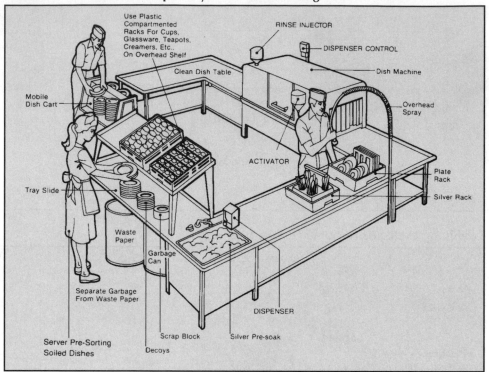

Courtesy of Ecolab, St. Paul, Minnesota.

them on dishes prepared by other cooks. In some operations, the fryer cook also works the grill; in this case, the range oven or grill (4) should be located close to or in the work station.

Redesigning Other Areas

Food service managers also may be involved in redesigning receiving and storage areas, dining room areas, and lounge areas.

When redesigning dining room and lounge areas, managers should include accommodations for guests with disabilities if they have not already been made. Examples include widened doorways, lowered or full-length mirrors in restrooms, grab bars near toilets, no raised thresholds in doorways, and access to facilities without steps. These and other accommodations are required by law in many localities and must be provided for when facilities are remodeled.

Receiving and Storage Areas

The receiving area should be as close as possible to the receiving door, and it should be large enough to handle all items ordinarily received. There should be room for a scale, dolly or cart, and other receiving equipment.

Exhibit 5   Parallel Layout for Frying Station

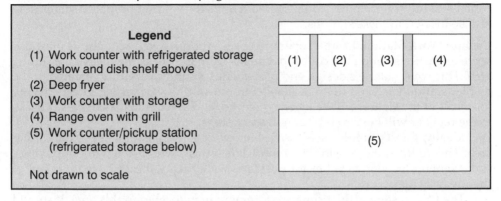

Legend

(1) Work counter with refrigerated storage below and dish shelf above
(2) Deep fryer
(3) Work counter with storage
(4) Range oven with grill
(5) Work counter/pickup station (refrigerated storage below)

Not drawn to scale

Storage areas include spaces for dry, refrigerated, and frozen products. Some large properties have separate storage spaces for produce, meats, seafood, and dairy products. For security reasons, dry storage areas should be designed with floor-to-ceiling walls and with ceilings that cannot be entered from an adjoining area. Some facilities have a lockable *precious storage* area for expensive items. It is common to have centralized walk-in refrigerators and freezers for all items needing cold storage.

Dining Room Areas

The planning team must pay special attention to the redesign of dining room areas. Guest reactions to food and its service often depend on the atmosphere of the dining room. Many things contribute to atmosphere: cleanliness; dining room furniture; dining room lighting; the amount of natural light (if any); the type of fabric and color(s) of tablecloths (if any); the types and color(s) of glasses and dishware; the type of flatware used; paintings, photographs, wall hangings, or other decorations; artificial, natural, or no plants; style of table settings; and many other factors.[1]

The size of the dining area must be matched with the kitchen's production capacity. Traffic patterns of employees and guests are affected by aisle width, location of restrooms and other public areas, and location of reception and cashier stations.

Servers in the dining room may need access to bar areas. Servers should not have to go through the kitchen, dishwashing area, or lobby to obtain drinks. This wastes steps and time, and lowers the speed and quality of guest service.

Two work areas of special concern in the dining room are server supply stations and the cashier work station.

Server Supply Stations. Many table-service operations have server supply stations in dining areas. These stations are often screened from guests and can store soiled and clean dishes, as well as the supplies (such as condiments, take-home containers, and table linens) needed for dining room service. Equipment items that might be located in food server supply stations include microwave ovens, beverage service equipment, calculators, and point-of-sale equipment. Ice bins, coffee-making equipment, and refrigerated units for holding prepared salads may also be located in these stations.

Cashier Work Station. In small operations, receptionists who seat guests may also serve as cashiers, who may collect payments from guests as they leave the dining area. This work station's design and placement should be carefully planned. If the cashier station is placed in an available but out-of-the-way corner, guests paying for meals at the station will be inconvenienced, and servers who take guest checks to the register will have to take unnecessary steps.

Ideally, guests should pass the cashier work station as they leave the dining area. This reduces the possibility of *walk-outs* (guests who leave without paying). A convenient location is better for guests as well; they will not have to go out of their way as they leave.

The POS system is the primary equipment item located in this area. It should be placed so the cashier and the guest can see the transaction rung up in the display window. Other items that should be located in this area include the following:

- *Telephone.* A telephone enables the cashier to take reservations.

- *Payment card terminals.* These terminals allow cashiers to process guest payment cards.

- *Miscellaneous items for sale.* Some food service operations have a variety of items for sale at the cashier's work station, including recipe books and items featuring the property's logo.

- *Menus.* Guests may wish to examine the menu while waiting to be seated. Offering take-home menus is another option.

- *Dining room sketch and server station assignments.* Space for a dining room sketch and a list of server station assignments may need to be available.

Lounge Areas

The atmosphere in the lounge should be exactly what the property wishes to project. Many of the factors discussed for dining room atmosphere, including cleanliness, furniture, lighting, and decorations, also apply to lounges.

Keep in mind that beverage service personnel may have to interact with the restaurant cashier/receptionist (for example, when processing beverage transfers). Therefore, the location of the lounge relative to the cashier's work station may be important. If food is served in the lounge, the lounge's location relative to the kitchen or food pickup areas is a concern. Guests who want only food service will ideally not need to pass through the lounge to get to the dining room, because nondrinking guests may not wish to enter the lounge. A foyer, coatroom, or public restroom may be used to separate the lounge from the dining room. Server traffic flow is also important.

Bars. The design of a bar is just as important as the design of the kitchen, dining, and lounge areas. The bar is an integral part of the food and beverage operation and generates sizable profits. It is unwise to allocate space to the bar based only on what is left after food service needs are met.

There are three basic types of bars: service bars, public bars, and combination public/service bars. Exhibit 6 shows a layout for a public/service bar that accommodates two bartenders. One works the service bar to provide drinks to employees who then serve guests in the restaurant or lounge. A second bartender serves guests seated at the public bar. The primary work stations are arranged around the two speed rails, which hold bottles of the most frequently ordered liquors. Other often-used items (soda gun, ice, and glassware) are also located in these areas. The

Exhibit 6   Sample Layout of Public/Service Bar

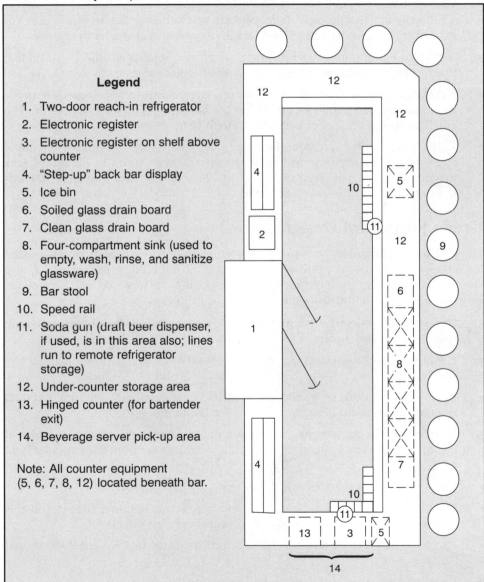

Legend

1. Two-door reach-in refrigerator
2. Electronic register
3. Electronic register on shelf above counter
4. "Step-up" back bar display
5. Ice bin
6. Soiled glass drain board
7. Clean glass drain board
8. Four-compartment sink (used to empty, wash, rinse, and sanitize glassware)
9. Bar stool
10. Speed rail
11. Soda gun (draft beer dispenser, if used, is in this area also; lines run to remote refrigerator storage)
12. Under-counter storage area
13. Hinged counter (for bartender exit)
14. Beverage server pick-up area

Note: All counter equipment (5, 6, 7, 8, 12) located beneath bar.

refrigerator and sinks are installed in a location convenient for both bartenders. The overall design and look of the bar must be compatible with the lounge as a whole.

Beverage preparation areas are designed by first developing individual work stations. The length of a public bar may be determined by the need for equipment space behind the bar, rather than the need for a specific number of seats (or amount of standing room) for guests.

Work simplification should be built into a bar's design. The task of preparing a variety of drinks in a short time requires carefully placed equipment, and the bar's layout influences a bartender's speed. Here are some bar layout guidelines:

- The bartender should be able to perform related activities in one place. For example, fruit garnishes can be cleaned, prepared, and stored in one area.

- Sufficient lighting and work counters at proper heights should be provided. Countertops should be approximately thirty-four inches from floor level.

- Doorways or pass-throughs should be wide enough to accommodate products and supplies to be placed behind the bar. Too often, half-barrels or even smaller sizes of draft beer kegs are difficult to bring into bar areas.

- Work space should accommodate employees. Bartenders should have ample space to produce drinks, and beverage servers need room to place and pick up orders. Space is also required to store items that servers may need, including napkins, bar picks, and ashtrays.

Green Restaurant Design

The best time to consider ways to be environmentally friendly is during planning for initial construction or extensive remodeling. Sustainability, conservation, and energy efficiency can be incorporated when planning addresses these concerns. Examples of construction strategies include the following:

- Use of solar-reflective roofing materials to reduce heat absorption and, therefore, cooling needs.

- Development of rainwater reuse systems to collect water for use during dryer seasons.

- Installation of smart irrigation systems that assess ground moisture and then regulate the amount of water required for landscaping.

- Installation of energy management systems to electronically control (manage) building zone temperatures and lighting schedules without the need for light switches.

- Use of light-emitting diode (LED) lighting for parking lots.

- Installation of variable speed, demand-based ventilation exhaust controls with sensors that monitor cooking to control exhaust fan speeds.

- Use of more efficient windows and window glazes to help cut cooling and heating costs.

- Installation of water aerators on hand sink faucets.

- Use of digital demand controllers to manage the operation of a large number of equipment items and prevent most of them from operating at the same time. This avoids power-demand spikes and resulting higher monthly demand charges.

Construction materials including special adhesives, sealants, paints, floor systems, and composite woods are available to reduce environmental challenges. The goal of zero waste in building construction may not yet be attainable, but the hospitality industry is quickly moving toward it.

Food and Beverage Equipment

Food and beverage employees cannot effectively store, prepare, or serve products without the right equipment. Today there is a wide range of food and beverage equipment available. Equipment is often expensive, and equipment decisions will affect the property for a long time: the useful life span of many items is more than fifteen years. How can managers decide which item is best? Part of the answer is to involve supervisors and employees in the decision-making process. They are the ones who use the equipment and know how it works and what is needed, so managers should solicit their ideas about equipment selection.

LEED and Green Restaurant Design/Operations

Leadership in Energy and Environmental Design (LEED) was developed by the U.S. Green Building Council (USGBC). LEED created a voluntary rating system of standards to guide the construction industry and promote sustainability for construction projects.

There are an increasing number of LEED-certified restaurants, thanks in large part to the "green restaurant" movement. These businesses save energy and generate less waste to reduce costs and decrease their impact on the environment. Very importantly, they appeal to consumers who support sustainability efforts.

To become LEED certified, a restaurant must register with the USGBC prior to beginning its construction project, and the restaurant's developers use the rating system to guide construction so as to earn rating points. Points can also be earned for using green energy, environmentally friendly landscaping, and organic methods to reduce waste.

Some LEED-certified U.S. restaurants are part of multi-unit chains such as Subway, Arby's, McDonald's, and Dunkin' Donuts. One small franchise operation, Pizza Fusion (www.pizzafusion.com), requires all new franchise owners to meet LEED standards even if they don't seek LEED certification.

Not surprisingly, the Internet is a great source of information about sustainability and green restaurant design. For example, to learn what one quick-service chain does to promote sustainability in restaurant operations and building design, look for the current year's "Global Best of Green" report at www.aboutmcdonalds.com.

The National Restaurant Association (NRA) has also developed excellent information for restaurants that wish to "go green." Go to the NRA's website at www.restaurant.org and type "green restaurants" into the search box to access online articles and other information about green restaurants.

Factors in Equipment Selection

There are numerous factors to consider when purchasing equipment, and many are similar to those considered when designing kitchens. While some factors address broad concerns important to every equipment purchase, other factors are specific to the property and the item in question. The factors important for most equipment purchases include:

- Cost

- Sanitation and safety

- Design and performance

- Operating efficiency

- Maintenance

- Capacity

- Construction

- Other factors

Cost. The purchase price is not the only cost to assess. Financing charges can dramatically increase equipment costs. Operating costs, including utility charges, can also be substantial. As energy costs increase, this factor will have an even greater impact on purchase decisions. Installation expenses can be high because some equipment may need a new ventilation, plumbing, or electrical system. Managers should consider repair, depreciation, and insurance expenses as well. All relevant costs must be identified and considered in the purchase decision.

Sanitation and Safety. Equipment should be easy to clean. NSF International (a nonprofit, nongovernmental standards development agency) periodically develops and issues guidelines on sanitary aspects of equipment design and construction.[2] These guidelines can help with the equipment selection process.

Buy equipment made of materials that can withstand normal wear, including the corrosive action of food and beverages and cleaning compounds. Equipment must not transfer odor, color, or taste to food. All food contact surfaces should be smooth, easily cleanable, corrosion-resistant, nontoxic, stable (no wobbly tables, for example), and nonabsorbent. Nontoxic solder should be used in all food contact areas. Some materials used for food service equipment include:

- *Wood.* While lightweight and economical, wood is difficult to keep clean because it is porous. Wood can easily absorb food odors and stains, so its use in food preparation areas should be restricted. It frequently is used for shelving in production and storage areas and for dining area tables and fixtures.

- *Metal.* Metal, especially stainless steel, is commonly used for food preparation equipment and food contact work surfaces. Steel, copper, or brass can be plated with chromium, tin, or nickel. These treatments frequently are used on food service equipment items to produce a shiny finish. Copper utensils are usually plated to help them resist corrosion, and steel plating is often used to line equipment. Steel sheets can be treated, covered with zinc, and used

NSF International (www.nsf.org), founded in 1944 as the National Sanitation Foundation, is known for the development of standards, product testing, and certification services in the areas of public health safety and protection of the environment. The NSF mark is placed on millions of consumer, commercial, and industrial products annually and is trusted by users, regulators, and manufacturers alike.

to make galvanized metal for sinks, tables, and related service equipment. Over time, however, this metal is subject to wear and the steel can be exposed, resulting in rust and corrosion. Sanitation-related codes and regulations limit the use of galvanized metal equipment in food preparation and service areas.

- *Glass.* Glass is sometimes used in equipment doors.

- *Plastic or rubber-based products.* Plastic or rubber-based equipment items are very popular. These materials resist cuts and odors and are lightweight, non-porous, and easy to clean. Plastic or rubber-based equipment items are often much less expensive than metal-based products.

Equipment must also be safe to use. The Occupational Safety & Health Administration (OSHA) has established regulations to help ensure that equipment is free of hazards. These regulations can provide meaningful safety information to guide purchase decisions.

Check for Underwriters Laboratories (UL) approval on electrical equipment and American Gas Association (AGA) approval on gas equipment. Look for such features as safety catches on steamer doors, safety pilot lights on gas equipment, and overload protection on electrical equipment.

Exhibit 7 lists some government and industry groups that are concerned about equipment safety and sanitation.

Design and Performance. Equipment should be simple to use, provide value (price relative to quality), incorporate sanitation and safety standards, and help employees provide high-quality products in the volume and with the speed that are necessary.

Multipurpose equipment with optional features can often be purchased at little additional cost. For example, a mixer with the proper attachments can be used to slice, grind, or shred food products. On the other hand, some equipment may have built-in features that increase the purchase price but will never be used. Performance features might best be assessed by talking with industry professionals using similar equipment and with manufacturers and vendors at trade shows.

Since some equipment is easier to operate than others, the skills and abilities of employees must be considered. Buy equipment that is designed to be easy to operate.

Operating Efficiency. The emphasis on minimizing harm to the environment and reducing energy consumption and costs begun during construction planning should continue as equipment purchase decisions are made. Examples of energy-saving equipment and features include the following:

- *Steamers.* Connectionless steamers operate without a boiler and drain and consume less water and energy than steamers with boilers.

- *Broilers.* Since these consume large amounts of energy, sometimes more energy-efficient thermostatically controlled griddles can be substituted

Exhibit 7   Government/Industry Groups Concerned with Equipment Safety and Sanitation

Name of Group	Type	Special Concerns
1. Occupational Safety & Health Administration (OSHA)	Government	Equipment and facility safety and related concerns
2. NSF International	Private	Equipment sanitation
3. Underwriters Laboratories (UL)	Private	Electrical equipment safety
4. American Gas Association (AGA)	Private	Safety for gas-fueled equipment
5. Municipal and state agencies	Government	Safety and sanitation
6. National Electric Manufacturers' Association (NEMA)	Industry	Electrical equipment safety
7. Food and Drug Administration (FDA)	Government	Sanitation
8. American Society of Sanitary Engineers	Industry	Facility design

when preparing applicable menu items. Grooved griddles can sear "grill marks" onto food to make it look like it was broiled.

- *Ovens.* Combination (combi) ovens are more versatile than space saving since they combine the functions of ovens and steamers. However, they use a significant amount of energy and water when they operate in the combi mode. The best recommendation is to use the manufacturer's suggestions and to limit cooking in the combi cycle.

- *Griddles.* Thermostatically controlled griddles cost less to operate than their manually controlled counterparts.

- *Fryers.* A unit that has earned an Energy Star is more energy efficient than units that have not.

- *Braising Pans.* Some come with insulated walls.

- *Holding Cabinets.* Cabinets that have earned Energy Stars are available.

- *Refrigerators and Freezers.* Energy Star units can reduce energy costs by up to 45 percent compared with less-efficient models. Purchase units with required capacity.

- *Ice Machines.* Larger units are more efficient than smaller ones, so purchase one with the correct capacity.

Several websites listed in the Internet Sites section at the end of the chapter provide additional information about energy-saving, environmentally friendly food service equipment.

Maintenance. Most equipment requires careful scheduled periodic maintenance to operate effectively. Can maintenance be done by on-site staff or must skilled technicians be contracted? How often and at what cost must these activities be performed? How long does maintenance take? If the equipment being considered is a newer model of current equipment, managers should review the old equipment's maintenance and repair record. (See Exhibit 8 for a sample record. Today, such records are increasingly computerized. To view additional samples, enter "preventive maintenance and repair record images" in your favorite search engine.) Excessive repairs suggest that either the equipment is unsuitable or it is being used improperly. Equipment that is frequently down is of little value.

Capacity. Managers must select equipment that has the right capacity for the operation. Inadequate equipment can impair efficiency because production staff may need to prepare several batches of food instead of one, for example.

Construction. NSF International has developed detailed construction specifications for many types of food service equipment. Consult this source when considering equipment construction standards. Reputable manufacturers and suppliers are more likely to provide high-quality equipment.

Properly constructed equipment is more expensive than lower-quality equipment. However, because of its extended life and other advantages, properly constructed equipment may be worth the additional investment. When a dishwashing

Exhibit 8   Preventive Maintenance and Repair Record

Service	Type Machine	Equipment Number
Location	Serial Number	Model Number
Make	Date Purchased	Purchase Cost

Preventive Maintenance Procedure	
Function	Interval

Special Instructions

Specifications	
Voltage	Drive
Amperage	Belts
Phase	Fuse
Pressure	Lubrication
Horsepower	Filter
RPM	Fluids

Spare Parts Required			
Part	Mfr. Part Number	Stock Number	Quantity

machine can cost as much as an automobile, the importance of proper design and construction is clear.

Other Factors. Normally, food service equipment should be made for commercial use, not home use, so it will be more durable.

Appearance is important for serving and production equipment that will be visible to guests. New equipment should be compatible with existing space and other equipment items already in use. For example, a dishwashing machine that fits into the old dishwashing machine's space is convenient. In some operations, the quietness of equipment and/or its mobility will be an important concern.

Generally, stock is a better choice than custom equipment. Stock equipment is available in catalogs and can be ordered through dealers without modification to basic designs. Custom equipment tailored to the operation is much more expensive, and managers must allow considerable lead time when ordering it.

Types of Food Service Equipment

Food service equipment items include:

- Refrigerated equipment

- Ranges

- Ovens

- Tilting braising pans

- Steam-cooking equipment

- Broilers

- Deep fryers

- Other equipment

Refrigerated Equipment. The two basic types of refrigerated equipment are walk-in units and reach-in or roll-in units.

Walk-in units. Refrigerated **walk-in units** are refrigerated rooms used for central storage purposes. They can also hold items awaiting production or service. Walk-in freezers are used to store items awaiting production and frozen leftovers.

For safety reasons, it should be possible to open the doors of walk-in refrigerators and freezers from the inside even if the door is locked. A thermostat, perhaps with an accompanying high-temperature-alert device, can monitor the internal temperature of the unit.

Walk-ins can be sectional (installed in sections after the building is constructed) or built-in. Separate refrigeration systems should generally be used for walk-in refrigerator and freezer compartments. Refrigeration systems feature water- or air-cooled compressors. The compressor, condenser, and evaporator must be fitted to the size of the refrigeration unit.

Walk-in refrigeration units should be built with locking panels to ensure an airtight, durable seal. Normally the manufacturer warrants refrigerated units for several years under normal usage. Insulation is usually foamed in place or made of a froth-type urethane. Like other equipment, refrigeration units are becoming

Technology and Restaurant Refrigeration

Equipment technology is increasingly helping food service managers to better control product quality and reduce utility costs. Here are some examples of new technology for refrigerated units:

- Remote e-monitoring systems using electrical, temperature, pressure, and water sensors can alert restaurateurs to wasted energy. Managers can be alerted by text messages if heating and cooling systems are operating at the same time, if open doors are causing a refrigeration unit to short-cycle, or if refrigerator or freezer temperatures are excessive. (See www.powerhousedynamics.com for more information.)
- An "e-cube" system manages refrigerator temperatures based on the internal temperature of the food stored within the refrigerators rather than the interior temperature of the refrigerators. This increased control reduces energy costs. (See www.powersolutions.com for more information.)
- Glycol rack refrigeration can be used in food service operations with multiple refrigeration units on-site. Instead of needing a refrigeration system on each device, all refrigeration units are supported from one centrally located rack that distributes glycol rather than refrigerant throughout the restaurant. (See www.standex.com for more information.)

more energy efficient with specialized insulation and electrical components. If prefabricated units are installed on concrete floors, a floor made of insulated panels may also be necessary. To prevent floor distortion, a flooring load of at least 300 pounds per square foot is generally recommended. Metal plates or floor coverings should be used when there is continual use of heavily loaded transport equipment.

Reach-in or roll-in units. Smaller refrigerated units are referred to as **reach-ins** or **roll-ins.** They are used to store food products at their points of use in production areas. These units are often used in server or guest areas as well. They may also be used as central storage units at small operations.

Reach-ins have doors that swing open like a home refrigerator or swing up like a chest-type freezer. Reach-ins or roll-ins may open on one side only or be a pass-through type with doors on each side. They may have from one to three or more sections of full-length doors or two to six or more sections of half-size doors. Reach-ins may have fixed shelves or slides for modular pans. Some reach-ins are designed to accommodate roll-in carts. Under-the-counter units used to store small quantities of food items in preparation/service areas are also available.

A pass-through reach-in is generally located between a preparation area and a service area. In a cafeteria operation, salads, sandwiches, and refrigerated desserts can be prepared in the kitchen, placed in the pass-through, and retrieved through the other side by servers or guests.

As with walk-in refrigerators and freezers, the proper size of the compressor, condenser, and evaporator for reach-in or roll-in units is essential. Foamed-in-place or froth-type urethane insulation is necessary. Reach-ins or roll-ins should have a seamless interior construction with self-closing doors. Adjustable legs that make the equipment level with the floor, an automatic defroster-timer for the freezer, an exterior-mounted thermometer, and locking doors are useful options.

Ranges. A **range** can be used to do almost any type of cooking. Ranges may be operated by either gas or electricity.

Ranges have been very popular and widely used in commercial and institutional food service operations for years. However, specialized equipment has reduced dependence on ranges. Several ranges installed in a straight-line work station are being replaced in some operations by a work station consisting of one range, a high-speed pressure steamer, a pressure fryer, and other specialized equipment items.

There are two basic types of ranges: solid-top and open-top. Solid-top ranges apply heat uniformly over the entire top section of the range. Open-top ranges have individually heated units that can be adjusted separately. Combination solid-top/open-top ranges are also available. While most ranges come equipped with ovens underneath, some countertop models have shelves or storage cabinets below.

Specialized ranges include chop suey ranges and range griddles. A griddle or a grill can be purchased as a separate piece of equipment, but it is usually placed close to the range. Griddle-top units are usually equipped with a grease collection pan underneath and a splashback to prevent spillage.

Carbon dioxide or nontoxic chemical fire extinguishers that meet applicable regulations should be placed near ranges. Generally, ventilation systems above ranges have fire extinguishing systems built into them. The danger of a grease fire is always present when cooking with range equipment. Managers should stress safety to employees and provide them with safety training.

Ovens. There are many types of **ovens.** Range ovens have been a traditional and versatile piece of production equipment in most food service operations. Many ranges have ovens beneath them.

Deck ovens are decked (stacked) on top of each other to increase capacity without requiring additional floor space. These units are available with single or multiple decks and in combination with roasting or baking ovens.

A roasting oven typically has an interior cavity twelve to fifteen inches high, while the interior cavity of a baking oven is usually about eight inches high. However, both types of ovens are available in a wide range of interior lengths and widths.

Convection ovens have fans or blowers to circulate heat and air in the closed oven chamber. This allows heat to penetrate food products more quickly and shortens cooking time, and permits the use of lower oven temperatures. Convection ovens are available in these types: single-deck, double-deck, and roll-in ovens that allow a mobile rack to be wheeled directly into the oven.

Many items that can be prepared with a conventional range or deck oven can also be prepared in a convection oven. Since items can be cooked in a shorter time and at a lower temperature in convection ovens, food quality is often enhanced. This also increases output, and, because the convection oven itself is smaller than a conventional deck oven, more efficient use is made of available floor space.

Rotary or revolving tray ovens use flat shelves suspended between two reels. Food items to be roasted or baked are loaded onto the trays as they appear at the

Food Service Equipment Photos and Information on the Internet

Equipment Available	Company and Website
Convention ovens, combi ovens, hydrovection ovens, deck ovens, range equipment, steam equipment, conveyor ovens, rotating rack ovens	Blodgett www.blodgett.com
Range ovens, convention ovens, broilers, countertop cooking equipment, deep-fat fryers, pizza ovens, refrigerated bases, griddles, pasta cookers, stockpot stoves	The Montague Company www.montaguecompany.com
Baking ovens, proofers, toasters, griddles, backshelf broilers, convection ovens, microwave ovens, hot plates, mixers, meat saws, grinders, choppers, tenderizers, peelers, slicers, salad dryers, tenderizers, scales, refrigerators, freezers, heated cabinets, dishwashers, pot and pan washers	Hobart www.hobartcorp.com
Steam table equipment, buffet and table-service smallwares, carts, countertop cooking equipment, mobile equipment, cookware, pots, pans, utensils, underwashing accessories	The Vollrath Company, LLC www.vollrath.com
Walk-in, reach-in, roll-in, and undercounter refrigerators and freezers, blast chillers, cafeteria/buffet dispensing equipment, refrigerated work stations, display cases, work tables, pizza proofers, thermalizers, compartment steamers, steam-jacketed kettles, tilt skillets, braising pans, combination steamers/ovens, cook-chill equipment, rotisseries, broilers, deep fyers, hot plates, sinks, cabinets, heated holding cabinets, beverage dispensing equipment, ice-making equipment, ice cream units	Manitowoc Foodservice www.manitowocfoodservice.com
Coffee- and espresso-making equipment, cold and frozen beverage equipment	Bunn www.bunn.com

door opening. These ovens are designed to prevent the escape of hot air when the door is opened. Rotary ovens are frequently used in large food service operations.

Microwave ovens use radiation (electromagnetic waves) to heat food. As the waves penetrate food, they cause molecules in the food to move, producing friction and heat. The advantages of microwaves include fast cooking, easy cleaning, and fewer fire hazards. Microwaves have many uses. They can be used for many products that do not need browning. Some microwave ovens are even equipped with browning units that impart characteristic color to bakery and other products.

Technology Helps Managers Learn About Food Service Equipment

Assume you are a food service manager considering the purchase of a deep fat fryer. What companies manufacture this item? What are desirable features? What other purchasing considerations are important?

These and related questions can be easily answered through a quick computer search which, among other sources of information, will uncover numerous restaurant equipment buying guides developed by equipment supply companies. One example of an equipment buying guide is from Central Restaurant Products (www.centralrestaurant.com). When you reach the company's site, click on the type of equipment you want to learn about. For alternative information sources, enter "restaurant equipment buying guides" in your favorite search engine.

Typical applications for microwave ovens in quantity food operations include cooking short-order products, and thawing, heating, and reheating small portions of food.

Infrared (quartz) ovens may be used to heat, roast, and brown products. They are especially useful for reconstituting frozen foods packaged in bulk. A quartz oven can be used for broiling and for browning dishes that have been heated in a microwave.

Recon ovens are used to reconstitute frozen, prepared entrées. They can also be used as high-speed conventional ovens. Recon ovens have many uses and come in various sizes to accommodate most needs.

Combi ovens (combination ovens) are a blend of a steam and convection oven. Combi ovens have three functions: convection, steam, and combination cooking. Chefs use a combi oven in the convection mode to circulate dry heat, such as for baking. They use it in the steam mode to inject water into the oven (for cooking fish, vegetables, and rice). In the combination mode, dry heat and steam are used to maintain exact humidity levels.

Tilting Braising Pans. A **tilting braising pan** is flat-bottomed and can be used as a kettle, griddle, fry pan, steamer, oven, or warmer/server. The bottom of an electric tilting braising pan is a heavy stainless steel plate heated by an electric heating element.

A tilting braising pan can reduce the total cooking time of many food products by as much as 25 percent. It is flexible and can be used for a wide variety of food products. Since it tilts, both pouring and cleaning are easy.

Steam-Cooking Equipment. **Steam-cooking equipment** is used in many food service operations. There may be a self-contained boiler that produces steam for the equipment. It is a common practice to purchase steam equipment with a larger-than-necessary boiler so that more steam equipment can be added. Steam equipment can also be purchased without a boiler and is then connected to a centralized steam source. The steam may or may not come into direct contact with the food being cooked.

Steam-jacketed kettles. Steam-jacketed kettles are large cooking pots that range in capacity from several quarts to 100 or more gallons. They are generally used to steam, boil, or simmer. Steam-jacketed kettles have a double wall: food is heated by steam that is in a jacket surrounding the interior wall of the kettle. In some kettles, the double wall extends only approximately three-fourths of the way up the side. In other kettles, the double wall extends up the entire side. As with any steam equipment, proper safety features are a must, including pressure-reducing and safety valves.

Steam-jacketed kettles can be used to prepare meats, poultry, casseroles, eggs, soups, fresh or frozen vegetables, sauces, and pie fillings. They reduce the amount of range space and number of top-of-range cooking utensils necessary. Large kettles allow cooking in one vessel rather than many. Because steam-jacketed kettles tend to heat evenly, scorching problems are reduced.

Some steam-jacketed kettles can be tilted to remove food products and draw off water used to clean the kettle. Tilting kettles may also have draw-off valves. In nontilting kettles, food or water must be removed by ladling or by a draw-off valve.

Steam-jacketed kettles should be placed near a water source because water is a common ingredient in many items prepared in the kettles, and is also used to clean it. A nearby drain makes it easier to clean kettles.

Compartment steamers. A compartment steamer cooks food directly with steam. It works like a pressure cooker. It can be used to cook almost any food except those that need to be deep fried, sautéed, or cooked with dry heat.

A conventional low-pressure compartment steamer usually operates at approximately five pounds per square inch (psi) of steam pressure. Low-pressure compartment steamers are used in the kitchens of many large-volume food service operations. They can be used to prepare large quantities of food and are excellent for cooking vegetables, macaroni, and eggs. Low-pressure compartment steamers also thaw frozen products and perform many of the same tasks as steam-jacketed kettles.

High-pressure compartment steamers are often placed on cooking lines in commercial properties. These equipment items operate at approximately fifteen psi. They are designed to cook small quantities of food quickly. High-pressure compartment steamers are used to prepare such convenience foods as frozen or refrigerated pre-portioned items in pouches, fresh shellfish, and a variety of other items that can be reconstituted on an as-needed basis.

Convection steamers. Room-pressure convection steamers are very useful for cooking seafood, vegetables, and other items for which nutrient retention is especially important.

Broilers. Broilers use radiant heat to cook foods rapidly and can be fueled by gas or electricity. There are two common types of broilers.

Overhead broilers. Overhead broilers have heating units that radiate heat down to foods placed on a shelf below. The shelf is usually adjustable so that food can be placed closer to or farther away from the heat source to change the broiling time. A thick piece of meat placed close to the heat source might burn on the outside before it is done on the inside, so the shelf should be placed farther away. A thinner cut of meat might be placed closer to the heat source.

Food Production and Energy Consumption

Restaurants typically consume a lot of energy. However, there are an ever-increasing number of options to save energy, "go green," and reduce operating costs. To help reduce energy use and lower utility bills, many restaurant equipment manufacturers are producing new commercial appliances that consume less energy than older models. For example, steam cookers use a lot of energy and water to prepare food; some new models are 90 percent more efficient than older models.

Some states offer rebate programs for restaurants purchasing commercial equipment with the Energy Star label. Energy Star is a voluntary program administered by the U.S. Environmental Protection Agency to, in part, identify and promote energy-efficient products to reduce energy consumption. Eight categories of restaurant equipment carry the Energy Star label:

- Dishwashers
- Fryers
- Griddles
- Hot food holding cabinets
- Ice machines
- Convection and combi ovens
- Refrigerators and freezers
- Steam cookers

For more information, go to www.energystar.gov.

A small overhead broiler, also called a shelf broiler or salamander, can be mounted on top of a range. While the capacity of shelf broilers is small, they are adequate in operations with low broiling loads. They are usually used as finish broilers (for example, to melt cheese or brown bread crumb toppings) and as auxiliary broilers during slow periods.

Charbroilers. Underfired charbroilers use a heat source under the food. Items to be charbroiled are placed on a grate above a radiant-hot surface. During cooking, the food juices drip directly onto the hot surface and burn, creating the typical charcoal flavor and appearance. Since this process produces smoke and odors, charbroilers—like most other pieces of cooking—must be placed under an efficient ventilation system. Charbroilers with small cooking surfaces are available for light use. Some larger units have an expandable grate area.

Deep Fryers. Deep fryers can be fueled by electricity or gas. Conventional fryers (tabletop models) may hold fifteen pounds or less of frying fat. Large freestanding fryers may hold 130 pounds or more of frying fat.

Pressure fryers have sealed lids. When the unit is in operation, pressure builds up within the fryer. This reduces frying time and is ideal for such items as deep-fried chicken.

Large-volume operations may use a continuous-type deep fryer with a conveyor to move products through the fat. The food's position on the conveyor determines the cooking time. Items that require more cooking time are placed at the end of the conveyor so that they remain in the fat longer.

High-quality fat enhances food flavor and lasts longer. A fat's quality and smoke point (the temperature at which the fat disintegrates and smokes) are important concerns in selecting frying fat.

Deep fryers must have a rapid recovery rate, which is the amount of time it takes a deep fryer to reheat the fat to proper cooking temperatures after cold food is added. Without rapid recovery, food products will absorb grease, and food quality will suffer.

Conventional and pressure deep fryers are often equipped with two frying baskets. This is useful for frying large quantities at one time or for alternating baskets. Many models are equipped with automatic filtering systems and computerized controls to automatically lower frying baskets into the fat, time the food while it is frying, and then raise the baskets.

Many kitchen fires originate at the deep fryer, so the area must be well ventilated and have fire extinguishing equipment nearby. Personnel should be carefully trained in proper fryer use. Since breading or other preparation activities are frequently necessary for products being deep fried, sufficient work space close to the fryer is important. Work space must also be available so employees can set down products removed from the unit. In too many operations, this work space is across the aisle from the fryer, and the aisle quickly becomes unsanitary and unsafe because breading, batter, and frying fat drips on the floor as products are removed.

Other Equipment. The equipment discussed to this point cooks food. Other food service equipment includes:

- Mixers

- Cutters, choppers, and slicers

- Coffee-making equipment

- Dishwashing machines

- Preparation and other tables

- Inexpensive equipment/tools

Mixers. A mixer is a mechanical device used to combine or blend foods. An electric motor drives a mixing arm. Mixers are commonly used in preparation areas for making salad dressings, whipping potatoes, and blending casserole mixtures. In the baking area, a mixer is necessary for making dough and batter.

Mixers are of two general types: table models with a capacity of five to twenty quarts, and floor models with a capacity of twenty to eighty quarts or more.

Special attachments can be used with a mixer to cut, shred, grind, or chop food products for casserole dishes, salads, and other items. A floor-model mixer has three standard attachments: (1) a paddle beater for general mixing that can be used to mash, cream, mix, or blend food products; (2) a whip that incorporates air into light mixtures and can be used to blend dry mixes, whip cream or egg whites, or mix light icings; and (3) a dough hook to mix heavy dough with a folding and stretching action.

The drive shaft of a mixer can also be used to operate a wide array of food-processing attachments such as knife sharpeners, juice extractors, and food slicers. Three other popular mixer attachments are cutters, choppers, and grinders. Cutters and choppers cut vegetables and other food as the food passes against or between rotating blades. Grinders push food items through grinding plates or blades. If properly used, these attachments can significantly increase kitchen staff productivity.

Cutters, choppers, and slicers. Cutters, choppers, and slicers can also be purchased as stand-alone pieces of equipment. Food cutters/mixers are available in table and floor models.

A table-model food chopper is another popular item. Items to be chopped are placed in a bowl that revolves and pushes the products through revolving knives. The chopped food is removed when the bowl has turned once. For finer chopping, the bowl is allowed to turn additional times.

Some stand-alone food slicers automatically move food across a blade. Manual slicers are more common, however. Slicers can be very dangerous if used improperly. The manufacturer's instructions should always be followed. Managers must train employees in safe operation and cleaning.

Coffee-making equipment. A wide variety of coffee-making equipment is available to meet the needs of almost any food service operation. Manual, semi-automatic, or automatic equipment can produce one cup or many gallons at one time. Equipment can be stationary, mounted on a counter or directly on the floor, or mounted on a cart for mobile use.

Small coffee-making units for hotels and restaurants use manual, pump, or siphon systems to pour water over and through coffee grounds into glass carafes. Urns ranging in size from 3 to 150 gallons are also available for use in banquet and institutional operations.

Proper maintenance of coffee-brewing equipment and procedures for correctly making and handling coffee are a must. Coffee distributors usually offer a wide variety of information for use in employee training programs.

Dishwashing machines. A dishwashing machine is a valuable and expensive appliance available in many types. The most basic is a rack-type machine in which dishes are racked and inserted into the machine for washing. Most machines have an automatic washing and sanitizing cycle to eliminate the need for operator control of these cycles. Large rack-type machines are also available. With these machines, dishes are racked and placed on a conveyor that pulls the racks through the machine. They are then removed from the conveyor belt at the other end by a dishwashing machine operator.

Dishwashing machines typically have automatic dispensers for detergent and other chemicals such as drying agents. Most machines require a booster heater to bring the water temperature up to required minimum temperatures necessary for sanitization. Some units use lower temperatures and sanitize dishes with chemicals.

Preparation and other tables. Food production and service areas may use a wide range of stationary (without wheels) or mobile tables and counters of varying lengths and widths. They may feature shelves and/or drawers below and, sometimes, utensil racks or shelves above. If they are stationary and against a

Dishwashing Is Expensive!

The dishwashing machine is the single most expensive piece of equipment in many food service operations. Associated costs include those for counters, disposers, racks, dish carts, and the dishwashing area itself (plumbing costs, ventilation costs, and so on). Proper layout and design are important to ensure that employees can work efficiently in the dishwashing area.

Here's a question to consider: "Would you give the keys to your expensive car to someone who is almost a stranger?" While just about everyone would say, "No!" managers do something similar when they hire dishwashers, provide almost no training to them, and then turn them loose to wash the dishes. This shows very poor judgment on the part of such managers.

Equipment that was expensive in the first place gets even more expensive when poorly trained employees damage it through improper operation. And consider the question of food safety: the operation's financial future will surely be negatively affected by news reports of foodborne illness, and then there are the financial repercussions of lawsuits filed by harmed guests and employees. As you can see, managers should be sure to train their employees to correctly and safely use the dishwashing machine!

wall, they are typically manufactured with a backsplash edge to eliminate the possibility of food or other soil contaminating the space between the table and wall. They may also rest on a closed base or on legs that keep bottom shelves at least six inches off the floor to facilitate cleaning. Self-cleaning and germ-killing tables and counters may be available in the future, thanks to a thin layer of titanium dioxide that, when activated by ultraviolet light, destroys any organic molecules it touches, including dirt.

Inexpensive equipment/tools. The list of inexpensive food service equipment is long and includes toasters, warmers, ladles, peelers, scales, knives, pots and pans, egg beaters, measuring spoons, pastry brushes, rolling pins, muffin and pie tins, funnels, strainers, thermometers, can openers, mixing and chopping bowls, graters, poultry shears, cutting boards, butter spreaders, and much more. There are no universal guidelines for the types and quantities of inexpensive equipment items an operation should have; each operation must assess its own needs.

Types of Beverage Equipment

Most operations need far less beverage equipment than food service equipment. Common beverage equipment includes refrigerators, frozen drink machines, glass storage areas, sinks, blenders, and hand tools such as bar strainers, shakers, and corkscrews.

In recent years, a wide variety of automated beverage equipment has become available. Automated beverage control systems may enhance production and service capabilities while improving accounting and operational controls. A **beverage control unit** is the brain of an automated system. This control unit is generally located close to a beverage storage area and is primarily responsible for regulating all essential mechanisms within the system. The unit communicates requests from order entry terminals to the system's delivery network and directs the flow of beverages from a storage area to a dispensing unit.

Automated beverage control systems may employ different types of sensing devices. A **glass sensor** is located in a bar dispensing unit, and will not permit liquid to flow from the dispensing unit unless there is a glass positioned below the dispensing head to catch the liquid. A **guest check sensor** prevents the system from filling beverage orders unless they are first recorded on a guest check or entered into a point-of-sale system. When a server or bartender places a beverage order whose ingredients are out of stock, an **empty bottle sensor** relays a signal to the order entry device.

Sophisticated systems can record data input through order entry devices, transport beverage ingredients through a controlled delivery network, dispense ingredients for ordered items, and track important service, sales, and revenue data for inclusion in reports for managers.

Components of an automated beverage control system include an order entry device, a delivery network, and dispensing units.

Order Entry Device. The primary function of an order entry device is to initiate activities involved with recording, producing, and pricing beverage items requested by guests. There are two basic order entry devices, one with preset buttons and one with a keyboard unit:

Restaurant Kitchen Equipment Trends

Kitchens are becoming smaller as operators seek to maximize front-of-the-house space. In response to this trend, kitchen equipment will continue to get smaller and more complex. The combi oven is an example of a multifunctional piece of equipment that can cook, steam, and hold food, and it is now available in small stackable models for countertop usage.

Energy costs continue to rise, with back-of-the-house energy consumption comprising more than half of a food service operation's energy expenditures. The EPA's Energy Star standards are inspiring numerous examples of new energy-saving equipment. One example is heat-recovery systems for dishwashers and refrigeration units; with these systems, the heat given off by this equipment is captured and recycled to preheat incoming water or air. In another example, new controllers allow equipment to be powered down during off-peak energy usage hours. Converting to LED lighting in display cases or reach-in coolers not only saves energy, it also reduces lamp replacement costs.

High turnover of preparation personnel and less time for training means that equipment isn't always operated properly. Increasingly, technology focuses on making equipment easier to operate. One example of this trend is the touchscreen now commonly found on convection and combi ovens. These touchscreen systems help ensure proper cooking, and they are easier to use for new employees who may also have language barriers.

Source: Adapted from "Kitchen Trends," *Restaurant Business*, February 1, 2013.

- *Preset buttons.* A group of preset buttons located on a beverage dispensing unit is the most popular order entry device. However, since dispensing units may support relatively few preset buttons, the number of beverage items under the control of the automated beverage system is limited.

- *Keyboard units.* Keyboard units (which can be touchscreens) function like pre-check terminals with beverage dispensing performed by a separate piece of hardware. Since they support a full range of preset keys, price look-up keys, and modifier keys, these units place a large number of beverage items under the control of the automated system.

Delivery Network. An automated beverage control system relies on a **delivery network** to transport beverage item ingredients from storage areas to dispensing units. The delivery network must be able to regulate temperature and pressure conditions at various locations and stages of delivery. To maintain proper temperatures, the delivery network typically employs a cooling system to control cold plates, cold boxes, and/or cold storage rooms.

Most automated beverage control systems deliver beverage ingredients by controlling pressure sources such as gravity, compressed air, carbon dioxide, and nitrous oxide. Gravity and compressed air are used for delivering liquor, nitrogen or nitrous oxide for wine, compressed air for beer, and a carbon dioxide regulator for post-mixes. A post-mix soft drink dispenser mixes syrup and carbonated water together at the dispenser.

Almost any type of liquor and accompanying liquid ingredient can be stored, transported, and dispensed by an automated beverage control system. Portion sizes of liquor can be controlled with remarkable accuracy. Typically, systems can be calibrated to maintain portion sizes ranging from one-half ounce to three-and-one-half ounces.

Dispensing Units. Once beverage item ingredients are removed from storage and transported by the delivery network to production areas, they can be dispensed. Automated beverage control systems may have several types of dispensing units.

Touch-bar faucet. A **touch-bar faucet** can be located under or behind the bar, on top of an ice machine, or on a pedestal stand. Typically, touch-bar faucets dispense only a single beverage type and are preset for one specific portion size

---

Want to Learn More About Automated Beverage Dispensing Systems?

The Berg Company is one of the largest manufacturers of automated beverage dispensing systems. Its website (www.bergliquorcontrols.com) provides a wide variety of information. For example, it provides detailed information about dispensing products and applicable software, as well as information about the need for liquor control.

The Internet provides a great deal of information about automated beverage dispensing systems. For example, see Easybar (www.easybar.com) and Wunder-Bar (www.wunderbar.com).

output per push on the bar lever. A double shot of bourbon, therefore, may require the bartender to push twice on the bar lever.

Console faucet. Console faucet dispensing units can also be located in almost any part of the bar area or up to 300 feet from beverage storage areas. They can dispense various beverages in a number of portion sizes. Using buttons located above the faucet unit, a bartender can trigger up to four different portion sizes from the same faucet head.

Hose and gun device. The **hose and gun device** has control buttons on the handle of the gun that can be connected by hoses to liquors, carbonated beverages, water, and/or wine tanks. These dispensers can be installed anywhere along the bar and are frequently used on portable bars and at service bar locations. Depressing a button produces a premeasured flow of the desired beverage. The number of beverage items under the control of a hose and gun dispensing unit is limited to the number of control buttons the device supports.

Mini-tower pedestal. The **mini-tower pedestal** dispensing unit combines the portion-size capabilities of console faucet units with the button selection technique of hose and gun devices. In addition, the mini-tower offers increased control of bar operations. A button must be pressed for a beverage to be dispensed, and a glass-sensing device requires that a glass be placed directly under the dispensing head. This unit has been popular for dispensing beverage items that need no additional ingredients before service, such as wine, beer, and call brand liquors. A mini-tower unit can also be located on a wall, ice machine, or pedestal base in the bar area.

Bundled tower unit. The most sophisticated and flexible dispensing unit is the **bundled tower unit**. It is designed to dispense a variety of beverage items. Beverage orders are entered on a point-of-sale device. Bundled tower units may support in excess of 110 beverage products and contain a glass-sensing element. Each liquor has its own line to the tower unit, and a variety of pressurized systems can be used to enhance delivery from storage areas. The bundled tower unit can simultaneously dispense all ingredients required for a specific beverage item; bar servers merely garnish the finished product. This unit can be located up to 300 feet from beverage storage areas.

Endnotes

1. For more detailed information about sanitation aspects of food service design, see National Restaurant Association Educational Foundation, *ServSafe Coursebook*, 6th ed. (Chicago: National Restaurant Association Educational Foundation, 2012).

2. To learn more about NSF International and its standards for food service equipment, check out its website: www.nsf.org.

Key Terms

beverage control unit—Part of an automated beverage control system, located close to a beverage storage area and primarily responsible for regulating all essential mechanisms within the system.

broiler—Food service equipment that cooks with radiant heat from above or below the food.

bundled tower unit—A machine in an automated beverage control system designed to dispense a variety of beverage items. Also referred to as a *tube tower unit*.

capital costs—Expenditures for equipment, fixtures, and other items that will provide benefits for more than one year.

console faucet dispensing unit—A machine in one kind of automated beverage control system that can dispense various beverages in a number of portion sizes. Using buttons located above the unit, a bartender can trigger up to four different portion sizes from the same faucet head.

deep fryer—Food service equipment that cooks food by submerging it in hot fat.

delivery network—Part of an automated beverage control unit that transports beverage item ingredients from storage areas to dispensing units.

empty bottle sensor—Optional part of an automated beverage control unit that relays a signal to the order entry device when a server places a beverage order calling for ingredients that are out of stock.

glass sensor—An electronic mechanism located in a bar dispensing unit that will not allow liquid to flow from the dispensing unit unless there is a glass positioned below the dispensing head.

guest check sensor—A beverage control sensor that prevents the system from fulfilling beverage orders unless they are first recorded on a guest check.

hose and gun device—An automated beverage dispensing unit that features control buttons connected by hoses to beverages being dispensed.

mini-tower pedestal dispensing unit—A machine that combines the button selection technique of hose and gun devices with the portion-size capabilities of console faucet units. Part of one kind of automated beverage control system.

oven—Food service equipment that cooks food in a heated chamber. Examples include range, deck, roasting, convection, rotary, microwave, infrared, and recon ovens.

range—Food service equipment with a flat cooking surface used to fry, grill, sauté, etc. Two basic types of ranges are solid-top and open-top.

reach-in or roll-in refrigerator—A small refrigerator used to store food products at their point of use in production areas or in server or guest areas. May be used for central storage at small operations.

return on investment (ROI)—The amount of profit relative to the investment required to generate the profit; usually expressed as a percentage.

steam-cooking equipment—Food service equipment that cooks food by the direct or indirect application of steam, such as steam-jacketed kettles and compartment steamers.

tilting braising pan—Flat-bottomed cooking equipment that can be used as a kettle, griddle, fry pan, steamer, oven, or warmer/server. The bottom of an electric tilting braising pan is a heavy stainless steel plate heated by an electric element.

touch-bar faucet—Part of an automated beverage control unit, typically dedicated to a single beverage type and preset for one specific portion size output per push on the bar lever.

walk-in unit—A large refrigerated room used for central storage purposes.

work flow—The traffic patterns staff members create as they work. Good design and layout seek to minimize backtracking, intersections where several staff member paths cross, and other traffic pattern problems.

work station—A place in which one staff member works or where one menu item is made.

Review Questions

1. What concerns should managers and owners address when redesigning a kitchen?
2. What are four types of work-area layouts?
3. What are some things a food service manager should keep in mind when redesigning receiving and storage areas?
4. What are some factors that contribute to a dining room's atmosphere?
5. What items are typically found at a cashier work station?
6. What are three basic types of bars?
7. What are some bar layout guidelines?
8. What are some factors managers must consider when selecting food service equipment?
9. What are some common types of food service equipment? beverage service equipment?
10. What are some common types of ovens?
11. How has an emphasis on green kitchen and restaurant design changed traditional equipment and layout decisions?

Internet Sites

For more information, visit the following Internet sites. Remember that Internet addresses can change without notice. If the site is no longer there, you can use a search engine to look for additional sites.

Standards and Regulations

American Gas Association (AGA)
www.aga.org

American Society of Safety Engineers (ASSE)
www.asse.org

Foodservice Consultants Society International (FCSI)
www.fcsi.org

National Electric Manufacturers Association (NEMA)
www.nema.org

North American Association of Food Equipment Manufacturers (NAFEM)
www.nafem.org

NSF International
www.nsf.org

Occupational Safety & Health Administration (OSHA)
www.osha.gov

Underwriters Laboratories Inc. (UL)
www.ul.com

Kitchen Design Consultants

Mise Design Group, LLC
www.mdgrestaurantconsultants.com

Next Step Design
www.nextstepdesign.com

Robert Rippe Associates, Inc.
www.robertrippe.com

TriMark SS Kemp
www.sskemp.com

Restaurant Facility (Interior) Designers

Cahill Studio
www.cahillstudio.com

Deborah Goolsby Interiors
www.debroahgoolsbyinteriors.com

Maxey Hayse Design Studios, Inc.
www.maxeyhayse.com

Quantified Marketing Group
www.quantifiedmarketing.com

Slifer Designs
www.sliferdesigns.com

Environment Concerns: Layout and Equipment

Consortium for Energy Efficiency, Inc.
www.cee1.org

Energy Star
www.energystar.gov
(enter "restaurants" in the site's search box)

EPA Green Building
www.epa.gov/greenbuild
(enter "restaurants" in the site's search box)

EPA WasteWise Program
www.epa.gov/wastewise

EPA WaterSense
www.epa.gov/wastesense
(enter "restaurants" in the site's search box)

Food Service Technology Center
www.fishnick.com

Green Restaurant Association
www.dinegreen.com

NRA Conserve Initiative
www.conserve.restaurant.org

Chapter 13 Outline

Competencies

1. Describe the origins and the advantages of uniform systems of accounts. (pp. 359–360)

2. Explain how an operations budget is used as a standard. (pp. 360–364)

3. Identify the components and uses of income statements and balance sheets. (pp. 364–373)

4. Describe and calculate liquidity, solvency, activity, profitability, and operating ratios. (pp. 373–379)

5. List and briefly discuss fundamental accounting tasks typically performed by software programs. (pp. 379–380)

13

Financial Management

FINANCIAL MANAGEMENT deals with the economic aspects of food service operations. In today's fast-paced world of business, food service managers need to know as much as possible about their operations' finances. Fortunately, effective computerized accounting systems can ease the food service manager's financial management responsibilities.

In the United States, groups such as the American Accounting Association and the American Institute of Certified Public Accountants establish rules and standards used by all businesses. In the hospitality industry, food service operations can use accounting systems developed by professional associations for their specific type of operations. The major purpose of accounting systems is to generate accurate and timely information to help managers make decisions. These uniform accounting systems are discussed early in this chapter.

The existence of uniform accounting systems does not mean that accounting should be left completely to the accountants. Controllers and other accountants are most often in a staff or advisory relationship to the restaurant manager and other line managers. Knowledge of accounting principles and basic financial statements helps line managers gauge the soundness of their accountants' analysis and advice.

This chapter focuses on the financial aspects of a food service operation that managers need to understand in order to perform their jobs effectively. The **operations budget**—management's profit plan and control tool—is examined in some detail. The income statement and the balance sheet are discussed from a management perspective. A section on selected financial and operations ratios illustrates how these ratios help a manager evaluate the success of the food service operation.

Uniform System of Accounts

Several major trade associations serving the food service industry have published manuals defining accounts and accounting statements. A food service organization using the uniform system of accounts designed for its segment of the hospitality industry may select accounts that apply to its operations and ignore those that do not. A **uniform system of accounts** serves as a turnkey accounting system because it can be quickly adapted to the needs and requirements of new and expanding food service businesses.

The idea of a uniform system of accounts is not new, nor is it unique to the hospitality industry. The *Uniform System of Accounts for Hotels* was first published in 1926 by hoteliers with the foresight to recognize the value of the system.

Although there have been numerous revised editions since the 1926 publication, the fundamental format of the original uniform system has survived. This is a testament to the success of the system in meeting the basic needs of the industry.[1]

Following the lead of the lodging industry, the National Restaurant Association published the *Uniform System of Accounts for Restaurants* in 1930. Its objective was to give restaurant operators a common accounting language and to provide a basis upon which to compare the results of their operations. This uniform accounting system has been revised several times, and today many restaurant operators find it a valuable accounting handbook.[2]

Additional uniform accounting systems serve the needs of other food service segments such as conference centers, private clubs, and hospitals. The systems are revised as necessary to reflect changes in accounting procedures and in the business environment. The systems now enjoy widespread adoption by the industry and recognition by lending institutions as well as the courts.

Food service managers gain many benefits from adapting the uniform system of accounts appropriate for their operations. Perhaps the greatest advantage is that the uniformity of account definitions provides a common language with which managers from different food service operations within the same industry segment can discuss their operations. This common language permits useful comparisons among properties of the same size and service level. When managers and executives from businesses using the same uniform system of accounts gather to discuss the industry, they know that they are all speaking the same language.

Another benefit of a uniform accounting system is that regional and national statistics can be gathered and the industry can be alerted to possible threats and/or opportunities posed by developing trends. Industry statistical reports also serve as general standards that managers can compare to the results of their operations. For example, assume managers of two different food service operations compare their food costs. If these costs have been determined by including and excluding the same factors, it is possible to detect significant differences between the costs in the operations. If so, the manager with the higher food cost may want to analyze his or her operation to determine whether improvements can be made (food costs can be reduced) without compromising quality requirements.

The best standard against which to measure the financial performance of a food service operation is its own financial plan developed by management in an operations budget.

The Operations Budget

The operations budget is a profit plan and control tool for a food service operation that addresses all revenue and expense items appearing on the business's income statement. Annual operations budgets are commonly divided into monthly plans. These monthly plans become standards against which management can evaluate the actual results of operations each month. Thus, the operations budget enables management to accomplish two of its most important functions: planning and control.[3]

In small food service operations, the manager/owner generally develops the budget. In larger operations, other staff members (such as controllers or accountants) provide important help. Supervisors might budget expenses for their areas

---

Who Uses Financial Information?

Food service managers require financial information to help them analyze and make decisions about their operations. Others may also want to review the operation's financial information. They will require financial statements and proper definitions of accounting terms that accurately reflect the operation's financial status.

Those concerned about an operation's financial status include:

- *Top-level managers.* Managers of units in chain organizations report to off-site higher-level managers who use financial information, defined and collected in the same way at each unit, to help determine the financial status of the units for which they are responsible.

- *Owners.* Owners have invested a significant amount of money in the business and want to assess whether the returns on their investments are worthwhile. If owners discover otherwise, they might decide to use their investments for other purposes.

- *Investors.* Investors have put their own money into another person's business. They have two goals: to retain the money they have invested and to earn income from their investment. Like owners, they have investment alternatives, and want to know if the money they have invested in a business is generating a competitive income.

- *Creditors.* Persons or financial institutions that lend money to a food service organization must know about its financial health to be confident that they will be repaid according to the terms of the lending contract.

---

of responsibility after meeting with senior managers, or a budget committee may review each department's revenue and expense plans before a property-wide budget is approved. When staff members are allowed to provide input into the budget process, they often become more motivated to implement the property's profit plan and are less likely to resist budget numbers that they feel are imposed on them.

The Budget as a Profit Plan

The operations budget is developed by projecting revenue, determining profit requirements, and estimating expenses for each month of the upcoming fiscal year. These plans are then combined to form the annual operations budget. Many managers **reforecast** expected results of operations and revise operations budgets throughout the budget year. This reforecasting is necessary only when actual results vary significantly from the operations budget due to changes that occur after the budget has been prepared.

Projecting Revenue. Revenue is projected by forecasting food and beverage sales for the budget period. Sales history information from point-of-sale systems and past monthly income statements are among the sources of information managers use to project revenue. However, other factors must also be considered, including new competition, planned street improvements, and other activities over which the operation has little or no control but that may affect future sales. Also, changes in economic and social conditions or changing lifestyles within the local or broader community may affect the operation. In addition, sales promotions, remodeling, and other activities scheduled for the upcoming year may affect revenue projections for the budget period.

Determining Profit Requirements. If you were to ask commercial food service managers how much profit they wanted to generate, answers might include "as much as possible," "at least as much as last year," or "as much as my competition is making." These answers indicate a passive approach to determining profit requirements. Most passive approaches view profits as "leftovers": whatever is left after expenses have been subtracted from revenue.

A better approach to determining profit requirements subtracts profit requirements from projected revenue to arrive at allowable expense levels. This approach ensures that the operations budget takes into account the expectations of owners and investors who provide the financial support necessary for the food service operation to remain in business.

Many not-for-profit noncommercial food service operations must generate revenue in excess of direct operating expenses to pay their share of overhead, equipment, and other costs. This excess of income over direct expenses is often referred to as a "surplus." The managers of noncommercial food service operations should factor the required surplus into their operations' budgets, just as commercial food service managers factor profit requirements into their budgets.

Estimating Expense Levels. Many expenses are directly related to sales volume and vary as sales volume changes. For example, food costs and beverage costs increase as sales increase, because more food and beverage products must be purchased. These types of variable expenses can be estimated by comparing past expenses with projected sales levels. Other types of expenses do not fluctuate with sales volume and are easier to estimate because they do not change as frequently as variable expenses. These expenses, often referred to as fixed costs, include rent, depreciation, insurance, and license fees.

The Budget as a Control Tool

Developing a thorough operations budget reminds managers that they are responsible for meeting revenue, profit (or surplus), and expense goals. The operations budget helps pinpoint responsibility and encourages managers to use the budget as a control tool.

The process of budgetary control identifies and analyzes variances (differences) between budgeted figures and actual results of operations. Variance analysis may indicate that additional investigation by management is required to determine causes of the variances. Once causes are identified, management can take corrective action.

Budget reports are generally prepared monthly, and are useful only when they are timely and relevant. Reports issued weeks after the end of an accounting period are too late to allow managers to investigate significant variances, determine causes, and take corrective action. Relevant reports include the revenue and expense items for which the food service manager is responsible.

Reports should include sufficient detail to allow managers to make reasonable judgments about the budget variances. Budgeted revenue and expense items on the report will differ (hopefully, only slightly!) from actual results of operations. Figures describing the actual results of operations that can be compared with budgeted amounts are obtained from monthly income statements. Differences are to be expected since no budgeting process is perfect, but only significant variances require management analysis and action.

With assistance from the operation's controller, if applicable, top management should define significant variances. When significant variances are expressed in terms of dollars or percentages, the format of the monthly reports should include dollar and percentage variance columns so managers can easily identify which variances are significant.[4] Exhibit 1 shows the first line of a sample monthly operating report for March 20XX.

When you review Exhibit 1, notice that the first line of the report relates to food revenue. It shows information for March (in columns 2–5), for year-to-date (January–March 20XX, in columns 6–9), and for March of the previous year (in column 10). The manager can learn much about food revenue by reviewing this information. For example:

- Food revenue for March was $45,800 less than expected, as shown in column 4. This amount was calculated by subtracting the actual revenue ($329,400 in column 2) from the budgeted revenue ($375,200 in column 3). The actual revenue for March 20XX was 12.2 percent lower than expected ($45,800 budget variance in column 4 ÷ $375,200 budgeted revenue in column 3).

- The year-to-date (January–March) revenue was $85,250 less than expected. This was calculated by subtracting the actual food revenue (in column 6) from the budgeted revenue (in column 7). Not surprisingly, the year-to-date percentage of actual food revenue generated was 8.7 percent lower than expected ($85,250 budget variance in column 8 ÷ 980,450 budgeted revenue in column 7).

- The food revenue from March of last year ($361,410 in column 10) was also greater than for March of the current year ($329,400 in column 2).

There is an old saying, "Managers cannot solve a problem until they are aware of it." The manager of the food service operation with the food revenue detailed in Exhibit 1 must determine, with the help of his or her management team, why

Exhibit 1   Sample Format for a Monthly Operating Report

March 20XX									
	This Month				Year-to-Date				Last Year (This Month)
Revenue	Actual	Budget	Variance		Actual	Budget	Variance		Actual
			$	%			$	%	
(1)	(2)	(3)	(4)	(5)	(6)	(7)	(8)	(9)	(10)
Food	329,400	375,200	(45,800)	(12.2)	895,200	980,450	85,250	(8.7)	361,410

food revenue was significantly lower than anticipated during March and for the first three months of the current year, and also why revenue was lower for March of this year than for March of last year.

The Income Statement

A food service operation's **income statement** provides important financial information regarding the results of operations for a stated period of time, usually one month.[5]

Information reported on income statements is developed through a bookkeeping process. As transactions occur, bookkeeping entries are made in the appropriate accounts. At the end of the month, trial balances and various adjusting entries are made to ensure that account balances accurately reflect the month's activity.

Since the income statement reveals operating results, it is an important measure of the effectiveness and efficiency of management. A later section in the chapter examines common ratios used to evaluate management's effectiveness. Many of the figures needed to calculate important ratios come from the income statement.

Restaurant Income Statement

The income statement for a restaurant operation summarizes the revenue, cost of revenue, and gross profit generated by the sale of food and beverages. Exhibit 2 shows a sample income statement for the fictional independent Brandywine Restaurant for January.

Note that the income statement also lists amounts for controllable expenses (those generally within the control of managers). Recall that fixed costs (called *occupation costs* in Exhibit 2) are not controllable by the food service management team.

Most restaurant operations prepare supporting schedules for the income statement to provide detailed information about major line items. For example, the Brandywine Restaurant may prepare a supporting schedule detailing food revenue for the month of January. Depending on the manager's needs, the supporting schedule could document food revenue by meal period (breakfast, lunch, dinner) and/or by location (dining room, lounge, take-out counter, banquet room, etc.). The total food revenue shown on the supporting schedule would represent the same total food revenue amount that appears on the income statement for food revenue ($533,250). (These calculations are discussed in more detail later in the chapter.)

Information in Exhibit 2's percent column is calculated in two different ways. Percentages for food cost of sales and beverage cost of sales are calculated by dividing, respectively, food costs by food revenue and beverage costs by beverage revenue. Percentages for the remaining items are calculated by dividing each line item by the total food and beverage revenue. (Examples of these calculations are shown later in the chapter.)

Hotel Food and Beverage Department Income Statement

The income statement for a hotel consolidates the income and expenses reported on separate departmental statements. It also includes nondepartmental items.

Exhibit 2   Sample Income Statement for the Brandywine Restaurant

Brandywine Restaurant Income Statement Month Ended January 31, 20XX		
Sales	**Amount ($)**	**Percent**
Food	533,250	71.9
Beverages	208,500	28.1
Total Sales	741,750	100.0
Cost of Sales		
Food	217,033	40.7
Beverages	58,172	27.9
Total Cost of Sales	275,205	37.1
Gross Profit		
Food	316,217	59.3
Beverages	150,328	72.1
Total Gross Profit	466,545	62.9
Other Revenue	8,250	1.1
Total Revenue	474,795	64.0
Controllable Expenses		
Salaries and Wages	203,981	27.5
Employee Benefits	35,604	4.8
Direct Operating Expenses	48,214	6.5
Music and Entertainment	6,676	0.9
Marketing	14,093	1.9
Utility Service	18,544	2.5
General and Administrative Expenses	40,055	5.4
Repairs and Maintenance	12,610	1.7
Total Controllable Expenses	379,777	51.2
Profit Before Occupation Costs	95,018	12.8
Occupation Costs		
Rent, Property Taxes and Insurance	35,604	4.8
Interest	6,676	0.9
Depreciation	17,060	2.3
Other Additions and Deductions	(2,967)	(0.4)
	56,373	7.6
Net Income Before Income Tax	38,645	5.2

For example, income taxes are not allocated to any specific department. Exhibit 3 shows a year-end income statement for the fictional Hotel Doro.

Since the income statement is the first financial statement prepared, it is designated Schedule A (upper right hand corner in Exhibit 3). All schedules that support it are assigned the prefix A and a sequence number. For example, "A2" (on

Exhibit 3   Sample Income Statement for the Hotel Doro

Hotel Doro, Inc.
Statement of Income
For the year ended December 31, 20XX   Schedule A

	Schedule	Net Revenue	Cost of Sales	Payroll and Related Expenses	Other Expenses	Income (Loss)
Operated Departments						
Rooms	A1	$ 897,500		$ 143,140	$ 62,099	$ 692,261
Food and Beverage	A2	524,570	$ 178,310	204,180	54,703	87,377
Telecommunications	A3	51,140	60,044	17,132	1,587	(27,623)
Other Operated Departments	A4	63,000	10,347	33,276	6,731	12,646
Rentals and Other Income	A5	61,283				61,283
Total Operated Departments		1,597,493	248,701	397,728	125,120	825,944
Undistributed Expenses						
Administrative and General	A6			97,632	66,549	164,181
Marketing	A7			35,825	32,043	67,868
Property Operation and Maintenance	A8			36,917	24,637	61,554
Utility Costs	A9				47,312	47,312
Total Undistributed Expenses				170,374	170,541	340,915
Income Before Fixed Charges		$1,597,493	$248,701	$568,102	$295,661	$485,029
Fixed Charges						
Rent	A10					28,500
Property Taxes	A10					45,324
Insurance	A10					6,914
Interest	A10					192,153
Depreciation and Amortization	A10					146,000
Total Fixed Charges						418,891
Income Before Income Taxes and Gain on Sale of Property						66,138
Gain on Sale of Property						10,500
Income Before Income Taxes						76,638
Income Taxes						16,094
Net Income						$ 60,544

Source: Raymond Cote, *Accounting for Hospitality Managers*, 5th ed. (Lansing, Mich.: American Hotel & Lodging Educational Institute , 2007), p. 196.

the second line of the "Schedule" column in Exhibit 3) refers to Schedule A2—the year-end food and beverage department income statement shown in Exhibit 4.

Note that Exhibit 4 presents detailed information about the hotel's food and beverage department that is summarized only on the Food and Beverage line of the consolidated income statement in Exhibit 3. Most hotel accounting systems combine food and beverage operations into one operating department because of shared costs. However, separate information is provided about revenue and cost of revenue for food and for beverages in the departmental income statement (Exhibit 4) to allow analyses of the gross profit margins for both of these operational areas.

Note in Exhibit 4 that the cost of food and beverages is reduced by the cost of meals provided to all employees of the hotel because each department is charged for its share of employee meal expenses.

Exhibit 4   Food and Beverage Department Income Statement for the Hotel Doro

Hotel Doro, Inc.
Food and Beverage Department Income Statement
For the year ended December 31, 20XX   Schedule A2

	Food	Beverage	Total
Revenue	$360,000	$160,000	$520,000
Allowances	1,700	130	1,830
Net Revenue	358,300	159,870	518,170
Cost of Sales:			
Beginning Inventory	5,800	3,000	
Purchases	145,600	40,310	
Available	151,400	43,310	
Ending Inventory	7,000	2,800	
Cost of Goods Used	144,400	40,510	184,910
Cost of Employee Meals	9,200		9,200
Cost of Goods Sold	135,200	40,510	175,710
Net Other Income			3,800
Gross Profit			346,260
Operating Expenses:			
Total Payroll and Related Expenses			204,180
Total Other Operating Expenses			54,703
Departmental Income			$ 87,377

Source: Raymond Cote, *Accounting for Hospitality Managers,* 5th ed. (Lansing, Mich.: American Hotel & Lodging Educational Institute, 2007), p. 229.

Payroll and employee benefits expenses associated with food production staff, service staff, and other food and beverage personnel are charged to the food and beverage department, as are the other applicable operating expenses reported in Exhibit 4. Finally, note that the food and beverage departmental income ($87,377 in Exhibit 4) is carried on to the hotel's income statement. (See the "Income (Loss)" column for "Food and Beverage" in the second line of the "Operated Departments" section of the income statement shown in Exhibit 3.)[6]

Calculating Actual Food Costs. A carefully planned operations budget establishes revenue and cost goals, and information in the income statement shows actual operating results.[7] A critical part of a food service manager's job involves control: developing standards (in the operating budget), assessing actual results (in the income statement), and making comparisons between the budget and the income statement to see if corrective action is needed. Even if the operation has an accountant or food and beverage controller, the manager must understand and take an active part in the process. Let's look at one cost—food—and see how actual costs shown in the income statement are assessed.

To ensure that actual food costs are comparable to budget costs, several rules must be followed:

- Actual costs must be stated in the same manner as budgeted (or "standard") costs. If budgeted food costs are stated as a percentage of revenues, actual food costs must be stated the same way.

- Both actual costs and budgeted costs must cover the same meal periods. If budgeted costs are expressed as a specified percentage of revenue across all meal periods, so must actual costs.

- All factors used to estimate budgeted costs must be included in the calculation of actual costs. If complimentary meals are excluded from budgeted cost estimates, they must also be excluded from actual costs.

- Actual costs must be assessed on a timely basis. Decision-makers must know as soon as possible if and to what extent actual costs differ from budgeted costs.

The technical term for "food cost" is "cost of sales": the cost of the food used to generate the food revenue produced during the accounting period.

The basic monthly cost of sales for food (the process to calculate beverage cost is essentially the same) is calculated as follows:

$$\text{Cost of Sales} = \text{Beginning Inventory} + \text{Purchases} - \text{Ending Inventory}$$

For example, assume:

		Food
Beginning Inventory		$124,500
Purchases	+	85,000
Ending Inventory	−	112,000
Cost of Sales (Food Cost)		$ 97,500

The **food cost percentage** is calculated by dividing the cost of sales by the food revenue and multiplying by 100:

$$\frac{\text{Food Cost of Sales}}{\text{Food Revenue}} \quad \times \quad 100 \quad = \quad \text{Food Cost Percentage}$$

For example, assume that food revenue is $284,500 and cost of food sales is $97,500. The food cost percentage can be calculated as follows:

$$\frac{\$97,500}{\$284,500} \quad \times \quad 100 \quad = \quad 34.27\%$$

Exhibit 5 illustrates the sources of information used to calculate the basic cost of sales. Note that the value of inventory is calculated only once monthly. The value of ending inventory on the last day of the month is the same as the value of beginning inventory on the first day of the next month.

The value of monthly food purchases can be obtained from the daily receiving reports for the period. Delivery invoices may be attached to these documents. If the daily receiving reports are completed correctly, they will separate food and beverage purchases to reduce the time needed to make these calculations. If a daily

Exhibit 5 **Information for Basic Cost of Sales (Food or Beverage) Calculation**

Required Information	Source
Beginning Inventory	Physical Inventory Forms (last month)
+ Purchases	Daily Receiving Reports and Delivery Invoices
− Ending Inventory	Physical Inventory Forms (end of current month)

receiving report is not used, the value of purchases is the sum of delivery invoices, adjusted by applicable request-for-credit memos.

Values of ending inventories for food items can be taken directly from a physical inventory form. When taking inventory counts, be consistent with the procedures used in each fiscal period:

- The method used to calculate the cost of inventory items must be the same.

- Decisions about the consideration and value of food supplies in work stations must be the same.

- Decisions about whether items in broken cases, in miscellaneous storage areas, or in process should be considered "inventory" must be consistent.

Adjustments to Basic Cost of Sales. A manager calculates cost of sales to determine the cost incurred in generating revenue. To make the information more useful, some adjustments to the basic cost of sales can be made to include costs not directly related to generating revenue. For example, in operations where meals

---

Just Add Up the Payments?

This chapter describes a process to calculate food and beverage costs that involves determining beginning and ending inventory costs. Wouldn't it be simpler and faster to just add the total of the checks and cash used to purchase food and beverages each month?

The answer is "yes," it would be simpler and faster, but it would also be far less accurate. The reason is that the products in inventory on the first day of the month were purchased (paid for) before the month began and other products placed in inventory during the month will be purchased (paid for) in future months. This check and cash payment method cannot, therefore, accurately determine what the food cost was that generated the revenue for the current month.

Food and beverage managers want to follow an accrual system of accounting, which requires that revenue generated during the month be matched with the actual expenses incurred to generate the revenue. That is why the chapter describes a method that considers both changes in inventory costs and purchases during the month to make the food or beverage cost calculations for a specific accounting period.

are provided free or at reduced charges to employees, the food cost (and food cost percentage) will be overstated if no adjustment is made to reduce the food cost for employee meals. These food expenses were incurred to feed employees, not to generate revenue. This cost is more appropriately considered a labor or benefits cost rather than a food cost.

Some food service managers use the unadjusted cost of sales as their monthly food and beverage costs because they do not believe the increased accuracy warrants the time it takes to make the adjustments. However, even operations with relatively small annual revenue levels may note a significant difference in product costs when adjustments are made to yield a more accurate picture of the cost of generating revenue.

When adjustments are made to the basic cost of sales, the amount deducted must be charged to some other expense category. Managers who want a more accurate identification of the costs of food products that generated revenue may make any or all of the adjustments listed in Exhibit 6. These adjustments are examined in the following sections. Note, however, that to make comparisons meaningful, any of these adjustments must also be reflected in the way budgeted food costs are calculated. The actual monthly cost of food should be compared with budgeted performance expectations and, if useful, past financial statements.

Food transfers. Transfers from the kitchen to the bar decrease the cost of food. Examples include fruits used as drink garnishes or ice cream used for after-dinner drinks. These transfers were used to generate beverage revenue, and can be charged to the beverage operation to decrease food expense and increase beverage expense.

Beverage transfers. Transfers to the kitchen from the bar increase the cost of food. Examples include wine used for cooking or liqueurs used for tableside flaming of desserts. Although these expenses were initially charged to the beverage operation, they increased food revenue rather than beverage revenue and can be more appropriately charged to food. This adjustment would increase food costs and decrease beverage costs.

Employee meals. Employee meal costs are usually calculated by multiplying a fixed amount representing the food cost per meal by the number of employee

Exhibit 6   Adjustments to Basic Cost of Sales

Cost of Sales: Food	Charge to:
Value of Beginning Inventory + Purchases − Value of Ending Inventory	
Unadjusted Cost of Sales: Food	
+ Transfers to Kitchen − Transfers from Kitchen − Employee Meal Cost − Value of Complimentary Meals	Food Cost Beverage Cost Labor Cost Promotion Expense
Net Cost of Sales: Food	

meals served. This food cost may be deducted from the cost of food sales and charged to the labor or employee benefits account. Procedures for calculating employee meal costs are beyond the scope of this chapter. They can be complicated and have both legal (involving wage and hour laws) and income tax implications. Interested readers should contact their state restaurant association, department of labor, or an accountant for current information.

Complimentary food and beverages. Complimentary meals may be provided to prospective guests touring the operation or for other purposes. These costs might be considered a marketing department (promotion) cost. If so, the cost of food sales can be reduced by their value, and the costs can be transferred to the appropriate marketing account.

The Balance Sheet

A **balance sheet** reports the financial position of a food service operation on a specific date by showing its assets, liabilities, and equity. Understanding how this statement reveals the financial position of a business is the key to understanding the sequence of categories on the statement. The major categories that appear on the balance sheet are:

- Assets
- Liabilities
- Equity

Assets represent anything a business owns that has commercial or exchange value; **liabilities** represent the claims of outsiders (such as creditors) on assets; and **equity** represents the claims of owners on assets. On every balance sheet, the total assets must always agree (that is, balance) with the total of the liabilities and equity sections. Therefore, the format of the balance sheet reflects the fundamental accounting equation:

$$\text{Assets} = \text{Liabilities} + \text{Equity}$$

Exhibit 7 presents a sample year-end balance sheet for the fictional Deb's Steakhouse, a small independent property. The following sections briefly describe the major line items of the assets and liabilities sections of the balance sheet. The owner's equity section of a balance sheet varies in relation to the type of business organization: a sole proprietorship, a partnership, or a corporation.[8]

Assets

Assets are arranged on the balance sheet according to whether they are current or noncurrent. Current assets are those assets that are cash or can be converted to cash within twelve months of the balance sheet date. All other items in the assets section are noncurrent assets.

Current assets are usually listed in the order of their liquidity, that is, the ease with which they can be converted to cash. The item "Cash" includes cash in house banks, checking and savings accounts, and certificates of deposit. "Accounts Receivable" includes all amounts due from guests on open charge accounts.

Exhibit 7   Balance Sheet for Deb's Steakhouse

Deb's Steakhouse
Balance Sheet
December 31, 20XX

ASSETS

CURRENT ASSETS

Cash	$34,000	
Accounts Receivable	4,000	
Inventories	5,000	
Prepaid Expenses	2,000	
Total Current Assets		$ 45,000

PROPERTY AND EQUIPMENT

	Cost	Accumulated Depreciation	
Land	$ 30,000		
Building	60,000	$15,000	
Furniture and Equipment	52,000	25,000	
China, Glassware, Silver	8,000		
Total	150,000	40,000	110,000

OTHER ASSETS

Security Deposits	1,500	
Preopening Expenses	2,500	
Total Other Assets		4,000
TOTAL ASSETS		$159,000

LIABILITIES

CURRENT LIABILITIES

Accounts Payable	$11,000	
Sales Tax Payable	1,000	
Accrued Expenses	9,000	
Current Portion of Long-Term Debt	6,000	
Total Current Liabilities		$ 27,000

LONG-TERM LIABILITIES

Mortgage Payable	40,000	
Less Current Portion of Long-Term Debt	6,000	
Net Long-Term Liabilities		34,000
TOTAL LIABILITIES		61,000

OWNER'S EQUITY

Capital, Deb Barry—December 31, 20XX	98,000
TOTAL LIABILITIES AND OWNER'S EQUITY	$159,000

Source: Raymond Cote, *Basic Hotel and Restaurant Accounting,* 6th ed. (Lansing, Mich.: American Hotel & Lodging Educational Institute, 2006), p. 67.

"Inventories" includes products held for resale, such as food and beverage items and operating supplies. Prepaid expenses may include prepaid interest, rent, taxes, and service contracts.

The property and equipment section of the balance sheet lists noncurrent assets. As indicated in Exhibit 7, the costs for building and for furniture and equipment are decreased by amounts shown under the heading "Accumulated Depreciation." Depreciation spreads the cost of an asset over the term of its useful life.

The other assets section of the balance sheet includes assets that do not apply to other line items. For example, security deposits include funds deposited with public utility companies and other funds used for other deposits.

Liabilities

Liabilities are also reported according to their current or noncurrent status. Current liabilities are obligations that will require an outlay of cash within twelve months of the balance sheet date. Noncurrent liabilities are often referred to as long-term liabilities or long-term debt.

The "Total Current Liabilities" line alerts the restaurant operator to cash requirements and is often compared with the total figure for current assets. A major line item of interest to food service managers is "Accounts Payable," which shows the total of unpaid invoices due to creditors from whom the operation has received merchandise or services.

Ratio Analysis

A ratio is a mathematical relationship between two figures. Ratios and ratio analysis help make financial statement information more meaningful, informative, and useful.

To be useful as financial measurements, ratios must be compared against some standard. The three standards commonly used to evaluate an operation's ratios are: ratios from a past period, from industry averages, and from the budget developed for the specific food and beverage operation.

Comparing present ratios with those calculated for past periods may reveal significant changes that management should address. For example, if the monthly food cost percentage is significantly higher than in previous months, managers may need to investigate reasons and take corrective action.

Industry averages provide another useful standard against which to compare ratios. Investors may want to compare the return on investment (ROI) for the operation with the average ROI for similar food service operations. This can provide an indication of management's ability to use assets effectively to generate profits for investors.

Ratios are best compared against planned ratio goals. For example, to more effectively control the cost of labor, managers project a goal for the current year's labor cost percentage in their budget. If the budgeted labor cost percent is slightly lower than the previous year's level, the expectation of a lower labor cost percentage reflects management's efforts to improve scheduling, increase productivity, or control other labor-related factors. By comparing the actual labor cost percentage with the budgeted percentage, managers can assess how successful they are in meeting their goal of doing a better job controlling labor costs than in previous years.

Different evaluations may result from comparing ratios against these different standards. For example, a food cost of 33 percent for the current period may compare favorably with the prior year's ratio of 34 percent and with an industry average of 36 percent, but may be judged unfavorably when compared with the operation's planned goal of 32 percent. Therefore, care must be taken when evaluating the results of operations using ratio analysis.

Ratios are generally classified by the type of information they provide. A full discussion of ratios is beyond the scope of this chapter. What follows is a general introduction to the ratios included in five common ratio groups.[9]

Liquidity Ratios

Liquidity ratios reveal the ability of a food service operation to meet its short-term obligations. The most common liquidity ratio is the **current ratio**, which is the ratio of total current assets to total current liabilities. Using figures from Exhibit 7, the current ratio for Deb's Steakhouse can be calculated as follows:

$$\text{Current Ratio} \quad = \quad \frac{\text{Current Assets}}{\text{Current Liabilities}}$$

$$= \quad \frac{\$45{,}000}{\$27{,}000}$$

$$= \quad \underline{\underline{1.67}} \text{ or } 1.67 \text{ to } 1$$

This result means that, for every $1 of current liabilities, Deb's Steakhouse has $1.67 of current assets. In other words, there is a cushion of $.67 for every dollar of current debt.

Owners and stockholders prefer a low current ratio to a high one, because they view most current assets as less productive than investments in noncurrent assets. Creditors normally prefer a relatively high current ratio, because it suggests they will receive timely payments. Managers are caught in the middle, trying to satisfy both owners and creditors.

Solvency Ratios

Solvency ratios measure the extent to which the food service operation has been financed by debt. If an operation carries a lot of debt, its ability to meet its long-term obligations may be questionable. A food service operation is solvent when its assets exceed its liabilities. The most common ratio in this group is the solvency ratio, which is total assets divided by total liabilities. Using figures from Exhibit 7, the solvency ratio for Deb's Steakhouse is determined as follows:

$$\text{Solvency Ratio} \quad = \quad \frac{\text{Total Assets}}{\text{Total Liabilities}}$$

$$= \frac{\$159{,}000}{\$61{,}000}$$

$$= \underline{\underline{2.61}}$$

This result shows that Deb's Steakhouse has $2.61 of assets for each $1 of liabilities, or a cushion of $1.61. As with the current ratio, owners and stockholders normally prefer a low solvency ratio. Creditors, on the other hand, prefer a high solvency ratio, as it provides a greater cushion should the operation experience financial problems. Managers are again caught in the middle, trying to satisfy both owners and creditors.

Activity Ratios

Activity ratios reflect management's ability to use the assets of the food service operation. Managers are entrusted with inventory, fixed assets, and other resources to generate earnings for owners while providing products and services to guests. One important activity ratio for food service operations is inventory turnover.

The **inventory turnover ratio** shows how quickly inventory is used. Generally, a faster inventory turnover is better, because inventory can be expensive to maintain. Maintenance costs include storage space, freezers, insurance, personnel expense, recordkeeping, and the cost of opportunities lost because the money tied up in inventory is unavailable for other uses.

Food inventory turnover is calculated by dividing the cost of food used by the average food inventory. The average food inventory is computed by adding the inventory at the beginning of a period to the inventory at the end of the period and dividing by two. Assume that, during a particular month, Deb's Steakhouse had a beginning food inventory of $5,000; an ending food inventory of $6,000; and food cost of $18,975. Inventory turnover for that month can be calculated as follows:

$$\text{Average Food Inventory} = \frac{\text{Beginning } + \text{ Ending Inventory}}{2}$$

$$= \frac{\$5{,}000 + \$6{,}000}{2}$$

$$= \underline{\underline{\$5{,}500}}$$

$$\text{Food Inventory Turnover} = \frac{\text{Cost of Food Used}}{\text{Average Inventory}}$$

$$= \frac{\$18{,}975}{\$5{,}500}$$

$$= \underline{\underline{3.45}}$$

This means that food inventory for the month turned over 3.45 times, or approximately once every nine days (thirty days per month $\div$ 3.45 = 8.7 days [rounded]).

A high food inventory turnover may be desired because the operation requires a relatively small investment in inventory; however, too high a turnover may indicate possible stockout problems. Failure to provide desired items to guests may not only immediately result in disappointed guests, but may also result in reduced business if the problem persists. Too low an inventory turnover may suggest that food is overstocked and, in addition to the costs of maintaining the inventory, the cost of spoilage and/or theft may become a problem.

An inventory turnover for beverage supplies should be calculated separately from food supplies. A beverage inventory turnover is calculated similarly to the food inventory turnover. Some food service operations calculate beverage turnovers separately for the different types of beverages (beer, wine, and liquor) that they sell.

Profitability Ratios

Profitability ratios show management's overall effectiveness as measured by returns on revenues and investments. One common profitability ratio is the **profit margin**, a measure of management's ability to generate profits on revenues. Profit margin is determined by dividing the net income before tax by total revenue. Net income is the income remaining after all expenses have been deducted from revenue. Using figures from Exhibit 2, the profit margin for the Brandywine Restaurant in January can be determined as follows:

$$\text{Profit Margin} = \frac{\text{Net Income Before Taxes}}{\text{Total Food and Beverage Revenue}}$$

$$= \frac{\$38,645}{\$741,750}$$

$$= \underline{\underline{5.2\%}}$$

If the profit margin is lower than expected, expenses and other areas should be reviewed. Poor pricing strategies and low revenue volume can contribute to a low profit margin.

Operating Ratios

Operating ratios help managers analyze their food service operation. Many operating ratios relate expenses to revenue and are useful for control purposes. For example, an actual food cost percentage is calculated and compared with the budgeted food cost percentage to evaluate the overall control of food costs. Any significant deviation is investigated to determine causes for the variation between actual costs and budgeted costs. Exhibit 8 shows some operating ratios useful to food service managers. The following sections examine some common operating ratios.

Food Cost Percentage. As discussed earlier, the food cost percentage compares the cost of food sold with food revenue. Most food service managers rely heavily on this ratio for determining whether food costs are reasonable. Using figures described in the discussion of Exhibit 2, the January food cost percentage for the Brandywine Restaurant can be determined as follows:

Exhibit 8   Common Operating Ratios

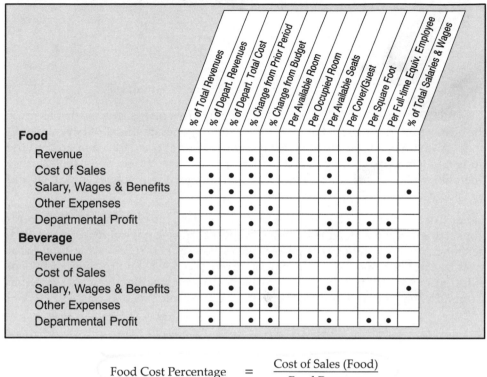

	% of Total Revenues	% of Depart. Revenues	% of Depart. Total Cost	% Change from Prior Period	% Change from Budget	Per Available Room	Per Occupied Room	Per Available Seats	Per Cover/Guest	Per Square Foot	Per Full-time Equiv. Employee	% of Total Salaries & Wages
Food												
Revenue	•			•	•	•	•	•	•	•	•	
Cost of Sales		•	•	•	•		•					
Salary, Wages & Benefits		•	•	•	•			•	•			•
Other Expenses		•	•	•	•			•				
Departmental Profit	•			•	•			•	•	•	•	
Beverage												
Revenue	•			•	•	•	•	•	•	•	•	
Cost of Sales		•	•	•	•							
Salary, Wages & Benefits		•	•	•	•			•				•
Other Expenses		•	•	•	•							
Departmental Profit	•			•	•			•		•	•	

$$\text{Food Cost Percentage} \quad = \quad \frac{\text{Cost of Sales (Food)}}{\text{Food Revenue}}$$

$$= \quad \frac{\$217,033}{\$533,250}$$

$$= \quad \underline{\underline{40.7\%}}$$

This means that for each $1 of food revenue, $.407 is needed to cover the costs of purchasing the food required to generate the $1 of food revenue. The actual food cost percentage should be compared with the budgeted food cost percentage for the period. A significant difference in either direction should be investigated. Managers should be just as concerned about a food cost percentage that is significantly lower than budget as they are about a food cost percentage that exceeds budgeted standards. A lower food cost percentage may indicate that the quality of food served is lower than desired, or that smaller portions are being served than are specified in standard recipes. A higher food cost percentage than the budgeted standard may be due to poor portion control, excessive food costs, theft, waste, spoilage, or a host of other factors.

Beverage Cost Percentage. The **beverage cost percentage** results from dividing the cost of beverages sold by beverage sales. Using figures from Exhibit 2, the January beverage cost percentage for the Brandywine Restaurant can be determined as follows:

$$\text{Beverage Cost Percentage} = \frac{\text{Cost of Sales (Beverages)}}{\text{Beverage Revenue}}$$

$$= \frac{\$58,172}{\$208,500}$$

$$= \underline{\underline{27.9 \text{ or } 28\% \text{ (rounded)}}}$$

This result shows that for each $1 of beverage revenue, $.28 is needed to cover the costs of purchasing the beverages required to generate the $1 of beverage revenue. As with the food cost percentage ratio, this ratio is best compared to the budgeted (standard) beverage cost for that specific time period. Some food service operations also calculate a beverage cost percentage by type of beverage sold and by beverage outlet.

Labor Cost Percentage. Labor is one of the largest expenses in food service operations. Labor expense includes salaries, wages, bonuses, payroll taxes, and fringe benefits. A general **labor cost percentage** is determined by dividing total labor costs by total revenue. Using the payroll figure ($203,981) and the employee benefits figure ($35,604) from the Brandywine Restaurant income statement (shown in Exhibit 2), the January labor cost percentage can be calculated as follows:

$$\text{Labor Cost Percentage} = \frac{\text{Labor Costs}}{\text{Total F\&B Revenue}}$$

$$= \frac{\$203,981 + \$35,604}{\$741,750}$$

$$= \underline{\underline{\$.32 \text{ or } 32\%}}$$

This result indicates that of every $1 of food and beverage revenue, $.32 goes toward covering the cost of labor required to generate the food and beverage revenue. As with the food cost percentage ratio, this ratio is best compared with the budgeted standard for the same time period. Some food service operations calculate labor costs by type of labor or by type of food and beverage outlet (dining room, lounge, banquet room, etc.).

Average Food Service Check. The **average food service check** ratio is determined by dividing the revenue generated during a meal period by the number of guests served. If the Brandywine Restaurant generated $1,500 of revenue from the sale of food and beverage items during a specific meal period and served 100 guests, the average check is calculated as follows:

$$\text{Average Check} = \frac{\text{Total F\&B Revenue}}{\text{Number of Guests Served}}$$

$$= \frac{\$1,500}{100}$$

$$= \underline{\underline{\$15}}$$

Check averages are often calculated for different dining areas and/or for separate meal periods. In addition, managers often separately track the average beverage service check for their operations.

Seat Turnover. Seat turnover is the number of times that one seat in a sit-down dining area is occupied during a meal period. This ratio is determined by dividing the number of guests served during a meal period by the number of seats available. If during one meal period the Brandywine Restaurant served 100 guests with 38 available seats, the seat turnover can be calculated as follows:

$$\text{Seat Turnover} = \frac{\text{Number of Guests Served}}{\text{Number of Available Seats}}$$

$$= \frac{100}{38}$$

$$= \underline{\underline{2.6}} \text{ times}$$

This result indicates that each available seat was occupied 2.6 times during the meal period. As the seat turnover rate increases, more guests are served during a meal period and more sales revenue should be generated.

Technology and the Accounting Process

Food service computer systems vary in the type of general accounting software programs they provide. Four major back-of-the-house software programs relate to accounts receivable, accounts payable, payroll accounting, and financial reporting.

Accounts Receivable Software

The term *accounts receivable* refers to obligations owed to the property from sales made on credit. Accounts receivable software typically performs the following functions:

* Maintains account balances
* Processes billings
* Monitors collection activities
* Generates aging of accounts receivable reports
* Produces an audit report indicating all accounts receivable transactions

Accounts receivable software generally maintains a customer master file that contains guest data and billing information, including the number of days elapsed between payments and the invoice to which the last payment applied. Many accounts receivable programs also maintain an accounts aging file that segments each account according to the date the charge originated.

Accounts Payable Software

The term *accounts payable* refers to liabilities incurred for food, supplies, equipment, or other goods and services purchased on account. An accounts payable program maintains a supplier master file, an invoice register file, and a check register file, and typically does the following:

- Posts supplier invoices
- Monitors supplier payment discount periods
- Determines amounts due
- Produces checks for payment
- Facilitates the reconciliation of cleared checks

Accounts payable software often generates a cash requirements report that lists all invoices selected for payment and the cash required to pay the invoices.

Payroll Accounting Software

Payroll accounting is an important part of an integrated food service computer system. Payroll accounting software streamlines payroll accounting tasks and can manage the tasks required to process time and attendance records, employee benefits, pay rates, withholdings, deductions, and payroll reports. Payroll accounting software typically:

- Maintains an employee master file
- Calculates gross and net pay for salaried and hourly employees
- Produces paychecks
- Prepares payroll tax registers and reports

A single employee may perform different tasks over a number of work shifts at separate pay rates. Payroll accounting software must be able to handle job codes, employee meals, uniform credits, tips, taxes, and other data that may affect the net pay of employees.

Financial Reporting Software

Financial reporting software (also called general ledger software) lists financial statement accounts and account numbers used by the food service operation. The software maintains account balances, prepares trial balances, computes financial and operating ratios, and produces financial statements and other management reports.

Generally, financial reporting software can track accounts receivable, accounts payable, cash, and adjusting entries. To do this, the software must have access to account balances maintained by other back-of-the-house software programs. With a fully integrated food service computer system, daily file updates ensure that the balances in the financial reporting files are current.

Endnotes

1. *Uniform System of Accounts for the Lodging Industry*, 11th rev. ed. (Lansing, Mich.: American Hotel & Lodging Educational Institute, 2014).

2. *Uniform System of Accounts for Restaurants*, 8th rev. ed. (Washington, D.C.: National Restaurant Association, 2014).

3. For more information on operations budgets for food and beverage operations, see Jack D. Ninemeier, *Planning and Control for Food and Beverage Operations*, 8th ed. (Lansing, Mich.: American Hotel & Lodging Educational Institute, 2013).

4. The budget process is discussed in more detail in Raymond S. Schmidgall, *Hospitality Industry Managerial Accounting*, 7th ed. (Lansing, Mich.: American Hotel & Lodging Educational Institute, 2011).

5. For a more complete discussion of income statements, see Raymond Cote, *Basic Hotel and Restaurant Accounting*, 6th ed. (Lansing, Mich.: American Hotel & Lodging Educational Institute, 2006); and Raymond Cote, *Accounting for Hospitality Managers*, 5th ed. (Lansing, Mich.: American Hotel & Lodging Educational Institute, 2007).

6. For more information on an income statement for a hotel food and beverage department, see Schmidgall.

7. Much of the material in this section was adapted from Ninemeier.

8. For a fuller explanation of the equity section of the balance sheet, see Cote, *Basic Hotel and Restaurant Accounting* and *Accounting for Hospitality Managers*.

9. For more information on ratios, see Schmidgall.

🔑 Key Terms

assets—Things a business owns that has commercial or exchange value.

average food service check—A ratio comparing the revenue generated during a meal period to the number of guests served during that same period; calculated by dividing total food revenue by the number of guests served.

balance sheet—A financial statement stating the account balances for assets, liabilities, and equity on a given date.

beverage cost percentage—A ratio comparing the cost of beverages sold to beverage revenue; calculated by dividing the cost of beverages sold by beverage revenue.

current ratio—Ratio of total current assets to total current liabilities; calculated by dividing current assets by current liabilities.

equity—The claims of owners on assets.

food cost percentage—A ratio comparing the cost of food sold to food revenue; calculated by dividing the cost of food sold by food revenue.

income statement—A financial statement that provides information regarding the results of operations, including revenue, expenses, and profit for a stated period of time.

inventory turnover ratio—A ratio showing how quickly an operation's inventory moves from storage to productive use; calculated by dividing the cost of products used by the average product inventory.

labor cost percentage—A ratio comparing the labor expense to the total revenue generated; calculated by dividing labor costs by total revenue.

liabilities—The claims of outsiders (such as creditors) on assets.

operations budget—Management's detailed plans for generating revenue, determining profit requirements, and estimating expenses for the food service operation.

profit margin—An overall measure of management's ability to generate revenue and control expenses; calculated by dividing net income by total revenue.

reforecasting—The process of reviewing the operations budget during the period to which it applies to reflect data not available when the budget was originally developed.

seat turnover—A ratio indicating the number of times that a given seat in a sit-down dining area is occupied during a meal period; calculated by dividing the number of guests served by the number of available seats.

solvency ratio—A measure of the extent to which an operation is financed by debt and is able to meet its long-term obligations; calculated by dividing total assets by total liabilities.

uniform system of accounts—A manual produced for a specific segment of the hospitality industry that defines accounts for various types and sizes of operations, provides standardized financial statement formats, explains individual accounts, and provides sample bookkeeping documents.

Review Questions

1. How do food service managers benefit from using the uniform system of accounts appropriate for their operation?

2. How is the operations budget used as a control tool?

3. Why is the income statement a measure of the effectiveness of food service managers?

4. How are food costs calculated?

5. What is the purpose of a balance sheet? What do the assets, liabilities, and equity sections of a balance sheet represent?

6. What standards can be used to evaluate the ratios computed for a food service operation?

7. Why would creditors of a food service operation prefer that the operation's balance sheet indicate relatively high current and solvency ratios?

8. How do food service managers determine whether food and beverage costs are reasonable?

9. What are some factors that could contribute to a high food cost percentage? A high beverage cost percentage?

10. What five common operating ratios are of interest to food and beverage managers? How are they calculated? How do the managers use them?

11. What types of software are available to help with accounting tasks?

Internet Sites

For more information, visit the following Internet sites. Remember that Internet addresses can change without notice. If the site is no longer there, you can use a search engine to look for additional sites.

Restaurant Accounting

Hospitality Financial and Technology
   Professionals
www.hftp.org

Krost, Baumgarten, Kniss, & Guerrero
www.restaurantaccountants.com

National Restaurant Association
www.restaurant.org

Restaurant Accounting Services
www.restaurant-accounting.com

Restaurant Resource Group
www.rrgconsulting.com

Restaurant Accounting Software and Systems

Altametrics
www.altametrics.com

Compeat Restaurant Management
   Systems
www.compeat.com

Horizon Payroll Solutions
www.horizonpayroll.com

PenSoft Business Solutions
www.pensoft.com

Problems

Problem 1

a.   Complete the following Monthly Operating Report for the Hilo Town Restaurant.

Month	Revenue	Actual	Budget	Variance $	Variance %	Year-to-Date Actual	Year-to-Date Budget	Variance $	Variance %	Last Year (This Month) Actual
Jan.	Food	124,000	130,250							133,400
Feb.	Food	131,000	125,400							129,250
March	Food	139,950	127,450							130,400

b.   What is your analysis of the operation based upon the financial information in the Monthly Operating Report?

Problem 2

a.   Given the following information, what is the "Net Cost of Sales: Food" during August 20XX for the Hilo Town Restaurant?

Value of ending food inventory, August 30, 20XX	$ 37,450
Value of ending food inventory, July 31, 20XX	$ 39,790
Value of purchases during August 20XX	$107,475
Value of transfers to kitchen	$ 6,470
Value of transfers from kitchen	$ 3,125
Cost of employee meals	$ 1,140
Value of complimentary meals	$ 990

b.   What is the Hilo Town Restaurant's food cost percentage for August 20XX, if its food revenue for the month was $317,410?

Problem 3

The following is balance sheet, income statement, and other financial information applicable to the Hilo Town Restaurant's operation in July 20XX.

Balance Sheet Information		Income Statement Information	
Current assets	$98,400	Food revenue	$155,000
Current liabilities	$71,200	Beverage revenue	$20,000
Total assets	$390,010	Net income before taxes	$10,900
Total liabilities	$217,100	Total labor costs	$52,400

Other Financial and Related Information	
Beginning food inventory	$12,480
Ending food inventory	$14,100
Cost of sales (food)	$41,075
Cost of sales (beverage)	$4,900
Number of guests served (average day) in July	452
Number of seats in restaurant	98

Use the preceding information to answer the following questions:

a.   What is the current ratio? What does it mean?

b.   What is the solvency ratio? What does it mean?

c.   What is the average food inventory?

d.   What is the food inventory turnover rate? How often (number of days) does the food inventory turn over?

e.   What is the restaurant's profit margin?

f.   What is the restaurant's food cost percentage?

g.   What is the restaurant's beverage cost percentage?

h. What is the restaurant's labor cost percentage?
i. What is the average food service check?
j. What is the seat turnover in July?

Index